PIGS MIGHT FLY THE INSIDE STORY OF PINK FLOYD

PIGS MIGHT FLY
THE INSIDE STORY OF PINK FLOYD

MARK BLAKE

This updated and extended paperback edition first published in 2013 by Aurum Press

First published 2007 by Aurum Press Limited
74–77 White Lion Street, Islington,
London N1 9PF
www.aurumpress.co.uk

A catalogue record for this book is available from the British Library.

ISBN 978 1 78131 057 1

10 9 8 7 6 5 4 3 2 1
2017 2016 2015 2014 2013

Designed in Spectrum and Gill Sans by Rich Carr
Typeset by SX Composing DTP, Rayleigh, Essex
Printed and bound in Great Britain by CPI Group (UK) Ltd, Croydon, CR0 4YY

CONTENTS

CHAPTER ONE **PIGS HAVE FLOWN**

'It would be fantastic if we could do it for something like another Live Aid. But maybe I'm just being terribly sentimental – you know what us old drummers are like.'

Nick Mason

'I really do hope we can do something again.'

Richard Wright

'I don't think we'd get through the first half an hour of rehearsals. If I'm going to be on stage playing music with people, I want it to be with people that I love.'

Roger Waters

'I think Roger Waters has my phone number. But I've no interest in discussing anything with him.'

David Gilmour

J ust when it seems as if rock music has long lost its power to offend, Pink Floyd's reunion has thrown the establishment into a panic. It is 2 July 2005, and the band are due to perform at the Live 8 charity concert in London's Hyde Park, but the event has already over-run by nearly an hour. In the words of the 1960s counter-culture from which Pink Floyd emerged, 'The Man' is not happy. Except 'The Man' is now Tessa Jowell, Secretary of State for Culture, Media and Sport. Word filters back to the media that she has called an emergency meeting backstage and is threatening to end the show early, fearful that a crowd of 200,000 people spilling into the capital's streets in the small hours will constitute an act of public disorder.

The last time David Gilmour, Richard Wright, Nick Mason and Roger Waters fell even remotely foul of a politician was some twenty-five years earlier. Then, Pink Floyd's hit single, 'Another Brick in the Wall Part 2', featured a choir of London inner city schoolchildren shouting a chorus of 'We don't need no education', much to the disgust of the then Prime Minister, Margaret Thatcher.

In 2005, though, the political landscape has undergone a seismic shift. Live 8 has been staged to raise awareness about Third World deprivation and to urge world leaders, convening for the following week's G8 Summit, to tackle the issue of poverty. However, one of those very same leaders, Prime Minister Tony Blair, has just let slip that, regardless of the band's political motivation, he is looking forward to watching Pink Floyd's performance at Live 8. Blair is a rock fan, a sometime guitar player and, briefly, the lead singer in a band while at university. When press articles about the PM's rock 'n' roll years appear, they're predictably accompanied by a photo of the youthful Blair in 1972, beaming behind ripples of unkempt long hair. If it wasn't for the grin, he could even pass for a member of Pink Floyd, or, at worst, a member of their road crew, perhaps one 'let go' for being too cheerful by half and getting under Roger Waters' feet.

Who knows whether the Floyd-loving Prime Minister lent his voice to the argument? But, after the emergency meeting, which involved the Metropolitan Police and the Royal Parks Agency, Tessa Jowell allows the show to continue. There is even talk of blankets being distributed to those audience members wishing to spend the night in the park. News of the near-cancellation will only make it back to the viewing public in the following day's newspapers. But to anyone even dimly aware of the shared history between Pink Floyd's members, the real miracle is that they have agreed to be here in the first place.

Live 8 has been a day filled with glowing and not-so-glowing performances, alongside the usual car-crash moments that occur when pop stars get anywhere near a worthy cause. Organiser Sir Bob Geldof has rounded up the heads of pop's royal family, using the same persuasive tactics deployed when staging Live Aid in 1985: namely, the implied suggestion that any band that refuses will dent their credibility for ever. U2, Madonna, Sir Elton John, Sir Paul McCartney and numerous younger, unknighted rock stars have agreed to give their services for free. The bill is random, newcomers following old hands, but, as the day wears on, a pecking order of sorts emerges.

Around the world, nine further concerts are taking place in cities such as Rome, Berlin and Philadelphia. For many gathered at these events, though, it is a single performance, taking place tonight in London, that generates the greatest anticipation. As Geldof grudgingly admits, 'In the US, why this band, with such a painful history of disorder, have agreed to do this, is a far bigger story than Live 8 itself.' On the day that Pink Floyd's appearance is announced, whispers circulate of a promoter guaranteeing $250 million for the four to tour.

Pink Floyd's recording career began in 1967. They have since sold over 30 million copies of their 1973 album, *Dark Side of the Moon*, alone. Yet their public falling-out has sometimes threatened to overwhelm their artistic achievements. It has been more than twenty-four years since the four members shared a stage. In the meantime, Gilmour, Wright and Mason have forged ahead with the Floyd name, releasing albums and staging tours, while Roger Waters, previously the group's bass guitarist, but also their most prolific songwriter and acknowledged ideas man, has raged from the sidelines, once declaring that his former colleagues 'took my child and sold her into prostitution, and I'll never forgive them for that'.

Forgiveness may not be on the agenda, but today, the four have struck a truce, of sorts. Pink Floyd haven't made an album since 1994, and, under normal circumstances, coaxing what guitarist David Gilmour describes as 'this great lumbering behemoth to rouse itself out of its torpor' would have been an arduous process. Yet with the lure of a good cause and Geldof's expert arm-twisting, it has taken just three weeks between the reluctant Gilmour agreeing to play and the re-formed Floyd arriving on stage in Hyde Park.

At 10.17 p.m., David Beckham, officially the biggest footballer in Britain, introduces Robbie Williams, officially the biggest pop star in Britain, on stage. Williams's voice is noticeably frayed, but he slips easily into his routine – part boy band heart-throb, part Norman Wisdom – camping it up, and making it difficult to imagine anyone having the crowd quite so on their side.

Under the circumstances, it doesn't bode well for next act, The Who. In 1964, Pink Floyd's drummer Nick Mason, then studying architecture at Regent Street Polytechnic, watched The Who perform 'My Generation' and experienced a moment of epiphany: 'Yes, *that's* what I want to do.' With two of their number now gone, The Who's surviving members, Pete Townshend and Roger Daltrey, plus hired hands, plough through 'Who Are You' and 'Won't Get Fooled Again'. They avoid any direct communication with the crowd and, in the case of Townshend and his impenetrable, wraparound shades, any eye contact. The Who's performance is ferociously tight, with glimpses of their former chippy glory, but it seems to be over almost before it has begun.

The show is approaching its tenth hour, the park is submerged in inky darkness, McCartney is still to play the closing slot and, on the sidelines, presumably, Tessa Jowell's blankets are being unpacked for those planning a long night under the stars.

At 10.57 p.m., without any fanfare or a celebrity introduction, an eerie yet familiar sound begins drifting across the park. Any remaining roadies on stage suddenly disappear into the wings. The sound rises in volume: the steady, metronomic pulse of a heartbeat. Searchlights sweep over the audience, the video screen behind the stage flickers into life, and the heartbeat grows louder. Then comes the voice: '*I've been mad for fucking years.*' A snippet of speech from a Pink Floyd roadie recorded nearly thirty years earlier at Abbey Road Studios. It's followed by the ominous whirr of helicopter blades, a ringing cash register, and a disengaged cackle of laughter repeated again and again, before segueing into a long, hysterical scream; the closing moment of 'Speak to Me', the very first track on *Dark Side of the Moon*.

The goosebumping scream seems to rise in pitch and volume, then is replaced by the soothing opening bars of 'Breathe'. As the searchlights dim and the stage is bathed in light, the audience are allowed their first proper view of the men on stage. In a curious reversal of the decree by the Wizard of Oz to 'pay no attention to the man behind the curtain', the men are all we're left with. The flying pig and aerial shots of Battersea Power Station drifting on the video screen behind the stage are familiar Floyd motifs, but, for once, they fail to draw the attention away from the group themselves. In the past, Pink Floyd thrived on their anonymity. As their success grew so did their stage sets; all designed to divert an audience's gaze away from the four unremarkable-looking, long-haired men on stage. By 1980, they played behind a specially constructed wall, as part of Roger Waters' lordly protest at the dehumanising nature of the music industry. When Gilmour coaxed 'the lumbering behemoth' back into service in the eighties and nineties, he, Mason and Wright were augmented by younger session musicians, shimmying female backing singers and a Spielberg-style stage show of blinding lasers that overwhelmed the original band members.

Tonight, Pink Floyd look curiously real. They could be any group of fifty-something businessmen on a dress-down Friday, or assembled in the clubhouse waiting for the rain to subside and a round of golf to commence, even if their shared uniform of faded jeans might contravene club rules. At the back, Nick Mason, his expression frozen somewhere between studious concentration and a knowing smile, patters around his kit. The recent author of a book about the band, Mason has become the group's most publicly visible and media-savvy member, although his decision to continue in Pink Floyd after Waters' departure led to a rift with his close friend that only healed in recent years. The group's self-appointed diplomat ('I'm the Henry Kissinger of rock,' he informs journalists later), Mason has also been instrumental in helping Geldof broker this reunion.

Mason gave up studying architecture in 1966, when the fledgling Pink Floyd signed their first management deal. He always planned to go back to it, if playing drums in a rock 'n' roll band didn't work out. Now, three decades on, the walrus moustache and crown of long dark hair that were his visual traits throughout the early seventies are long gone. Clean-shaven, a little jowly, with his grey hair undiminished but cut short, the sixty-year-old drummer now resembles the architect he nearly became. His white shirt even displays a few telltale creases, suggesting that it's fresh out of a box.

Stage left, Richard Wright hunches over his keyboards. Wearing a dark linen jacket over a white shirt, Wright's rather hangdog demeanour once prompted an observer to liken him to 'an ex-champion jockey down on his luck'. In truth, while briefly studying to become an architect himself, Wright has an artier air about him still, and looks more like a semi-retired seventies rock star than his drumming counterpart. A gifted musician, Wright found himself relegated in Pink Floyd, a victim of his own reticence and the strong personalities surrounding him. In 1979, he suffered the ignominy of being forced out of the band by Roger Waters, on the grounds that he wasn't contributing sufficiently to the recording of their latest album, *The Wall*. Wright endured a period of depression and a spell in exile, before slowly being reintroduced into the band under Gilmour's aegis, and eventually acquiring a stake in the group he'd helped to form.

In worn-out denim and black T-shirt, David Gilmour gazes imperiously into the middle distance. More than any of his bandmates, Gilmour has always looked like the quintessential seventies hippie musician: barefoot, laid-back, one hank of his long hair usually tucked behind his ear to keep it off his face as he fussed with the settings on his amp, or nudged an effects pedal with his toes. The hair is long gone, the remains shaved tight to the scalp, and the waistline is thicker. But Gilmour seems to carry himself with greater confidence now. Cradling his guitar, he sets about singing lyrics written by his one-time nemesis – Roger Waters. Gilmour has been Pink Floyd's only frontman since the mid-1980s. The target for most of Waters' ire, he has overseen two platinum-selling Floyd albums and record-breaking tours without his former partner. He exchanges thin smiles with Mason and the crowd, including his wife and some of his children watching from the enclosure in front of the stage, but barely glances at the bassist.

Just a few feet away, Roger Waters mans his own corner. His greying hair is longer, still touching the collar of a washed-out blue shirt. His sleeves are rolled up, revealing an expensive-looking watch that jangles every time he moves. Waters doesn't seem so much to play his bass as assault it. Chin jutting regally, he scowls and jerks his head in time to the music while wringing the neck of his instrument. He smiles frequently, but bares his teeth and the grin becomes disconcertingly aggressive. Despite this threatening demeanour, Waters looks delighted to be back on stage with the same men he threatened with legal action twenty years previously. Tellingly, while Gilmour sings, Waters mouths the words, as if reminding all those watching that these are *his* songs.

'Breathe' is a balmy, low-key overture. The sweet guitar figure prompts the obligatory raising of glowing cigarette lighters above the heads of the crowds, while beatific smiles appear on the faces of those who've spent the past ten and a half hours hunkered down in their vantage points waiting for this moment. Written by the then thirty-year-old Waters, 'Breathe' set out the lyrical agenda of *Dark Side of the Moon*; a plaintive exploration of the fears and insecurities of early adulthood, the realisation that, in the bass player's own words, 'you've been sitting around waiting for life to start only to suddenly realise that it's already started.' That it's being rendered by the same men thirty years later makes it seem all the more prescient.

With barely a word of acknowledgement to the crowd, 'Breathe' segues into 'Money', the US single that helped to break Pink Floyd in America. In contrast, this is loud, overdriven hard rock. The lyrics have since become a predictable target for those dismissive of Floyd's multi-millionaire status. But its subject matter is pertinent for Live 8 and, as Mason later explains, 'Sir Bob wanted us to do it.' Either way, the sheer drive and tempo of the song makes it ideal for an outdoor event. Gilmour solos restlessly, before the song is hewn in two by a saxophone solo from Dick Parry, the same musician who played on the original track, who ambles on stage, also looking as if bound for the ninth hole. As the pair negotiate the song's final bend, there is a flicker of eye contact between Gilmour and Waters. Then it's gone.

Backstage earlier, Nick Mason had calculated that there would be 'over three hundred years of old rock 'n' roll experience' on stage. But it's the group's life experience that's important. As one Floyd insider once put it, 'Pink Floyd's music is like a beautiful girl walking down the street who won't talk to you.' For a band notable for their corseted English reserve and inability to communicate with each other outside the music, this outbreak of peace has brought all the humanity and emotion concealed in their songs to the surface. Suddenly, it all makes perfect sense.

In the context of today's performance, 'Wish You Were Here' sounds like what it is: a simple love song to a departed friend. Gilmour and Waters both play acoustic guitars, while another Floyd familiar, second guitarist Tim Renwick, steps out of the shadows to help them along. Waters sings the second verse, his harsher, cracked voice a contrast to Gilmour's sweeter tone. The song is short, simple and rapturously received. Its inspiration and meaning is not lost on this audience. It is a song partly about the one member of the original Pink Floyd not on stage tonight.

The closing song is as inevitable as it is anticipated. To have not played it would have been seen as heresy. 'Comfortably Numb' is taken from *The Wall*, a concept album about a rock star's tortuous decline. Sharing the lead vocals again, Waters and Gilmour sing of *The Wall*'s burnt-out muso, slipping into pillowy, drug-induced nirvana, before Gilmour delivers the pay-off moment – a guitar solo that carries the song to a grand, Hollywood climax, the sort plundered inexpertly by so many rock bands since. It's grandiose, spectacular and oddly moving.

Previously stoic expressions break into relieved grins as the four wander to the centre of the stage. Waters, his arm already around Mason and Wright, gestures towards an uncomfortable-looking Gilmour, mouthing the words, 'Come on.' Hesitantly, the guitarist allows himself to be embraced, and the reunited Pink Floyd take their bow. A slogan in the audience captures the moment: 'Pink Floyd Reunited! Pigs Have Flown.'

At 11.15 p.m., Sir Paul McCartney strides on stage to play Live 8's closing set. But even he can't shift the attention away from what has come before. In the US, there is speculative talk of lucrative reunion tours and the possibility of another Pink Floyd album. In the UK, the *Guardian* more irreverently concedes that although the band members 'look like senior partners in a firm of chartered accountants . . . twenty-four years after they last shared a stage, they sound fantastic.'

Watching their performance on TV, backstage at the Canadian Live 8 event in Barrie, was Bob Ezrin, Floyd's effusive long-time collaborator and co-producer of *The Wall*. 'I thought it was stunning, the stuff legends are made of,' he enthuses a few weeks later. 'I was so overjoyed and, yeah, I have to admit, I cried. Then I became slowly aware that everyone was watching *me* watch Pink Floyd.'

For the band's followers, record companies, dewy-eyed former colleagues, everyone, Live 8 offered hope of a longer-term reconciliation. David Gilmour swiftly quashed any such speculation. 'It's in the past for me. Done it. I don't have any desire to go back there,' he said. 'It's great to put some of that bitterness behind us, but that's as far as it goes.'

Before rehearsals for Live 8, David Gilmour and Roger Waters had last spent time in each other's company on 23 December 1987, in the words of the guitarist, to 'thrash out the terms of our divorce'. Convening on Gilmour's houseboat-cum-studio, the pair finalised the deal with an accountant and a computer to settle the terms of a legal document relating to use of the name Pink Floyd.

Previously, Waters had filed law suits against both Gilmour and Mason, believing that the band name should have been put to rest following his official departure in 1985. For nearly twenty years, Waters had been the group's dominant songwriter, devising the original concepts behind albums such as *Dark Side of the Moon* and *The Wall*, writing the bulk of the lyrics and, in his own words, 'driving the band'. Refusing to cede to his demands, Gilmour and Mason had elected to continue as Pink Floyd. Three months before this final meeting, the pair had released a new Floyd album, *A Momentary Lapse of Reason*, signing up Richard Wright to play on the subsequent tour. Two months later, despite being denounced by Waters as 'a fair forgery', the album had notched up platinum sales, confirming that the Pink Floyd brand was strong enough to weather even the loss of a key member.

Then again, it wasn't the first time the band had lost one of its number. At Live 8, Roger Waters had acknowledged the one Pink Floyd member missing that night, dedicating 'Wish You Were Here' to 'everyone that's not here, but particularly, of course, Syd'.

Syd Barrett, once Pink Floyd's lead singer, guitarist and guiding light, had dropped out of both the band and the music business some three decades earlier. As his former bandmates performed to over 100,000 fans in Hyde Park and to a television audience of over 2 billion people around the world, Syd Barrett remained at home in a semi-detached house in suburban Cambridge. At his own request, Barrett no longer had any direct contact with Pink Floyd or wished to be reminded of his time in the band. For him, it had long been over.

CHAPTER TWO THE ENDLESS SUMMER

'Freedom is what I'm after.'

Syd Barrett

t was made public four days after the event. On Friday, 7 July 2006, Syd Barrett died. The cause of death was given as pancreatic cancer, though his health had been declining for many years. Syd's family informed David Gilmour, who relayed the news to his former bandmates and others in the Floyd's circle of friends. Respecting Syd's family's wishes, none of Pink Floyd had seen or spoken to Syd in many years. When the news finally broke worldwide on Tuesday, 11 July, photographs of Barrett appeared on the front pages of newspapers across the world. It was an extraordinary and unprecedented reaction to the death of a man who had not made a record in over thirty years, and had not spoken about his time as a pop star for just as long.

In the spring of 1968, Pink Floyd had parted company with their original singer and childhood friend. By then, David Gilmour had joined the group to provide some musical stability, as Barrett's drug use and increasingly fractious state of mind had rendered him a liability. In January that year, on their way to perform a show, the rest of the band took the decision not to collect Syd, a decision that would have a profound effect on the rest of their lives.

The week before Pink Floyd's Live 8 performance, the *London Evening Standard* despatched a journalist to Barrett's house in Cambridge, in an attempt to interview the band's elusive former singer. Barrett refused to answer the door. His sister Rosemary revealed that she had told her brother of Pink Floyd's imminent reunion, only to be met with a blank response. 'That is another life for him,' she explained, 'another world in another time.' The nickname of Syd, acquired in that previous life, had been abandoned. For many years Syd had been known once again as Roger Barrett.

The anonymous semi-detached house at 6 St Margaret's Square, Cambridge, where Barrett spent his final years, gave away very little about the identity of its sole occupant. There were none of the trappings beloved by rock stars of all generations: no wall-mounted gold discs to be glimpsed through the gaps in the curtains or expensive sports cars lined up in the driveway. Yet there was none of the neglect some might expect after hearing the rumours and whispered half-truths about the mental state of its owner. Barrett had lived there alone since the death of his mother in 1991. He had never married, fathered any children or held down a job for a significant length of time since his alter ego left Pink Floyd in the 1960s.

Every so often the outside world would impinge on his private universe. Pictures of the navy-blue front door would be splashed across the newspapers, alongside an image of the occupant himself. Caught unawares on his doorstep by photographers, Syd always looked baffled, sometimes angry or scared, invariably half-dressed with a middle-age paunch on display. Any glimpse of his down-at-heel appearance supplied more grist to the Syd Barrett rumour mill.

Syd would undergo these intrusions whenever his past life became a topic of interest in the present day. When Pink Floyd reconvened without him to play Live 8, it was inevitable that the press would descend. Previously, during the media frenzy surrounding acid house raves in the late 1980s, Barrett was held up by the *News of the World* as a cautionary example of the dangers of taking LSD. Of course, they knew he would never sue. But then, who knew what he might do? Neighbours spoke of hearing deathly screams in the middle of the night, while others said they'd heard him bark like a dog. Since the early nineties, though, Roger Barrett simply spent his days painting, reading and cycling to the local shops. He led a quiet, though not completely reclusive existence. Invariably, after each intrusion on his privacy, the trail would go cold again and Syd would be left alone, with only the occasional uninvited fan knocking on his door.

Yet, whatever their context, the photographs of the old Syd Barrett that accompanied these newspaper exposés were still unavoidably compelling. Those same pictures appeared again after his death. Taken almost forty years earlier, they showed Syd dolled up in his best Kings Road clothes, wavy hair teased into an explosive halo, eyes smouldering into the camera, as he blueprinted the image of the doomed rock star, a cliché adopted by countless would-be Syds ever since.

'He was someone that people would point out on the street,' recalls David Gilmour of his childhood friend. 'Syd had that charisma, that magnetism.'

The shared history of Pink Floyd's three chief protagonists – Barrett, Gilmour and Waters – is irrevocably tied to the city of their youth.

Cambridge's reputation as a seat of learning began as early as the thirteenth century. With the striking architecture of its colleges and the River Cam winding its way through the city, it retains a traditional English quality. Yet as a counterpoint to any quaintness, the landscape around the city comprises rugged fenland. The atmosphere seeped into Pink Floyd's music from the start. The title of the group's first album, *The Piper at the Gates of Dawn*, was taken from *The Wind in the Willows*, Kenneth Grahame's 1908 children's novel set on a riverbank. In the chapter of the same name, two of the book's animal characters embark on a bizarre spiritual quest. 'Grantchester Meadows', Roger Waters' softly played interlude on the band's *Ummagumma* album, was named after the beautiful, heavily wooded riverbank area tucked away towards the south of the city, near David Gilmour's family home.

At the time of the three principal Floyds' arrival into the world, Cambridge was, as one of their childhood peers now describes it, 'a place where licensed eccentricity was considered permissible. You'd see all these brilliant but rather odd people such as Francis Crick who discovered DNA, cycling eccentrically down the street.' Syd's father was another familiar, eccentric figure, often to be seen cycling on an upright bicycle down Hills Road.

Dr Arthur Max Barrett, known to all as Max, was a university demonstrator in pathology at the local Addenbrooke's hospital. Later, he would take up the position of morbid anatomist at the university. In his spare time he was a noted amateur painter and botanist, with the privilege of his own set of keys to the city's botanical gardens. Displaying the musical talent for which his son would become better known, Dr Barrett was also a member of the Cambridge Philharmonic Society.

He was married to Winifred Garrett, the great-granddaughter of Elizabeth Garrett Anderson, the country's first female physician in 1865. The Barretts had five children: Alan, Donald, Ruth, Roger (later known as Syd) and Rosemary. Syd was born on 6 January 1946 in the first family home at 60 Glisson Road, near to the centre of Cambridge. Three years later, the family moved to a nearby five-bedroom house at 183 Hills Road.

A few minutes' walk from the Barretts' new home was Rock Road, where the family of George Roger Waters would settle when he was just two years old. Roger's father, Eric Fletcher Waters, had grown up in County Durham, the grandson of a coal miner and prominent Labour Party agent. He became a schoolteacher and, being a devout Christian and conscientious objector, refused to join up at the outbreak of the war. Instead he did voluntary work and drove an ambulance during the Blitz and joined the Communist Party. But halfway through the conflict, Eric had a change of heart and decided to sign up for the war. He eventually joined the City of London Regiment, 8th Battalion Royal Fusiliers as a second lieutenant.

Preceded by one brother, John, Roger was born on 6 September 1943. His mother, formerly Mary Whyte, was also a schoolteacher. When Eric was posted overseas, Mary moved with her sons from Great Bookham, in Surrey, to Cambridge, believing they would be safer from German bombing raids over London.

Eric Waters was declared missing presumed dead on 18 February 1944, during the Allies' assault on the beaches of Anzio, on the Italian coast. Roger was just five months old at the time.

David Jon Gilmour arrived in the world on 6 March 1946. The Gilmours' home at the time was a village outside Cambridge called Trumpington. The family moved several times, before finally settling at 109 Grantchester Meadows in the Newnham district, near the River Cam, when David was ten years old. His father, Doug, and mother, Sylvia, met at Cambridge's Homerton College, where both were training to be teachers. Sylvia went on to become a film editor, eventually working for the BBC. Doug Gilmour became a senior lecturer in zoology at the university. The couple had four children: David, his brothers Peter and Mark, and a sister, Catherine.

'Cambridge was a great place to grow up,' says Gilmour. 'You're in a town dominated by education, you're surrounded by bright people. But then it's also got this rural heart that spreads practically to the centre. There were great places to meet up with friends.'

While Gilmour has no memory of the meeting, he first encountered Barrett and Waters when the three were enrolled by their parents at a Saturday morning art club at Homerton College. Both Waters and Barrett attended Morley Memorial primary school in Blinco Grove, where Mary Waters was working as a teacher. It was here that Syd's precocious talents first became apparent. Noted for his gift of mimicry, he and sister Rosemary (known to most as Roe) also won a shared prize for playing the piano when Syd was seven years old.

Nick Barraclough, a fellow Morley Memorial pupil, later to become a musician and BBC broadcaster, remembers Syd as 'a beautiful boy and incredibly artistic. My sister was in his class. They would have been about ten or eleven, and the pupils were asked to paint their impressions of a hot day. Most of the children drew a beach or a sun. Roger – as he was still called then – drew a girl lying on a beach in a bikini with an ice-lolly dripping over her, which all seemed terribly advanced considering his age.'

All three boys sat and passed their 11-plus, the then compulsory test which divided British schoolchildren into those deemed intelligent enough for a grammar school education, or, if not, the secondary modern school system. 'My father was a primary school teacher,' remembers Barraclough, 'and the two Rogers both came to him at different times to be coached in advance for the 11-plus.'

Waters was enrolled at Cambridgeshire High School for Boys (formerly the Cambridge and County School) in Hills Road in 1954. Now reinvented as Hills Road Sixth Form College, back then 'the County' was, as one former pupil described it, 'a grammar school that thought it was a public school, with masters, mortar boards and sadism'. The school had a record for high academic achievement, with a similarly impressive Oxbridge output.

Roger became a noted sportsman: a wicket keeper in the school's first XI cricket team, and an impressive fly half in the rugby team. He also joined the school's Combined Cadet Force, initially against his wishes, spending some time at the weekend naval training school at HMS *Ganges*. Part of the Force's training involved target practice and marksmanship, to which he was better disposed. However, although he was smart and witty, his sharp tongue and overbearing streak could also make him unpopular. On at least one occasion his fellow pupils beat him up. 'I think I was roundly hated by most of the people involved,' admitted Waters later.

'Roger was in the year above me,' remembers fellow County boy Seamus O'Connell. 'I was friends with another chap called Andrew Rawlinson, whose nickname was Willa, and who was a great friend of Roger's. The relationship between Roger and I was a bit fraught at school as he wasn't always that pleasant, but we still counted each other as friends.'

Later, tiring of the Cadet Force, and in a fit of pique, Roger simply handed in his uniform and refused to attend further training, leading to a dishonourable discharge. Fellow County pupil Tim Renwick, who would go on to work with Pink Floyd as a guitarist, recalls the scandal: 'I was a couple of years younger than Roger, but everyone in the school heard about it. He caused rather a fuss. Though I'm sure I can remember hearing that Roger told them he was leaving on the grounds that he was a conscientious objector.'

Waters' childhood experiences would find their way time and again into Pink Floyd's music, leaving even the most inattentive listener in little doubt about his feelings for life at the County.

'Roger tolerated his schooling,' said Mary Waters. 'His attitude was, "You have to get on with it and make the most of it."'

'I hated every second of it, apart from games,' Roger insisted. 'The regime at school was a very oppressive one. It was being run on pre-war lines, where you bloody well did as you were told, and there was nothing to do for us but to rebel against it. It's funny how, when you get these guys at school, they will always pick on the weakest kid. So the same kids who are susceptible to bullying by other kids are also susceptible to bullying by the teachers. It's like smelling blood. They home in on it. Most of the teachers were absolute swine.'

'I always presumed that Pink Floyd's *The Wall* was about the masters at the County,' says Nick Barraclough, who followed Waters to the school. 'The headmaster there at the time was a man named Eagling, who was, to this day, the scariest man I have ever known. The two Rogers would have been right in the thick of all that.'

Being schooled after the Second World War in an education system still behind the times, hampered by pre-war attitudes, and hardly attuned to a generation enjoying the peace and relative prosperity not afforded to their parents, the late fifties was an era of opportunity for teenagers, unlike any before.

Railing against the school system, Waters would later describe an episode that encapsulated this contempt. Deciding to seek revenge on the school's gardener for some real or imagined slight, he and a group of co-conspirators went into the school orchard with a stepladder and singled out the gardener's favourite tree. They then proceeded to eat every apple on the tree, taking care not to remove any from the branches. Recounting the incident for *Musician* magazine over thirty years later, Waters proudly recalled 'being filled with a real sense of achievement' after the elaborate prank.

Three years behind Waters, Syd Barrett's progress through the County was marked by an overriding passion for art and a keen interest in poetry and drama. Also displaying an anti-authoritarian streak, Barrett could charm his way out of trouble by being smart, good-looking and, as Gilmour recalls, 'a sharp cookie, very able in many areas'. Nevertheless, adhering to more conventional lines, Syd rose through the ranks to become patrol leader, Kingfisher patrol, in his local Scout troop.

In June 1961, aged fifteen, Syd began a relationship with Elizabeth Gausden (known by everyone as Libby), a pupil at the nearby Cambridge Grammar School for Girls. 'Syd actually had a girlfriend already, a very pretty, fluffy German girl called Verena Frances,' remembers Libby. 'But we hit it off. He always used to say, "You're not the prettiest, but you're the funniest girl ever". He was a wonderful boy. Everybody loved him.'

John Gordon first encountered Syd in the County's art class. 'He shone from the first day,' he remembers. 'His hair was longer than anyone else's. He spoke his mind to the teachers and would even walk out of a class if he was being told off.'

Syd frequently refused to wear his school blazer and was also notable for wearing his shoes without laces, a trait that continued into adulthood. Encouraged by his parents, Syd also indulged the keenly creative streak that had first surfaced at the Morley Memorial, participating in poetry readings and public speaking. But his adolescence would be blighted. On 11 December 1961, Dr Barrett died. 'His father had been ill for a long time,' says Libby Gausden. 'He had cancer and it was very painful, and I think it was almost a great relief to the children as he was suffering so much before he died. Syd was a great diary writer. Each page was about a foot and a half long, and he would fill every page. But on the day his father died, he just wrote "Poor Dad died today".'

Many people have speculated about the impact of his father's death on Syd. David Gilmour, who spent a great deal of time with his friend in those years, says that 'Syd never spoke about it. People say his father's death changed him, but at the time it was difficult to recall any great change.'

'I didn't know Syd's father or his brothers, so I never really knew where the men in the family got to,' recalls John Gordon. 'Syd always seemed more worldly than me, and had more freedom and experience, and, after his father died, he seemed to readily take on a lot more responsibility.'

Once his older siblings moved out of 183 Hills Road, Syd commandeered a large room at the front of the house as his bedroom, while his mother let out the former bedrooms to lodgers, many of whom were attending the university and who included at least one minor British aristocrat and a future Japanese Prime Minister.

If Waters and, to some extent, Barrett were displaying an anti-authoritarian streak, they now had an official excuse. With the advent of Bill Haley and The Comets' hit single 'Rock Around the Clock' in 1955, the media had officially announced the invention of the teenager, and their designated soundtrack – rock 'n' roll. Two years later, Elvis Presley would give this new music an iconic image and provide a role model for a generation. Syd's brother Alan played saxophone in a skiffle group, and Syd himself began messing around with a ukelele before persuading his mother to buy him a Hofner acoustic guitar.

'After school, Syd and I would meet in the corridor and I would go over to his, as he lived almost opposite the school,' remembers John Gordon. 'My father was a musician, but part of me didn't want to be like him, so I'd shunned learning the piano but wanted to learn guitar with Syd. He'd also got hold of some American imports and I had an older uncle who was bringing in Bill Haley and Eddie Cochran 78s and 45s. I would take them over to Syd's and we'd try and learn guitar from them. Syd was into everything. Everyone now talks about him liking Bo Diddley, but he was into much broader stuff than that.'

The fourteen-year-old Waters was the ideal age for rock 'n' roll, but was initially wary. Instead, his musical tastes skittered between Dixieland jazz and blues singers such as Bessie Smith. 'Anything,' he admitted later, 'but rock 'n' roll.' Having acquired a guitar from an uncle, Waters also began taking tentative classical lessons with a local female teacher, but later admitted that he'd given up 'as it hurt my fingers, and I found it much too hard'.

Meanwhile, David Gilmour shared none of his future bandmate's suspicion about rock 'n' roll. 'I'm not sure if "Rock Around the Clock" was the very first record I bought, but it must have been one of the first,' he recalls. (He later revealed that the 78rpm disc was destroyed when the family's au pair accidentally sat on it.) Gilmour was much more taken with Elvis Presley's 'Heartbreak Hotel', which followed a year later. At home, his parents' record collection included numerous blues 78s. Like Waters and Barrett, Gilmour had also discovered Radio Luxembourg, with its diverse mix of music that was outside the remit of any existing British radio station – 'All sorts of strange sounds' – and which would have a marked influence on a whole generation of English rock musicians.

While Gilmour's musical education was already underway, his education proper had begun at the age of five when he was sent to boarding school. Doug Gilmour decided to take a six-month sabbatical from Cambridge University and go to Wisconsin in the American

Midwest with Sylvia. The children were despatched to Steeple Claydon in Buckinghamshire where they remained until the end of the following school year.

'My parents loved each other and enjoyed each other's company, but, to be honest, I think they found us rather inconvenient,' Gilmour told *Mojo* magazine in 2006. 'We holidayed together when we were very little, but as soon as we got to the age where we could be bounced off into something else, like joining the Boy Scouts, we never went on holiday together again.' Years later, Gilmour would rediscover letters and a diary from the time, revealing that even when his parents had returned to Cambridge, David and his siblings remained in Steeple Claydon. 'These things seem perfectly normal at the time. It's only later when you think, "Hang on, that wasn't so great." '

At the age of eleven, just as Barrett made his way to the County, Gilmour was enrolled at the Perse School for Boys. Situated just a few doors down from Syd's family home, the Perse was a fee-paying grammar school run on strict authoritarian lines. Its old boys included Sir Peter Hall, founder of the Royal Shakespeare Company and director of the Royal National Theatre. Dating back to the seventeenth century, a quarter of the Perse's pupils were boarders, and all pupils were made to attend Saturday morning lessons, contributing to the atmosphere of, in the words of one of its former alumni, 'a rather snooty public school'.

Though naturally bright, Gilmour's approach to academia was found wanting. 'I was lazy,' he admits now. Elvis may have been a primary influence, but it was the arrival of a pair of guitar-playing, high-harmony singing siblings – the Everly Brothers and their 1957 breakthrough hit 'Bye Bye Love' – that was pivotal in Gilmour picking up the guitar.

'I loved the Everlys. When I was thirteen, our next-door neighbour's son was given a guitar, and he was completely tone deaf and had no interest in it whatsoever. So I borrowed it and never gave it back. I started plonking away on it, and my parents were pretty happy about that, and got me the Pete Seeger guitar book and record. These elementary lessons were wonderful.'

Also painstakingly working his way through the Seeger instruction manual was Gilmour's friend Rado Klose, who, using his middle name as Bob Klose, would later go on to become a member of the early Pink Floyd.

'David and I had known each other since we were born,' says Klose. 'His father had met mine before either of them even had families. I can't recall if David actually took lessons from me, but I can remember the two of us listening to that Pete Seeger record and scrambling around listening to Radio Luxembourg. We'd hear a record, and think: How do you play that? And then set about trying to find out. The Ventures' [1960 hit] "Walk Don't Run" was one of those. David instantly picked up how to play it, while it took the rest of us much longer.'

Klose was also a pupil at the County: 'At that time, your life is totally bound up in school. Syd was the year below me and Roger Waters was the year above. We all had similar musical tastes. For a while I was very much into jazz, but only jazz made up until 1935! Then Django Reinhardt. Roger was really into Jimmy Dufree. Discovering the blues, though, was a real moment of epiphany. I remember going into a record shop after school and finding a record by Leadbelly. I didn't know what it was. I just liked the name, so the guy in the shop let me take it into the booth and listen. And it was like the essence of everything I'd ever liked in music – but more concentrated.'

While Leadbelly would become a shared favourite for Klose, Gilmour and Waters, the latter found his musical interests went unappreciated at home. From the age of twelve, Roger had regularly attended jazz concerts at the local Corn Exchange, but, unlike Syd's mother, Mary Waters had little time for music.

'She claimed to be tone deaf,' her son recalled. 'She had no real interest in the arts. She was very political. Politics was more important than anything else. I certainly didn't feel encouraged in music either at home or at school.'

In 1961, the same year that Syd Barrett lost his father, Gilmour's home life underwent a major upheaval. As part of what was commonly known as 'the brain drain', in which British academics were lured abroad by high-paying teaching posts, Doug Gilmour was offered a position at New York University, where he was eventually appointed Professor of Genetics. He and Sylvia announced their decision to go for a year. Gilmour's ten-year-old brother Mark went with them, while his siblings stayed in England; sister Catherine was already attending university. The fifteen-year-old David was invited to the States, but, already fired up by the musical possibilities around him, he chose to stay in Cambridge, where he lodged with a family in Chesterton. Left unsupervised, Gilmour still found it easy to sneak out to attend gigs instead of studying for his O-Level exams. Waters, Barrett and Gilmour, with their shared academic backgrounds, all now had absent fathers, and were striking out independently, muddling towards the beginnings of what would become Pink Floyd.

If Gilmour was the first to embrace rock 'n' roll, his future Floyd partners weren't slow in seeking out a rebellious antidote to the strictures of Cambridge school life, even without Elvis to encourage them. If Waters' meticulous raid on the Cambridge County orchard seems more like an art prank than a simple act of vandalism, then it's little wonder. As a university town, Cambridge was perfectly placed to welcome the influence of a new school of non-conformist American underground writers and poets, 'the Beat Generation'. The writers in question – Allen Ginsberg, Jack Kerouac and William Burroughs – always balked at the title, frequently protesting, 'Three friends does not make a generation.' Nevertheless, they shared enough of a like-minded vision to warrant the comparison. Ginsberg's *Howl and Other Poems* (1956) and Burroughs' novel *The Naked Lunch* (1959) both gained widespread over-exposure after running up against obscenity laws. Yet it was Kerouac's *On the Road*, finally published in 1957 in the wake of the *Howl* trial, that helped establish the Beat Generation's wider popularity. The story of a poetic drifter, hitching lifts and jumping freight trains across America, popping pills and enjoying casual sex to a soundtrack of bebop jazz, it became required reading material for smart teenagers growing up in a university town.

The Beats' frantic creativity, anti-conformist stance and spirit of adventure appealed to both Barrett and Waters. In letters to his girlfriend Libby Gausden, Barrett enthused about *On the Road*. Experimenting with his appearance, he adopted the uniform of black trousers and fisherman's sweaters, which was popular among art students and jazz fans. Sometime after the death of his father, he began to refer to himself occasionally as 'Syd the Beat', the 'Syd' taken from one Sid Barrett, the unrelated drummer in a jazz band he'd encountered playing the local YMCA and the Anchor pub.

'There was at the time,' Waters explained years later, 'this idea of going east in search of adventure.'

Andrew 'Willa' Rawlinson accompanied Waters and others on various trips around Europe. 'We took Roger's mum's car and drove to Istanbul via France, Italy and Greece,' he recalls. 'It took us about three months.' Aged nineteen, Waters joined Rawlinson and others on a jaunt to the Middle East. 'We went in an ambulance called Brutus,' says Rawlinson. 'We knew nothing about engines, put no water in it and it blew up in Beirut. So the five of us went our separate ways. Roger hitched back to England on his own.' It was a trip that would provide an inspiration for his 2003 solo song 'Leaving Beirut', which opened with the line: 'So we left Beirut, Willa and I . . .'

By 1962 Syd Barrett's scepticism about rock 'n' roll had diminished. His musical interests now included Americans such as Chuck Berry and Bo Diddley, but also the homegrown instrumental guitar band The Shadows, a key influence on every aspiring guitarist in the early sixties. The release of the first Beatles single, 'Love Me Do', in 1962 and debut album, *Please Please Me*, a year later, gave another inspirational boost to the Cambridge music scene. The Beatles were English, nearer to home, 'more like us', and even the usually sceptical Waters said that 'the songs on their first album were just so good.' Barrett became an evangelical Beatles fan, and, having acquired his first electric guitar and the Holy Grail of learning manuals – the Pete Seeger record and book – started to think about a group of his own.

While Syd and John Gordon would spend time thrashing around on guitars, Syd's first serious attempt came with the formation of Geoff Mott and The Mottoes, centred around their gregarious lead singer Geoff Mottlow, another ex-Cambridge County boy and Roger Waters' rugby team-mate. The group had an ideal rehearsal space in Syd's front room/bedroom and commandeered it for regular Sunday afternoon sessions. Barrett and Nobby Clarke played guitar, Mottlow sang lead vocals, while Clive Welham (who sadly died in 2012) played drums.

'It was quite possible that when me and Syd first started I didn't even have any proper drums and was playing on a biscuit tin with knives,' says Clive Welham. 'But I bought a kit, started taking lessons and actually got quite good. I can't even remember who our bass player was.' Welham is certain that, contrary to most existing reference books, it wasn't Tony Sainty, a local bassist who would end up playing in bands with David

Gilmour. 'I played in bands with Tony later,' insists Clive, 'but not with Syd. There were a lot of people who used to drop by and have a blow. Roger Waters was always round Syd's house, but it was before he was doing music.'

The Mottoes' repertoire revolved around covers of songs by Buddy Holly, Chuck Berry, The Shadows and Eddie Cochran. Years later Barrett would tell the music press that 'the band did a lot of work at private parties', but The Mottoes only played one ticketed event, a fund-raising gig in March 1963 for the Campaign for Nuclear Disarmament at the local Friends Meeting House, advertised with a poster designed by Roger Waters. The connection was political as well as musical. Roger had followed his mother's interest in left-wing politics by becoming a fundraiser for the *Morning Star* and chairman of the youth section of the local CND. (He later took part in CND marches to Aldermaston.) 'We all behaved ourselves if Roger Waters was around,' laughs Libby Gausden. 'It was like a teacher coming into the room. Being older, Roger certainly looked the part. He had a motorbike before any of us even had driving licences *and* he owned a leather jacket.' The band wouldn't last, but, in 1965, Mottlow's next group, The Boston Crabs, would score a minor hit with the future Northern Soul classic 'Down in Mexico', while Clive Welham would become a fixture on the Cambridge circuit.

At the age of sixteen, Syd's days at the County were drawing to an end and he announced his intention to go to art school. His mother worked in the office of the Cambridge School of Art and to help her son's progress, arranged for Syd and John Gordon to attend extra-curricular Saturday morning art classes. Their diligence paid off, and, in the summer of 1962, both boys enrolled at the school, where Syd, studying Art and Design, would remain for the next two years, cutting a swathe through the school and making a lasting impression on lecturers and pupils alike.

'Syd was a very big personality,' remembers fellow student John Watkins. 'I mean this in the nicest possible way, but he had a real mouth on him. John Gordon reckons it was probably because his dad had died. But Syd really pushed it. He wouldn't take bullshit, and he was always pissing about.'

Situated in East Road, the Cambridge School of Art had been founded in the nineteenth century. Ronald Searle, the cartoonist and illustrator of the popular St Trinian's series of books, was a pupil, as were Spitting Image creators Peter Fluck and Roger Law.

'Syd reminded me of a Spanish gypsy,' says Richard Jacobs, a pupil in Barrett's illustration class. 'Later on he used to claim his grandmother *was* a gypsy. Though I'm not entirely sure we ever believed him. The first time I saw him was in the summer of 1962, and he was carrying an acoustic guitar and wearing Levi's. I was very impressed. This was when the rest of us were all still dressing very straight. There was a common room in the basement area of the college and Syd seemed to commandeer it at break times. He was always sat on the window sill, playing guitar. He used to sing this old music hall thing – "just because my hair is curly, just because my teeth are pearly . . ."' (A 1910 jazz song, 'Shine', later recorded by Ella Fitzgerald and Louis Armstrong.)

The school also brought Barrett back into contact with David Gilmour. With Gilmour's parents briefly returned from the US, David was now studying Modern Languages at the Cambridgeshire College of Arts and Technology next door. As John Watkins recalls, he seemed to spend most of his time between lectures in the art school. 'There were several of us who played or, in my case, *half*-played guitar, and we started having sessions in the art school at lunchtimes,' says Watkins. 'Dave started sitting in on these, and spending more and more time with us. Before Cambridge, I'd come from Egypt and Cyprus, so I didn't know what was going on in the English music scene. I had a guitar and I started to pick up stuff from Syd, who gave me a few lessons, and I was always hassling Gilmour for new chords. The Beatles were just starting, so Syd would have just learned something like "Twist and Shout", and Dave turned me on to Dylan.' Gilmour had discovered the American singer-songwriter when his parents returned from the US with a copy of his latest album.

'In all the time I saw him there,' says Stephen Pyle, another pupil, 'I never saw Gilmour without that guitar in his hand. He was so single-minded about it, even then.'

While Gilmour was a more reliable teacher for learning new chords, Syd was prone to wilder tricks. 'He took this experimental approach to playing,' remembers another of his Cambridge peers, David Gale. 'One time in his room, I recall Syd picking up a Zippo lighter, which he might have got off an American serviceman, and running it up and down the guitar neck. I also think someone had a Zippo with a musical box inside it that played a few notes, and he ran that up and down the neck of an amplified guitar, getting that bottleneck effect but with the music box tinkling away inside – which was the type of thing he'd end up doing in Pink Floyd.'

In the classroom, Syd was known for his high jinks. One lecturer regularly had his slide show art history lessons disrupted, as Syd led the class out through the rear windows of the darkened room and back in through the door, ensuring a constant stream of reappearing pupils. On other occasions, he would hide his guitar under his desk and begin strumming it with his feet, infuriating the lecturer, who couldn't understand where the noise was coming from.

'I remember Syd as being obstinate and rebellious with tutors,' says Richard Jacobs. 'He liked to make a scene and would storm out of a lecture hall. He just had this thing where he didn't want to be told what to do. We were all going on a field trip one day and for some reason Syd refused to get on the coach. No idea why. He wouldn't say. He'd just have these tantrums. It was quite feminine in a way.'

John Watkins also observed the unconventional dynamic in the Barrett household: 'Syd had become the man of the house after his dad died. He loved his mum, but he was very funny and very rude to her. I think he was challenging her and seeing how far he could go. His bedroom at home was his domain, and if his mother brought in a cup of tea, he'd start shouting, "Get out of the room, woman!"'

'Syd's mother, Win, was a hearty, wonderful woman,' recalls Libby Gausden. 'She only saw the good in people which is why Syd was allowed to get away with murder. She was also older than all our mothers. She had had Syd's brothers, Don and Alan, very early on. Don was in the RAF and Alan was an academic. They were both bald by thirty! Completely different from Syd. But he was just different from the rest of the family. But Syd had been the same before his father died. Syd's dad was *always* in his study. So Syd had always been left alone to do as he pleased.'

Away from the lunchtime music sessions, Syd's approach to his art was frequently erratic but often yielded results. To the frustration of others, Syd spent more time painting in his back garden than in the college, but, with an assessment looming, would show up at the last possible moment with a masterpiece. 'One minute his pictures would be figurative, the next abstract,' recalls John Gordon. 'He was always experimenting, trying out different styles. Somewhere I have a black-and-white photo I took in his back garden of Syd holding a canvas that's nearly as big as him, and it's an abstract, in dark ochre colours, of a bit of fabric – possibly a shirt – slapped on the canvas with paint thrown all over it.'

Syd's behaviour was still, at this point, viewed as nothing more than mildly eccentric, and his drug use was far from public.

'Syd loved his cannabis,' says Libby Gausden. 'He was certainly smoking it at a time when you could still get away with smoking it on the top deck of the bus, which he did. I never smoked it. None of the Cambridge girls did at the time, though I think that changed when some of them went to London.'

'I never saw Syd smoke dope but we knew it was around,' says John Gordon. 'I moved out of home when I went to art school and although I never got into dope, my flat in Clarendon Street was a crash pad, where people used to drop by to smoke. It was one of those places where you'd wake up in the middle of the night and find people baking banana skins in the oven and trying to smoke them. There was a bunch that used to come round that included two local guys, Pip and Emo, who both ended up working for Pink Floyd. They could show up any time of the day or night.'

Ian Carter, known as Pip, was, in the words of one acquaintance, 'a wild boy from the Fens', with a broad East Anglian accent that sometimes rendered him incomprehensible to those outside his immediate circle. Like others in Pink Floyd's network of associates, Carter would make up the numbers in the road crew, employed as a lighting tech (though he would later be described by Nick Mason as 'one of the world's most spectacularly inept roadies').

Iain 'Emo' Moore is remembered by another of his contemporaries as 'a gurning, gesticulating, knob-crazed guy, with most of his teeth missing'. Like his friend, Pip, Emo would become a close confidant of both Syd Barrett and David Gilmour. Emo would spend the seventies and early eighties working as a live-in housekeeper for Gilmour and his first wife Ginger. An occasional actor, he later appeared in numerous pop videos, and had a blink-and-you'll-miss-it cameo in the film of Pink Floyd's *The Wall*, playing best man at the wedding of the character played by Bob Geldof. No longer part of Gilmour's inner circle, he now lives a much quieter life on the English south coast.

'Pip and Emo nurtured Syd and, later, David,' explains one of their peers. 'They looked after both of them, but also enjoyed the benefits of that friendship, especially with Dave Gilmour.' In Pip's case, this would mean various drug rehab courses paid for by the Floyd guitarist, while Emo enjoyed the expert ministrations of Gilmour's dentist.

'Everybody in town knew Pip and Emo,' laughs John Gordon. 'Back then, they were mods, always haring around on scooters and hanging around outside Miller's music shop. If you've seen the film *Quadrophenia*, they were both like the character played by Phil Daniels, while Dave and Syd were like the character played by Sting – the cool guy.'

'I met Syd when he was sixteen and I started to get to know Dave when he was seventeen,' says Emo, who was then working in a Cambridge coal yard. 'I used to go round to Syd's and smoke dope all day. Dave knew all these people from school but he didn't know any working-class people like me. I went to a terrible school and didn't learn anything. But we got on well, because I would have liked to have been more like Dave, and there was a part of Dave that I think would have liked to have been more like me. His parents were always pushing him, and he wanted to be free of all that. Whereas I wanted to be pushed and given all the stuff he had been given.'

Among Emo's other well-heeled acquaintances was Nigel Lesmoir-Gordon, a former pupil of Oundle public school, a couple of years older than Emo, and then living in Cambridge with his divorced mother. At Oundle, Lesmoir-Gordon had staged concerts, including a coveted appearance from jazz trumpeter Humphrey Lyttelton. In Cambridge he would arrange a series of poetry readings above the Horse and Groom pub, and was, in the words of one of the Cambridge set, 'terribly hip, with the benefit of looking like a young Alain Delon'.

Syd Barrett intrigued Nigel. 'I went round to some of those Sunday afternoon sessions at Syd's house,' he recalls. 'Syd was younger than us. But we were all very interested in him on account of his extraordinary looks and the fact that he had this strange, charismatic quality.'

Among Lesmoir-Gordon's associates were 'a gang of very hip boys', largely comprising pupils from the County and the Perse, including, among others, Andrew Rawlinson, Paul Charrier, David Gale, Seamus O'Connell, Dave Henderson, John Davies, John 'Ponji' Robinson, Anthony Stern, future Pink Floyd sleeve designer Storm Thorgerson and the writer Nick Sedgwick, whose 1989 novel, *Light Blue with Bulges*, would offer a thinly disguised account of the author and his friends' experiences in Cambridge at the time.

'Syd always thought Dave Gale was a bit of a lad, and he worshipped Nigel Gordon,' recalls Libby Gausden. 'I think that lot all thought we were a bit of a teenybopper crowd because we were a bit younger. But they were all very taken with Syd.'

The group's favoured haunts included Miller's music shop, the El Patio and the Guild coffee bars, the Criterion pub (known locally as 'the Cri'), the Dorothy Ballroom and varying spots along the River Cam. Between 1963 and 1965, as John Davies recalls, 'we made the transformation from schoolboys to aspiring beatniks', swapping school uniforms for black polo necks and leather jackets, listening to Miles Davis, riding Vespas and smoking dope purchased from American GIs on the neighbouring airforce bases at Lakenheath and Mildenhall.

'The El Patio was one of the first expresso bars,' explains Anthony Stern. 'I bunked off school at the Perse to do a washing-up job there, as I wanted to rebel. The idea of growing up normally was off the case. So we would spend a lot of time doing things that were likely to annoy one's parents. That's how we developed this fascination with the blues. It was the rebellious aspect that appealed. Ah, good! Another way to twist the knife into our parents.'

'In 1962 we were all into Jimmy Smith,' explained Storm Thorgerson. 'Then 1963 brought dope and rock. Syd was one of the first to get into The Beatles and The Stones. Syd used to take his guitar and busk at parties.'

'I was a couple of years older than Syd and at the Perse,' recalls David Gale. 'By the time I was sixteen, Syd and I were on nodding acquaintance. The thing to be in those days was to look bohemian – which Syd did very well. There were two or three cliques that went down to the river during the school holidays. Each clique would have their favoured spots, but there would be commerce between the camps. We'd be on the green near the Mill Pond, next to two pubs – the Mill and the Anchor. Storm's crowd used to go further up near the men's bathing sheds on Sheep's Green where there were some banks and willow trees. The thing to do was hire a punt at one of the boatyards at the Mill and take it down to Grantchester Meadows.'

Aubrey 'Po' Powell would go on to form the Hipgnosis design company with Storm Thorgerson. He had been educated at King's School in neighbouring Ely, and had first encountered County and Perse boys Storm and David Gale during inter-school cricket and rugby matches.

'Later we had a mutual friend in Cambridge, a Liverpudlian drug-dealer named Nod,' recalls Po now. 'Which is how I got to know those guys again.' On leaving school, he took a tiny room in the same Clarendon Street house where John Gordon had been living. 'There were loads of people in and out of there,' he remembers. 'The comedian Peter Cook's sister, Sarah, had the basement flat, so we used to hang out with her. Storm's mother's house was next door in Earl Street, so there was a little enclave where we used to congregate.'

Storm Thorgerson's mother, Evangeline, was a potter and school-teacher at Ely Grammar School for Girls, and a friend of Mary Waters. She was separated from Storm's father, and, like Syd, Storm enjoyed the run of the family home. He had spent the early part of his life in the highly liberal Summerhill Free School in Suffolk, an establishment later dubbed by the media 'The Do What You Please School'. 'This meant that Storm always seemed terribly advanced for his years,' recalls one of his peers.

'Storm used to make films, using his friends as actors,' recalls Anthony Stern. 'He made one called *The Meal* which he shot at my parents' house. It was a surreal fantasy, and at one point Nick Sedgwick got "eaten". So there was Nick's semi-naked body lying on my parents' table, which raised a lot of tut tuts from my father and lots of "For God's sake, Anthony, what are you doing?"'

As well as coming from highly academic families, many of the group had another thing in common. Storm's father, like Nigel's, was separated from his mother. Meanwhile, Syd, Roger Waters and John 'Ponji' Robinson had lost their fathers. 'There was,' as John Davies explains, 'a lot of us with fathers that were physically or emotionally absent. Or both.'

'Almost all of us had parents that had gone through World War Two,' elaborates Anthony Stern. 'My father suffered from a complete inability to talk about his experiences in the war. Added to this was the fact that in Cambridge you were surrounded by this enormous weight of history and all these brilliant people. My parents were also academics at St John's College. So as the children of academic parents, as was Syd, we grew up feeling as if nothing we did was ever going to be considered good enough. I think many of us suffered from what I now call "The Cambridge Syndrome".'

Left to his own devices, Storm Thorgerson's bedroom at Earl Street became, as one of the crowd described it, 'a fuelling station' for the aspirant beatniks. 'The main event of the evening was to go to Storm's place,' explains Emo. 'You could just about fit ten people in his bedroom, and we'd all be sitting on the floor, smoking, trying not to wake his mother – asleep next door.'

'Storm had this amazing room,' recalls Po. 'It was covered in graffiti and montages of surreal pictures cut out of magazines, and that sort of thing was absolutely unheard of back then. But then Syd's room was amazing, too. Syd's was full of paintings and little model cars and model aeroplanes, and all sorts of things you might associate with a typical art student. But then I went there one day and there was this dodecahedron, quite big, about eighteen inches across, made out of balsa wood, and then another one, nine inches across, and another smaller, all just hanging from the ceiling. He'd made them himself – these absolutely perfect models.'

Po was similarly intrigued by Syd's appearance and manner. 'I always have this memory of him in his room, walking around barefoot, but standing in this weird way of his on his tip-toes, sort of hovering, with his hair hanging down and a cigarette in his hand. Almost elf-like in a way. He had this style of dressing, terribly arty. He'd turn up in the pub wearing some blue and white matelot shirt, looking as though he'd just walked out of Montparnasse in the 1920s.'

Yet Barrett could be as elusive with his old schoolfriends as he was with his newer art school companions.

'He could be with a crowd of people and then suddenly disappear – gone,' says Po. 'He wouldn't tell you where he was going, and then you'd be with a crowd of people later on and he would suddenly appear. I don't think it was deliberate. I think he got easily bored and liked to go off and do his own thing. He had a great sense of humour but he could also suddenly withdraw from everything. One minute you'd be sitting in a room, getting stoned, and then the next minute he'd disappear.'

Libby Gausden recalls Barrett's disappearing acts: 'Instead of going to all the things we'd been invited to, he'd drive off and just sit in the Gog Magog hills. As soon as he bought his first car, he was always taking me to look at rivers and hills, which at the time I thought was all terribly boring. But Syd was into nature, when all the trendy people weren't.'

By late 1962, David Gilmour had played some gigs with a local band called The Ramblers, which already included rhythm guitarist John Gordon and ex-Mottoes' drummer Clive Welham. 'We were a semi-pro band, playing and earning,' says Welham now. 'Dave had come on a hell of a lot. I'd seen him playing about a year before and he wasn't up to it then, but you could tell he'd put a lot of work in since.'

'Dave and Syd were two of those guys you couldn't miss,' remembers Rick Wills, who would play bass guitar in one of Gilmour's later groups. 'I used to run into Dave at Ken Stevens' music shop. We'd both be trying out guitars and making a bloody nuisance of ourselves. Dave had an air about him, though – quite arrogant sometimes, an air of "I know it all". Syd had a look that was all his own. To be frank, I never took him seriously. He was one of those arty types who walked around with a Bob Dylan LP under one arm. Not a proper rock 'n' roller, I thought.'

However, others, including Mick Jagger, disagreed. Libby Gausden accompanied Syd to a Rolling Stones gig in a village hall in nearby Whittlesey. 'It must have been something the Stones had been con-tracted to do before they became famous,' says Libby. 'After the show, Mick Jagger came straight up to us out of everybody in the crowd. I remember it because he had this awful, put-on voice, and being from Cambridge we all spoke properly. He was asking about my clothes but he was also fascinated by Syd. He thought Syd looked like a very young Bill Wyman – the same dark hair and very thin.'

At a Bob Dylan show at London's Festival Hall, fashion designer Mary Quant, also in the audience, was, as Libby now puts it, 'very taken with Syd'. Back in Cambridge, older women at the parties they attended would be enchanted by Barrett, and pass him their telephone numbers. 'He used to ring them up,' admits Libby. 'But we'd both listen to what they said, and laugh ourselves silly when he arranged to meet them, then didn't turn up.'

At the same time, Gilmour was also moonlighting with another local group, The Newcomers, previously Chris Ian and The Newcomers. 'Dave had a poxy old Burns guitar and a crappy amp, but you could see he'd got it even then; he was bloody good,' their lead singer Waterson later recalled.

With Syd Barrett's stint at the Cambridge School of Art coming to a close, his future plans still involved art rather than music. 'But I always thought his art was something to do while he was waiting for something to happen with his music,' says Libby Gausden.

In the summer of 1963, Syd travelled to London to attend an interview for Camberwell School of Art, even though it meant missing a Beatles gig. The sacrifice paid off and he was accepted. 'Syd desperately wanted to go to Chelsea art school but he couldn't get in,' reveals Libby. 'Then he found out that Camberwell was even trendier.'

That summer, he and Anthony Stern had staged an exhibition of their work above the Lion and Lamb pub in nearby Milton. Now studying at St John's College, Stern had been granted the use of a studio space by the provost of the neighbouring Kings College. 'They were friends of my parents, so I was immensely privileged,' says Stern. 'Having this room offered me another chance to escape from my parents and gave me the opportunity to meet girls.'

Unfortunately, the exhibition was less successful. 'Syd's paintings were wild abstracts and still lives in oil on canvas; mine were rather feeble attempts at psychotic surrealism. We didn't sell anything.'

However, Stern's makeshift studio would provide a bolthole for Barrett to escape to. 'Syd and I would spend ages in there, having endless conversations about the nature of film and art and music. There was a man at St. Catherine's College called Reg Gadney, who made light boxes in his room. He showed us these things – they were like huge television screens behind which there were a series of mechanical gadgets and light projections. These were the sort of ideas that later became part of psychedelia, and which the Floyd used in their light shows. Syd and I were fascinated.'

Syd had previously experimented with home-made light shows with his art school friend John Gordon. When John moved into a flat in Clarendon Street, he and Syd would delight in projecting images on to the windows of the house opposite.

Through Anthony, Syd would make contact with another aspiring artist that year. Recently graduated from the university, Peter Whitehead was renting a studio in Cambridge's Grange Road. Later, as a film-maker, he would shoot the defining footage of the Syd-era Pink Floyd. For now, though, Barrett and his musical friends were simply 'the nameless group' that rehearsed in the room next to his studio. 'I think Syd was having an affair with the daughter of the owners of the house,' says Peter now. 'The louder his group rehearsed, the louder I put on my Bartók, Janáček and Wagner albums. I didn't like pop music. When Syd discovered I was a painter, he used to drift in and chat and ask me what I was listening to. I had no idea our paths would cross again.'

In the autumn, Barrett moved to London and began his degree course at Camberwell, where he was remembered as an enthusiastic, if single-minded student, surprising his tutors and other pupils with his insistence on using the same-sized brush for all his paintings. Among his compositions from the summer of 1964 was a portrait of pop singer Sandie Shaw, which he lovingly sent to her record company, only to hear nothing in response. London was exciting, but regular trips back to Cambridge brought him into contact with his old sparring partners.

Back at home, Andrew Rawlinson had become involved in staging some 'happenings' at the Round Church. Integral to these events was the participation of the audience. In the same spirit, Rawlinson bought a large map of the world, traced the outlines of fifty countries onto sheets of paper and then sent them out to other like-minded individuals with the message, 'Decorate this how you like and send back to me'.

Syd was sent Russia, which he duly painted blue and returned. He later sent Rawlinson a book he'd crafted called *Fart Enjoy*. Comprising seven sheets of cardboard taped together, its contents included snippets of poetry, doodles, pictures torn from magazines, a possible spoof letter entitled 'Dear Roge'. ('How did the group get on at Essex?') A photo of a bare-breasted model is scrawled with the words 'Fuk, Suk and Lik'. Rawlinson described it as 'a mixture of austere bordering on the abstract and blazing whimsy'.

However committed Syd may have been to his art, he still found himself drawn back to his old musical haunts in Cambridge. During the summer holidays, he began playing guitar with The Hollerin' Blues (sometimes known as Barney and The Hollerin' Blues), during a return trip to Cambridge. Here, he came into contact with sixteen-year-old

Matthew Scurfield, the half-brother of Ponji Robinson and a school-friend of The Hollerin' Blues' harmonica player, Pete Glass.

Scurfield would go on to become a theatre, TV and film actor. 'My father was what you might call "a romantic socialist", and sent me to a very rough secondary modern school in Cambridge,' he says now. 'I'd failed my 11-plus and ended up almost dropping out. My aunt was a very prominent psychiatrist in the area and I ended up at the Criterion, peddling pills that I'd taken from her medicine cabinet.'

Through what Matthew describes as 'the trafficking of medical contraband', he came into contact with Pip and Emo. They introduced him to Syd one evening in the Criterion. 'We clicked straight away because we were both interested in theatres, and Syd and I discovered we'd both built our own model theatres. Ponji and I both became good friends with him. I didn't even know he was a musician until I went to see The Hollerin' Blues at somewhere like the Dorothy Ballroom and there was Syd on guitar. He wasn't the best player in the world, but he certainly had an aura about him.'

By early 1965 The Hollerin' Blues had turned into Those Without, and Syd was back, playing guitar during the holidays. 'We played a couple of our best gigs ever with Syd, at the University Cellars and the Victoria Ballroom,' recalls drummer Stephen Pyle. 'He was on a visit from London and he'd got himself kitted out with a new Fender and a big Vox amp. The Kinks' single "You Really Got Me" had come out and Syd was thrilled with that. He kept playing it over and over again during band practice.'

Meanwhile, David Gilmour was making his own plans. If he passed his A-levels, it would mean going to university, which would take him away from the local music scene. Gilmour chose to drop out halfway through his exams. By now, his parents had returned permanently to the US and he was living alone in a flat in Mill Road. He'd also helped form a new band, Jokers Wild, which had coalesced around Gilmour, John Gordon and Clive Welham.

While Syd upped sticks to London, Gilmour stayed put. Jokers Wild's forte was five-part harmonies. 'We came together in the first place because we could all sing,' says Welham. Their set centred around songs by The Four Seasons, Sam and Dave, and The Beach Boys, performed in as many clubs, parties and neighbouring airforce bases as would take them, including a regular Wednesday night booking at Les Jeux Interdits, a club in Cambridge's Victoria Ballroom, popular with foreign students from the neighbouring colleges. 'I think at one time we all had foreign girlfriends,' recalls Clive.

The line-up originally comprised Gordon, Welham, keyboard player and saxophonist Dave Altham, and bassist Tony Sainty, later replaced at odd times by either Rick Wills or David's brother Peter.

Gilmour may have come across as shy and unassuming, but his appearance got him noticed. 'Dave was always more clean-cut than Syd,' remembers John Gordon. 'He had a collegey look, a style of American dress – a bit preppy – with white Levi's. It went down well with the women.'

'All the girls absolutely drooled over him,' says Christine Smith (formerly Bull), who first encountered the band as a seventeen-year-old in Cambridge. 'We used to call him the Adonis.' With Gilmour's parents overseas, Christine's family would welcome David and Peter into their home, including a Christmas Day evening 'when they brought round their guitars and kept us entertained for hours'.

A personal ad in an early-sixties issue of the pop magazine *Rave* offers a glimpse of Gilmour's popularity at the time. Placed by Libby Gausden's schoolfriend Vivien Brans (known by the nicknames Twig and Twiggy), it read: 'Last June I met a boy called David Gilmour in Cambridge. He played in a group called Jokers Wild. He said he planned to go to London, and always wore blue jeans with patches on them. If anyone knows where he is, please tell him to write to the girl with long blonde hair who pushed his van up Guest Road to get it started. Tell him Vivien is anxious to hear from him, if he remembers her.' (Vivien would become David Gilmour's long-term girlfriend in 1964.)

The guitarist's growing reputation was also enough to attract the attention of Beatles manager Brian Epstein, who sent a talent scout to the Victoria Ballroom. Epstein decided not to sign him, but, with his reputation preceding him, Gilmour was the obvious understudy for other players on the circuit. Hugh Fielder, now a music critic, but then singing with Cambridge band The Ramblin' Blues, hired Gilmour when his own group's guitarist dropped out at the last minute for a gig at a local girls' school in 1965. 'We'd had girls screaming at us before,' recalls Fielder. 'And we really didn't want to miss out on it again. Gilmour was fantastic.' There was, it transpires, only one problem: 'Unfortunately, he charged us as much for his services as we were getting for the whole gig.'

For Roger Waters, the arrival of The Beatles and The Rolling Stones had thawed his resistance to rock music. One evening, he and Barrett had travelled to London to see a package rock 'n' roll show featuring The Rolling Stones, Helen Shapiro and Gene Vincent, at the Gaumont State Cinema in Kilburn. The brooding, leather-clad Vincent had none of Elvis's pretty boy charm. An alcoholic who'd permanently damaged his left leg in a motorcycle crash and walked with a pronounced limp, stories circulated of Vincent being rolled up in a carpet by his bodyguard and forcibly carried on stage after he refused to perform. Maybe something about Vincent's outsider image and damaged persona made its mark on Barrett and Waters. Whatever the catalyst, on the train back to Cambridge, the two sat together, sketching a picture of the amps they would need when they started their own rock 'n' roll group. Yet by the time Syd arrived in London, Roger was already part of a band.

Without Barrett's flair for painting or Gilmour's for playing guitar, Waters found himself pondering his next move on leaving the County. When he saw Syd perform with The Mottoes, Waters would talk later of 'wanting to be a bit further towards the centre of things'. After abandoning plans to study Mechanical Engineering at Manchester University, he submitted to a series of aptitude tests for the National Institute of Industrial Psychology, who suggested he might be cut out for a career in architecture.

As a precursor, Waters spent a few months working in an architectural office in neighbouring Swavesey, before enrolling on a degree course at Regent Street Polytechnic in London's Little Titchfield Street, near Oxford Circus. Waters brought his guitar and billeted himself in a number of downmarket student houses, including a cold-water squat near the Kings Road. As one of his future bandmates would later explain, 'Roger wanted to free himself but he didn't know how to do it.' By the spring of 1963, though, Waters had drifted into the orbit of a group of like-minded fellow students, which included a drummer, Nick Mason, and a keyboard player, Richard Wright.

Nicholas Berkeley Mason was born on 27 January 1944 in Edgbaston on the outskirts of Birmingham. His father, Bill, was a Communist Party member and former shop steward for the Association of

Cinematographic Technicians. Accepting a job as a documentary film director, he moved with his wife Sally to Downshire Hill in Hampstead Garden Suburb, North London, when Nick was aged two. Three daughters, Sarah, Melanie and Serena, completed the family.

Bill collected vintage cars, and was a motor racing enthusiast who competed at an amateur level. On a similar theme, his early film-making credits included *Le Mans*, a 1955 documentary about the French sports car race. The Masons' car collection wasn't the only evidence of their wealth. Like the rest of his future bandmates, Nick's upbringing was comfortable. Though, in his case, a little *more* comfortable. As Pink Floyd's first manager Peter Jenner recalled, 'I remember being amazingly impressed that Nick's parents had a swimming pool.'

Nick's musical education also began with Bill Haley, Elvis Presley and regular scanning of the airwaves in search of Radio Luxembourg. He learned to play the violin and piano, but showed no great aptitude at either. A drum kit followed later, and Mason became part of an ad-hoc school group called The Hot Rods, whose repertoire rarely extended beyond tireless renditions of the *Peter Gunn* TV theme.

At the age of eleven, Mason was enrolled at Frensham Heights, a co-ed boarding school near Farnham in Surrey. Today, the school prides itself on 'No uniforms, no competition, teachers and pupils all on a first-name basis.' And even in the 1950s, compared to Waters' experiences at the strait-laced, boys-only Cambridge County, Nick's time at Frensham Heights was a good deal more relaxed. 'I enjoyed my time at Frensham,' he wrote in 2004. 'It was fairly traditional, in terms of blazers and exams, but it had a far more liberal approach to education.'

Mason didn't apply himself quite so vigorously to his academic work as might have been expected. At Frensham, his interest in music was stirred by the modern jazz and, later, bebop records played in the school common room. By the time he was fourteen, he was playing drums again, albeit on his own terms. 'I never had any formal training,' he said later. 'And I think that was a big mistake. The easiest way to learn something properly is to be taught it.'

After leaving school, Nick 'drifted into a five-year architecture course' at Regent Street Poly in the spring of 1962. Perhaps tellingly, Frank Rutter, the father of Nick's then girlfriend and future wife, Lindy, was an architect of some note. Even then, while drumming again, he seemed to share none of David Gilmour's burning ambition to become a musician. As Mason would tell one interviewer some years later: 'I'm a very bad example of how things can still go right without trying – how you can still get lucky.'

More than architecture or music, Nick's passion was cars, one of which, a 1930 Austin 'Chummy', he used to drive himself to and from the Poly. Mason wrote in his 2004 book that this car was the reason Roger Waters first 'deigned to speak to me'. Waters wanted to borrow the vehicle; the protective Mason refused, claiming it was currently out of action. Shortly after, Roger spotted Nick behind the wheel. Nevertheless, when the two were given a shared assignment, they struck up a friendship.

In September 1963, Poly students Keith Noble and Clive Metcalfe were casting around for like-minded students and placed a notice on the college noticeboard. 'It said, "Anyone want to start a group?"' recalls Clive Metcalfe. At the time Noble and Metcalfe were already some way ahead of their new rhythm section. 'Keith and I used to sing together in a bar in Albemarle Street in Piccadilly. We were doing everything from The Beatles to Peter, Paul and Mary, R&B, twelve-bar blues. I was actually at the Chelsea School of Art, but at the time it was being rebuilt so they put us into Regent St Poly.' Keen to expand beyond a duo, Noble and Metcalfe began rehearsing in the student common room with 'the people that saw our notice and turned up'. These included Mason and Waters (then playing rudimentary guitar), and Keith Noble's sister Sheilagh.

'Sheilagh used to sing with Keith, but I don't remember her doing very much with us,' says Metcalfe. 'Roger wasn't very well developed as a musician, so although I originally played lead and rhythm guitar, when we realised we needed a bass player, I switched to bass.'

The band took the name of The Sigma 6 after expanding to a sextet with the arrival of another Poly student, pianist Richard William Wright. Born on 28 July 1943, Wright was the son of a biochemist, Robert, who was employed at the local Unigate Dairies, and his wife Daisy. The Wrights lived in Hatch End, Pinner, North London. Pinner was also home to Reg Dwight, who would become Elton John, and, much later, Duran Duran's future lead singer Simon Le Bon.

After a stint at the local prep school, St John's, Richard was enrolled at Haberdashers Aske's, a fee-paying grammar school, then located in Hampstead. (It later moved to Elstree.) By the time Richard reached his teens, he'd learned trombone, saxophone, guitar and piano, and was a frequent visitor to trad jazz gigs at the Railway Tavern in neighbouring Harrow and Wealdstone, where The Who would later launch their career. 'I wasn't into pop music at all,' he said later. 'I was listening to jazz. The music I first listened to that made me want to be a musician was back in the days of Coltrane, Miles Davis and Eric Dolphy.'

A brief stint as a messenger boy for the local Kodak factory in Harrow and Wealdstone ensued, but, unsure of what he wanted to do with his life, Richard sheepishly followed his careers master's advice and, in 1962, signed up to study architecture at Regent Street Poly. Years later, he would admit that 'being an architect never really interested me'.

Not owning a keyboard at the time, Wright's role in the band was dependent on whether a piano was available at the venue. Bookings were mostly student birthday parties and private functions in and around the Poly. With Sheilagh Noble gone, Wright's girlfriend Juliette Gale, then also studying at the Poly, stepped in as an occasional singer.

'Juliette was lovely and she sang brilliantly,' remembers Clive Metcalfe. 'She'd sing blues, things like "Summertime". Rick Wright was just incredibly quiet. I don't think I ever really got to know him.'

By the end of the year, the group had acquired a manager and some-time songwriter in another student, Ken Chapman, who'd push his own compositions on to the band to fit in with their repertoire of R&B numbers. ('There was one that was set to the tune of Beethoven's *Für Elise*,' recalled Waters.) Chapman also hustled an audition with Gerry Bron, then a music publisher and later the founder of Bronze Records. 'He said the songs were quite good but to forget the band,' remembered Nick Mason. 'I think if we'd listened to anyone who had any taste at the time we'd have folded up right there and then. But we were so egocentric we just carried on.' Throughout the coming year there were many name changes, including, supposedly, The Megadeaths and The Screaming Abdabs (later shortened to The Abdabs). Interviewed for an article in the student magazine, The Abdabs were photographed posing awkwardly beside a lamp-post in Great Titchfield Street, Waters –

denouncing rock as 'beat without expression' – wearing his regulation Dylan-style black leather box jacket and best sneer.

'I struggled with Roger,' admits Clive Metcalfe. 'Nick Mason was very easy-going but I found Roger rather acerbic, and I was an easy target. I'd grown up in the country and had had a rather sheltered background. Roger didn't suffer fools gladly, and I'm afraid he could make a fool of me rather easily.'

'I'm not sure if I was aware of being menacing,' Waters explained later. 'Although I think that in my insecurity I probably tried cultivating it. I was so frightened of everything as a young man that I became quite aggressive.'

At the same time as he was attending the Poly, Wright was taking private lessons in musical theory and composition at the Eric Gilder School of Music, but realising architecture was not his vocation, he jumped ship (or was pushed, according to some sources) at the end of his first year.

'I gave up in boredom,' he later explained. 'So I started going abroad to places like Greece, and then came home to earn a bit of money in jobs like interior designing and private decorating. But I was very unhappy and turned to studying music.' Wright eventually enrolled at London's Royal College of Music.

Meanwhile, Waters and Mason struggled to apply themselves to their studies. Waters, especially, seemed as frustrated with his teachers at the Poly as he had been with those at the County, clashing repeatedly with his Architectural History lecturer. 'I must have been horrible to teach,' he admitted years later. 'I was very bolshie. It was just like school, and I hoped I'd escaped all that.' Yet there were two lecturers that didn't attract Waters' withering contempt. The first, his head of year, encouraged him to bring his guitar into class, and allowed him to play it during study time. The other was architect Mike Leonard, who taught part-time at the Poly and at the Hornsey College of Art. He was an accomplished pianist and, although some fifteen years older than his pupils, shared an interest in the more avant-garde areas of music. Much to Waters' curiosity, Leonard was also experimenting with lighting effects; designing and building contraptions out of glass and Perspex, and experimenting with oil slides. Leonard's house at 39 Stanhope Gardens, Highgate, was large enough to double as a rehearsal space, but he also needed tenants to help pay the mortgage. Mason and Waters were the first to move in.

The arrival of guitarist Bob Klose, David Gilmour's childhood friend, in the summer of 1964 proved timely. Klose had been playing regularly in a Cambridge band, Blues Anonymous, and had become a highly rated guitarist. However, his arrival prompted Clive Metcalfe and Keith Noble to return to working as a duo. 'Bob was one of those guitarists that I thought got overly clever,' says Metcalfe. 'With me and Keith in the band the sound really wasn't gelling.' Metcalfe and Noble would go on to write 'A Summer Song', a US Top 40 hit for Chad and Jeremy later that year. Klose moved into Stanhope Gardens and took over as guitarist, while Waters switched to bass.

Bob Klose wasn't the only Cantabrigian to move down to the capital. After enrolling at Camberwell School of Art, Syd, too, moved into Michael Leonard's house in Stanhope Gardens, sharing a downstairs bedroom with his old schoolfriend Roger Waters. Richard Wright would soon move in with Juliette Gale, and Nick Mason would return to the relative sanctuary – and swimming pool – of his parents' Hampstead home.

For the Cambridge contingent, their first visit to the drummer's parents' home came as surprise. 'The band barely had any money for petrol to make the journey,' recalls Libby Gausden. 'When we arrived at Nick's we were made very welcome by the sort of people you didn't think would make you feel welcome at all. There we were, all black clothes and hair, thinking we were beatniks. I recall Nick had a very good drum kit and money for amplifiers and his parents were quite happy for him to be playing in a group. It seemed to us coming from Cambridge that London people had money.'

Mike Leonard's house was an Aladdin's cave of exotic musical instruments, suits of armour, beatnik books and jazz records, shared with his cats Tunji and McGhee. The set-up appealed to Syd's sense of the bizarre. While Leonard lived and worked on the upper floor, Barrett, Mason, Waters and Klose rehearsed below. 'The noise was phenomenal,' Leonard said in 1991. 'The neighbours sent round the police and council officials. Then they had a lawyer's letter saying someone's health was being damaged.' Undeterred, the band, now calling themselves The Spectrum Five, continued the din, while a fascinated Barrett and Waters helped Leonard with his prototype lights machines. The group would also supply the music for Mike's experiments at Hornsey College of Art's Sound and Light Workshop.

Mike would sit in on some rehearsals and play organ, but, despite a couple of performances with the band in a local pub, had no desire to become a pop star: 'I was a bit too old and didn't have the right image.' Instead, he was content to encourage the band while marvelling at Barrett's practical jokes and fumbled attempts to cook Sunday lunch: 'Half an uncooked cabbage would end up on your plate.' The band briefly adopted the name Leonard's Lodgers in their landlord's honour.

In the meantime, Barrett had tired of sharing a room with Waters and moved in with his Cambridge friend David Gale. The two shared a bed-sit in a decrepit house at 12 Tottenham Street, where another of the Cambridge gang, Seamus O'Connell, was already living with his mother Ella.

'It was this rundown crappy tenement block just off Tottenham Court Road,' says Seamus now. 'I did well at the County up until O-levels, but then I went a bit off my nut due to family troubles. My mother decided to move to London and I went with her. So I was living in this place and studying for my A-Levels, when David and Syd moved down.'

While Barrett disappeared each morning to Camberwell, Gale was studying film at the Royal College of Art and working part-time in the Better Books shop on Charing Cross Road, then the capital's main emporium for beat literature and magazines. At night, they would repair to what Gale remembers as 'our scummy little room' with a mattress either side. As one visitor recalls, 'While domesticity was not a priority in any of the places we lived, that flat in Tottenham Street was the only one I recall in which there were cockroaches.'

Meanwile, having taken a break from his studies, the briefly absent Richard Wright was soon back playing keyboards in Leonard's Lodgers on a permanent basis. He had also enjoyed a musical breakthrough of his own, selling one of his own songs, 'You're the Reason Why', to Liverpudlian harmony trio Adam, Mike and Tim, for the princely sum of £75.

Nevertheless, the role of a proper lead singer was still unfilled. Juliette Gale had left the Poly to attend university in Brighton. Barrett and Klose muddled through on lead vocals, but soon realised that they needed a proper frontman. Syd approached Geoff Mottlow, but he'd just had a hit with The Boston Crabs, and turned them down. At Klose's suggestion, they sought out another Cambridge refugee.

Chris Dennis had sung in a local band called The Redcaps, worked as a technician for the RAF, and had the rare distinction of having sung with Malta's first electric group, The Zodiacs, during a posting on the island. He was older than his penniless student bandmates, and had the benefit of owning a Vox PA system.

'It was very much a case of me joining them,' says Dennis now. 'They wanted to play strictly blues – Slim Harpo, Lightnin' Hopkins, Howlin' Wolf – stuff that was unheard of in the UK at the time. I was much more into rhythm and blues after seeing The Rolling Stones at the Rex Ballroom in Cambridge. That was much more my style.'

Dennis attended rehearsals at Mike Leonard's place and stuck with the group for six months, playing around a dozen gigs, including an opening slot for Jeff Beck's group The Tridents. 'With a lot of bands you find there's someone in the group who's there only because they're a friend, and, at first, I thought Syd was surplus to requirements. He used to sing some numbers, like Chuck Berry's 'No Money Down', but he didn't have any presence. Roger was the leader. It was Roger who told me what to sing and what songs to learn.'

Subsequently, the band have claimed that Dennis's jokey stage banter, including announcing his own made-up song titles for the likes of Howlin' Wolf's 'Smokestack Lightning', became a problem. Dennis takes a different view. 'They didn't have much of a sense of humour,' he insists. 'But a lot of those old blues songs are funny. They used to tell me not to make up song titles, that we should tell people exactly what they were. And I used to say, "Why? They don't know what it is anyway." To be honest, I don't think audiences then were ready for stomping blues with weird lyrics.'

It was during Chris Dennis's tenure in the group that they assumed a variation on what would be their lasting name. Syd had spliced together the monikers of two North Carolina bluesmen, Pink Anderson and Floyd Council, also utilised as the names of his two pet cats, Pink and Floyd. At various points during 1965 and early '66 the group were said to have been called The Pink Floyd Blues Band, The Pink Floyd Sound and The Tea Set, sometimes spelled T-Set.

'I don't *ever* remember us being called The Tea Set,' insists Chris

Dennis. 'But I do remember Syd coming down to rehearsals and telling us he'd come up with a name – Pink Floyd. I didn't like it at first. I got used to it later, but to start with, I didn't think it rang true.'

It's widely believed that the first gig performed by the band under the Pink Floyd name, in whatever variation, was at the Count Down, in Palace Gate, Kensington in February 1965. The band performed three ninety-minute sets and landed a pitiful £15 fee. To cloud the issue of the band's name still further, Barrett's Cambridge art school friend, Richard Jacobs, is adamant that Syd had coined the name as early as 1963. 'I distinctly recall him coming into the common room one afternoon and telling me he had a name for the band he was going to start – Pink Floyd. He said it as if he'd had some revelation in his lunch hour.' By 1967 the story had changed again and Syd was spinning yarns to gullible interviewers that the name had been transmitted to him from a flying saucer while he was meditating on a leyline.

Yet there were further changes afoot. Unhappy with the spoof song titles Chris Dennis created for their blues standards, Waters insisted that Bob Klose fire him. Before he had the chance, the singer announced that the RAF had posted him to Bahrain. 'I wouldn't have stuck with them for much longer anyway,' he claims. 'When I came back from Bahrain, there was a Pink Floyd LP in the shops. When I heard it, I didn't relate to it at all. The kind of music Syd would end up doing came as a complete surprise to me.'

With Dennis gone, Barrett was reluctantly pushed into the role of frontman. Through a contact of Richard Wright's the band scrounged some free time at a West Hampstead recording studio to record a demo. Alongside Slim Harpo's 'I'm A King Bee' were Barrett's own 'Butterfly' and 'Double O Bo' (a barely disguised tribute to Bo Diddley) and 'Lucy Leave', which, with its stolid Rolling Stones groove, gave little indication of the fanciful wordplay and *outré* musicality that lay ahead.

Then again, the wider musical competition was daunting. 'I can remember seeing The Who on *Top of the Pops* doing "My Generation", and thinking: Yes! Now that's what I want to do,' recalls Mason. 'That would have been in 1964, but I couldn't have imagined that it would have been possible with what we were doing.'

Chris Dennis wouldn't be Pink Floyd's only casualty that year. By the summer of 1965, Bob Klose was gone. 'Bob was a far better musician than any of us,' said Richard Wright. 'But I think he had some exam problems and felt he ought to apply himself to work, whereas the rest of us weren't so conscientious.'

'Bob heard those dreaded words from his mother and father: "Finish your exams and then do it",' recalls Libby Gausden.

'I felt adrift and I needed to get to grips with things,' says Klose now. 'Syd had just begun to write and was coming through with these songs of his own. At the time, though, it was like, "Oh, Syd's written a song." But it was only later on that I was able to hear the originality of it. Roger would lay these fantastic concepts before us – and later he would make them happen. The grandness of his vision was extraordinary then. But the music we were playing before was influenced by the fact that I was such a facile guitar player – always whizzing around. Syd writing gave them the push to stop doing R&B covers and go off in a more original direction.'

'It was a major switch when Bob left the band,' said Mason. 'That sent us spiralling into another direction. Syd and Roger were listening to John Mayall and Alexis Korner, but, somewhere along the line, Syd had discovered writing songs, and his songs were not in that vein at all.'

'Bob Klose was a man with a great wealth of blues runs in his head,' explained Waters. 'And when he left we hadn't anyone who had any blues knowledge, so we had to start doing something else. Syd took over on lead guitar, and I'm sure it was the noises that Pete Townshend was making then, squeaks and feedback, that influenced Syd. So we started making strange noises instead of the blues.'

Later, claims would be made that Klose was uncomfortable with the psychedelic direction the band's music was starting to take. 'That's way too glib,' he insists. 'Also the idea that Syd and the Floyd were a drug-sodden shambles is an absolute nonsense. Syd didn't have to be stoned to play the music he did.'

The summer holidays found Barrett back in Cambridge and hooking up with his old friends. While the Floyd were far from 'drug-sodden', the cliques along the River Cam had found a new obsession: Lysergic Acid Diethylamide, known as LSD, the then still legal hallucinogenic, whose greatest advocate was the American writer and psychologist Dr Timothy

Leary. The co-author of *The Psychedelic Experience*, published in 1964, Leary expounded the merits of the drug as offering 'a journey to new realms of consciousness'.

By 1965, dope had been smoked by some in the circle for at least two years, and one of the crowd had also acquired a subscription to a medical journal, unavailable to the general public, which listed various legal pharmaceuticals and outlined their effects when taken in excess. The exact circumstances of LSD's arrival in Cambridge in the sixties are still the subject of speculation. Anthony Stern first took LSD in 1963, with an acquaintance then studying at Cambridge who had acquired the drug through contacts in America. 'He sat with me in our house in Fisher Street and prepared me for what was going to happen, and, boy, when it happened . . . Cambridge was a wonderful place to take LSD, as there were loads of fascinating places you could go. We used to wander through the Fitzwilliam Museum, staring at the exhibits, and many an acid trip culminated in the Kings College chapel, which had this extraordinary medieval ceiling.'

'At that time, we'd all begun to read about Timothy Leary and the emergence of this wonder drug, and all wondered how we could get hold of it,' adds David Gale. 'Without very much effort, people simply brought it down from London. It was usually on blotting paper, and each blot had 500 micrograms, which was quite a whack back then.'

In truth, it was a British scientist, Michael Hollingshead, who had first turned Timothy Leary onto the drug in 1961. Four years later, Hollingshead opened the World Psychedelic Centre in a plush Mayfair flat, attracting a networked set of old Etonians, Oxbridge alumni and well-connected musicians and poets, including William Burroughs and Paul McCartney, eager to discuss the merits of the new drug.

It was through the Hollingshead connection that Nigel Lesmoir-Gordon, now studying at the London School of Film Technique, took his first trip. 'I first tried LSD in London in March 1965,' he recalls. 'My first trip was absolutely ghastly, my second one much better. After that I started selling it on to other people, I was evangelical about it – selling it for a quid a trip and not making very much money.'

As well as LSD, it was discovered that the seeds of the Morning Glory flower contained a rough strain of the hallucinogenic drug when taken in sufficient quantities, and chewed to a pulp. Florists in Cambridge reported a boom in the seeds' sales, though the plant had its drawbacks. As Emo explains: 'You had to endure two hours of the most excruciating stomach cramps and nausea before you started tripping.'

That summer, David Gale's parents disappeared to Australia for six months, leaving him free run of the family home. Among those to take full advantage was Emo, who had, in Gale's words, 'become the working-class jester in a group of largely middle-class dopeheads'. Emo promptly commandeered a room in his friend's house, from which, according to Gale, 'he used to go down the Mill, bring a girl back, shag her, then go back and get another one.'

One afternoon, Emo, Barrett, Storm Thorgerson and another friend, Paul Charrier, convened in Gale's parents' garden. Emo is convinced that, on this occasion, both he and Syd had taken Morning Glory. David Gale maintains that some of them were tripping on liquid LSD that they'd taken in droplets on a row of sugar cubes. In a previous experiment with phials of the drug, Emo had made the discovery that LSD could be absorbed through the skin, when he accidentally handled impregnated sugar cubes, resulting in 'hours of fucking chaos and us not having a clue which cubes you could trip on and which ones you couldn't'.

Whatever he'd ingested that day, Barrett's imagination was gripped by a matchbox, a plum and an orange, which he'd found in David Gale's kitchen, and spent the next four hours contemplating, until, depending on who's telling the story, Charrier stamped on the fruit or Emo ate it.

'That was when Paul and Syd then went into the house, and started jumping up and down in Dave Gale's bath shouting, "No rules, no rules!"' recalls Emo. 'Syd always had this thing about breaking free of rules. He thought that when he joined a group and made it, there'd be no rules and he could come and go as he pleased. But, of course, once he got there, he found it was the same as anywhere else – one of the things that probably screwed him up.'

In the meantime, Syd's frequently on-off relationship with Libby now seemed to be permanently off, though they remained friends. She began seeing artist Pablo Picasso's son Claude ('He loved Syd, and would often suggest we go and visit him on a Sunday'), and went to Germany that summer to study. Barrett continued to visit Cambridge at weekends. His hometown was still full of interesting distractions, some of which were evident when he returned to London.

'I never touched acid, scared stiff of it,' says Seamus O'Connell. 'But I remember when we were in Tottenham Street, Syd had been back to Cambridge for a weekend and had some strange drug experience there at the Arts Theatre with one of his mates. When he came back to London, one of his eyes looked dead. He had very lively eyes, normally, very bright, but one of them wasn't quite right. We all remarked on it, and he came out with some fanciful explanation.'

That same summer, with Libby gone, Syd began seeing Lindsay Corner, another ex-pupil of Ely Grammar School for Girls, whose father had been a friend of Dr Barrett's. Their mutual friend Po had introduced the pair at the Dorothy Ballroom. Lindsay was also more sympathetic to Syd's 'consciousness-expanding' adventures. At this time Nigel Lesmoir-Gordon filmed Syd purportedly tripping on magic mushrooms. Nigel had borrowed an 8mm camera from college and headed for a disused quarry near Cambridge's Gog Magog Hills, with his wife Jenny, Syd, Roger Waters' friend Andrew Rawlinson, David Gale, Rawlinson's girlfriend Lucy Pryor and future Floyd lighting tech Russell Page.

The footage is grainy, the camera angles sometimes unsteady, but a surprisingly dapper-looking Barrett, in white shirt and blue raincoat, is clearly visible, striding purposefully around the quarry one moment, before slipping into quiet contemplation the next. Later, he's seen pondering the leaf of a plant, bawling silently at the camera and appearing, rather self-consciously it seems, with mushrooms placed over his eye sockets and mouth. The film concludes with footage of a bonfire started in the quarry and some shaky footage of his co-conspirators. Now widely bootlegged and freely available to view on the Internet, the film was misleadingly given the name *Syd's First Trip*.

'We were just fucking around with a camera,' says David Gale. 'That film has a certain nostalgic charm. But we really were making it up as we went along. It certainly wasn't the first time Syd took a trip, and I'm not convinced that his first time was in my parents' back garden, either. Legend has moved in on that one. But it's quite possible that he'd taken it before in London. I wouldn't be surprised.'

David Gilmour would also try LSD that year. 'There were a lot of people experimenting with it as a way of finding a greater consciousness,' he said. 'The intention was to have a quasi-religious-cum-scientific experience, and I rather concurred with that. I'm an atheist, and I didn't start suddenly believing in God, but the claims were that it accessed parts of your brain that were not normally accessible, and the first couple of times I took it, I found it to be a very *deep* experience.'

For some of the Cambridge set, taking LSD would lead to that quasi-religious experience. 'Everyone seemed exciting at that time,' recalls Jenny Lesmoir-Gordon. 'There were several very charismatic characters around, not just Syd, but people like Andrew Rawlinson and Paul Charrier. Syd was just one of them.'

It was Charrier that would engineer a sudden, dramatic split in the group, and one that had a significant impact on Barrett. 'Paul was an energetic, bombastic, fat, loveable fellow,' says David Gale. 'But something happened to him while he was on that trip in my parents' garden. He went into the toilet and found a book called *Yoga and the Bible*, and, while having a shit, had this revelation that this book was where it was at. He came out of the toilet and announced that he was now going to India to find this guru. We thought it was the acid talking, but in his case it transformed his life. Within a few weeks he was off to Delhi, and came back after six weeks, having been initiated into this guru's outfit and given a series of spiritual tasks. He cut off his hair, bought a suit off the peg at Burton's, became depressingly ordinary-looking, and began proselytising like mad, at which point Andrew Rawlinson, Ponji Robinson and other key figures converted and fucked off to Delhi as well. Then they all came back, proselytising again, and converted a whole load more people. But the other half of us – me, Storm, Seamus – were all going, "This is bollocks!"'

The Sant Mat sect that so enraptured Charrier and friends was an offshoot of the Sikh religion, and dated back to thirteenth-century India. The guru in question was Maharaj Charan Singh, referred to as 'Master' by his followers, who were known as *satsangi*. The peace-and-love ethos of Sant Mat was perfectly pitched for the times. There were four main principles: abstinence from sex outside of marriage; a strict vegetarian diet; no drugs or alcohol; and a general catch-all instruction to lead a moral life. Initiates were also expected to undertake at least two hours of meditation a day. Over the course of the next twelve months, various members of the Cambridge set would find themselves drawn to Sant Mat.

'We'd all gone so far into ourselves with LSD that we wanted the journey to continue without drugs,' explains Emo. 'Paul Charrier went off to India, and when he came back and told us about the Master he was absolutely amazing. Then Ponji went, and when he came back, he had a sit-in in Nigel Lesmoir-Gordon's room when he was living in London, where he also told us what it was like. Dave Gilmour was there and said if he had the money he would have got on an aeroplane and flown out there and then. Syd also wanted to follow the path.'

'Syd would have read the book and have been forced to do so by Paul Charrier,' believes David Gale. 'Paul was insufferably full of it: "This guru is God. What are we waiting for?" According to Storm, Syd was quite impressed and wanted to meet the Master, who used to come to London now and again to meet his British followers, some of whom were quite ancient and were coming from the back end of the Raj era. The Master would check into a Bloomsbury hotel and give an audience – this pleasant enough bloke in his sixties with a big beard and wearing a turban. And Syd went along, met the Master to see if he could be initiated, and the Master told him he wasn't ready for it. So did the Master see in Syd something we were not yet seeing? Storm thinks that Syd was quite upset at not being considered spiritually ready.'

'To some extent I think it may have been a problem,' says Storm Thorgerson. 'In hindsight, you think all sorts of things about his fragile personality. But Syd's character was very mercurial. He tended to go into things with great gusto and then drop them.'

While the path being taken by his peers may have intrigued Barrett and Gilmour, their future Pink Floyd colleague was less enchanted. Still on the fringes of the hipster group and unimpressed by LSD or Indian mysticism, Roger Waters was, as Andrew Rawlinson recalls, 'a committed atheist, who took no interest in it at all'.

Whatever spiritual setbacks Syd may have been experiencing, 1965 also brought him back into contact with David Gilmour. That summer, in a break from Jokers Wild, Gilmour had hitchhiked through France to stay with friends near St Tropez. Syd and a contingent from Cambridge showed up in a Land Rover and set up home on a nearby campsite. During the two-week sojourn, Barrett and Gilmour got drunk, had fun, played their guitars and were arrested for busking.

That October, their paths would cross again when Jokers Wild and The Tea Set were booked on the same bill, performing at the twenty-first birthday party of Storm Thorgerson's girlfriend, Libby January, and her twin sister Rosie, at a country house in Great Shelford. Arranged by their father, Douglas January, a prominent local estate agent, the bands performed on two stages at either end of a marquee. Also playing that night was an unknown American singer-songwriter called Paul Simon.

'Paul Simon sang in the living room,' remembers Jokers Wild's new drummer (and Clive Welham's replacement) Willie Wilson. 'Nobody knew who he was, and he was a pain in the arse. He came up and said, "Can I play with you?" And we were like, "You're an acoustic folk singer; we're a rock 'n' roll band." He said, "I can do 'Johnny B. Goode'." So we eventually let him get up and have a go.'

Dope was smoked surreptitiously, as the partygoers inevitably fell into two camps. 'There were the young farmers and all those with money up one end of the marquee and us lot up the other end,' says Emo. 'Then Syd tried to pull a tablecloth off, and you've never seen so many expensive crystal glasses going everywhere.' Emo's sidekick, Pip Carter, jumped on stage to accompany Jokers Wild on the bongos. Not wishing to be left out, Emo followed suit. 'I actually got up with The Tea Set and did a Bo Diddley song, but I didn't know the words, so I sung them after Syd had sung them, until I fell off the stage, drunk, and came to, with Mr January standing over me.'

'It was the night I realised that everything was changing,' offers John Davies. 'I remember being very stoned, but very aware that we were all now heading off on our own personal journeys. I'm not sure we were such a unique group, but sometimes it felt as if we had to wait until 1967 for the rest of the world to catch up with us.'

As Cambridge's 'gang of very hip boys' undertook their own personal journeys, Barrett and Waters would have to wait another two and a half years before Gilmour came back into their lives. Four years later, the Januarys' country house would reappear in the Pink Floyd story, its lawn and French windows immortalised on the cover of the band's album, *Ummagumma*. By then, unknown to all at the time, Pink Floyd's charismatic and beguiling frontman would be replaced by one of his best friends.

CHAPTER THREE A STRANGE HOBBY

'Turn up, tune in, fuck off!'

Roger Waters

'What a rave! A man crawling naked through jelly. Girls stripped to the waist. Offbeat poetry. Weird music . . .'

Sixties gossip magazine *Titbits* was quick to recount the 'Spontaneous Underground Happening' in February 1966. The event took place at the Marquee club on Wardour Street, in the heart of London's Soho. Within weeks, one of the bands providing the music would be The Pink Floyd Sound, as they were now commonly billing themselves.

The year of 1966 would be a causal one for rock music and popular culture as a whole. The Beatles released *Revolver* – an album filled with exotic sounds that reflected the group's LSD experiences – Cream, rock's first so-called super-group, began inventing heavy metal; while Jimi Hendrix wowed London's clubland with his dazzling, pyrotechnic approach to playing the electric guitar. In London, a collision of fashion, art and music was slowly taking effect, and would peak during the following year's so-called Summer of Love.

The arrival of both Hendrix and Cream made an impact on Pink Floyd. 'I remember seeing them as a callow youth,' recalled Roger Waters. 'They both played the Regent Street Poly as part of our end-of-term hop, and it was astonishing to see and hear these long improvisations.'

Whatever their place might be in this new world, the band's personal situation was far from glamorous. Money was in perilously short supply, and the dilemma of juggling work and college commitments with gigs remained. Mason was slogging on at the Regent Street Poly but had arranged to work for Lindy's architect father, and Waters had put his studies on hold while he gained more practical experience at a firm of city architects. Wright and Barrett were both still ensconced at their respective colleges.

Pink Floyd's appearance at certain 'happenings' around the capital in early 1966 sprang from the activities of a group of London 'scenesters'. John 'Hoppy' Hopkins was a Cambridge graduate and one-time physicist for the Atomic Energy Authority. He took an unscheduled trip to Moscow, was subsequently interrogated by the security services, and ended up quitting his job. By the early sixties he was working as a freelance photographer for Fleet Street and *Melody Maker*.

'Hoppy got into outraging the bourgeoisie, smoking dope, and had an overall sense of anarchism,' claimed one contemporary. But, as another explains, 'Hoppy was also a natural organiser at a time when everybody else was just fooling around.' After a visit to the US in 1964, Hopkins returned to the capital with the idea of establishing an underground newspaper and what would become known as the London Free School. The school was the first to come to fruition. Set up in the basement of 26 Powis Terrace in Notting Hill, it was, as he explained in October 1966, 'a non-organisation, existing in name only, with no elected officers and no responsibilities'.

One of Hopkins' acquaintances, black activist Michael de Freitas, known as Michael X, arranged the loan of the building from its owner. First to move into the basement were squatters, who immediately gave the place a back-to-nature vibe. 'It was so wet and cold there that they ripped up the floorboards and put them on the fire,' remembers Hoppy. 'So one of the things the school was well known for was its earth floor.'

With its walls painted in psychedelic colours, it swiftly attracted musicians, poets, beatniks, liberal intellectuals, and the general flotsam and jetsam of London's artistic underground. Acting as an ad-hoc community centre, those involved were also available to offer practical advice to tenants on housing law, and even teach rudimentary English to local immigrants. Years on, some of those involved with the school would be instrumental in organising the first Notting Hill Carnival, while Michael X arranged for boxing legend Muhammad Ali to visit the area in 1966.

As Hoppy insists now, 'The Free School was an open-ended idea and the people that populated it filled it with whatever they wanted to.'

Among those involved were Joe Boyd, a twenty-five-year-old American who ran the UK office of Elektra Records, and Peter Jenner, a twenty-four-year-old who had graduated from Cambridge University with a first-class honours degree in Economics, and was currently lecturing at the London School of Economics. Jenner was a former flatmate of Eric Clapton's, and something of 'an avant-garde music nut'.

Hopkins, Jenner, Felix de Mendelsohn (another of the Free School alumni) and Hoppy's flatmate, the jazz critic Ron Atkins, had founded a production company called DNA, and recorded the free jazz group AMM. In what Jenner now describes as 'a spectacularly shit deal', they arranged with Boyd to release AMM's album, *Music from a Continuous Performance*, through Elektra.

'AMM would play guitars, pianos, but also radios and saws,' recalls Hoppy. 'They were working on the boundary between music and noise. After an hour of listening to them, you'd walk out into the street and it was as if it was all still carrying on. There was an improvised movie called *Shadows* made by John Cassavetes in the late fifties, and AMM was the musical equivalent of that. Absolutely hypnotic.'

AMM guitarist Keith Rowe's atonal approach, and his use of random objects to coax noises out of his guitar, would have a marked influence on Syd Barrett, who would later watch an AMM recording session. Yet by avoiding any recognisable semblance of melody, the group was unlikely to challenge The Beatles for commercial appeal, a drawback not lost on Jenner.

AMM would appear at one of the first of these happenings at the Marquee. English folkie Donovan, daubed in red and black eye make-up, and jazz organist Graham Bond were among those making up the entertainment at the inaugural event on 30 January 1966. The happening had been organised by Steve Stollman, whose brother Bernard ran the experimental music label ESP Records in New York.

'I was a twenty-two-year-old American let loose in London,' says Steve Stollman now. 'One of the first places I went to was Better Books, as they sold my brother's records. There, I got to know Hoppy and all these other interesting people. I wanted to help my brother get some visibility for his label. ESP put out records by Albert Ayler, Sun Ra and The Fugs – unusual stuff. Somebody, maybe me, said it would make sense to take this club that was unused on a Sunday afternoon. So I spoke to the Marquee's owners. The alleged rationale was to raise some money for Kingsley Hall [the community project of psychoanalyst R.D. Laing], as we had all read Laing's book *Knots*. I still think a few bucks we made went to the place.'

The event began at 4.30 p.m., admission was six shillings and sixpence, there was no official advertising to support the event, and the audience were individually invited: musicians, writers, poets, the underground cognoscenti. A promotional statement from the organisers suggested a dress code of 'costume, masque, ethnic, space, Edwardian, Victorian and hipness generally . . .' The dividing line between performer and audience was deliberately blurred.

'Halfway through, I was called to the front door as Robert Shelton, the *New York Times* critic, had showed up in a suit and tie,' recalls Stollman of one of the early happenings. 'We'd insisted everyone dress up bizarrely – even if it was just having a handkerchief hanging out your ear. As Robert was the guy who famously discovered Bob Dylan, I told him he had the best costume in the joint and let him in.'

It's since been widely reported that The Pink Floyd Sound performed at both the first Marquee happening in January and again on 27 February. However, other eyewitness accounts claim that the group actually made their Marquee debut at the third event on 13 March.

As Stollman readily admits now, 'I didn't know The Pink Floyd Sound from The Green Floyd Sound. I hadn't a clue who they were, but someone suggested them.'

'I knew Steve Stollman,' explains Nigel Lesmoir-Gordon. 'He was looking for experimental music, and nobody else wanted to play those Sunday afternoon sessions. That's how they got the Floyd.'

Stollman nevertheless maintains that the band's performance that night was recorded. 'I remember seeing a guy called Ian Somerville, who was a friend of William Burroughs, sat in the booth at the Marquee with headphones on the whole time. Nobody knows what became of that tape.' The band's set of blues standards and their own compositions, all delivered with Barrett's abstract guitar playing and extended instrumental jamming, was the ideal soundtrack for the occasion.

'Good sounds, good poetry, a lovely event,' offers Stollman. 'I swear the Floyd played for nearly three hours. Nobody wanted to stop them, as it was so much in the spirit of what was going on at the time.'

'Floyd's music was new but it wasn't completely foreign to what was happening elsewhere,' elaborates Hoppy. 'We were all listening to avant-garde jazz, and my girlfriend at the time had brought back tapes of The Velvet Underground from New York. John Cage had also given a concert at the Saville Theatre in 1964 or 1965, and that had made a dent on people's musical consciousness. Floyd were different, but they fitted right into all that.'

Further Sunday afternoon happenings ensued, with the future David Bowie – then still just plain David Jones – among those who encountered the group and was impressed by the 'strange presence with his white face and black eyeliner singing in front of the band'.

But Stollman's interest in staging such happenings quickly waned when the Marquee's management proposed opening a bar during the events. 'I thought fights would break out,' he laughs. 'A lot of people were stoned, so I didn't think there should be alcohol available with all this stuff happening. So my interest faded.'

Stollman would later end up having to leave the country after being named in a tabloid newspaper exposé, following his involvement in a BBC-funded documentary about LSD: 'There I was, on the front page, with my eyes blacked out. A scandal!'

For Floyd, though, a vital connection had already been made. One Sunday in June, weary of marking LSE exam papers, Peter Jenner headed to the Marquee. 'I knew who Steve Stollman was, and I think I'd seen an ad for this thing in the *Melody Maker*,' he recalls. After observing 'various people sliming around in jelly', Peter encountered The Pink Floyd Sound: 'The Floyd were mostly doing blues songs, but instead of having howling guitar solos with the guitarist leaning back, like all guitarists did back then, they were doing cosmic shit. They weren't doing interesting blues songs. But it was what they did with them that was interesting. I think what Syd was doing was a way of being distinctive and filling in the gaps where you should have had a howling Clapton or Peter Green guitar solo. I was very intrigued.'

Peter's interest was driven by something more prosaic than just the music. 'By this time I'd added up the figures at DNA and, unless we sold a lot of records, it was never going to survive. Basically, we needed a pop group.' A year before, Peter had even approached The Velvet Underground, having heard Hoppy's tapes of the band, only to be told by the group that artist Andy Warhol already had the job of managing them.

Realising that the Floyd were without management, Jenner made an approach. 'I got their number from Steve Stollman, and I went up to Highgate where they were living with Mike Leonard. I didn't know Mike so I didn't know what was going on there, but it all sounded a bit arty – and that was part of the appeal. The first person I talked to seriously was Roger. I said, "Do you want to be on our label?" And Roger said they were all going off on holiday and to come back in September.'

Jenner's impression then was that the group were 'quite serious in a semi-pro way', but that their future was far from certain. 'They'd bought a van and some gear with their grant money, but they were on the verge of splitting up,' he claimed in 1972. Certainly, without any bookings on the immediate horizon and with college work and career choices to be made, the band had plenty to contemplate when they went their separate ways for the summer.

Mason was the first to leave, following girlfriend Lindy to New York where she was now working with the Martha Graham Dance Company. Here, Mason would experience the US jazz scene beyond just hearing the music on record, catching celebrated pianists Thelonious Monk and Mose Allison on the same bill, before he and Lindy headed off to the West Coast. If Mason was experiencing serious doubts about the future of the band, he was buoyed by the discovery of an article in the New York underground magazine, *East Village Other*, name-checking The Pink Floyd Sound. As he later recalled: 'It made me realise that the band had the potential to be more than simply a vehicle for my own amusement.'

Juliette Gale had also disappeared to the States that summer, leaving boyfriend Richard Wright at a loose end. Some of the Cambridge set had spent the past three summers in the Greek and Balearic Islands, hopping between Mykonos, Ibiza and Formentera, working on their tans, puffing strong weed and setting the world to rights. Richard and Juliette had also been to Lindos, Rhodes. In the summer of 1966, Wright joined Roger Waters for another Greek excursion.

'There was Nigel and me, Russell Page, David Gale, Rick, Roger and Judy,' recalls Jenny Lesmoir-Gordon. The Judy in question was Judy Trim, a former pupil of the Cambridge County School for Girls and the daughter of a research scientist at the university. She and Roger had been together since their teens. 'Rog, Andrew Rawlinson and me were all after Judy,' recalls Storm Thorgerson. 'And Rog got her.'

'It was on that holiday that Roger took his first acid trip,' continues Jenny. 'We set off across Europe in this old American car and in the middle of the night woke up to discover that it would only go backwards. The mechanic we took it to actually used the word, "*Kaput*". So we caught a slow train across Yugoslavia to Greece. Eventually, we found this villa and we let Rog and Ju-Ju — as they called each other then — have the best room in the house. Roger insisted on it, though I do believe they found a scorpion under the bed. Roger was a very forceful character but in other ways he could be rather shy. I remember he and I being alone on the beach one day, and he seemed terribly nervous. He was with Judy but he seemed rather shy around women.'

Unlike most of the party, Waters had never tried LSD. On the Greek island of Patmos, he decided to take a drop from Nigel's bottle and pipette. 'It was an extraordinary experience,' recalled Waters. 'And it lasted about forty-eight hours.' He would later say that he only took acid once after that.

Regrettably, the Greek sojourn also revealed the first indication of Waters' fraught relationship with Richard Wright, a rift that would have a significant implication for Pink Floyd years later. 'Rick was a shy, sweet chap,' remembers Jenny. 'He had a girlfriend who was in America at the time, whom he seemed to think an awful lot of. But Roger was always putting him down. It was as if he was using Rick as his punchbag.'

Reconvening at Stanhope Gardens after their respective holidays, the band members found Peter Jenner still keen to get involved. When Waters informed him that what the band really needed was a manager,

Peter shelved his plans to sign them to DNA and enlisted an old friend and fellow London Free School colleague, Andrew King. 'Pete and Joe Boyd were going to run DNA together, and I was going to manage,' recalls Andrew King. 'But when the label didn't work out, Pete suggested he and I manage Floyd together.' Jenner arranged for a twelve-month leave of absence from his LSE post, with an option to return if his pop management career failed to take off.

Andrew King and Peter Jenner had been at school together and had spent time travelling in the United States after leaving university. They were, as King explains, 'middle-class, liberal intellectuals involved in the London avant-garde scene'.

'I didn't listen much to pop music,' admits Jenner. 'I just about got into Bob Dylan and The Byrds. But I didn't think that white men could sing the blues.'

At the time, King was working in public relations for British European Airways, but, crucially, had some family money to invest. Pleading poverty, Waters persuaded the new management to splash out on a band PA, which they did, only for the equipment to go missing immediately. King and Jenner dug into their wallets again. Later, Waters would reveal that he initially thought the pair were high-class drug-dealers on the make.

Meanwhile, the Free School needed money. 'One of the things we did was put out a newsletter,' says Hoppy. 'I was paying the production costs, and although I'd been doing rather well in Fleet Street as a photographer in the early sixties, by this time I was doing other things and getting poorer and poorer, so to keep the school and the newsletter going we decided to hold a benefit, which turned into a series of benefits.' Peter Jenner booked The Pink Floyd Sound to play these benefits at the All Saints Church Hall, just off nearby Westbourne Park Road. A significant venue in the area, the hall would later stage musicals and plays, and provide a general meeting place for the Notting Hill community. At the time, it also hosted one of London's first pre-school playgroups.

John Leckie, who would go on to engineer sessions for Pink Floyd, later producing such luminaries as The Stone Roses and Radiohead, grew up in nearby Ladbroke Grove: 'I saw Floyd a few times at the All Saints Hall. Fantastic. The only thing was that it *was* a school hall. There were all these tiny kids' tables and chairs set up, which always seemed very funny every time someone suddenly jumped up, freaking out and idiot-dancing to this far-out music.'

It was at the All Saints Hall that Andrew King had his first Pink Floyd experience. 'I think that's where I first saw them,' he says now. 'They were still doing fifteen-minute versions of "Louie Louie" and I remember thinking how weird it all sounded. I knew about the blues and the roots of rock 'n' roll and this wasn't right. But those musical inconsistencies were what worked. I also thought Syd exuded a certain magnetism.'

Also in attendance was fledgling author Jenny Fabian, who would go on to write the 1969 music biz novel *Groupie*. 'I had just run away from my first husband, and was living in Powis Square,' she says now. 'I was always on the lookout for something extraordinary, and was drawn into All Saints Hall by the people I saw going in. The music was interesting, the guys on stage looked interesting, and the lead singer looked more than interesting.' Recognising Jenner and King 'as a couple of public schoolboys I'd known in a past life', Jenny said she 'allowed Andrew to seduce me', before befriending the real object of her affections, Barrett, who would later appear in her novel in the thinnest of disguises as Ben, while the band were recast as Satin Odyssey.

Adding to Syd's magnetic performance during these gigs was a then exotic light show, courtesy of Joel and Toni Brown, an American couple on a visit from Haight-Ashbury, the hippie district of San Francisco. Though rudimentary by today's standards, the couple's use of coloured slides and a projector was a far cry from the standard overhead lights of most theatre venues. When the Browns returned to the US, Peter Jenner and his wife, Sumi, set about fashioning a copycat set from 'half-inch-thick timber shelving, domestic fixed spotlights from Woolworths, drawing pins and plastic gel'. Joe Gannon, a seventeen-year-old American from the All Saints Hall gigs, was co-opted into becoming the group's first lighting tech.

While the Jenners' lighting rig might seem hopelessly primitive by today's standards, at the time it gave Pink Floyd a distinct visual edge over their competitors, as well as tapping into what Peter Jenner describes as the 'mixed-media world'. The band members were receptive to the idea, having been used to providing musical accompaniment to Mike Leonard's light and sound workshop at the Hornsey College of Art. In March, they had played the University of Essex's rag ball to a projected backdrop of footage filmed by a student in a wheelchair, as he was pushed around London.

With their avant-garde lightshow and back projections, word gradually spread of the All Saints Hall's shows, even if one early gig was so sparsely attended that Syd ended up jokily reciting a speech from *Hamlet* to the handful of punters. 'There were about twenty people there when we first played,' admitted Roger Waters. 'The second week one hundred, and then three to four hundred, and then, after that, many couldn't get in.'

In keeping with both their own and their management's left-leaning politics, the band would soon find themselves playing an Oxfam benefit gig (on the same bill as comedians Peter Cook, Dudley Moore and Barry Humphries) and a Majority Rule for Rhodesia show at the Camden Roundhouse. Yet with the Free School floundering, Hoppy's tireless campaigning began again in earnest. Inspired by New York's *Village Voice*, Hopkins enrolled Barry Miles (later just Miles), among others, into the idea of launching a free newspaper for the alternative community. Miles had started the Indica Bookshop and Gallery, both respective Meccas for the hip community and a popular stopover for visiting American beatniks. He was also friends with Paul McCartney. The paper, *International Times*, was created, in the words of Miles, to 'link London to New York and Paris and Amsterdam . . . to unite the painters, the music people, the dance people . . .'

On 15 October 1966, *International Times* was set up in the basement at Indica and launched with a party at London's Roundhouse in Chalk Farm, a one-time turning station for steam locomotives and a former gin distillery. Hoppy and Miles charged ten shillings on the door and punters were given a free sugar cube, which they were told may or may not have been spiked with LSD (in truth, none of them was spiked). Inside, amid the treacherous ruins of the distillery, its missing floorboards and abandoned horse-drawn carts, around two thousand people, some tripping, some *thinking* they were tripping, marvelled at the sight of mini-skirted actress Monica Vitti, Marianne Faithfull in a bum-length nun's habit, Paul McCartney and Jane Asher dressed as Arabs, and, as *New Society* magazine later reported, 'trendy people, beatniks, beards, dollies and gold lamé cavemen'. The Pink Floyd Sound were booked to headline, with support from The Soft Machine, an experimentally inclined jazz-rock band, who used the sound of a revving motorcycle in their performance that night. Before the Floyd's performance, there was an accident, in which Syd and roadie Pip Carter are supposed to have destroyed a 6ft jelly art installation, either by backing the group's van into it, or removing a plank of wood vital in keeping the mould upright.

'I remember the jelly,' laughs Jeff Dexter, then a club DJ in London. 'The Roundhouse gig was the first time I saw The Pink Floyd. I didn't think much of the show but the *people* show was fantastic. I was intrigued by Floyd's little entourage, mainly the girls around Syd.'

Glammed up in their best satin shirts and silk scarves, according to one eyewitness, the Floyd 'honked and howled and tweeted' while a primitive light show and projected slides blinked and dripped psychedelic colours around them.

'Their music was almost entirely a very loud psychedelic jam that rarely seemed to relate to the playing of any introductory theme, be it "Road Runner" or some other R&B classic,' wrote Miles in 2004. 'After about thirty minutes, they would stop, look at each other, and start up again, pretty much where they'd left off, except with a new introductory tune.'

'I think it was a stroke of good fortune that we couldn't work out how to play covers,' admitted Roger Waters. 'It forced us to come up with our own direction, our own way of doing things.'

As Richard Wright elaborated: 'Everything became more improvised around the guitar and the keyboards. Roger started to play the bass as a lead instrument.'

Whatever the group's musical shortcomings, Peter Jenner was delighted with the outcome of the Roundhouse gig. 'There was a great feeling that night,' he recalls. 'We'd made contact with lots of other like-minded souls; other bands, other people. There was this sense of, "Wow, this is our place."'

By Jenner's own admission, he and Andrew King wanted to court 'the posh papers'. For them, 'this was a cultural thing, not just pop music'. A week later, The Pink Floyd (the Sound had been dropped at Peter Jenner's suggestion) gained their first mention in the national press with a surprisingly sympathetic review in the *Sunday Times*, in which an interviewed Waters talked of 'co-operative anarchy' and of the band's music 'being a complete realisation of the aims of psychedelia', a quote he later disowned as 'obviously tongue-in-cheek'. 'Co-operative anarchy' aside, Floyd and their new management still understood the importance of a business deal.

At the end of the month, Jenner and King signed a six-way partnership with the four band members, establishing the company Blackhill Enterprises. (The name was taken from a cottage owned by King's family in the Brecon Beacons.) Barrett, Waters, Wright and Mason finally gave up their studies. Though, as Bob Klose later recounted, 'Syd had a real battle with himself over the decision to leave art college. He went through agonies over that.' Not for the first time, those close to Syd wondered why this talented artist was giving it up for music.

'I always thought it amazing that Syd and Roger's mothers were both OK about them dropping out of art school and architecture,' recalls Libby Gausden. 'Especially Mary Waters, as Roger was on his way to becoming an architect.'

Blackhill Enterprises established a base in Jenner's flat at 4 Edbrooke Road, Notting Hill, hiring June Child, who lived in the flat below, to answer the phone. For Jenner and King, the personalities of their new charges were becoming clearer. 'Sometimes it felt like it was Syd and the three blokes he was playing with,' admits King. 'You could say, though, that initially Nick and Rick were along for the ride and Roger was lurking.'

'Syd was a good-looking chap and the singer, so he was always the one you would focus on,' elaborates Jenner. 'Syd was the creative one, and, at first, very easy to get along with. But Rick was very pretty as well, so it wasn't *just* Syd. Rick I liked a lot. He was very gentle and it's a classic management situation: he wasn't any trouble so you didn't notice him. You were always more aware of the people that were high maintenance. Nick was easy to get along with and the one who could talk to all of the others. But he was Roger's mate, so would always side with him if something was put to a vote. Roger was the organisation. He would be the one you went to for sorting out practical issues. He was very questioning and wanted to know exactly what was going on.'

'Roger organised *everything*,' recalls Libby Gausden. 'Years later when I heard he was fighting for the name of Pink Floyd, I remember thinking, "You bloody well deserve it, you do".'

Barrett and Waters had both begun to write songs while still in Cambridge. One of Syd's earliest attempts, 'Let's Roll Another One', would later be retitled 'Candy and a Currant Bun' – to deflect accusations of a pro-dope message – and end up as the B-side of the group's first single. Waters had made his compositional debut with the still unrecorded 'Walk With Me, Sydney', a hokey duet intended to be sung by Barrett and Juliette Gale. By November 1966, the band's repertoire would include such Barrett compositions as 'Matilda Mother' and 'Astronomy Domine', as well as Waters' early effort, 'Take Up Thy Stethoscope and Walk'. 'They were all encouraged to write,' says Jenner. 'But it was Syd who came out with the great songs.'

The autumn of 1966 marked both a highly creative period for Barrett, and also, it seems, a time of personal contentment, in stark contrast to the mania that would ensue just months later. Syd had now taken over a room in a narrow, three-storey house at 2 Earlham Street, near London's Cambridge Circus.

Then 'a typical 1966 hippie pad, from its purple front door to the psychedelic graffiti on the walls', according to one visitor, 2 Earlham Street has long since been renovated, and a newsagents now trades on its ground floor. It was the first of several successors to 27 Clarendon Street, the Cambridge dope den from a couple of years earlier. The building's prime tenant was the late Jean-Simone Kaminsky, an absconder from the French army who'd wound up in England, and, via a sympathetic MP, had first found lodgings in Cambridge, next door to Matthew Scurfield.

Kaminsky moved to London, and took over the rent at 2 Earlham Street. While holding down a job at the BBC, he also had a sideline producing so-called 'intellectual sex books' on a couple of printing presses at the flat.

Later, when one of the presses caught fire, the building had to be evacuated. When the blaze was stopped, the fire brigade discovered Kaminsky's illegal literature, and called the police. The rest of the building's tenants swiftly stashed the offending books in the back of a van and drove round London throwing the sodden remains into all available gardens.

With furniture fashioned from discarded crates found in neighbouring Covent Garden, conditions were Spartan. John Whiteley, a former guardsman from the north of England, then working as a handyman at Better Books ('I was the only one among those intellectuals who could change a lightbulb'), was living there on and off with his girlfriend Anna Murray when the Cambridge contingent descended en masse. 'That lot all seemed to arrive at the same time,' recalls Whiteley now, 'Ponji Robinson, Dave Gale, Seamus O'Connell, which is how I came to know Syd.' With the help of his hip mother, the eminently sensible Seamus ('I was into beer and jazz and blues') organised a controlled rent for the whole place of five pounds five shillings and five pence a week.

Anna Murray and Barrett shared an interest in painting, and the two struck up an immediate friendship. 'Anna painted as well,' explains John Whiteley, 'and she and Syd became great friends. They used to smoke a hell of a lot of dope together – as we all did back then.'

Syd commandeered the attic room at Earlham Street, becoming close friends with the house's other prime tenant, Peter Wynne-Willson and his girlfriend, Suzie Gawler-Wright. Wynne-Willson had left his public school after taking part in the Aldermaston March and was then working as a lighting technician during the first run of the stage musical *Oliver!* Suzie would be accorded the nickname of the Psychedelic Debutante. Wynne-Willson once arranged a group trip during a performance of Handel's *The Messiah* at the Royal Albert Hall. The pair would be quickly absorbed into the Floyd's entourage, with Wynne-Willson taking over as the band's lighting tech when Joe Gannon disappeared back to the United States. 'When the theatres I was working in threw stuff out, I'd take them home and renovate them,' explains Wynne-Willson, who was now in charge of the Jenners' homemade lighting rig.

One of his earliest onstage lighting gimmicks would involve stretching a condom over a wire frame. He would then drip oil paint on to it, through which light would be shone, creating one of the first oil slide effects. This became a defining feature of Pink Floyd's live shows. In another burst of creativity, he fashioned a pair of what became known as 'cosmonocles'. These were a pair of welding goggles with the dark lenses removed and replaced by clear glass and two glass prisms, giving a distorting, disorientating view.

'I can remember putting a pair on and walking down Charing Cross Road – or rather, trying to walk down Charing Cross Road,' recalls Emo. 'A copper asked me what I was doing, and I think we made him put them on as well. Of course, the view was even worse if you were stoned. Or tripping.'

'1966 in London was fantastic,' remembers Storm Thorgerson. 'We were all full of hormones and life.'

At Earlham Street, Syd played guitar, wrote songs, smoked dope and hung out with girlfriend Lindsay Corner, who'd moved from Cambridge to London to pursue a modelling career. Under the tutelage of Seamus O'Connell's mother, he had become enamoured with *I-Ching*, the mystical Chinese *Book of Changes*, and the Chinese board game 'Go'. Stoned sessions of each would be followed by restorative chocolate bars from Café Pollo in nearby Old Compton Street.

I-Ching would be one of Syd's many musical inspirations at that time, alongside tarot cards, Hilaire Belloc, The Beatles, Mothers of Invention, Aldous Huxley . . . As Roger Waters later explained, 'Syd was never an intellectual, but he was a butterfly who would dip into all sorts of things.'

Cambridge boy John Davies was now in London training to become a veterinary surgeon and recalls that 'the Earlham Street flat was a lovely place to hang out on a Saturday. It was all happening. Syd would play us records and new songs he'd just written. I can remember sitting there, incredibly stoned, listening to him strumming "Scarecrow" on an acoustic guitar.'

'There was something that happened at Earlham Street that sums Syd up for me,' says Po. 'He had this little room – bedroll in one corner, guitar in the other, a rail with some velvet trousers and flowery shirts hanging off it. Nothing else. And I remember sitting there playing "Go" with him. There was a bare lightbulb overhead and it was a bit too bright. I was like, "Sydney, isn't there something you can do about that light?" He said, "Yes, there is." He had some oranges in a brown paper bag. He tipped them out, made a hole in the bag, screwed the light bulb in around it, and we now had a beautiful lampshade, giving this soft light on our game. He was always able to do these effortlessly artistic things that would have taken the rest of us ages to think about.'

Blackhill set about getting its new charges to record a demo tape that could be pitched to record companies, 'despite the fact', as Jenner admits, 'that we didn't really know anyone in the business apart from Joe Boyd'. At Thompson's Recording Studio, Hemel Hempstead, Floyd recorded, among other things, 'Candy and a Currant Bun' and a newer composition, 'Interstellar Overdrive'. The first was typical Carnaby Street acid-pop, the ideal soundtrack for mini-skirted podium dancers ('Don't touch me, child,' declares Barrett campily in its chorus). But it was 'Interstellar Overdrive' that would become Floyd's signature song, an instrumental 'freak-out', growing out of a guitar figure reputedly inspired by Love's version of the Bacharach and David standard 'My Little Red Book', which Jenner is said to have hummed to Syd.

Anthony Stern was now living in Carlisle Street in London's West End and working with film-maker Peter Whitehead, the artist Syd had encountered in his Cambridge studio some four years earlier. Running into Peter Jenner one day in Soho, the Floyd's manager handed Anthony a copy of the band's demo for 'Interstellar Overdrive'. 'I thought it was absolutely right for the sort of films I wanted to make,' says Stern. On a trip to America the following year, Stern secured funding for his film, *San Francisco*, which featured the rough, early version of 'Interstellar Overdrive' set to abstract, flashing images of America in 1967, which, in Stern's words, 'attempted to duplicate the Pink Floyd's light show'.

With management, a booking agent, and now a demo tape, a rejuvenated Pink Floyd went back to Cambridge in December 1966 to play the art school's Christmas party.

In attendance that night was future photographer Mick Rock, then in his first year at Cambridge University. With a taste for dope and hallucinogenics, Rock had made a connection with Pip and Emo: 'They kept talking about their friend Syd and his band Pink Floyd and how they were named after two bluesmen I'd never heard of. They raved about this guy Syd. I was completely blown away when I first saw Pink Floyd. But it was all Syd. You didn't even notice the rest of the band. Pip and Emo took me to meet him, but first I met Lindsay Corner. We hung out, smoked a joint, and I remember being very taken with her. And when I found out after the show that she was Syd's girlfriend, I was even more impressed.'

After the gig, Rock joined Barrett and friends back at Hills Road to smoke more dope and ponder the merits of Timothy Leary's *Psychedelic Review* and that year's hippest novel, Arthur C. Clarke's *Childhood's End*. A friendship began between Rock and Barrett that would endure into the next decade and some time after Syd's departure from Pink Floyd.

Another of Syd's former college friends was also in the audience. John Watkins had helped to organise the event. He recalls: 'I went up to Syd afterwards, full of praise – "It's fantastic what you're doing." And he looked at me and said, "Thanks, but I think I need to kick the drummer and the keyboard player up the arse." But then, that was his way. It felt as if he started a new band every week at art school. I could never imagine him staying in one group, playing the same songs, night after night . . .'

Back in London, Hoppy and Joe Boyd had formed a partnership of their own. Boyd had seen Pink Floyd's shows at All Saints Hall and was searching for a regular venue in which to stage similar events. Boyd found his ideal venue in the Blarney Club, an Irish showband ballroom beneath the Berkley and Continental Cinemas on Tottenham Court Road. Boyd struck a deal with the Irish owner, Mr Gannon, on a handshake and agreed to pay £15 a week for the use of the venue every Friday night. Originally billed as 'UFO-Night Tripper', before becoming known simply as UFO, the club opened its doors on 23 December 1966, with performances from Pink Floyd and The Soft Machine (in support). UFO would become a weekly event from the New Year, with Pink Floyd and The Soft Machine establishing themselves as its so-called 'house bands', the former securing 60 per cent of the gross takings for their first three appearances.

Unusually for the time, the club's organisers found themselves making money, with much of the surplus being put towards paid advertisements in *International Times*, which helped keep the paper afloat. In return, *IT*'s staff, such as it was, would run the door at UFO. The club ran from ten o'clock at night until eight in the morning, its fashionable clientele, psychedelic soundtrack and then space-age lighting effects disguising the fact that the polished dancefloor and overhead mirror ball were firmly rooted in showbiz tradition. There was no alcohol licence, but a small stall dispensed macrobiotic food to hungry clubbers, while a German drug-dealer, known only as Marlon, was on hand to sell trips. UFO's in-house lighting wizard, the late Mark Boyle, had been a regular at Mike Leonard's sound and light workshop at Hornsey College of Art. Boyle worked on a makeshift platform, mixing together different substances between clear slides to be warmed by a projector lamp, before, effectively, melting and spreading across the band on stage.

'Nowadays, UFO would make a 1970s disco look sophisticated,' says Mick Farren, then writing for *International Times* and singing with his own band, The Social Deviants. 'But at the time, the ambience was mind-blowing.'

'You'd drop acid and arrive blotto,' says Jenny Fabian. 'It was like descending into a subterranean world of dreams. There were people floating about with that beatific gaze in their eyes, or flat out on the wooden floor. I often lay there myself, absorbed in the old black-and-white films they showed between music. There was also something regressive about the whole thing. If you went to have a pee, beyond this hall of dreams lay a dark, winding corridor, brightly lit, but black and dripping with condensation, which led to a garish Ladies, and I'd look in the mirror and be amazed at what I saw . . . It was always a relief to get back into the womb of make-believe.'

As well as live music, the club staged performance art – jugglers and mime acts – as well as screening avant-garde film shows. But as time progressed, the live bands became an increasingly important part of UFO's appeal. Despite the club's womb-like ambience, an element of competition arose between the respective bands' audiences, if not the groups themselves. 'Floyd were very trippy, very druggy, but very white rock. They were for people who liked Tolkien and went looking for UFOs on Hampstead Heath,' says one Soft Machine devotee. 'The Soft Machine were more avant-garde in a European sense. They fitted the bill at jazz festivals in France. Their audience seemed more socially conscious – into black civil rights and the working-class revolution.' For some, the merits were purely musical and visual. 'There was always competition between my friends as to who was better,' says John Leckie. 'We always argued about who was most stretching the boundaries. Soft Machine could certainly play better. But Floyd were more abstract and, of course, they had Syd.'

Even among their own entourage, not everyone was convinced by the Floyd's musical worth. 'To be completely honest, I was never a fan,' laughs John Whiteley. 'I helped do the lights for them at UFO, but I can still recall Syd playing away and shouting out the chords to the others – telling them what to play.'

Yet The Soft Machine's drummer Robert Wyatt remembered his rivals with affection: 'There was an at-easeness about the Floyd, which I rather liked. Soft Machine's equipment would always blow up and Floyd would let us use theirs, which didn't usually happen between rock bands at the time. Most of them were in their cocoons. I was still listening to John Coltrane and not buying rock records. But I was amazed when I saw Floyd play, at their nerve in taking their time to get from one note to the other. I couldn't do it, but Floyd were always in control.'

With both bands free to perform the music they wanted, for as long as they wanted, Floyd and Soft Machine had the advantage of playing to, as Wyatt puts it, 'people who didn't know what year it was, let alone what time it was.'

The distortion of time that accompanies an acid trip made Floyd the ideal soundtrack for the LSD experience. Prior to their performances at UFO, their crew would clear the crowd away from the area directly in front of the speakers. As Miles later wrote in *New Musical Express*, 'This was originally designed to prevent stoned hippies from burning out their eardrums, but it soon assumed a curious, ritual significance, like a Zen ceremony, the emptying of the space into which the Floyd's mysterious music was about to spurt.'

On stage, they performed with their homemade spotlights up close and projections slipping across the backdrop behind them, casting shadows over the band and adding to the mystique. Syd's abstract guitar riffs battled with Richard Wright's unearthly-sounding keyboards. Roger Waters, gangling and aloof, delivered a thudding bass to underpin the din, and some ungodly screaming when the mood demanded it. One night, Joe Boyd recalled seeing a tripping Pete Townshend crouched by the side of the stage, pointing at Waters and claiming the Floyd bassist was 'going to swallow him'.

'I tripped three times at UFO,' recalls Townshend now. 'I thought Roger was very handsome and very scary, and what I was really afraid of was that he was going to steal my girlfriend, whom he openly fancied, while I was weakened by acid.' The girlfriend in question, Townshend's future wife Karen Astley, was a beautiful art student who had already featured on the inaugural UFO club poster. She routinely attracted attention at UFO, according to The Who's guitarist, on account of 'dancing in a dress that looked like it had been made out of a cake wrapper'.

Trouble at UFO erupted rarely. Visiting mods sometimes took exception to the prevalent peace-and-love vibes, though many would end up dropping acid themselves and joining the party. On other occasions, tripping bikers became heavy-handed with the female clientele. A greater threat to public order came when some of the beautiful people broke free from the pack, hippie bells tinkling, kaftans askew, ending up on Tottenham Court Road in the small hours and attracting the interest of the passing constabulary.

Sam Hutt, London's first 'alternative doctor', later to become country singer Hank Wangford, was a UFO regular and still marvels at how much the club's clientele could get away with: 'The Irishman who owned the place was incredibly pragmatic. He literally turned a blind eye to what was going on – very Irish. To him it was no different to the local pub staying open late.'

'You have to remember that this was a rented Irish showband joint,' adds Mick Farren: in those days the police had to be sweetened, 'even in the normal run of things – without hippies all over the joint one night a week.' A crate of whiskey at Christmas was the accepted sweetener.

In January 1967, Barrett's path crossed again with Peter Whitehead, who was now making films, assisted by Syd's art exhibition partner Anthony Stern. *Wholly Communion*, a movie of the 1965 Royal Albert Hall poetry reading, featuring Allen Ginsberg, and *Charlie is My Darling*, the following year's documentary of a Rolling Stones tour, would establish Whitehead as a diarist of the so-called counter-culture. 'Mr Trendy', as Andrew King later described him, even if, as Peter insists, 'I didn't really like pop music and had never been to a pop concert before in my life.'

Whitehead was halfway through making another film, *Tonite Let's All Make Love in London*, which spliced together interview snippets and footage of Mick Jagger, Julie Christie, Michael Caine, David Hockney and more, as a time-capsule document of the pop stars, movie stars and artists of the time. What it needed, though, was a suitably *now* soundtrack. 'There was no way I wanted to put the bloody Rolling Stones on it,' says Whitehead. 'Anthony knew I liked The Soft Machine, and told me about how Syd was in The Pink Floyd, who were doing something similar.'

Peter ventured out to the UFO club and encountered Syd backstage –

'He was already a little out of it' – though his attention was more drawn to Barrett's escort, a beautiful girl from Cambridge named Jenny Spires.

'Jenny was the first girl who totally encapsulated the vibe at UFO,' offers Anthony Stern. 'She lived in my flat for a while, and I was sitting there one night, when I heard a door open and this lovely sound of bells jingling, like a reindeer. It was Jenny. She had these bells on her ankles, and she was the most wonderful vision of a new type of woman. I didn't hear such a lovely sound again, until I went to a town called Herak in Afghanistan in 1972, where the horses had the exact same bells on, and I suddenly had this flashback of Jenny coming through the door of my flat again.'

Jenny and Syd had met during one of Barrett's visits to Cambridge, and had been together from the end of 1964 through most of 1965. Their relationship has been on and off until spring 1966, but the two remained close friends. When Jenny moved to London, she regularly hung out with Syd and Lindsay at Earlham Street.

'I started seeing Jenny Spires as well,' explains Peter Whitehead. 'Back at my flat one night I showed her a lot of the images I'd cut for the film, and told her how I needed some music. She suggested the Floyd, but they didn't have any proper recordings.'

Arranging the deal with Syd and Blackhill, Whitehead stumped up £85 for two hours of recording time at Rye Muse studios, later renamed Sound Technique, in Kensington, and filmed the group's performance of 'Interstellar Overdrive', the earlier demo of which had so impressed Anthony Stern. 'I liked it because it was very dark, druggy, mysterious and semi-classical,' says Whitehead. Like Stern, Peter believed the piece would be ideal for his film also.

In the ensuing footage, Barrett can be seen playing dissonant, freeform guitar, his baggy red-and-black T-shirt and spidery pencil moustache rendering him rather less stylish than his bandmates that day. Mason, in particular, looks, as one Floyd insider puts it, 'very Carnaby Street'. With extra time to fill, the band jammed their way through another piece, entitled 'Nick's Boogie', though only 'Interstellar Overdrive' would find its way into the finished film. Years later, Whitehead's additional footage of the band performing at UFO and the Alexandra Palace would appear on the commercially released video and DVD, *Pink Floyd London 1966–1967*.

At Sound Technique, Pink Floyd cut more songs, including another new Barrett composition, 'Arnold Layne', under Joe Boyd's guidance. The group filmed a promo clip for the song, featuring the four goofing around with a shop window dummy on a freezing Sussex beach. It now offers a rare snapshot of the band in light-hearted mode, even if Barrett seems strangely upstaged by a showboating Roger Waters, who hams it up unselfconsciously for the camera, gangling across the sand in slightly too short drainpipe trousers.

Peter Jenner blithely admits that 'back then, we didn't know what we were doing', but the vague plan was for Boyd, in his capacity as an A&R man, to secure a deal for the band. According to Jenner, Boyd had brought over his boss, Jac Holzman, label manager of Elektra Records, who'd signed Peter Jenner's new favourites Love, to see the band, 'but he didn't like it, and blew us out'. However, Nick Mason recalls that Holzman had offered 'a rather grudging one and seven-eighths percentage'.

Yet Polydor Records pitched in with a better offer, which included Joe being retained as an independent producer. (He had now formed his own independent production company Witchseason, the name taken from Donovan's 'Season of the Witch' single). A contract was drawn up. Within days, though, the deal would fall apart.

Bryan Morrison was one of the country's shrewdest booking agents. Working out of an office on London's Charing Cross Road, Morrison managed The Pretty Things, as well as handling publishing and agency bookings for a variety of acts, including all the bands that appeared at the fashionable Speakeasy. Jeff Dexter was among those who first invited Morrison to the UFO club to see Pink Floyd.

Speaking in 1982, Joe Boyd recalled that Morrison and two of his aides, Tony Howard and future Floyd manager Steve O'Rourke, visited him and the band while they were rehearsing. 'There was an immediate, intense dislike between myself and those three,' he said. Later, Boyd would recall 'velvet jackets, scarves knotted around their throats, tight trousers . . . the dandyism only made them more sinister.'

This combination of old-school mores and elements of the prevalent 'head culture' made for a formidable mix. 'Joe would have been intimidated by Morrie, Steve and Tony,' concedes Jeff Dexter, 'because they were a force to be reckoned with.'

It would prove a significant encounter. Morrison had already approached Blackhill with a view to representing the band, had looked over The Pink Floyd's contract with Boyd and Polydor and told them they could do better. Before Joe could raise any objection, Blackhill had backed out of the Polydor deal and signed with Morrison, who would then fund an independent recording to be pitched to record companies.

'The trouble was that Joe was the only person we knew in the industry,' admits Jenner. 'And, for us, he'd rather blotted his copybook with the Jac Holzman business. Along comes Bryan Morrison and he seemed to know everybody . . . In those days it was EMI or Pye or Decca. EMI were considered much hipper because they had The Beatles and they owned Abbey Road. Bryan told us, "You go with the company with the most money", and that saves you from thinking.' Bryan Morrison had hooked EMI after receiving a letter from EMI Parlophone's new producer Norman Smith, who was scouting for bands.

'I'd sent out letters to all the managers and agents I could think of,' Norman Smith told this writer in 2005. 'I got one back from Bryan Morrison, who invited me to go and see Pink Floyd. I'd never heard of them and, to be honest, I had no real interest in psychedelia. But he took me to the UFO club, and, while the music did absolutely nothing for me, I could see that they did have one hell of a following even then. I figured I should put my business hat on, because it was obvious to me that we could sell some records.' The proposed deal hit a snag when Jenner and King requested an advance. 'They wanted some front money – £5,000,' says Smith. 'But EMI didn't usually pay an advance. It was difficult to get it past the company's management but eventually I did.'

According to Smith, EMI's then head of A&R, Beecher Stevens, 'rowed himself in on the deal', and has since been wrongly credited with signing the group. Nevertheless, Jenner recalls that the label was 'very excited to be seen as so hip and so groovy by landing the band'. Better still, The Pink Floyd had secured an album deal rather than one dependent on hit singles.

The spurned Joe Boyd had nobly produced the new versions of 'Arnold Layne' and its B-side 'Candy and a Currant Bun' (with, as he later recalled, 'Roger over my shoulder, extending his big index finger on one of the faders'). However, EMI's regulations did not include using outside producers, while the Morrison Agency hiked up the band's fee for playing the UFO club. Joe Boyd's involvement with Pink Floyd was all but over. As he complained: 'It was a case of, "Thanks a lot for doing 'Arnold Layne', Joe. See you around." '

'There was always a little bit of needle between Joe and ourselves after that,' says Jenner. 'But we didn't have time to be doing UFO every time they wanted us to. So now we're having the conversation of, "Well, how much money are you going to pay?" Joe felt he'd been done over, which, it has to be said, he had been. I like to think we've all got over it now.'

Boyd wrote of the coup in his book, *White Bicycles: Making Music in the 1960s*: 'Like me, Jenner and King were out of their depth. None of us imagined that decades later you could go to the remotest part of the globe and find cassettes of *Dark Side of the Moon* rattling around in the glove compartments of Third World taxis.'

A song about a fetishist whose 'strange hobby' involves stealing women's underwear, Pink Floyd's debut single, 'Arnold Layne', was released on 11 March 1967. The Kinks and The Who were already dabbling with more outlandish lyrical ideas as well as blazing a trail for quirkily English bands that were happy to sound quirkily English. 'Arnold Layne' was a creepier addition to the pack. The lyrics were supposedly inspired by a real incident in Cambridge, where an unidentified knicker-thief had raided Mary Waters' washing line. Roger had regaled Syd with the story.

The music employed a woozy, merry-go-round rhythm, with Barrett's vocals sounding defiantly English, bordering on the deadpan. It is Richard Wright's Farfisa organ that provides the clearest link to psychedelia, splashing colour in place of a traditional guitar solo, and dominating the song. In the spring of 2006, touring as keyboard player in David Gilmour's solo band, Wright would sing Syd's lead vocals on a version of the song.

'Arnold Layne' is a reminder of just how integral the quiet, diffident Wright was to Pink Floyd's earliest work. 'Everyone, including me, underestimated Rick,' admits Peter Jenner. 'But he was so important to those early records. I remember him sorting out those harmonies and arrangements, telling people what to sing, tuning Roger's bass . . . I also felt there was a lot more to the way Rick and Syd worked together than history allows for.'

With a little help from the management ('We spent a couple of hundred quid trying to buy it into the charts,' admitted Andrew King), 'Arnold Layne' reached number 20 in the UK, and was banned by Radio Caroline and Radio London, due to its supposedly risqué content. 'We can't think what they're so perturbed about,' protested Waters in *Disc and Music Echo*. 'It's a song about a clothes fetishist who's obviously a bit kinked. A very simple, straightforward song about one sort of human predicament.'

UFO's former house band had gone decidedly overground, even if a mooted appearance on the BBC's flagship *Top of the Pops* was cancelled when the single began reversing down the charts. 'We want to be pop stars,' Waters told one interviewer. On the surface, the band seemed willing to jump through the requisite hoops: high-kicking in their best shirts and boots for a promotional photo outside EMI's Manchester Square HQ; posing self-importantly with EMI bigwig Beecher Stevens in his office; and, above all, submitting to a punishing tour schedule, courtesy of the Morrison Agency, that found them zigzagging across country and frequently playing two gigs a night.

'Arnold Layne' aside, much of the group's set still consisted of the less chart-friendly 'freak-outs' that wowed the mightily stoned in the UFO club. The reception was markedly different in the provinces: disgruntled punters poured beer on the band from the balconies, and Waters, who was unafraid to offer a withering aside to even the most hostile crowd, took a deep gash to the forehead one night from a thrown coin. Aubrey 'Po' Powell spent six months driving the band's van to gigs, and saw how badly The Pink Floyd's music could go down: 'You'd play to a bunch of, say, twenty mods, who all stood around looking horrified by this psychedelic band that didn't mean fuck all, when they just wanted to listen to Junior Walker.'

As The Pink Floyd became EMI's trophy underground band, the scene that spawned them was changing. By the spring of 1967, Keith Richards of The Rolling Stones had been busted for drugs, and the music business's preoccupation with illicit substances became perfect tabloid fodder. The *News of the World* splashed headlines such as 'POP SONGS AND THE CULT OF LSD', and The Pink Floyd were misquoted as describing themselves as 'social deviants'. The paper had confused them with Mick Farren's band, The Social Deviants. Lawyers were consulted and The

Pink Floyd received an apology. Holding their nerve, they even managed to convince EMI that their music was in no way recreating the experience of tripping, as accused. ('Quite how we managed that, I don't know,' admitted Nick Mason.)

While The Pink Floyd escaped, others were less fortunate. Caught up in the furore, John 'Hoppy' Hopkins was arrested for possession of marijuana and jailed for six months. ('I was careless, incredibly careless,' he says now.) Before going to Wormwood Scrubs prison, he arranged for Joe Boyd to take sole control of the UFO club. As an A&R man, Boyd understandably decided to focus on booking new bands rather than staging more mixed-media happenings.

In the following years Boyd would help orchestrate the careers of Fairport Convention and Nick Drake, among many others. But for some, this more commercial approach to UFO was indicative of the schism that existed in the underground scene – simply that it was no longer 'underground'. The Pink Floyd's move to EMI dovetailed with this change. 'I thought it was a shame that the Floyd weren't "ours" any more,' says Jenny Fabian.

Mick Farren takes a more pragmatic approach. 'It was pretty obvious to the more rational among us that the Floyd would end up on a major label, but some of the freaks saw it as a sell-out. I remember the words "Pink Finks" being painted on the wall of the UFO toilet. But it did bother me how they seemed to back off in major haste from the drug culture in which they'd made their name when the shit really started going down – the Stones being busted, Hoppy going to jail, major street harassment . . . That seemed like a cop-out.'

Yet for the group themselves, the scene had given them a launch pad for their music rather than a lifestyle philosophy. Having opted out of college and work to pursue a musical career, the pursuit of that career was more important than the fortunes of the London Free School or *International Times*.

'There were elements of the "underground" that we did tune into,' says Nick Mason now. 'You supplied the music while people did creative dance, painted their faces, bathed in a giant jelly. But probably through being middle-class, reasonably well-educated people, we could talk our way through a certain amount of stuff, including making ourselves sound as if we were part of the current movement.'

Roger Waters felt an even greater distance. 'To this day I still don't know exactly what a lot of that stuff was about,' he admitted. 'You'd hear the odd thing about a revolution, but nothing specific. I read *International Times* a few times, but what was the Notting Hill Free School actually all about? What was it meant to do? I never gathered what it was, apart from a few "happenings". The "happenings" that we put on were always a joke.'

EMI may have been persuaded to pay for the band's new Ford Transit and a new Binson Echorec, the box of tricks that helped create those space-age sound effects, but splashing out for a hotel was unheard of. Gigs in the far north still meant a night drive back to London. The ramshackle crew mucked in together. Peter Wynne-Willson loaded gear and patched together Floyd's homemade lighting rig between gigs. Peter had yet to pass his driving test, however, so Blackhill's secretary, the late June Child, would often drive the van instead. The pretty, blonde-haired June would prove an integral part of Pink Floyd's set-up, and a shoulder for Syd to cry on. June would later marry Barrett acolyte and Blackhill client Marc Bolan.

'I would buy a lot of equipment and materials to experiment with for different lighting effects,' recalls Peter Wynne-Willson, 'and each month June would come to Earlham Street to go through the mass of receipts. To make this boring process more interesting we developed a system whereby, on either side of a little table under the high-level bed, we would sit with our feet in each other's crotch. Such a delightful little ritual we had. June wore the shortest of skirts.'

Nevertheless, the whirlwind of gigs was soon taking its toll on Blackhill's star player. 'I saw Floyd's touring schedule years later,' said one Floyd confidant. 'Whoever programmed them to run around England in the way they did in the condition they did? Sheer madness. It would have been debilitating for anyone, never mind someone on drugs.'

Matthew Scurfield was now about to start his acting career in theatre rep, but followed his brother Ponji to Earlham Street, and saw, up close, the effect of Syd's new workload. 'Syd was someone who wasn't totally in the groove, like the other members of the group,' he says. 'He wasn't ambitious in the way Roger was. I always thought Syd was like an outsider even within the Floyd. It was very obvious at times that a lot of their ambition thwarted his art. It was always, "Come on Syd. It's time to go!"'

Barrett's drug use from the time remains the subject of much speculation. What was Syd taking, how much was he taking and how often? And what about the rest of the band? 'Back then I don't think Roger and Nick hardly ever took drugs,' recalls Andrew King. 'I always thought Roger was a "down the pub for a couple of pints" chap. Rick was smoking some dope. Syd was trying everything.'

'Syd, Andrew and I smoked dope,' says Peter Jenner. 'Although I don't recall Syd ever saying to me, "Let's take a trip", I knew he was doing LSD. How much, I don't know. I've always been told that he had what you might call "religious acid friends", yet I don't remember Syd being evangelical about LSD. But I do think it was a trigger for his problems.'

'Syd definitely wasn't taking LSD every day in Earlham Street,' insists Peter Wynne-Willson. 'It may have been the dope rather than the acid that brought on problems. I know the dope is a lot stronger these days, but young men who smoke dope between the ages of eighteen and twenty-two are particularly susceptible to mental trouble if they are of a sensitive disposition. With Syd, I don't remember a trip that was a turning point or anything like that. He sometimes had a hard time on dope, but not on acid. In England there was mostly hash available. Syd and I would generally smoke joints, sometimes chillums; we rarely smoked pipes of pure hash together.'

For Peter Jenner, Pink Floyd's (at some point that year they seemed to lose the definitive article) appearance at 'The 14-Hour Technicolor Dream' at Alexandra Palace in April 'coincided with the height of acid use that summer'. Staged as a fundraiser for *International Times*, which had just been raided and all but closed down by the police, it would be John Hopkins' last organisational feat before going to prison.

'I was the one that parlayed the rent of the hall,' says Hoppy now, 'and they were *still* looking for me years after. It was a gas. Ten thousand people must have gone through the doors at some time. Michael X's friends were de facto security. What we didn't realise till later was that they pocketed the money that people were paying. So very little made it back to central control.'

Pink Floyd were billed to play alongside The Pretty Things, The Soft Machine and the underground's latest overground star, Arthur Brown, soon to enjoy his first hit single, 'Fire', and performing while wearing a burning head-dress. There were avant-garde film shows, beatnik poetry readings, a fairground helter-skelter and the opportunity to smoke banana skins in a fibreglass igloo. John Lennon was among those who turned up to watch the madness.

That same night the Floyd had played a Dutch TV show before catching a flight back to London and driving at breakneck speed to Alexandra Palace in Muswell Hill. Peter Jenner, eager to make the most of the event, had dropped a tab of LSD a little too early. 'I was still driving the van while I was coming up,' he says. Meanwhile, Peter's old university pal, 'the alternative doctor' Sam Hutt was in a similar state. 'I drove up with Rick Wright, and I was tripping,' he recalls. 'Driving on acid? Not something I would recommend to anyone. All I can remember is being transfixed by this shiny cape Rick was wearing – or at least I *think* he was wearing.' Inside the venue, Hutt would become similarly transfixed by the helter-skelter. 'I just kept going up and down, up and down, getting reborn every time,' he laughs.

For The Soft Machine's Robert Wyatt, Pink Floyd's 4 a.m. performance 'must have been one of the greatest gigs they ever did. It completely blew my mind.' Others have wrongly claimed that Syd was too incapacitated to perform, yet photographs from the night also show Barrett with his hands on his guitar, clearly lucid enough to play, even if Richard Wright's cape isn't quite the shiny creation of Dr Sam Hutt's memory.

For organiser John 'Hoppy' Hopkins, Pink Floyd's dawn performance, good or otherwise, took a back seat to other events happening at the same time. 'One of our friends was a chemist,' he recalls, with some relish, 'and he came along with some stuff which we now think was a cousin of DMT [the hallucinogenic, diemethyltryptamine]. Whatever it was, my girlfriend and I had a nice warm glow and ended up outside Ally Pally in the dawn light looking down across London. I never saw Pink Floyd play that night. Or if I did, I can't remember a thing.'

Peter Jenner's reference to 'Syd's religious acid friends' may well refer to some of his flatmates that year. In late 1967, Syd left Earlham Street for a room in one of the flats at 101 Cromwell Road. The Lesmoir-Gordons had taken the first-floor flat some twelve months before, moving in with another Cambridge émigré, Bill Barlow, landlord of the notorious 27 Clarendon Street in Cambridge, home to numerous local hipsters. The

Cambridge 'scene' now spread to this new party house in the capital, located in a now-demolished Victorian building close to the West London Air Terminal coach station in Earls Court.

Nevertheless, with Nigel studying at the London School of Film Technique and moving in the most fashionable circles, number 101 became a Mecca for the capital's overlapping art, music, movie and drug crowds. The poet Allen Ginsberg, the film-maker Kenneth Anger, and singers Donovan and Mick Jagger were among those who dropped by.

From 1965 onwards, the building's various rooms had offered a rehearsal space for Pink Floyd and, briefly, lodgings for Roger Waters. It would also play host to various exotic tenants. These would include, at various times, John Esam, the New Zealand-born beatnik and an early link in London's LSD distribution chain, and Prince Stanislas Klossowski de Rola, aka Stash de Rola, the son of the prominent French artist Balthus. Stash was a confidant of The Rolling Stones, who would later be arrested on drug charges with Brian Jones, and would also take a memorable acid trip with Syd Barrett – of which more later.

The artist Duggie Fields had briefly studied architecture at Regent Street Poly, where he met the Cambridge contingent through Juliette Gale. Sometime in 1965 he moved into 101 Cromwell Road. 'Pink Floyd used to rehearse in one of the rooms,' he recalls now. 'And I used to go downstairs and put on an American R&B record as loud as I could because I thought they had no sense of rhythm and subtlety, and I rather hoped some of it might find its way into what they were doing.'

Duggie was still living at Cromwell Road, in a room papered with Marvel Comics, when Barrett took the room next to his.

'The house had seven rooms on those two top floors, and there were nine or ten people living there,' says Fields now. The living-room's walls, ceilings and floor were painted white (an idea lifted from the 1965 movie *The Knack . . . and How to Get It*), and films were often projected on the walls – sometimes deliberately running backwards. The room was routinely occupied by the building's lodgers, their friends and sometimes complete strangers.

'I can remember coming home from college to find maybe twenty people sitting around. I wouldn't know any of them and there'd be nobody there that actually lived at the flat,' says Fields. 'And this could be happening during the day as well as the night.'

On the floor below lived a lecturer ('poor Mr Poliblanc' as one of the residents now refers to him), who was totally unconnected with the group. 'One of our number worked out a way of wiring up the meter so we were effectively stealing his electricity,' admits Duggie. 'The landing also became a rubbish dump, as it was several floors up and nobody could be bothered to take the rubbish out. To this day I have no idea where the rubbish at 101 actually went.'

As well as housing such doyens of the capital's counter-culture, number 101 also offered shelter to Pip and Emo. There was a false ceiling installed in the hallway, with enough room above it to create a claustrophobic hidey-hole, big enough for a mattress.

'Cromwell Road was always a last resort,' groans Emo. 'We went there when we'd been kicked out of everyone else's flats. I still remember that platform suspended over the corridor. Girls were always terrified to get up there, and there was always a rush between me and Pip to get to that bed if it was the only one available.'

In the words of one of his acquaintances, 'Duggie Fields was not into self-annihilation', but while he stayed sane, many of the Cromwell Road regulars did not. Although stories about the house's occupants may have been exaggerated, Mick Rock, another regular visitor, recalls a general air of drug-induced chaos: 'Apart from Duggie's room, the rest of the place was full of acid burn-outs.'

Communal trips at Cromwell Road were certainly commonplace, whether during Barrett's residency or not, with one eyewitness recalling a bottle of LSD and pipette kept in the fridge of the Lesmoir-Gordons' flat. On at least one occasion a party of trippers were said to have marched the wrong way down the perilous entrance to the coach station, convinced of their invincibility despite the risk of oncoming vehicles. The spiked iron railings surrounding 101 Cromwell Road proved an even greater hazard to anyone believing they were inde-structible while under the influence. One night Nigel Lesmoir-Gordon found another of his old Cambridge drug buddies, Johnny Johnson, naked, disorientated and hanging on to the drainpipe outside 101's bathroom window. Nigel managed to persuade him back in. Johnson had previously attempted to commit suicide by throwing himself out of a window, and would succeed the next time he tried.

In May that year, Joe Boyd claims to have come across Lindsay Corner and a 'crazy-eyed' Syd in London's West End. Lindsay told him that Barrett had been taking acid every day for a week.

Barrett's supposed daily acid use has long been the subject of wild speculation. Some think he *was* taking it every day; most claim he wasn't. However, others in Pink Floyd's entourage were concerned that his flatmates might be encouraging his drug use by 'spiking' his drinks with LSD. 'Cromwell Road was full of heavy, loony, messianic acid freaks,' said Peter Jenner.

Two of the occasional people around Syd at Cromwell Road were known as 'Mad Sue' and 'Mad Jock'. In the real world, 'Jock' was Alistair Findlay. 'Sue', his then girlfriend, was Susan Kingsford, a model, who had first encountered Barrett and Gilmour while at the Cambridge Technical College. After appearing in a TV advert, as one of the first Cadbury's Flake girls, she moved to London and paired up with another of 101 Cromwell Road's residents, who had worked for Robert Fraser, the art gallery owner who got busted with some of The Rolling Stones. This friend 'fell in with the druggies,' says Sue now, 'and I fell in with him.' She also makes a fleeting appearance in Peter Whitehead's film footage of 'The 14-Hour Technicolor Dream', wearing, in her own words, 'a musquash coat and nothing else, holding a daffodil and beaming beatifically'.

'I remember Sue and Jock floating about,' says Mick Rock. 'Sue was this incredibly beautiful girl who'd taken too much acid.' But Duggie Fields recalls that 'Sue really wasn't mad at all, possibly just a little wacky.'

While asserting that her LSD use was prodigious – 'We took it constantly – enormous quantities' – Sue insists that they never spiked anyone. 'Why would anyone do such a thing?' she insists. 'In those days, if you took acid it was all very serious. You did it and then listened to Bach, or watched Kenneth Anger's latest film, or read the *Tibetan Book of the Dead*.'

'Spiking was a heinous crime,' Alistair Findlay told Syd Barrett biographer Tim Willis. 'You just wouldn't do it.'

'If they were spiking everyone,' asks Duggie Fields, 'why didn't they spike me? It never happened.'

Whatever his later problems, Syd was certainly *compos mentis* when he started work on Pink Floyd's debut album. The group were quickly ensconced at EMI's Abbey Road Studios. Widely regarded as one of the best studios in the world, Abbey Road was run along strict lines: white-coated technicians were on hand to deal with any equipment malfunctions, and tape ops and engineers were taught every aspect of the trade, from how to wrap up cable properly to the correct positioning of microphones. Best of all was the inspiring mix of musicians passing through its doors on a daily basis. As Abbey Road tape op and later engineer Jeff Jarratt recalls, 'You could come in one day and find the classical composer and conductor Otto Klemperer in Studio One, The Beatles in Studio Two, and Pink Floyd in Studio Three.'

In keeping with company policy, the Floyd's designated producer was their A&R executive Norman Smith, a dapper ex-RAF man, experienced jazz musician and sometime studio engineer for The Beatles. 'He was old-school with a very dry sense of humour,' recalled Roger Waters, 'and always gave the impression of being a retired song-and-dance man. I liked him enormously.'

Sessions for what would become *The Piper at the Gates of Dawn* album began in Abbey Road's Studio Three in January 1967. At various times during the next few months, The Beatles would be next door in Studio Two creating *Sgt Pepper's Lonely Hearts Club Band*. Smith had staked his reputation on Pink Floyd, but, as he recalled, 'It was not the easiest of associations.' To break the ice, the producer sat at the piano playing jazz and 'bashing away while the band joined in'. These jamming sessions worked well, but Syd was less receptive to taking advice about his own music. 'With Syd it was like talking to a brick wall,' said Smith. 'He would do a take, come back into the control room and have a listen. I'd make some suggestions, and he would just nod, not really saying anything, go back into the studio, do another take and it would be exactly the same as the one before. Roger was very helpful, and the others were fine, though I remember Rick was extremely laid-back, but with Syd I eventually realised I was wasting my time.'

Jeff Jarratt worked as a tape op during the sessions. 'My memories are different from Norman's,' he says now. 'Syd was clearly the band's main creative force, and I thought he was fantastic. When I was asked to do the sessions I went to see Floyd play live, and I was absolutely amazed. It was so fresh and exciting; I hadn't heard anything like it. Norman would have been directing them in the best way for that stuff to sound good on record. So perhaps there were things he said that challenged their way of thinking.'

Similarly, Waters remembers that 'despite him [Syd] doing a lot of acid there were no real problems at that stage.' Nevertheless, all agreed that the band's more outlandish musical ideas jarred with the traditionally minded Smith.

'I wasn't that knowledgeable about the sort of music they were playing,' admitted Norman. 'Psychedelia didn't interest me. But I felt it was my job to get them to think more melodically.' On that score, Smith succeeded in 'discouraging the live ramble', as Peter Jenner calls it. Instead, freeform live numbers such as 'Pow R Toc H' were hacked down to a more manageable length, though a 'licensed ramble' was permitted with the 9 minute 41 second version of 'Interstellar Overdrive'. According to the late Abbey Road engineer Pete Bown, this was the song he heard Floyd rehearsing when he first checked in to begin working on the album. 'I opened the door and nearly shit myself,' he recalled years later. 'By Christ it was loud. I had certainly never heard anything quite like it before.'

'Peter Bown was an unbelievable character,' remembers Jeff Jarratt. 'A fun, extrovert guy. He was older than the band, but he was very receptive to new ideas.' 'Pete had a much more creative attitude than perhaps Norman did,' offers Peter Jenner. 'He was also extremely gay, ragingly gay, which seemed quite unusual back then.' Andrew King recalled Bown seated at the mixing desk painting the tips of his fingers with a plastic skin compound used to repair cuts and grazes, as he was concerned that endless sessions working the desk would 'wear them out through over-use'.

Stories of Pink Floyd meeting The Beatles during these sessions are steeped in apocrypha. They range from the fictitious — that Barrett secretly played on *Sgt Pepper* — to the simply mundane — that the Floyd were taken in to meet The Beatles, encountering a grumpy Lennon and a cheerier McCartney. Nick Mason wrote of 'sitting humbly as they [The Beatles] worked on a mix' of what would become 'Lovely Rita'. Norman Smith added a new tale to the collection. He was in Studio Three, attempting to bond with Floyd at the start of the *Piper* sessions, when 'the door opened and who should walk in but Paul McCartney. He introduced himself to them, though they obviously knew who he was, and then tapped me on the shoulder as he left and said, "You won't go wrong with this chappie." I think the boys were impressed.'

'What you have to remember,' says Jeff Jarratt, 'is that bands were running into each other all the time at Abbey Road. Who knows how many times Floyd and The Beatles might have met?'

Aubrey 'Po' Powell also recalls a meeting between Barrett, Waters and Paul McCartney at the UFO club: 'There was this little corridor by the side of the stage, and I was sat there when McCartney came in, smoking a joint. Paul was a very affable guy and he passed the joint around. After he'd gone Syd was like, "Wow, that was Paul McCartney and he's come to see Pink Floyd." I was surprised, because I was like, "Syd, you're pretty cool as well now." I also remember that Roger, who I'd never seen smoke before, took a huge hit off that joint. He knew when to play the game.'

The Beatles' success at Abbey Road certainly enabled 'the boys' to make *The Piper at the Gates of Dawn*. Following The Beatles' *Revolver*, the studio's engineers had become used to phasing, multi-tracking, and all manner of what Jenner calls 'weird shit'.

'Roger was especially interested in the studio itself and the development of sound,' recalled Smith.

But Andrew King remembers Syd showing a similar interest: 'One of my strongest memories is of Syd mixing the song "Chapter 24". I remember him at the desk operating the faders for the final mix. And he was very good at it. He knew what he wanted and he was totally capable of getting what he wanted – at a technical level.'

While Barrett is said to have written off several microphones in the course of the recording, and had the 'meters frequently screaming in the red', out of the occasional chaos came eleven songs for the album, and, most importantly, an additional single. 'When I heard "See Emily Play", I finally thought: This is it. This is the one,' says Smith.

Pink Floyd premiered the single, then still titled 'Games for May', at a performance of the same name in London's Queen Elizabeth Hall on 12 May. Jenner had secured the show at the capital's prestigious classical music venue through his wife Sumi's friendship with the promoter Christopher Hunt. It was here that the band chose to premiere their new gizmo, the Azimuth Coordinator. Effectively the first quadraphonic sound system, the Coordinator had been built for the band by one of the boffins at Abbey Road. It comprised four rheostats contained in a large box and was equipped with a 'joy-stick', which would be operated by Richard Wright to pan the sound around 270 degrees in whatever venue the band were playing. The sheer volume at which Pink Floyd played that night was an issue, but it was their use of a bubble machine and the scattering of flowers that caused the most concern. 'A combination of squashed daffodil stems and burst bubbles left this smeary liquid all over the leather seats and the floor,' says Jenner. 'We were immediately banned, and I don't think they let pop groups back into the South Bank for some time after that.'

Just days later it would be the issue of volume that preoccupied the interviewer on the BBC1 arts show *Look of the Week*. Following a snippet of Pink Floyd performing 'Pow R Toc H', Barrett and Waters submitted to some incredulous questioning from the Austrian musician and string quartet fan Hans Keller. The exchange now plays like a quaint period piece: the earnest, suited musicologist versus the flowery-shirted pop upstarts. 'Why does it all got to be so terribly loud [sic]?' enquires Keller. 'That's the way we like it,' counters Waters. Barrett, in a nice contrast to the strung-out Syd of legend, is as alert and well spoken as his bandmate. Keller remains singularly unimpressed, but does offer one sharp observation on Pink Floyd's music: 'My verdict is that it's a little bit of a regression to childhood.'

Shunning Abbey Road, the band returned to Sound Techniques Studio, where they'd worked with Joe Boyd on 'Arnold Layne', to cut the new single, 'See Emily Play'. But there was a problem. 'The trouble with "See Emily Play" was it didn't do a thing for Syd,' explained Norman Smith. 'In fact, I don't think he was happy about recording singles full stop.'

On the day of the session, Syd took a telephone call from David Gilmour. The guitarist was on a brief visit to London, buying equipment for his own band Jokers Wild, then playing a residency in a Paris nightclub. Barrett sounded perfectly normal on the phone and invited Gilmour to the studio. On arrival, Gilmour was shocked by what he saw. 'He looked very strange, glassy-eyed,' he recalled. 'He wasn't terribly friendly, didn't seem to recognise me. I stayed for an hour or two and then left. I knew about LSD, as I'd taken it myself, but I didn't connect it to this. He was in a very strange state.' Gilmour returned to France, troubled by his friend's condition but unaware of just how much impact it would soon have on his own career.

'See Emily Play' was released on 16 June 1967. EMI bigwig Roy Featherstone would coin the slogan 'Straight to Heaven in '67' to accompany the single's release, and, as Peter Jenner recalls, 'while that now sounds incredibly naff, as a slogan it worked at the time.' The song included a dash of typical Syd experimentation – the sound of a plastic ruler being scraped along the guitar fretboard – but, as Norman Smith explained, 'it had this wonderful melody, this amazing tune.'

The perfect amalgam of psychedelic excess and pure pop, 'See Emily Play' was brighter than 'Arnold Layne' on all levels, without the seamier subject matter of its predecessor, but with just enough of Wright's spooked-sounding keyboards and Syd's fey, disengaged vocals to prevent a complete slip into easy listening pop. As *New Musical Express* raved: 'It's full of weird oscillations, reverberations, electronic vibrations, fuzzy rumblings and appealing harmonies.'

Not as whimsical as some of his other compositions on *The Piper at the Gates of Dawn*, the song was still steeped in random images from Syd and Roger's Cambridge childhood. 'I know which woods Syd's talking about in "See Emily Play",' said Waters in 2004. 'We all used to go to these woods as kids. It's a very specific area – one specific wood on the road to the Gog Magog Hills.'

The Emily in question is similarly steeped in Floyd myths. Some claim it was Emily Young, one of the Notting Hill Free School and UFO club's regular alumni, now a noted sculptress. While Emily met Syd on occasion, she claims to have no specific knowledge that the song was written about her. Jenny Spires has since recalled that 'Emily' was Barrett's favourite name should he ever have a daughter. At the time of the song's release Waters told one radio interviewer, in the wonderful parlance of the era: 'Emily could be anyone. She's just a hung-up chick, that's all.'

Two weeks after the song's release, Pink Floyd were invited to play *Top of the Pops*. Andrew King would later say that Syd's decline could be plotted through the group's appearances on the show: two reluctant performances and one final non-appearance. Peter Wynne-Willson was with Syd in Trafalgar Square prior to one of the performances. 'It was getting later and later. In the end, I said to him, "Isn't it time we got going?" We hailed a cab and Syd asked it to go somewhere entirely different.'

Norman Smith was on hand to chaperone the band as they went to the show's Lime Grove Studios in West London for their debut appearance. 'I told them they'd have to mime, as that was what all the groups did back then,' he recalled. 'I don't think Syd was happy, but the others accepted it. So they went off to have their hair washed and their make-up done. Normally, I didn't think Syd cared how he looked, but when he came back, he looked like a pop star. I told him he looked fantastic. So he went straight over to the mirror, messed up his hair and grabbed a load of tissues to wipe off the make-up . . . A week later, we went back again, and the same thing happened. He just stood there on the show, letting the guitar dangle in front of him. I had a go afterwards, told him he was going to destroy our recording career if he carried on. But it just went in one ear and out the other.'

The single peaked at number 5. Taken back to the studio for a third appearance, the following week, Syd initially refused to go on. 'We finally discovered that the reason was that John Lennon didn't have to do *Top of the Pops*, so we didn't,' Roger Waters told *Melody Maker*.

Sue Kingsford encountered Syd on the afternoon of one of his scheduled *Top of the Pops* appearances. She and Jock were now living in a flat in Beaufort Street, South Kensington, near to Cromwell Road. 'Suddenly we heard this banging on the door,' she recalls. 'And there was Syd. He had no shoes on, which was not unusual in those days, but his feet were filthy and bleeding. He looked completely off of his head. He didn't say a word. He just came in and we gave him some Sugar Puffs and a cup of coffee. He still didn't say anything. He just sat there. About an hour after he arrived, there was another bang on the door. It was some of the Floyd's people: "Is Syd here?" We answered, "Yes, he's in the kitchen but he's not very well." They were like, "I don't give a fuck if he's not very well." They just dragged him out. Later that evening I discovered they'd dragged him off to do *Top of the Pops*. The reason he was sitting on a cushion during the show is because he was so out of it he couldn't stand up.'

Despite their *Top of the Pops* appearance, the BBC invited the group to guest on the *Saturday Club* radio show at the end of July. Having been ferried to the recording studio, Syd again decided that he didn't wish to participate. This time he offered no explanation. 'When we got the call that it was our turn to go on, nobody could find Syd,' remembers

Norman Smith. 'The doorman told us they'd seen someone that looked like him leaving. Roger Waters and I went out into the street and, sure enough, there he was, just turning the corner. That was the end of that.'

Inevitably, Barrett's behaviour was souring his relationship with the rest of the group. Aubrey 'Po' Powell, who was driving the band's van, agreed to pair up with Syd for a night drive back from the South Coast after a gig. 'I drove back from Portsmouth with Syd, as the others didn't really want to be with him. I remember it was pouring with rain, and he smoked a joint, and he must have laughed for about two hours, but hardly spoke. He was obviously losing the plot.'

In August, Blackhill issued a statement to the press following the cancellation of several Pink Floyd dates. 'It is not true Syd has left the group,' Andrew King told the *New Musical Express*. 'He is tired and exhausted, and has been advised to rest for two weeks.'

Peter Jenner called on Sam Hutt for advice. That summer, Hutt was fresh out of medical school and acquiring a reputation as London's hippest doctor. 'The idea was to send Syd to see "the good doctor",' explains Hutt now. 'The idea being, "He knows all about the drugs and he takes them as well, but he's not going to freak out."'

Hutt had rented a *finca* on Formentera, which then represented the western end of the hippie trail for those that didn't fancy making the full journey East. Syd and Lindsay, Richard and Juliette, Sam, his wife and their young son headed off to the island for a fortnight, later to be joined by Roger and Judy Trim, who were staying on neighbouring Ibiza. The plan was for Barrett to kick back, play guitar, bask in the sun, enjoy himself. Syd duly obliged and seemed quite content during parts of the holiday, but there was one snag. As Hutt remembers, 'He was munching acid all the time.' The idyllic retreat was also prone to electrical storms, a freak weather condition that did little to improve Syd's raddled state of mind. 'You get sheet lightning behind the clouds and the whole sky lights up fluorescent,' Hutt recalls. 'It could affect you even if you weren't taking anything at all. Add acid to the equation and Syd was, quite literally, trying to climb the walls. His fingernails were clawing the wall, as he was trying to get himself off the floor.'

'I thought it was fucking awful.' The Who's Pete Townshend was among those unimpressed by *The Piper at the Gates of Dawn* on its release that August.

Townshend's main gripe was that the record didn't do justice to the group's wall-of-sound live show. But Norman Smith had done the job asked of him. He'd curbed some of the band's excesses and helped realise Peter Jenner's dream of an avant-garde pop group. Less than twelve months earlier, Pink Floyd's repertoire included the likes of 'Louie Louie', yet barely a trace of the blues was to be found in their first album. Richard Wright's classical and jazz influences seem to have taken their place, the keyboards filling in the spaces usually occupied by a lead guitar, giving most of the record a sinister undertow. Childhood nursery rhymes permeate 'Bike', 'The Gnome' and 'Flaming' ('Watching buttercups come to life . . . sleeping on a dandelion'), but on 'Matilda Mother' and 'The Scarecrow' there's a hint of menace as well; like Grimm's Fairy Tales set to music. A sixties spy movie theme burbles away on 'Lucifer Sam', with its cryptic mention of one Jennifer Gentle, in reality Jenny Spires.

Nocturnal sessions with *I-Ching* at Earlham Street find their way into 'Chapter 24', accompanied by droning keyboards and percussion, the band making use of the treasure trove of odd musical instruments scattered around the studio. In the bleaker, noisier corner were 'Interstellar Overdrive' and 'Astronomy Domine'. The latter was, in the words of Nick Mason, similar to 'what Roy Lichtenstein was putting into his paintings'. With Peter Jenner reciting astronomical co-ordinates from a children's book of the planets through a megaphone and Roger Waters' primitive bass runs, it sounded like pop art and science fiction condensed into a rock song.

While Barrett's songs had a wistful, child-like charm, 'Pow R Toc H' and Waters' solo composition 'Take Up Thy Stethoscope and Walk' now sound like dummy runs for some of the bassist's later ideas. The shivery suggestion of madness and the frantic howling would be revisited on *Dark Side of the Moon* and *Animals*.

Yet Syd's fairy-tale contributions to the album immediately struck a chord with those from his hometown. 'There was something very Cambridge-like about it all,' says Seamus O'Connell. 'When we first heard these extraordinary songs, things like "Bike", we all made that connection.'

'I always thought Syd got stuck in a curious sort of protracted childhood,' offers Anthony Stern. 'So it was always there in the music. Childhood had been an idyllic time, and I think he found the idea of growing up and dealing with your parents' world frankly terrifying.'

For Sue Kingsford, Syd's hankering for his hometown was all too familiar. 'I always thought he was out of his comfort zone when he wasn't in Cambridge,' she ventures. 'Both of us often used to go back at weekends. I can remember us tripping one night in Cromwell Road, and Syd, who hadn't said a word for hours, suddenly asked, "Are you going home this weekend?" I told him I was, and he replied, "Do you know, that's all I want to do. I just want to go home."'

As steeped in 1967 as *Sgt Pepper*, Pink Floyd's debut also translates for subsequent generations of listeners. Reviews were favourable, even if some of what *Record Mirror* called its 'mind-blowing sounds' were still a step too far for many pop fans.

Photographer Vic Singh, hired to shoot the band for the album's cover, was similarly unsure. 'Their music seemed alien and quite surreal,' he says now. 'When I first heard it, I thought: This is never going to work.' Then sharing a studio with, among others, David Bailey, Singh was an up-and-coming society photographer and friends with George Harrison. 'George had been given a prism lens. He didn't know what to do with it, so he passed it to me.' Singh told Jenner and King to raid whatever boutiques they could to get the brightest clothes in which to dress the band. This time, even Syd seemed happy to play by the rules. Vic relaxed the band 'with a few joints and a couple of shots of Scotch in the coffee – and then snapped away'. The Quiet Beatle's prism lens split the finished image, rendering the Floyd in duplicate. 'It was unusual and different, and they were delighted with it,' says Singh. 'And Syd did his own little drawing on the back cover.' *The Piper at the Gates of Dawn* would be one of the few Pink Floyd studio album sleeves actually to feature the group on its front cover.

Vic Singh's experiences with Syd that year contrasted with those of Andrew Whittuck. A freelance photographer, shadowing the likes of The Beatles and the Maharishi in London that summer, Whittuck photographed Pink Floyd at Abbey Road and at his parents' house. 'I'd actually been to primary school in Hampstead with Nick Mason,' he says now. 'Though of course we were both too cool to mention it.' The band and a roadie arrived with their lighting rig and set up in Whittuck's bedroom: 'They played me the album, which was quite unlike anything I'd ever heard, and there was lots of talk about the composer

Stockhausen, which was where it was at, apparently. They all crashed out in my brother's room and Syd was practically asleep after wedging himself into a corner between the door and the bed. Eventually, my mother came in, took one look at him and announced, "That chap looks like he needs a strong cup of tea." She went off and brought him a cup. Of course, I was embarrassed, but, to be fair, Syd did actually perk up a bit after that.'

Pink Floyd were now attracting the attention of the music press, and interviews from the time see both Waters and Mason more forthcoming than their singer. 'I lie and I'm rather aggressive,' announced Roger to *Disc and Music Echo*. 'I want to be successful and loved in everything I turn my hand to,' Nick told the same interviewer. In contrast, Barrett is shyer and far less verbose. 'Our music is like an abstract painting,' he offered in a brief moment of insight. 'It should suggest something to each person.'

Back from Formentera, Syd and the band reconvened at Sound Technique Studios, as EMI were already looking for another single. Among the new songs on offer was Barrett's horribly prophetic creation 'Scream Thy Last Scream'. Abbreviated from its original title, 'Scream Thy Last Scream Old Woman with a Casket', the song featured Nick Mason on vocals shadowed by insidious, creepy Pinky and Perky-style vocals, the music swaying and lurching. 'Vegetable Man' was hardly any brighter, with a desperate Syd declaring, 'I've been looking all over the place for a place for me' against a tuneless oompah rhythm. 'He was singing about himself. It was an extraordinary document of serious mental disturbance,' says Peter Jenner. 'A song of amazing mad grandeur,' counters a more sympathetic Andrew King. Dr Sam Hutt dropped in while the band was recording the track. Unfortunately, he was tripping: 'All I can remember thinking was: Uh-oh, here come the demons!'

'We were probably the only people in Los Angeles that had a copy of *The Piper at the Gates of Dawn*,' insists Alice Cooper. Pink Floyd's debut was released in the US at the end of October 1967, when Alice was still just plain Vincent Furnier, the nineteen-year-old singer in a band called The Nazz and 'utterly fixated by all British bands'. Alice's and Pink Floyd's paths would cross within weeks of the album's release.

Andrew King, in his capacity as tour manager, flew to the States in advance of Floyd's inaugural US tour. As he now explains, 'Everything went wrong from day one.'

In San Francisco, King discovered that the group's work visas had not yet arrived. Under union rules, a visiting British band had effectively to swap with an American group visiting the UK, in this case Sam the Sham and The Pharoahs. 'I had to explain the situation to our promoter Bill Graham,' says King. 'Which made me feel like a complete prick.' Graham, a formidable figure on the American West Coast, was not a man to be trifled with. He had arranged for Pink Floyd to play club dates and theatre shows alongside Janis Joplin's band, Big Brother and The Holding Company. The absent visas meant the first six West Coast dates had to be cancelled. 'An irate Bill ended up getting the American ambassador out of his bed in London at 4 a.m. to sort out the visas,' continues King. 'The band were on the next plane out. If there was one consolation, I got to see the Ike and Tina Turner Revue, whom Bill booked to play the first night instead of the Floyd.'

Arriving in the US with only their guitars, the band were confronted with two major problems. Their US label Capitol ('who hadn't a fucking clue about us or our music', according to Peter Jenner) hadn't organised any instruments and the band were forced to hustle the local music shops into lending replacements. Arriving at the 5,500-seater Winterland Auditorium, where they were due to open for Janis Joplin and Richie Havens, King realised that the group's homemade light show, which they'd brought with them, 'would be absolutely fucking useless and more suited to a primary school play'. The headliners graciously allowed them to use their own.

In the UK, the West Coast music scene was romantically perceived as a counterpart to London's underground music clique. In the wake of The Beatles, any visiting British band intrigued the American music press. The just-launched *Rolling Stone* magazine sent photographer Baron Wolman down to Sausalito where Pink Floyd were staying. The band willingly played up for the camera. 'They were obviously pleased to be in San Francisco,' recalls Wolman now. 'At one time Syd grabbed a couple of sugar cubes and put them in his mouth, an obvious reference to his fondness for LSD and one of the more popular ways of ingesting that particular drug.'

However, as Waters would later protest, many of the West Coast's flagship groups were essentially country-blues bands. They might be given to lengthy jams and dope-smoking, but musically they were surprisingly conservative in their sound and influences. Pink Floyd's mind-bending mix of jazz, beat pop and electronic noodling was far removed from Janis Joplin. The contrast wasn't lost on the music press. As *Rolling Stone*'s star critic Ralph Gleason wrote: 'On the West Coast we have recently seen The Cream, The Who, Procol Harum, Jimi Hendrix and Pink Floyd. Three groups are winners. The other two just do not make it. In person, Pink Floyd, for all its electronic interest, is simply dull in a dance hall following Big Brother and Janis Joplin.'

The band found their smaller club shows, in which they could use their bijou lighting system, were better received – some of the time. Prior to flying out from London, Syd had had his hair permed at Vidal Sassoon's, and the resultant frizz was not to his liking. Lighting tech Peter Wynne-Willson had had his own hair permed at the same time. 'Syd, myself and a few others went to Vidal Sassoon's in London and had our hair permed. I wonder if Syd had an adverse reaction to the perm? I do remember that the horror look came into his eyes soon after.'

Before going on stage at the Cheetah Club in Santa Monica some reports claim Barrett, in a fit of pique, poured the contents of a tub of Brylcreem over his hair, into which he crushed a handful of (the barbiturate) Mandrax capsules. Wynne-Willson claims no memory of this. In the great spirit of rock myth and hearsay, others, including Sam Hutt, are adamant they'd seen him perform this trick on stage previously at the UFO club ('I remember being terribly impressed, and thinking: This is a man who has his finger on some kind of pulse.') Nevertheless, Nick Mason's memory of the show extends to Syd applying the hair gel but not the drugs. Once asked to comment on the likeliness of the story, David Gilmour quipped that he 'couldn't believe Syd would waste good Mandies'. Once on stage Barrett is said to have detuned his guitar, provoking Roger Waters to cut his own hand while hitting his bass in anger.

Cheetah Club regulars The Nazz approached the band after the show. 'The Floyd had run out of money in Los Angeles and ended up staying with us for a couple of nights,' claims Alice Cooper. 'We had a place on Beethoven Street in Venice. I remember getting up one morning and there was Syd staring at a box of cornflakes the way you or I would watch television. It was obvious that there was already something very, very wrong.'

'I don't think we'd run out of money,' corrects Andrew King. 'But we were feeling very lonely and dispirited. The Nazz invited us round to theirs to smoke some pot. They were incredibly kind to us when we most needed it. Though we did watch them play that club and they cleared the place.'

Offstage, Syd was also a liability: uncommunicative with reps from the band's American record company and appearing monosyllabic during an interview with Dick Clark on the popular US TV show *American Bandstand*. Tellingly, during a mimed performance of the Floyd's new song 'Apples and Oranges', Syd seems barely bothered to mouth the words beneath his bird's nest hair-do, the camera frequently cutting to a rather aggrieved-looking Roger Waters and an unflappable Nick Mason. It was, at least, an improvement on the day before on *The Pat Boone Show*, when Syd spent most of the time cutting his interviewer dead with a silent stare and a single-word answer to the question, 'What do you like?' Barrett: 'America.'

No one is entirely sure whether Syd took LSD while in the US (most think not), but there were other narcotic distractions.

'When we went to the States, the dope consumption went up,' says Peter Wynne-Willson. 'In California it was all grass, very strong and different, as it was always smoked without tobacco. So smoking straight grass in the States may have been that extra notch on the ratchet . . . Two young women took Syd and I off to some hillside . . . mountain . . . I couldn't call it a retreat, because it was phenomenal, a beautiful house. They plied us with prodigious amounts of dope, which wasn't so critical for me, as I only had to operate lighting equipment, but for Syd . . . to my memory that was the first time I saw Syd standing on the stage unable to play the guitar.'

Despite their singer's unpredictability, there had been some pleasant distractions on the tour for the others, with Waters and Mason initiated into the delights of Southern Comfort, courtesy of Janis Joplin, and several members of the travelling party enjoying the ministrations of obliging female fans, while kicking back at a groupie-friendly motel on Santa Monica Boulevard. One eyewitness claims that some individuals were obliged to book themselves appointments at the Middlesex Hospital's venereal disease clinic on returning to the UK.

Nevertheless, with their singer in freefall, Andrew King pulled the plug on the remaining East Coast gigs, and the dejected party flew back to Europe.

'There were a lot of criss-crossing emotions and feelings running about the place,' remembers King. 'We all had a number of conversations with Syd.' These included Waters demanding that Barrett be fired on the spot. Stopping off to play a festival in The Netherlands before continuing to the UK, the band tried to communicate with Syd backstage via handwritten notes. King found himself considering the possibility that 'we were all mad and Syd was the sane one.'

'I never really got a coherent story of what happened in America,' claims Peter Jenner. 'But I remember Andrew was shell-shocked when he got back . . . The trouble is I probably would have considered some of Syd's behaviour fine. It was avant-garde, and I thought avant-garde was cool.'

For some in the camp, the split was partly attributable to a division between those who smoked dope and those who didn't. Waters, with his drive and tenacity, was seen as 'not being cool'. 'A ridiculous thing when you think about it now,' says one of their associates, 'but in the hippie mindset of the time, we all thought that was the case.'

There was another, less tangible, division between Syd and his bandmates, according to Libby Gausden. In October, just back from the US tour, Syd visited Libby at her new job, working as a translator at the university. She was also just about to get married. 'Syd told me that everyone else in the band was being very sensible and wanting to buy flats with the money they'd made on the tour, but that he had spent every single penny he'd earned on a bright pink car which he was now having shipped over. He was doubled up with laughter at this and the thought of the others all putting their money towards flats and houses. He thought pop music was for fun and that he should spend everything.'

Libby's boss also walked into the office and saw Barrett. Unaware of who he was, but knowing that Libby was about to get married, her boss took her aside afterwards to offer some sage advice: 'He said, "Ooh, don't get tempted by that one. He's *very* peculiar".'

For Jenner, the 'Syd problem', as Waters was now calling it, escalated on the band's next run of dates. With barely twenty-four hours' respite after returning from the US, Pink Floyd were due to play the Royal Albert Hall, on the opening date of a tour supporting Jimi Hendrix. The rest of the bill included pop's latest movers and shakers: Amen Corner, The Move and The Nice. Each band was allotted an exact number of minutes for their set, with many venues requiring a matinée and evening performance. While Hendrix usually travelled alone, the support groups journeyed by coach, picked up from outside the London Planetarium in Baker Street. 'All these groups on one coach; it was rather like the Cliff Richard film *Summer Holiday*,' says Nick Mason, drolly, but Andy Fairweather-Low, then the teenage singer with Amen Corner, recalled the Floyd 'as unsociable buggers, who never spoke to anybody'. Fairweather-Low would go on to become a guitarist in Roger Waters' solo band, though at some point on that Hendrix tour there was an altercation between his manager and Waters. For Nick Mason, the Hendrix shows offered both good and bad experiences. 'We'd led a very solitary existence as a band before that tour,' he recalls. 'Mainly because we were playing our own strange music. So, on one level, it was wonderful to hang out with Hendrix and other musicians. But by the end of it, we were frazzled – and that was because of Syd.'

Even with their abbreviated time slot, Barrett behaved as if he'd rather be anywhere else. 'He used to go off on these long walks and then arrive two minutes before he was due to go on stage,' says The Nice's singer and guitarist Davy O'List. 'I'd seen this happen so I was aware that there was tension. Musically, I thought they were fabulous, and I used to watch them from the audience trying to work out what they were doing.' O'List's attention to detail would pay off. 'One day, possibly in Liverpool, Syd didn't turn up, so the band asked me if I'd stand in,' he recalls. 'I told them I knew "Interstellar Overdrive", so they produced Syd's hat and told me to put it on. I decided to play with my back to the crowd. The audience was full of fourteen-year-old girls who all started screaming, thinking I was Syd, so I decided not to turn around. Roger was smiling, thinking they'd got away with it. Which was the point at which I got a bit brave and turned around – and all the screaming stopped. As soon as Syd found out, he came back. I did notice that he wouldn't even look at me when we were on the coach after that.' Barrett's performances remained unpredictable, although O'List never stood in again. 'In the past I've exaggerated and told people I played more shows,' he admits now. 'But that's only because I wished it had been true.'

In November, the tour pitched up at Cardiff's Sophia Gardens. Nick Kent, the future *NME* writer, then a fifteen-year-old fan, was in the audience. 'It was the moment psychedelia arrived in the suburbs,' he recalls. 'Previously, all this stuff was only happening in London. The Nice had ten minutes, Amen Corner, fifteen . . . So everyone was pulling out their most flamboyant stuff, going in for the kill. Except the Floyd. They came on and played, I think, "Set the Controls for the Heart of the Sun". But I think they'd turned Syd's amp down, because you could hear this cacophony in the background while the other three tried to hold the thing together. It looked like he was unravelling.'

Backstage, visitors encountered Barrett sitting in the corner of the dressing room in what appeared to be an acid torpor, tentatively playing with a toy steam engine he had acquired, and looking terrified whenever anyone struck up a conversation.

Considering Barrett's condition, a stint of prodigious LSD use was perhaps not the best idea. During a rare few days off, a contingent of Cambridge and London hedonists set off in a rented Ford Zephyr for Blackhill Farm, Andrew King's family cottage in the Brecon Beacons, notable for a large penis sculpture in the garden, rendered by Eric Clapton's sometime pianist Ben Palmer.

The party included the Lesmoir-Gordons, Syd, Lindsay, Cromwell Road hipster Stash de Rola and a Cambridge fashion model known as Gai Caron, who would later marry Aubrey 'Po' Powell. Now the events of the trip have an absurd, cartoonish quality, but there's a bleaker undercurrent. The noise and odd behaviour attracted a warning visit from the police, Nigel and Jenny became lost in a snowstorm while tripping, and Stash, whose favoured garb included a Victorian night gown and a velvet cape, attempted to sit in the cottage's open fire, believing, according to Jenny, 'that if we really believed in the love, he wouldn't burn'.

The ridiculous antics took on a stranger hue where Syd was concerned. 'The first night tripping, he spent most of it perched on a wine bottle,' recalls Nigel. 'He had his two feet on it and his hands on a beam overhead and he somehow managed to keep his balance. Later that week, when tripping again, he did a shit on the doorstep, which we thought most peculiar. Even on acid that wasn't a terribly sane thing to do.'

Viewing his flatmates and neighbours as part of the problem, the Blackhill team had extricated Syd from Cromwell Road before the summer was over. Barrett and Lindsay had moved temporarily into Andrew King's family-owned flat on Richmond Hill with Rick and Juliette. Disturbing rumours circulated of Syd's pet cat being left at Cromwell Road where it was supposedly fed LSD and died. A second-floor property overlooking the River Thames, the Richmond Hill pad was supposed to provide a saner atmosphere. The pressing issue now, though, was to follow that up with another hit single, even if Syd didn't share the rest of the band's or their management's sense of commitment.

'Syd was beginning to feel deeply disappointed by what was happening with the Floyd,' says Anthony Stern. 'Around this time, he used to visit me in a flat I had in Norfolk Mansions in Battersea, and treat it as a sort of refuge. The thing about growing up in Cambridge was you never ever wanted to do what had been done before. Syd was innately revolutionary and creative, and he just didn't get the idea of commerciality.'

Instead of writing another hit single, Barrett would spend hours with Stern plotting out their ideas for a film, to which they gave the working title of 'The Rose-Tinted Monocle'. The pair had come across a book by the American author and inventor Buckminster Fuller, and had been especially taken with one passage referring to 'inherently regenerative constellar energy association events'. 'This was conceived as the basis for the film,' explains Stern. 'The energy association events would be episodes in a film. Syd and I wanted to make a film that had no linear structure but consisted of all these fragments which when viewed holistically would give you a sense of oneness – almost like something you might watch to aid you with meditation.'

While Barrett would never see the film through to completion, Stern would work with many of the ideas first devised for 'The Rose-Tinted Monocle', and create a movie of his own, which would later be offered to Pink Floyd. In the meantime, away from his fledgling film project, Syd was still being encouraged by others to think more like a pop star.

Syd's next creation, 'Apples and Oranges', had been released as a single to coincide with the US tour and hopefully nudge Floyd back into the UK charts for Christmas. Where previously Syd had sung of transvestite underwear thieves and mysterious 'hung-up chicks', this was, apparently, inspired by a more mundane occurrence: a girl he'd seen shopping in Richmond that, according to some, may have been Lindsay Corner. Jaunty psychedelia-by-numbers, but with none of the hypnotic charm of 'Arnold Layne' or 'See Emily Play', it barely made a dent on the charts. Syd may have been perceived as Floyd's resident songwriting genius, but it was Richard Wright's B-side, 'Paintbox', that now seems the better song.

'After "See Emily Play" there was that traditional music biz pressure of, "Where's the next hit?"' says Andrew King. 'Syd was the most likely person to come up with a hit single, so it was him we were pushing. I didn't think "Apples and Oranges" was *that* bad, but I suspect at the time we were thinking: Oh dear . . . but if that's the best they can come up with . . .' Producer Norman Smith admitted: 'I chose it. But it was the best of a bad lot.'

Quizzed about the song's lack of success, though, Barrett was unusually forthright. 'Couldn't care less,' he shrugged. 'All we can do is make records we like. The kids dig The Beatles and Mick Jagger not because of their music but because they always do what they want to do and to hell with everyone else.'

'We put Syd under a lot of pressure,' concedes Peter Jenner. 'But then we were also under financial pressure and that made everything worse.' Blackhill had moved out of the Edbrooke Street flat to a proper office in Alexander Street, Westbourne Grove, with some of the money from Floyd's EMI deal. Yet the company was now inadvertently paying the band and crew on a first come, first served basis. Cheques were regularly bouncing, prompting employees to collect theirs earlier in the week to cash them first.

'We hired an accountant, who started asking all these questions,' says Jenner. 'Like, "Can I see your books?" And we were like, "Books?" "Have you paid your National Insurance?", and we were going, "National Insurance?" The live market was also drying up for the Floyd. We weren't such an easy sell any more. We hadn't had another hit, so we couldn't play the pop clubs, [and] the blues clubs wouldn't have us any more.

Which just left the college gigs and there weren't that many and we'd played them all.'

A disillusioned Peter Wynne-Willson quit his role as the band's lighting tech at the end of the Hendrix tour. Tellingly, in the light of Blackhill's financial insecurity, his successor John Marsh was willing to work for a lower wage. Instinctively, Wynne-Willson also allied himself with Syd, whose position in the band was growing shakier by the day. As 1967 wound to a close, the naivety and blind optimism of just twelve months earlier seemed to be dissolving.

'By the end of 1967 the zeitgeist had changed,' ventures Wynne-Willson. 'And it wasn't the cosy, hippie thing any more.'

Accompanying the so-called Summer of Love, the *News of the World* had run a weekend expose on UFO, dubbing it 'a hippie vice den'. The police, who had turned a blind eye, informed Mr Gannon that if he opened the following Friday, his premises would be raided and his licence revoked. Joe Boyd moved UFO to the Roundhouse, but run-ins with local skinheads and the inflated rent took their toll. UFO effectively ended in October 1967. Meanwhile, its former house band and their star singer were in real danger of falling apart.

On 22 December, Floyd appeared on the bill alongside The Jimi Hendrix Experience, The Who and The Move at the 'Christmas on Earth Continued' show at Kensington Olympia. Inside the cavernous venue, 30ft lighting towers, fairground-style attractions and boutiques flanked the bands. But Syd was in no condition to perform. Bundled on stage by Jenner, King and June Child, he simply stood there, his arms hanging loosely by his side, his guitar draped around his neck but supposedly unplugged. As Nick Mason would later write, 'We had tried to ignore the problems, and will them to go away, but it was time to come out of denial. We were reaching breaking point.'

'It all happened so quickly,' says Peter Jenner. 'In just a few months Syd had gone from being a carefree student, living on his grant, having a smoke now and again, to having all these people wanting to be his best friend and relying on him to play the gig, do the interview, write the hit single, bring in the money . . . tell them the meaning of life.'

Asked for his thoughts by one pop magazine interviewer, Syd was already working up a new strategy. 'All I know is I'm beginning to think less now,' he said. 'It's getting better.'

CHAPTER FOUR WAKING THE GRAPEVINE

'I remember thinking I could knock Pink Floyd into shape.'

David Gilmour

The Olympia theatre on the Boulevard des Capucines in Paris has a sort of ruined splendour. Deep below the stage, in the basement of the building, lies a ragged circular lounge and tiny bar, serving red wine and *pastis* to thirsty rock stars and loitering members of the press. The sofas are threadbare, overlooked by pictures of the jazz and blues giants that have performed here over the past half a century. Tucked away in a tiny room, seated on a leather sofa and sipping from a mug of herbal tea, is David Gilmour.

It is 16 March 2006, ten days after Gilmour's sixtieth birthday, and almost a year since his truce with Roger Waters for Pink Floyd's Live 8 performance. The guitarist's third solo album, *On an Island*, has just reached number 1 in the UK. It's an album steeped in themes of encroaching old age and mortality, much of it inspired by the deaths of two close friends, including Tony Howard, one of the entrepreneurs who coaxed the young Pink Floyd away from their first managers in what must now seem like a past life.

A black T-shirt, Gilmour's uniform for the tour, disguises the extra weight acquired since hitting his thirties. But he's lost much of the ballast that accompanied Pink Floyd's comeback in the mid-1980s. Life is calmer now. In unfussy jeans, workman's boots and with a dusting of snowy-white stubble, Gilmour looks less like a rock star and more like someone you might find restoring antique furniture in a picture-postcard English town.

The guitarist has submitted himself to considerable press scrutiny to promote this new record. But it wasn't always this way. 'In Pink Floyd, we got away with talking to as few people as possible,' he admits. Today, he will answer questions about Roger Waters and Pink Floyd, after a brief quip – 'If we *really* must' – and the thinnest of smiles.

Understandably happier to talk about his own record, he bristles with boyish enthusiasm for the songs, before, unaccountably, slipping into some unprompted anecdote about Roger Waters and Pink Floyd. When he puts on his guitar to have his photograph taken, Gilmour visibly relaxes. The transformation is quite striking. Squinting at the framed posters overhead, and acknowledging Floyd's numerous visits to the Continent, Gilmour is insistent that Floyd never played L'Olympia. 'Absolutely not,' he says firmly. Yet before Floyd, Gilmour had plenty of misadventures in France. During tonight's show, he will address the audience in near-perfect French, a skill that once held him in good stead on an early trip to the Continent.

It is 30 July 1966, and for David Gilmour and friends, England's victory over Germany in the World Cup has been overshadowed by their current predicament. He and the remnants of what had once been Jokers Wild are on a slow train to Malaga, trundling through a Spanish heat haze, when the score is announced. Passengers congratulate the four dishevelled English teenagers, but are confused by their lack of interest. Since beginning their journey at London's Victoria Station days earlier, the group's precious cargo of guitars, keyboards, drums and amps has been unceremoniously dumped in the hold of a ferry from Dover; lost en route from Calais to Paris; retrieved in Paris; then lost again en route to Madrid.

Gilmour's fluent French has saved the day when dealing with railway officials, but each time their equipment has reappeared it is in more dilapidated condition than before. The human cargo hasn't fared much better.

The twenty-year-old Gilmour and his bandmates, drummer Willie Wilson, bassist Rick Wills and keyboard player and saxophonist Dave Altham, have shared their train carriages with donkeys and chickens, and been harassed by gun-toting border guards who, in the era of General Franco's Spain, have taken great exception to the length of their hair.

A year before, Jokers Wild had financed their own five-track album of Chuck Berry, Four Seasons and Frankie Lymon covers, but a record deal eluded them. By mid-1966, as Pink Floyd were signing their management deal with Blackhill, Jokers Wild were on their last legs. Since joining the band, Gilmour had supplemented his wages delivering wine, running a hot dog stall, loading sheet metal, and landing the very occasional £50-a-day gig as a photographer's model for the likes of *Varsity*, the Cambridge University magazine.

The Beatles' manager Brian Epstein hadn't offered the band a deal, but future DJ and musician Jonathan King, then a student at Cambridge University, saw them and invited Gilmour to London. The band recorded a cover of Sam and Dave's 'You Don't Know Like I Know', but when the original was re-released, the Jokers Wild version was shelved. 'Dave always told us that they wanted to sign him but not the rest of us,' says Willie Wilson. 'So he told us he told them to stuff it.'

'Jonathan King noticed Dave at this club,' recalls Rick Wills now. 'He hung out where there were good-looking boys, but he was also on the lookout for musical talent. I went to Jonathan's flat in London with Dave. He was on the phone talking to someone about getting a song played on Radio Caroline, and it happened right while we were there. We were like, wow! We knew someone in the music business that had real power.'

Through King, Gilmour was introduced to The Rolling Stones' former mentor Alexis Korner, who formed a partnership with another aspiring entrepreneur, Jean-Paul Salvatori, to manage the young guitarist. Salvatori offered him a six-week residency at the Los Monteros hotel and beach club just outside Marbella.

'Dave came back to Jokers Wild and said he'd been offered this gig,' says Willie Wilson. 'Who wants to do it? Are we all up for it? And most of the band said no. They all had day jobs. But Dave Altham and I both said yes. So we needed a bass player and Rick Wills was a mate who used to come to our gigs and was absolutely raring to go.'

Dave Altham had been playing keyboards, sax and guitar in Jokers Wild since 1964. John 'Willie' Wilson had first played in The Newcomers with Gilmour, and had, through Gilmour, landed a gig playing in another Cambridge outfit, The Swinging Hi-Fis, before taking over as drummer in Jokers Wild. Rick Wills played bass in another local band, The Soul Committee.

Before Marbella, though, Gilmour, Wills and Wilson would spend some time in London. 'We left in Willie's old Austin Cambridge,' remembers Rick Wills. 'Dave had got himself a flat in Moscow Road, near Queensway, but there wasn't room for all of us. So Willie and I ended up living in that car. It was terrible. We survived on bread and milk.' Nevertheless, under Salvatori's guidance, the band were whisked down the Kings Road, kitted out in bell-bottomed, sailor's trousers and blue Shetland jumpers, and put on stage at Sybillas, a nightclub in Swallow Street, where they immediately attracted attention. 'We were tasty young boys in tight trousers, so we were prime fodder,' says Rick. 'The chef took a particular shine to me, chasing us round the kitchen with a meat cleaver.'

But if male attention was forthcoming, a record deal was not.

'I don't think Jean-Paul Salvatori had the slightest idea what he was doing when he sent us to Spain,' says Willie Wilson. 'He saw Dave as a good-looking guy who sang and played guitar, and he just saw money. His brother-in-law was Tony Secunda, who was doing well managing The Move, and I think he fancied the same.'

Recruiting Dave Altham, the four-piece set off on their gruelling trek through France and Spain. When the band eventually arrived in Marbella, they discovered the promised beach accommodation was a concrete bunker that had acted as a bomb shelter during the Second World War.

'We also discovered that the club we were supposed to be playing hadn't been built yet,' says Willie, 'so they threw a party up at the golf club nearby and got us to play to people like Douglas Fairbanks Jnr and Monica Vitti. They were all part of that Marbella set.'

Despite their parlous living conditions, the band, later toying with the name Bullitt ('fast and flash-sounding, like the Steve McQueen movie'), began their residency at the soon-to-be-completed Los Monteros beach club, playing next to the open swimming pool and enduring the inevitable electric shocks.

'On one hand our situation was desperate, as we were sleeping in a bomb shelter,' says Rick. 'But we were young, and there were lots of extremely good-looking women around, so we were having the time of our lives.'

When the season was over, the band returned to Cambridge, where a frazzled Dave Altham chose to remain. 'Then we got another gig in Holland, playing a coming-out ball for Princess Beatrice, now Queen Beatrice,' says Willie. 'Next thing, Dave landed this two-month residency at a club called Jean Jacques in St Etienne, so Rick and I went with him. The gig was supposed to finish at Christmas, but in January we got a gig at Le Bilbouquet in Paris, and spent the next six months there.'

In between, the group played on demos for Johnny Halliday, the 'French Elvis', and at a party in Deauville, attended by sex symbol starlet Brigitte Bardot. 'I didn't meet her,' insists Willie, 'but Dave did. I think he went up to her and said, "Hello, I'm David", because that's exactly the sort of thing Dave would have done.'

It was in Paris that Gilmour also met Jimi Hendrix and was entrusted with squiring him around town. 'I was an Englishman in Paris,' Gilmour explained, 'and I could speak reasonable French.' Gilmour had seen Hendrix jamming at Blaises nightclub in London the year before and had raved about him.

'We became a different band in 1967,' explains Rick. 'We'd started to do Hendrix and Cream covers, and Dave had also started writing songs. His parents came over to France for his twenty-first birthday and bought him a cream-white Fender Telecaster. I don't think he ever took it out of his hands.'

When the band's van was broken into and their microphones stolen, Gilmour realised it would be cheaper for him to go back to London and pick up replacements than buy them in France. It was on this flying visit that he encountered Pink Floyd and a debilitated Syd recording 'See Emily Play'.

'Dave came back and told us these stories about the bizarre songs Syd was writing,' remembers Willie. 'I remember him singing them to us, and telling us, "You won't believe it, but Syd's written a song about his bike." '

'That summer we had *The Piper at the Gates of Dawn* and *Sgt Pepper* to listen to in France,' recalled Gilmour. 'When we'd left Cambridge in the summer of '66, Floyd hadn't got a record deal. Then I heard through friends that they had. Then I heard the album. I thought it sounded terrific and, yes, I was sick with jealousy.'

By the time Floyd's debut was released in August 1967, Bullitt had become Flowers, to capture the peace-and-love mood of the time. It was all to no avail. 'That was when it got really hand to mouth – sometimes our hands didn't even reach our mouths,' says Willie. To save money, the three shared a single hotel room. Then Gilmour became sick. 'Dave very rarely gets ill,' says Willie. 'But at the end he was so ill we couldn't do any work.'

'We hung on for as long as we could, but we had to come back when we were destitute,' says Rick. The crunch came when Gilmour was admitted to hospital. 'Dave had malnutrition and pneumonia, because he wasn't eating. We couldn't afford to. I weighed eight stone and Dave not much more.'

'We left the hotel we were staying in without paying as Dave was so sick,' says Willie. 'To his credit, Dave went back there five years later after he'd made money with Pink Floyd, found the hotel and the couple who'd looked after him when he was ill, and paid them.'

In a final twist, the dispirited band was forced to push their broken-down van off the ferry at Dover. Rick and Willie headed straight back to Cambridge; the dogged Gilmour chose to stay in London: 'To go back to Cambridge would have been admitting defeat.'

Instead Gilmour wound up sharing a flat in Kelvedon Road, Fulham, with Emo, before the pair commandeered another, more up-market pad in Victoria. Gilmour took a job driving a van for designers Ossie Clarke and Alice Pollock's Quorum fashion boutique. Emo submitted to a short spell of gainful employment, studding leather belts at the boutique's shop on the Kings Road. 'Dave Gilmour never really said very much,' Clarke's wife the designer Celia Birtwell later recalled. 'He just used to stand around. It was a bit unnerving.'

Gilmour's experiences in France had only toughened his resolve. He was still looking to start another band. In November, he headed to the Royal Albert Hall for Pink Floyd's opening slot for Jimi Hendrix. A few weeks later he showed up at the Royal College of Art where the band were playing alongside the Bonzo Dog Doo Dah Band. With various Cambridge refugees then enrolled at the college, it had almost become a home-from-home gig. But it was obvious to all concerned that something was wrong. 'They were awfully bad,' admitted Gilmour. 'Incredibly undisciplined.'

'I remember seeing Syd play, or rather not play, or rather play something inappropriate at that gig,' recalls Nigel Lesmoir-Gordon. 'I said to Susie Gawler-Wright, "What's going on?" and she said, "We don't know. Syd is very strange."'

In what would soon become a familiar pattern of confused and even non-communication, Nick Mason recalls approaching Gilmour after the art college gig, along the lines of: 'If we said we were looking for another guitarist, would you be interested?' Nigel Lesmoir-Gordon is certain he was asked by the group to telephone Gilmour about the job; something that Gilmour has since confirmed. Interviewed in 1973, the guitarist recalled, 'I knew all the guys in the band and they wanted to get rid of Syd. I was approached, discreetly, beforehand. It was put about in a very strange way.'

The final straw had been the 'Christmas on Earth Continued' show at Kensington Olympia. Barrett was there in body alone, appearing completely disconnected from his surroundings.

Long before his decline, Syd had struggled with the role of the traditional guitar hero. But it was the fact that he wasn't another Jimmy Page or Eric Clapton clone that had made him appealing to Peter Jenner and Andrew King. Those close to Barrett at the time believe he was well aware of his shortcomings. Syd had expressed some insecurity about his playing in a letter to his old girlfriend Libby Gausden three years earlier, even mentioning a desire to recruit David Gilmour – referred to in the letter by his nickname of 'Fred' – but bemoaning the fact that Gilmour had his own band.

However, since Bob Klose's departure, the idea of Floyd hiring another guitarist had never been mentioned. At a university gig in 1967, the late Tony Joliffe, a contemporary from Cambridge who'd played guitar in

The Swinging Hi-Fis and sometimes drove Pink Floyd's van, was coaxed on stage to perform. 'Tony was an amazing blues guitarist, and everyone was asking Syd to let him have a go,' remembers Emo. 'Roger, Nick and Rick wanted to see what he was like. Tony got up and he was amazing. But I don't think Syd wanted him up there, as he was aware that Tony was a better player.'

Nevertheless, whatever Syd's wishes may have been, Gilmour was recruited as an additional guitarist, on a promised £30 a week. An introductory jam was arranged at Abbey Road's Studio Two.

'Andrew [King] and I had never met Dave before,' says Peter Jenner. 'So we wanted to see if he could cut the mustard. He did this amazing impression of Jimi Hendrix, so it was clear he was an incredible mimic. Which was what they wanted at the time – someone who could cover for Syd onstage.' *New Musical Express* sent a photographer to the Victoria flat to take a picture of the Floyd's new guitarist.

Gilmour insisted on another change. 'Dave finally realised that as he was paying the rent, perhaps he should be the one sleeping in the bed and I should be sleeping on the sofa,' laughs Emo. 'It took him three months to realise, though.'

Bizarrely, Barrett had already proposed a change to the Floyd line-up. In a meeting at Blackhill's office, he had suggested hiring, in Roger Waters' words, 'two freaks he'd met somewhere. One of them played the banjo, the other the saxophone.' To this mix he also wanted to add 'a couple of chick singers'. Nick Mason would later write that Barrett viewed Gilmour 'as an interloper', but Syd's unpredictable behaviour during an early week of rehearsals in a West London school hall convinced them all that Gilmour's presence was necessary. Barrett spent a couple of hours attempting to teach the band a new song entitled 'Have You Got It Yet'. Each time the others reached the title in the chorus, Syd would change the song, turning it into the musical equivalent of an Escher staircase on which none of them would ever reach the top. 'I actually thought there was something rather brilliant about it, like some clever kind of comedy,' said Roger Waters. 'But eventually I just said, "Oh, I've got it now", and walked away.'

Publicity pictures were taken of the five-piece Floyd. In one, Syd is almost visibly fading into the background. In another, while the rest line up in suede jackets and dapper neck scarves, looking every inch the sixties rock group, a black-eyed, ghost-faced Barrett stares ahead beneath a mop of matted hair, as if he'd just surfaced from one of the Lesmoir-Gordons' acid benders.

'The light in his eyes was slowly going,' remembers Emo. 'He got those black circles underneath them, and you didn't know whether it was mascara or not sleeping or both.'

A handful of gigs were booked for January 1968, commencing with a show at Birmingham's Aston University. 'Sometimes Syd sang a bit, sometimes he didn't,' recalled Gilmour. 'My brief was also to play the rhythm parts and let Syd play what he wanted.'

Tim Renwick, then playing in a band called Wages of Sin, bumped into Gilmour on Denmark Street. 'He started telling me how odd it was standing in for Syd and how unpredictable Syd was on stage. Some nights Syd tended not to play anything. He was out of his crust.'

'I saw two of the gigs they did as a five-piece,' says Emo, who was then enjoying another rare spell of gainful employment as a Floyd roadie (on £15 a week). 'At the beginning Dave just played what was necessary. He'd learned the parts and just copied what Syd used to do. But you could tell Syd didn't understand what was happening. He was standing so close to Dave he was almost an inch from his face. Dave wasn't a physical person who'd have pushed him out the way, but you could see the look in his eyes, as if to say, "Help!" Syd stood like this in front of him, then started walking around him, almost checking that Dave was a three-dimensional object. That he was real. It was as if Syd was thinking: Am I dreaming this?'

As yet another compromise, the rest of the group hit on the idea of keeping Syd on board as a songwriter. 'Our idea was to adopt The Beach Boys' formula,' said Nick Mason, 'in which Brian Wilson got together with the band on stage when he wanted to. We absolutely wanted to preserve Syd in Pink Floyd one way or the other.' By 1968, The Beach Boys' similarly troubled composer had retired from live performances, while still writing many of the group's songs. 'There was no protest from Syd towards this idea,' elaborates Peter Jenner. 'But by that stage he'd become so detached that this was all going on around him. But I think that idea lasted about a week.'

'I think Roger didn't fancy that idea,' insists Andrew King. 'Because he fancied writing the songs instead.'

Barrett wasn't the only one struggling. 'I actually walked out of one of the first rehearsals,' says Gilmour. 'Roger had got so unbearably awful, in a way that I'd later get used to, that I stomped out of the room. I can't remember how long I was gone for. I eventually came back. But I don't think the band had fixed ideas of what I should do or how I should do it.'

It was on the way to a gig at Southampton University, on 26 January 1968, that the decision was taken not to call for Syd.

'Somebody said, "Shall we collect Syd?"' remembered Gilmour. 'And somebody, probably Roger, said, "No, let's not bother."'

'He was our friend, but most of the time we now wanted to strangle him,' admitted Waters.

Experiencing a sense of relief at being able to perform live without worrying about what their frontman was or wasn't going to do, the group decided to play the following night's gig without Syd also.

Richard Wright, who was still living in Richmond Hill with Barrett, was faced with the unwelcome task of lying to his flatmate: 'I had to say things like, "Syd, I'm going out to buy a packet of cigarettes", and then come back the next day.'

'Syd used to still turn up, even when they didn't pick him up,' says Emo. 'He must have still had the itinerary, because there was one gig when he was there when we arrived to set up – just sat there on the stage waiting. Eventually it sunk in that there was some other guy playing his part.'

Years later, though, Richard Wright would claim that David Gilmour hadn't been their only choice. 'When Syd left we actually asked Jeff Beck to join,' he said. 'But he turned us down.' Others claim the band were too shy ever to have asked Beck, and that he was even 'rejected on the grounds that he couldn't sing'.

Around the same time, Anthony Stern had run into Peter Jenner in Drum City, a music shop in London's Piccadilly. 'I played trumpet and had been into jazz, and while I could play the guitar, my playing wasn't up to much,' says Stern. 'But Peter was like, "Look, Syd's really falling behind, why can't you be a second guitar player in Pink Floyd? . . . You come from Cambridge . . . You know them all." Spontaneously, I just turned around and said, "Oh, no, I'm a film director"'.

Gilmour's self-confessed insecurity wasn't helped by the management's lack of faith. 'We consciously fought to keep Syd in the band,' agrees Peter Jenner. 'The idea that Roger was going to become the main songwriter didn't cross my mind. But I did think that Rick could have come into his own, and we did wonder if he and Syd would stick together.'

Wright shared the management's misgivings. 'Peter and Andrew thought that Syd and I were the musical brains of the group, and that we should form a break-away band,' he later told *Mojo*. 'And, believe me, I would have left with him, if I had thought Syd could do it.'

Despite the rest of the group's scepticism, Jenner and King still believed that Barrett was the band's golden goose, and aimed to establish him as a solo artist. Financially, Blackhill was still struggling, with Pink Floyd in debt to the tune of £17,000. At the end of 1967, the company had begun managing a young singer-songwriter, Marc Feld, now working under the name Marc Bolan, and his group Tyrannosaurus Rex. Feld had signed to Blackhill because they looked after his hero Syd Barrett, yet it would be another few years before he would become a bona fide pop star in his own right. An enterprising Jenner had also applied for a £50,000 grant from the Arts Council, supposedly to fund a hastily conceived rock opera featuring BBC underground rock DJ John Peel as narrator. When the tabloids got wind of the scam, they revived the previous year's headlines, claiming that Pink Floyd's 'sound equivalent of LSD visions' was reason enough to reject their application. The Arts Council agreed.

Unbeknown to Pink Floyd, the Morrison Agency was already circling. 'Bryan was very wily,' says Jenner. 'He was the man who told us, "If a musician ever asks you for any money, say yes, provided they sign a publishing contract. You can give any musician twenty-five pounds for a publishing contract." And Bryan acquired a lot of publishing contracts.'

In March 1968, Jenner and King formally dissolved their partnership with Pink Floyd, leaving the group free to secure a new management deal with Bryan Morrison. Morrison would eventually pass the job on to Steve O'Rourke, one of the 'sinister dandies' Joe Boyd had encountered the year before. Despite their previous misgivings, Boyd, Jenner and King had since warmed to both O'Rourke and Morrison's booking agent Tony Howard. Says Jenner: 'Knowing those two were involved was one of the reasons I felt confident that Floyd would get well looked after.'

Pink Floyd's enterprising new manager, twenty-seven-year-old Steve O'Rourke, was the son of an Irish fisherman and had originally trained as an accountant. He moved into the music business in his late teens, later hired by Morrison after a stint as a pet food salesman. It was a job O'Rourke would cite as a badge of honour, telling the band that he would often sample his products to demonstrate their nutritious value to prospective clients, declaring, 'If it's good enough for me, it's certainly good enough for Rover.' O'Rourke had also made a small appearance in the Bob Dylan documentary, *Don't Look Back*, which was deemed a point in his favour. However, later, O'Rourke's commitment to the idea that you could sell anything would prove a major stumbling block in his relationship with the more questioning Roger Waters.

'Steve was much harder than Peter and I,' admits Andrew King. 'And I was rather jealous of him. He sorted out some big mistakes we'd made in our contractual relationship with EMI. He had an eye for the main chance and used it to their advantage. Steve had one client – the band – and nothing would compromise him in what he would do for the band. They could not have had a better manager.'

'It was always a verbal agreement between Floyd and Steve,' says another of the group's confidants. 'The deal was done on a handshake. I always thought that was a clever move on the band's part. Somehow, it made Steve work that bit harder.'

On 6 April, Syd's departure was officially announced. A week later, Pink Floyd released a single, 'It Would Be So Nice', with Richard Wright on lead vocals, the first effort from their new line-up. A perky sub-Kinks affair (which Waters would later describe as 'complete trash'), it included a reference in the lyrics to the *Evening Standard* newspaper, which fell foul of the BBC's regulations. Happy to garner any publicity, the band contacted the newspaper, while agreeing to change the offending lyric. But even a little controversy couldn't save the song from barely denting the charts.

In Cambridge, the news of Floyd's line-up change was met with mixed emotions. Barrett's sister Rosemary had been appalled by her brother's rapid decline, and blamed the music industry for indulging his drug use.

She would later claim that after 'See Emily Play' she found Syd's music too painful to listen to.

Bob Klose, who'd concentrated on his studies after quitting the band, welcomed the change. 'Syd was the rocket fuel, but Dave was the steady burn,' he quips. 'I know that Roger Waters had the creative impulse, but a great band needs a great musician. You need someone who can sing and play and do all the very musical stuff, aside from the grand concepts.'

For Gilmour's former bandmates, the news of his recruitment came as no surprise.

'I was at home recuperating after the French trip when I heard,' says Rick Wills. 'I was disappointed, but it was a logical step. Next time I saw Dave, he'd come back to Cambridge after doing some gigs, and he had eighty pounds in cash on him – and this was when eighty pounds was still a lot of money. He was in Ken Stevens' music shop – long hair, velvet jacket, boots from Gohill's in Camden Town – buying a very expensive pair of headphones that you plugged straight into your guitar – and he'd got himself a Fender Strat by then. I thought: Christ, you look the part!'

On stage, though, the flashily attired, Fender Strat-wielding Gilmour was still understudying his predecessor, gamely singing Barrett's whimsical lyrics and replicating his guitar lines. A batch of mimed promo videos made by the band that year for Belgian TV captured the group's muddled situation. Waters mimes Barrett's vocals on 'Apples and Oranges' and 'The Scarecrow'. Wright half-mimes on 'See Emily Play', looking mortally embarrassed, while Waters upstages him by playing imaginary cricket and wielding his bass like a machine-gun. On each of the clips, Gilmour hangs around on the sidelines, looking swish and handsome, but not yet part of the gang.

Following UFO's closure, Middle Earth in Covent Garden had become the underground cognoscenti's club of choice. Jeff Dexter was one of the club's regular DJs. 'We put Floyd on at Middle Earth,' he recalls, 'and I thought the new line-up was brilliant. In those days lots of people thought the idea of showing you were out to lunch was kind of cool. But I thought David was, dare I say it, so much more professional.'

As Storm Thorgerson explains, 'You have to remember Syd couldn't play guitar very well. David could. Syd had an attractive voice but David had a great voice.'

Gilmour's professionalism certainly held him in good stead on the night Syd showed up at Middle Earth and spent the gig glowering at him from in front of the stage.

The real test for the group and their new recruit would come in the studio. EMI needed a second album. Pink Floyd reconvened with Norman Smith at Abbey Road. They'd already endured several recording sessions with Syd and had one Barrett-sung composition in the can, 'Jugband Blues', recorded just before Christmas. Syd had requested a Salvation Army band to play on the track and the redoubtable Smith knew just where to find one, though rumour has it that, on seeing the uniformed brass players, Barrett simply instructed them to play anything. Their contributions gave the song an even edgier quality. 'I think the track might have been playing in their headphones,' recalled Peter Jenner, 'but the brass band chose to ignore it.' It was agreed to include 'Jugband Blues' on the new album, but not Barrett's 'Vegetable Man' or 'Scream Thy Last Scream'. Waters vetoed their inclusion on the grounds that they were 'just too dark'.

The bassist had been especially prolific, delivering three self-penned songs: 'Let There Be More Light', a broody psychedelic wig-out, all about aliens landing in the Fens, which name-checked the Floyd's familiar Pip Carter; 'Corporal Clegg', the first of what would be many diatribes against the futility of war; and 'Set the Controls for the Heart of the Sun', a shivery, languid piece of what critics would later christen, to the band's despair, 'Space Rock'. Wright wrote and sang lead vocals on 'See-Saw' and 'Remember a Day', the last a slight piece of psychedelic pop originally intended for *The Piper at the Gates of Dawn*.

Still raw from his experiences with Syd, Norman Smith was impressed by Barrett's replacement. 'Dave Gilmour was a different story altogether,' he recalled. 'So much easier.' But while Gilmour may have been a more willing workmate than Barrett, collectively the band were more dogged than ever in their pursuit of experimental ideas, an approach that flummoxed the producer.

'I still didn't understand the music,' admitted Smith. 'But what I'd noticed is that they'd started developing their own tapes at home, so I encouraged this, as I always thought they should produce themselves in the long run.'

Smith backed off from the process, showing the band how to use the studio, while chipping in with advice, and, on 'Remember a Day', taking over the drums when Mason struggled to produce the required feel. But Smith's attitude jarred. 'Norman gave up on the second album,' griped Richard Wright. 'He was forever saying things like, "You can't do twenty minutes of this ridiculous noise."'

Peter Jenner now believes that the band's dissatisfaction stemmed from the fact that 'Norman was becoming "Hurricane" Smith, a pop star in his own right, and perhaps didn't feel he needed to be producing Pink Floyd.'

In fact, 'Hurricane' Smith's pop career wouldn't take off until the early seventies, but the noise in question probably referred to the album's title track. Divided into three movements, and filled with a cacophony of hammering pianos and cluttering percussion leading to a final, tuneful coda, it was the first fruits of Waters' decision to 'stretch things out and be experimental'.

For Pink Floyd's newest recruit, the experience was daunting and even alien: some versions of the songs had already been recorded with Syd; he barely contributed to the songwriting; and the harmony vocal skills that had been his forte in Jokers Wild weren't required. 'I didn't feel like a full member,' Gilmour said later. 'I was a little on the outside of it all.'

Syd Barrett's presence on the album – eventually called *A Saucerful of Secrets* – remains the subject of speculation. He's supposedly playing guitar on 'See-Saw', 'Remember a Day' and 'Jugband Blues', and Gilmour believes he's somewhere in the background on 'Set the Controls . . .' The final track, 'Jugband Blues', with its eerie, lurching brass arrangement, is the only song to feature Barrett's lead vocals. Sounding like a ghost, he utters the final prescient line, 'What exactly is a dream . . . and what exactly is a joke?'

'We could never write like Syd,' says Wright. 'We never had the imagination to come up with the kind of lyrics he did. I cringe at some of my songs, like "Remember a Day". But something like "Corporal Clegg", which was one of Roger's, is just as bad.'

'"Corporal Clegg" is a good piece of work,' insisted Waters later. 'We had to keep going. Once you're in a rock 'n' roll band, you weren't going to stop. That would have meant going back to architecture.'

Waters' doggedness is apparent throughout the album. Plotting the movements in the title track but unable to read music, he and Nick Mason scored the piece by inventing their own symbols, prompting Gilmour's comment that the song was mapped out 'like an architectural diagram'.

The album misses Barrett and, rather tellingly, one of its weaker tracks, 'See-Saw', was originally titled by the band 'The Most Boring Song I've Ever Heard Bar Two'. The record's true legacy now is the creeping influence of 'Let There Be More Light' and 'Set the Controls for the Heart of the Sun' on all those cerebral seventies rock bands that followed in the Floyd's wake.

Released in June that year, reactions to the band's latest creation were mixed. 'Forget it as background music to a party,' warned *Record Mirror* in an otherwise upbeat appraisal, while *New Musical Express* dismissed the title track as 'long and boring, and has little to warrant its monotonous direction'.

'I was surprised when *Saucerful* was criticised harshly in the press,' admitted Mason. 'I thought it had some very new ideas.'

But not everyone was so harsh about the new Floyd. DJ John Peel was moved to reverie by the group's performance of the title track at the Midsummer High Weekend festival in London's Hyde Park the day after the album's release. Having experienced the performance from a boat floating on the Serpentine, Peel announced in *Disc* magazine that 'it was like a religious experience . . . they just seemed to fill the sky and everything.' His lengthy ramblings earned him a place in the Pseuds Corner column of *Private Eye*.

The Midsummer High Weekend was the first free festival ever staged in Hyde Park, paving the way for free shows in the park from The Rolling Stones and Blind Faith. Its organisers were the ever-resourceful team at Blackhill Enterprises, who fared better with the Royal Parks Commission than they had with the Arts Council earlier in the year. Floyd performed alongside Roy Harper, Jethro Tull and Blackhill's great white hopes Tyrannosaurus Rex. 'Hyde Park in '68 was wonderful because it reminded us of our roots,' ventured Nick Mason. 'However spurious they may have been. It was a reminder that we were still part of this thing, which was by then a fairly commercial venture. So it gave us credibility.' An unofficial launch for the Syd-less Floyd, both of the group's hits, 'Arnold Layne' and 'See Emily Play', were conspicuously absent from the setlist that day.

While Pink Floyd road-tested a new sound, their former singer was in professional limbo. Peter Jenner had booked sessions for Syd at Abbey Road, but they'd proved difficult. Barrett's odd behaviour in the past had all but made him persona non grata at the studio. The King family's flat at Richmond Hill had provided a saner environment after Cromwell Road, but in his unwanted role as the freaks' pied piper, Barrett soon had disciples beating a path to its door.

By January 1967, the Lesmoir-Gordons had moved some 400 yards from Cromwell Road into Egerton Court, a rambling mansion block opposite South Kensington tube station near Brompton Road. Film director Roman Polanski had been so taken with the building's imposing décor and 1930s-era spiral staircase that he'd featured both in his 1965 movie *Repulsion*. David Gale, Dave Henderson, Aubrey 'Po' Powell, Ponji Robinson and Storm Thorgerson would soon occupy rooms at Egerton Court, its location being ideal for the Royal College of Art, where some of their number were now studying.

Nigel Lesmoir-Gordon was now working as an editor for the future film director Hugh Hudson, then directing commercials, but already responsible for the opening credits to the James Bond films. 'The flat became a focal point for a very arty set,' remembers Po. 'Mick and Marianne used to come round to drop acid with Nigel – all of them watching the reflection of crystals spinning on the walls. Donovan would drop round, and everyone was wearing Granny Takes a Trip clothes and looking terribly groovy. We were the original Kings Road hippies.'

'Nigel and Jenny took the biggest room at Egerton Court,' remembers frequent house guest Emo. 'David Gale had the smallest. It was so small, in fact, that he had to have a bed on stilts, so that there was somewhere for him to work. Storm was in a room that was about twenty-five feet long with an incredibly high ceiling. And he painted the walls bright orange and the window frames with red gloss paint. It was a complete horror-show, but he was like, "It's over the top, which is how I like it."'

'I was a student, negotiating everything from love affairs to illicit deals to supposedly working at college,' recalls Storm. 'I was not in the best emotional state personally.' Matthew Scurfield, another resident, says that 'For Storm, there was a lot of talking and dissecting of the cosmos and the universe.'

Throughout the remainder of 1967 and the early months of 1968, the occupants of Egerton Court continued their stoic consumption of narcotics. But, perhaps inevitably, something had to give.

'I spent three years sleeping on my brother's floor there,' recalls Matthew Scurfield, who took his first LSD trip at the flat. 'That was where I got to know Nigel and Jenny. A lot of the things that have been said about Egerton Court *are* true. It's not bending the truth to say there was a lot of acid-guzzling going on there. We took it in huge doses because no one knew what they were doing. But it wasn't just a load of people lying around doing it. We were all very existential people. So the front part of the brain and the intellect were very much to the fore of what was going on.'

'We often had great times on acid,' says Po. 'I can remember laughing myself silly for eight hours and wandering into pubs when I was on it and drinking pints of beer. But one of the cumulative effects of acid is that it opens your mind up to a lot of sensitive issues, and, after a while, those sensitive issues don't go away. What people refer to as "acid flashbacks" are really your mind and nervous system being opened up to sensitivities that wouldn't be opened up under normal circumstances. We all started to feel very raw. Whereas we used to smoke dope every day, now the dope was starting to open up those sensitivities as well. So suddenly you're smoking a joint, and that's making you feel paranoid as well. So the effects were kicking in for everybody. The joke was gone, and we were all feeling very edgy.'

When Nigel and Jenny left Egerton Court for a trip abroad, Syd and Lindsay took over their room. 'That was the start of a complete nightmare for the rest of the flat,' says Po. 'Because by that time Syd was not functioning very well. He could be charming, but he could also be anxious, withdrawn and aggressive.'

'I used to hear thumping noises and screams coming from their room. I knew what was happening,' recalls David Gale. 'Syd would start off tickling Lindsay and then it would quickly get much darker.'

'There are all these stories about him hitting her,' elaborates Po. 'He's supposed to have smashed his guitar and burnt her with cigarette ends, but I never actually saw that happen. I'd hear these furious rows, though, and I'd bang on the door. One night Syd opened it and came out, wearing a pair of red velvet trousers and nothing else. I thought he was going to hit me. I told him he had to stop as he was freaking the rest of us out. There'd be all these discussions in the kitchen the next morning, and I started locking my door at night, which I'd never done before.'

Emo and Matthew Scurfield were both there one night when they heard screams coming from Syd and Lindsay's bedroom. 'Matthew went in, as we could hear Syd banging Lindsay's head off the floor, and Syd nutted him,' says Emo. 'Matthew came out bleeding so I went in, picked Lindsay up, and Syd saw the look in my eyes and backed off. It was awful to see someone behaving like that. I don't think he knew what he was doing.'

'Lindsay would lock herself in the loo and Syd would tell you to fuck off when you tried to intervene,' says Matthew. 'In the end I thought: Fuck it! I don't want to be your mate any more. But it was odd, because sometimes he could be completely normal. It was like when you were kids at school and you saw a fight in the playground at lunchtime, and then, twenty minutes later, you'd see the same kid sitting in class, quite normal, as if nothing had happened. Syd was still thinking about his music at this time. I can remember seeing him at Egerton Court experimenting with a clock by putting it in a bath of water and recording the sound it made. But then the next minute it would all change again.'

Interviewed in 1988, the future critic and broadcaster Jonathan Meades talked of visiting a friend, Harry Dodson, at the flat, as a teenager. 'Syd was this weird, exotic and mildly famous creature by that time, who happened to be living in this flat with these people who were, to some extent, pimping off him both professionally and privately,' he recalled. 'I went in there and there was this terrible noise. It sounded like heating pipes shaking. I said, "What's that?" and he [Po] sort of giggled and said, "That's Syd having a bad trip. We put him in the linen cupboard".'

Meades says now that 'I must have gone to Egerton Court about three times. I'm always reminded of that Martin Amis book, *Dead Babies*, in which he describes this reckless group of drug-takers. That Cambridge lot made me think of them, especially extraordinary characters like Emo. They were all much more gung-ho in what they'd do than I was. Any sense of self-survival seemed pretty absent in that crowd.'

'I'll tell you what happened,' insists Po. 'I don't think Syd was still taking acid but he was smoking a lot of dope, and he used to get paranoid. What Jonty Meades called the laundry cupboard was, in fact, the toilet. There was no laundry cupboard. The toilet was like a cupboard – no window and one bare bulb. One day Syd was walking down the corridor, then the next thing I hear is him shouting, "Let me out! Let me out!" Somehow he'd locked himself in the toilet with the light off and had become very disorientated. He was probably very stoned and he began panicking. It took me twenty minutes to explain to him how to open the catch on the door. Jonty had walked into the flat and asked what happened. I think I said he'd locked himself in. When Syd came out he was hyperventilating, running in sweat.'

Meades' friend Harry Dodson now recalls meeting Syd only a few times, and that he 'seemed beyond all normal communication'.

Pop stardom, drug use and romantic entanglements would all become an issue.

'There's some suggestion that the women were as much of a problem as the drugs,' offers David Gale. 'Apart from the girlfriends, Syd would have lots of strange groupie girls coming round the house. Some of them specialised in making exotic shirts for rock stars and then shagging them – nice work if you can get it.'

'At one point he was wearing lipstick, dressing in high heels and believing he had homosexual tendencies,' David Gilmour told one writer years later. 'I remember all sorts of strange things happening.'

As Jenny Fabian attests, Syd's attitude towards sex seemed to be as distracted as it was for most other areas of his life. 'By the time I had my liaison with Syd, he was very far gone,' she told writer Mark Paytress in 2004. 'Everyone was *liaisoning* all over the place in those days. But Syd wasn't the sort of guy to flirt. I'd never seen him flirt. I wouldn't say he was madly sexual, he certainly wasn't predatory. If you were there and you were cool, there'd just be the smile or the indication that you were a friend enough to stay. It wasn't anything more than that.'

For those that had known Syd at art school in Cambridge, the change in his behaviour was especially troubling. The happy-go-lucky Barrett of three years earlier was now absent. John Watkins had last seen his friend playing at the art school's 1966 Christmas party. One evening, two years later, he ran into David Gilmour backstage at a Floyd show. 'I asked how Syd was and Dave said, "A bit weird." I got both their numbers and I phoned Syd up a week later, but he'd completely disappeared into himself. He probably knew who I was, but I couldn't get anywhere with him.'

Yet by the summer of 1968, Syd wasn't the only one experiencing the aftermath of the previous year's LSD use.

'Our group had split right down the middle,' says David Gale. 'With half of us going spiritual and half of us going to shrinks, myself in the latter half.'

That year, the Lesmoir-Gordons followed the lead of other Cantabrigians before them, disappearing to India to follow the Sant Mat path. Meanwhile, Matthew Scurfield and David Gale began attending sessions with colleagues of the celebrated R.D. Laing.

Earlier that year, Roger Waters claims to have driven Syd to an appointment with Laing, but says that Barrett refused to get out of the car. David Gale tried to engineer a repeat visit some months later. He remembers: 'I called Ronnie Laing from Egerton Court at the behest of everyone there, because we'd all said, "Enough", in spite of our absurd sixties coolness about "interrupting somebody else's trip, man". I told Laing that I was a friend of Syd Barrett's and that I thought he would benefit from some psychotherapy. Laing said he wasn't going to see anybody that didn't come of their own accord.' Promising Laing that Syd would attend, Gale booked a taxi. 'When it arrived, we said, "Oh, Syd, we've arranged an appointment for you with R.D. Laing" – who was considered the Elvis of psychotherapy – and Syd just said no and that was it.'

'When you're young and your friend goes off the rails it's hard to cope with,' says Thorgerson. 'We were not experts in analytical issues. Half of us were semi-crazy anyway, and, if not semi-crazy, had serious emotional defects and our own problems to bear.'

As well as Syd, John 'Ponji' Robinson would be among those who fell by the wayside. Ponji would go on to undertake an extraordinary form of therapy, which involved him taking LSD with his psychiatrist. Sadly, he eventually committed suicide.

In July 1968, as Pink Floyd embarked on their second US tour, Barrett left Egerton Court. Lindsay had already departed, finding a safe haven at Storm Thorgerson's new place in Hampstead after one especially violent outburst. In years to come, on the rare occasions she has been interviewed, Lindsay would play down the suggestion of Barrett's violence towards her. She would drop out of Syd's life completely by the end of the sixties, eventually marrying and raising a family.

Barrett, in turn, drove his Austin Mini back to Cambridge, reportedly taking a whistle-stop tour around Britain during which he may have shown up unannounced at various Floyd gigs. He would return to London sporadically, sleeping on old friends' floors, including Anthony Stern's Battersea flat, where rumours surfaced that he was experimenting with heroin. 'You'd see his mood declining as the evening wore on,' recalls Stern. 'Then he'd disappear into the lavatory and come back and his mood had changed. I don't think it was cocaine, which was completely absent at that time. The issue of whether Syd tried heroin has become a delicate one, but at the time *everything* was being tried.'

With Syd gone, the Lesmoir-Gordons returned to their old room at Egerton Court and made a discovery. 'I found a colour drawing Syd had left in our room,' recalls Jenny. 'It was a picture of a human head with a train going in one side and coming out the other, and at the top it had the words "That's Weird" written across it.'

During the ensuing months, Syd would occasionally show up at Blackhill's new offices in Princedale Road, Holland Park. Juliette Gale was now working in the same building, managing a modelling agency, Black Boy (later Black Boy And Blondelle), the first agency to represent black catwalk models. *Time Out*, London's new hip underground magazine, also rented an office in the house. 'I was at *Time Out*, which launched in the summer of '68,' says future BBC DJ Bob Harris. 'We had an office in the same building as Blackhill and Richard Wright's girlfriend Juliette. I'd seen Syd with Floyd at the UFO club many times, but the only times I saw him now he was comatose in reception, slumped in a corner with Juliette shrugging her shoulders as you wandered through. It seemed terribly sad.'

Jenner and King strived to keep a closer eye on their charge, but even they met with his suspicion.

'When he first left the band we had a rota of people who gave Syd supper one night a week,' recalls Andrew King. 'So he'd come and eat with us, as he'd known my wife since they were at art college in Cambridge together. I actually think he felt safer with her than me. I expect Syd saw me as part of "the business". The last time he came to ours for supper was one of the last times I ever saw him.'

Syd's former band were adjusting gingerly to their new handlers. Prior to undertaking their second US tour, Bryan Morrison sent Steve O'Rourke to see the band, claiming they needed to sign another agency contract as a formality for touring overseas. Waters was especially reluctant and suggested they sign a contract that lasted for the duration of the tour only. A day later, Morrison sold the agency to Brian Epstein's NEMS Enterprises. Steve O'Rourke was effectively sold to NEMS as part of the deal and, according to Waters, 'never got a penny out of it'.

Floyd's second US tour began almost as ignominiously as their first, with delayed work visas leading to the postponement of shows. Gigs alternated between underground hot spots such as Steve Paul's The Scene club in New York and the Detroit Grande Ballroom. Bussed into the backstage areas of these outdoor events, Floyd would catch the last moments of sets from fellow Brits such as The Troggs before being bundled on stage themselves. Elsewhere, they'd fight for the audience's attention between performances by homegrown heavies Blue Cheer and Steppenwolf. Midway through the dates, the money ran out, leaving the group stuck in Seattle until their US agency could settle their hotel bill.

'It also felt as if we could only get gigs at weekends,' said Roger Waters. 'So when it wasn't a weekend, we were stuck somewhere like the Mohawk Motor Inn on the outskirts of Detroit where you could get a room for eight dollars a night. Hour after hour spent sat by some crappy swimming pool with no money to go anywhere.'

Nevertheless, in New York, where the band stayed at the notorious Chelsea Hotel, Waters was tempted to try LSD again for the first time since his Greek holiday in 1966. While tripping, he ventured out to buy some food, and found himself frozen in the middle of Eighth Avenue, seemingly unable to move. Waters later claimed it was his last experience with the drug.

Even with Syd gone, Waters still felt moved to vent his ire on stage, developing his party piece of attacking the gong suspended behind Mason's drum kit with great gusto during 'A Saucerful of Secrets'. 'Roger would do some very strange things on stage,' recalls one eye-witness from the time. 'He was so very tall that he cut a very strong figure. And there was also the way he dressed . . .'

Roger had already had a slightly too-short pair of fashionably snug red trousers customised with gold braid tassels on the hems. In the US, he acquired a cowboy-style holster fixed to his belt and, with a piece of twine, to his thigh, in which he took to carrying around his cigarettes. 'The hippie clothes thing had a fairly narrow border,' recalls one friend of the band. 'But I guess we felt that Roger sometimes stepped outside it.'

Whatever his sartorial mishaps, Waters clearly helped to drive the band. Witnessing the group's performance at the 100,000-seater JFK Stadium in Philadelphia was future *Rolling Stone* writer David Fricke. A freak thunderstorm later that day would lead to the cancellation of headliners The Who, but the upstart English band lower down the bill grabbed his attention. 'From where I sat the Floyds were tiny moving matchsticks,' he recalled. 'Yet the music was big enough to move the air. For the forty or so minutes the Floyd were on stage they *were* the air.'

David Fricke's enthusiasm had yet to translate to his future pay-masters. Struggling with the live gigs, *Rolling Stone* also felt confused by the new album. 'The Pink Floyd are firmly anchored in the diatonic world, with any deviations from that norm a matter of effect rather than musical conviction,' complained reviewer Jim Miller.

By September, the band were back performing before more partisan crowds, revisiting Gilmour's old haunt, Le Bilbouquet in Paris, and their new home from home, the Middle Earth club in Covent Garden.

Slowly but surely Pink Floyd were changing, but not just musically. Earlier that year, they'd played the First International European Pop Festival in Rome alongside The Move and The Nice from the previous year's Hendrix tour. The Nice's Davy O'List, who'd understudied Syd on that tour, dropped into Floyd's hotel suite.

'I was rather shocked to see Dave Gilmour luxuriating on a double bed and holding a bottle of Scotch,' O'List laughs, 'because that was the first time I'd ever seen a member of Pink Floyd with a drink. Despite what was going on with Syd and the drugs, the rest of them had seemed so straight on that Hendrix tour.'

Faced with the challenge of filling Syd's shoes and standing up to the bass player, David Gilmour was similarly partial to a smoke. Later, when asked by a Canadian student newspaper whether they used drugs while they performed, the guitarist's answer was wonderfully obtuse: 'Sometimes. Usually. But not much.'

The Gypsy Moth and the First World War flying ace outfits certainly looked authentic. Standing alongside the biplane, Pink Floyd had swapped their Kings Road threads for grease-spattered flying suits and goggles, their collective plumage of hair the only reminder that this was 1968 rather than 1916. It was October and Pink Floyd were being filmed for a very literal promo clip to accompany their new single, 'Point Me at the Sky'. Unknown to them and EMI it would be their last UK-released single for eleven years. Unfortunately, like 'Apples and Oranges' and 'It Would Be So Nice', the Norman Smith-produced song showcased the group's insurmountable struggle to write a hit single. Worse still, the chorus sounded troublingly like that of The Beatles' 'Lucy in the Sky with Diamonds'.

Undeterred by the song's lack of performance on the charts, Pink Floyd simply savoured their chance to dress up like Biggles and fly in a Gypsy Moth.

'I never felt the band was finished when those singles flopped,' Nick Mason says. 'Blind optimism, I suppose. I think we just believed that we were right and everybody else was wrong. We were one of the first bands to benefit from the freedom that The Beatles had provided. After *Sgt Pepper*, we all had a lot more freedom.'

If EMI were happy to overlook Pink Floyd's failure in the singles charts, the band still had to consider the label's attitude towards *A Saucerful of Secrets*, an album that had hardly matched *Sgt Pepper* for sales. Roger Waters summed up EMI's approach as being, 'Yes, that's very nice . . . but now you have to get back to making some proper records.'

By the start of the New Year, they were already talking to *Melody Maker* about a planned double album, made up of individual compositions and group tracks. Yet an indication of where they were heading was already buried on the B-side of 'Point Me at the Sky' in an early version of a piece entitled 'Careful With That Axe Eugene'. Gradually expanded beyond its original two-and-a-half minutes, it would join 'Set the Controls for the Heart of the Sun' as another trial run for the wildly ambitious Floyd of the seventies: a slow-building melody, eerie effects, and complete avoidance of a conventional pop song structure.

'It was abstract music, not so song-orientated,' recalled Phil Manzanera, the future Roxy Music guitarist, then an avid Floyd fan. 'They were doing things with sounds, having fun with the traditions of *musique concrète* and the

Radiophonic Workshop. You have to remember a lot of people were lying down to listen to this stuff. It was a chill-out experience.'

To complement this abstract experience, *A Saucerful of Secrets* had been packaged in a suitably far-out sleeve. Just as the band's Royal College of Art pals had been on hand to design flyers and posters, they now contributed the sleeve design for the group's second album. Storm Thorgerson and Aubrey 'Po' Powell had formed a design partnership, though more by accident than design.

'Storm had a friend who worked in a publishing company,' recalls Po, 'and she introduced us to the people who did Penguin book covers, and they wanted to be part of a new, hip scene. We'd just discovered a thing called infra-red film and Storm said we should do them in infra-red. They were for cowboy book covers, so we photographed David Gale, Dave Henderson, Nigel and Jenny – everyone from Egerton Court – in Richmond Park, dressed up in western wear. It looked like *Stagecoach* on acid. We presented them to Penguin, who loved them and gave us £40 a cover – which was enough for us to live on for the whole summer. We ended up doing about ten covers. I think it was Roger Waters, who was very friendly with Storm, who suggested we do the cover for *A Saucerful of Secrets*. We'd been experimenting in dark rooms and had a few sketches and rough pages.' The suggested design – a tiny photograph of the band in Richmond Park surrounded by cosmic swirls – was intended to 'give the album a surreal, acidy feel'.

'At that point we were going to call ourselves Consciousness Incorporated, a very groovy name for the times,' explains Po, 'but you couldn't call yourself Incorporated as it was an American term for a limited company. Going up to Egerton Court one day we saw written on the outside of the door in biro the word 'Hipgnosis'. We were a bit pissed off about it as someone had graffitied on our nice clean door. But we both thought it was a great name – hip and gnostic. We never found out who wrote that on the door, but we always thought it was Syd. We called ourselves Hipgnosis and had a little card made, which said, "Photos, designs, artworks etc" and finished with the words "far outs, groovies, weasels and stoats". Don't ask me why.'

The duo were paid £110 for their efforts, and *A Saucerful of Secrets* would herald the start of their working relationship with Pink Floyd.

Yet before Floyd could head off into their own musical universe, there was the gravitational pull of their old singer to be negotiated. By January 1969, Syd was back in London, seemingly calmer, and settled in a new three-bedroom flat at Wetherby Mansions, a large block on Earls Court Square, just off the Old Brompton Road. His latest flatmates were a mutual friend by the name of Jules, who would soon move out, and the artist Duggie Fields, the former Regent Street Poly student and ex-Cromwell Road resident, viewed by those close to Syd as a calming influence.

'He seemed much happier having left the band, which is why I agreed to get a flat with him,' says Fields. 'Syd still had money coming in from the Floyd. It wasn't a lot of money, but it removed the pressure to get up in the morning and go to work. He seemed to be confused about what he should be doing.'

With Lindsay gone, Syd was now involved with Gilly Staples, another model from the Quorum boutique. He was also talking about making another record and contacted Malcolm Jones, head of EMI's newly launched subsidiary, Harvest. Jones had devised the idea of an imprint label dedicated to hip, underground music. With Floyd's success as its benchmark, Harvest would go on to enjoy success with Deep Purple and Roy Harper, alongside less successful waifs and strays from the Blackhill stable, including the Edgar Broughton Band.

Dedicated to making albums rather than chasing hit singles, Harvest would become synonymous with the progressive rock music of the next decade. More importantly, Jones was a Syd Barrett fan. Norman Smith was committed to Pink Floyd, so Syd asked Jones to produce some sessions, intending to revisit the songs he'd recorded with Peter Jenner (of which only 'Golden Hair' and 'Late Night' would appear on the finished album, *The Madcap Laughs*) and record new songs he claimed to have written.

'Initially, it was just to see if Syd had anything worth recording,' recalls Peter Mew, who engineered those first sessions at Olympic Studios. 'He would sit down, sing a couple of verses, then stop and have a wander around and then start something else. You could see there was the essence of some really interesting stuff there, but he didn't seem to be able to get it together enough to finish anything. Even stoned, musicians have some inkling of what they are going to be doing, even if it's very bad and they do it badly, but Syd didn't seem to have it together enough to sing a song from beginning to end, and he didn't seem to be able to analyse critically what he'd done and then maybe do another take.'

Later, Barrett roped in David Gilmour's former bandmate, Willie Wilson, and drummer Jerry Shirley, later of Humble Pie, to play on 'Here I Go' and 'No Man's Land'.

'Syd started playing these songs and I drummed along,' says Willie, who was now playing in a band called Bitter Sweet. 'The trouble was, the song was never the same twice. Then Jerry Shirley tried to dub a bass on top of it, but he couldn't follow it at all, as no two versions were the same.'

Jones booked more studio time, working on 'Terrapin' and 'It's No Good Trying'. From here on, the sessions became more problematic. Barrett showed up in the studio with an unusable recording of a revving motorcycle engine, which he wanted to dub onto a track. Later, he invited his old friends The Soft Machine to play on a song, but ignored their requests to know what key it was in, before walking out of the studio.

Jeff Jarratt was hired to engineer some of the sessions, but was stunned by the change in Syd since *The Piper at the Gates of Dawn*. 'It was tragic,' says Jeff now. 'One minute there was this guy who was this creative force and next he was like a vegetable.'

According to Malcolm Jones, EMI never called a halt to the *Madcap* sessions, but Barrett told the producer that he wanted his former bandmates to help out with the final sessions. Despite his attitude towards Gilmour at Floyd's Middle Earth gig the previous year, Syd was now in close contact with his successor. Gilmour had moved into a new flat at Richmond Mansions, also on Earls Court Square. He was hard to ignore, as Syd and Duggie's kitchen window afforded a perfect view into the guitarist's new pad.

'My memory is that EMI were going to shut the album down and shelve it,' said Gilmour. 'And I think Roger and I volunteered to rescue the project if they gave us more time. They gave us three days and it was very tricky to get anything done. Syd was in a very poor state in the studio, falling over, knocking mikes over. We put it out as best we could.'

'That was around the last time Syd and I communicated,' recalls Po. 'It was either just before or after his first solo album, I can't remember, but we all went down to Olympic Studios. There was Dave Gilmour, Nick Mason, Syd, myself and one or two others. I can't recall who was on bass but it wasn't Roger. But we played "Back Door Man", endlessly, for something like four hours. I was even playing guitar. It was being done to try and get Syd into a creative place, but it was obvious after several hours that it wasn't going to happen. He was dropping his plectrum, not knowing what was going on . . .'

With his album almost completed, Syd suddenly quit London and trailed a group of Cambridge friends to Ibiza. 'We saw him from a distance in the town square in San Fernando,' recalls Emo. 'Nobody knew he was coming. Someone said, "Hang on, isn't that Syd?" He was stood there in his rock star clothes and Gohill boots in the blazing sunshine. He had two bags with him – one was stuffed full of all these filthy, unwashed clothes, and the other had about five thousand pounds in English banknotes spilling out the top.' When the gang moved on to Formentera, Syd followed: 'One moment he'd be giggling and smiling, the next he wouldn't speak to anyone.'

Photographs remain from the trip: Barrett, beaming beneath curtains of unkempt hair, looking oddly incongruous against the Mediterranean landscape in his tight trousers and satin shirt. Later, having sustained bad sunburn after refusing to use any protective lotion, Syd returned to London, burnt and disorientated, while Gilmour and Waters did their best to patch his album together.

Adding to the pressure of completing their friend's record, Pink Floyd's trouble-shooters had already begun work on what would become the band's next album. Somehow, during a hectic 1969, Mason, Waters and Wright would find the time to get married to Lindy Rutter, Judy Trim and Juliette Gale, respectively.

Nevertheless, in March 1969, as Barrett prepared to start *The Madcap Laughs*, Pink Floyd had already recorded an immediate follow-up to *A Saucerful of Secrets* in a frantic nine-day burst. French film director Barbet Schroeder had commissioned the group to compose the soundtrack to his new movie, *More*. EMI agreed to release the record, but, as it was a private commission, Floyd were denied use of Abbey Road, booking into Pye Studios instead.

EMI's willingness to let the band make a film soundtrack, rather than 'a proper record', after their last three singles had flopped seems surprising in the twenty-first century. Yet the concept of Floyd as film soundtrack composers was no great leap. In their days in Stanhope Gardens, Floyd had performed music to accompany landlord Mike Leonard's light experiments and in December 1967 had appeared playing along to Leonard's light shows in an edition of the BBC's *Tomorrow's World*, and in 1968 had supplied some incidental noodling for a low-budget British film entitled *The Committee*. However, on 20 July 1969 Floyd found themselves hired by the BBC to improvise during a live broadcast of the first moon landings. 'There was a panel of scientists on one side of the studio, with us on the other,' recalled David Gilmour. 'The song was called "Moonhead" – a nice, atmospheric, spacey 12-bar blues.'

'Doing film music was a path we thought we could follow in the future,' said Gilmour. 'It wasn't that we wanted to stop being a rock 'n' roll group, it was more of an exercise.' Not to mention a potential safety net, should being a rock 'n' roll group not work out.

Barbet Schroeder, the son of a Swiss diplomat, was a left-wing film-maker who had begun his movie career assisting the director Jean-Luc Godard. *More*'s plot centred around the misadventures of a male hitch-hiker who succumbs to heroin addiction after encountering a beautiful female junkie. With scenes of drug use, wild bongo playing and the frequently bared breasts of its blonde star Mimsi Farmer, it is a film that perhaps could only have been made in the 1960s.

'I was a big fan of the first two Floyd records,' says Barbet Schroeder now. 'I thought they were the most extraordinary things I'd ever heard, and just wanted to work with them. I went to London and took a print of the movie *More*, and showed it to them. I didn't want typical film music – made to the minute and recorded with the image on the big screen. I didn't believe in film music. I wanted this to be the music the characters were listening to. At a party, the music came out of the loud speaker in a room, so we recorded it to sound as if it was playing in the room.'

'He didn't want a soundtrack to go behind the movie,' remembered Waters. 'He wanted it literally. So if the radio was switched on in the car for example, he wanted something to come out of the car. He wanted it to relate to exactly what was happening in the movie. I was sitting at the side of the studio writing lyrics while we were putting down the backing tracks. It was just a question of writing eight or nine songs with instrumentals.'

'Roger was the big creative force,' says Schroeder. 'I remember this incredibly hectic two weeks. The sound engineer couldn't believe the speed and the creativity of the enterprise.'

Of the instrumental tracks, 'Quicksilver' and 'Main Theme' explored the same 'abstract music' that had so enthralled fan Phil Manzanera on *A Saucerful of Secrets*. 'Green is the Colour' is a dainty acoustic reverie; the cosmic organ fills in 'Cirrus Minor' place it squarely in the box marked 'Space Rock'; while the Gilmour-sung 'Cymbaline' is very nearly a straightforward pop song. The biggest break with tradition came with 'The Nile Song' and 'Ibiza Bar', where Gilmour is finally let off his leash, and Mason clatters around the kit in the manner of his idols Ginger Baker and Keith Moon.

Hipgnosis chose a film still for the cover. No cosmic collage this time, just the movie's protagonists cavorting in front of an Ibizan windmill. The image was tarted up with a dark-room treatment that gave it the fuzzy edge experienced during the coming-up moments of an LSD trip.

More premiered at the Cannes Film Festival in May 1969, but sank without a trace, its copious sex and drugs denying it a proper UK release. Unexpectedly, for what the group considered 'a stop-gap album', the soundtrack made it into the Top 10 in June. Nevertheless, as David Gilmour later explained, 'EMI now thought we should cut out all the weird nonsense and get on with it.'

Weird nonsense had nevertheless become Pink Floyd's stock in trade during their live shows, as much as on record. Oddly, where Syd's reluctance ever to play the same thing twice had infuriated his band-mates, they in turn were now exploring a kind of controlled chaos, as well as realising Roger's vision to make Pink Floyd concerts an event. 'It was about more than watching a band stand in front of 600 watts of Marshall speakers,' said Richard Wright later. 'It was about an entertaining show.'

In June 1969, Waters' desire for a spectacle peaked with 'The Final Lunacy' at London's Royal Albert Hall. Whereas smaller haunts, such as North London's Fishmonger's Arms, were still mainstays on the Floyd gig sheet, the Albert Hall was roomy enough to accommodate their most grandiose ideas yet. For some time now the group had been performing segments from *The Massed Gadgets of the Auximines*, a suite divided into two main sections known as 'The Man' and 'The Journey'. The piece would never be recorded in its entirety, but many of the individual parts would be reworked for the *More*, *Ummagumma* and *Relics* albums.

The suite was premiered at the Royal Festival Hall in April 1969 and then expanded two months later for 'The Final Lunacy'. Taped sound effects, as well as the band's own performance, were panned 270 degrees around the venue by their personalised sound gadget, the Azimuth Coordinator. In a grand piece of performance art, a table was constructed on stage during the show, at which the crew sat and drank tea while listening to a transistor radio randomly tuned in and amplified through the speakers. Roger Waters would revive the same trick on later solo tours, playing cards with some of his band during a long instrumental passage.

Putting aside any misgivings he may have had about the album, producer Norman Smith was wheeled out on a mobile podium at the Albert Hall to conduct players from the Ealing Central Amateur Choir and Royal Philharmonic Orchestra during *A Saucerful of Secrets*. Richard Wright played the Albert Hall's church-style organ ('Fraught with difficulties, as there's a huge delay between pressing the keys and the noise coming out,' recalled Waters), one of the band's crew roamed the stage in a gorilla suit, a pair of cannons were fired (Waters: 'the same ones they used for *1812 Overture* – fucking great') and a smoke bomb exploded, prompting a life-long ban from the hall, something David Gilmour delightedly recalled when playing there again as a solo act in 2006.

Guitarist and Floyd friend Tim Renwick watched the performance from the audience. 'What you have to remember is that there was a lot of humour there. It was all very "art school" but very lighthearted. But talking to him, even back then, Roger always had this thing about wanting to do something more than just a rock show. He wanted a big presentation.'

'There was a period in the sixties where fame and fortune were irrelevant to people's lives,' explains Duggie Fields. 'It was all about the creativity.' For Pink Floyd, that period had ended. Their 'far-out sounds', to quote one review of the time, may have excluded them from the singles charts, but, with a new breed of discerning album buyer to pitch to, EMI viewed the group as a potential money-spinner.

'I remember once seeing Mick Jagger and Keith Richards plotting and talking about money,' says Nigel Lesmoir-Gordon. 'Which was something I never did in the sixties. Jenny asked Roger if he wanted to be rich and famous, and he turned round straight away and said, "Oh yeah!"'

'I had no idea that I would ever write anything,' Waters said years later. 'I'd always been told at school that I was absolutely bloody hopeless at everything. I took responsibility in the Floyd because nobody else seemed to want to do it. I know I can be an oppressive personality because I bubble with ideas and schemes, and in a way it was easier for the others to go along with me.'

Yet becoming rich and famous while staying true to their grand vision would prove trickier. Released in November 1969, Floyd's promised double album, *Ummagumma*, seemed like another stop-gap rather than a concerted move forward. The first record was given over to live recordings taken from two shows at Manchester College of Commerce and Mother's, the Midlands' answer to London's Middle Earth. The second record contained five solo compositions; two from Waters, one each from his bandmates. The live recordings of 'Astronomy Domine', a now fleshed-out 'Careful With That Axe Eugene', 'Set the Controls for the Heart of the Sun', and 'A Saucerful of Secrets' offer a time-capsule of Pink Floyd in the late sixties. By then, they had become, as Nick Mason said, 'a proper working rock 'n' roll band'. And it showed.

Yet the grand vision of the solo pieces worked less well. 'Someone suggested – probably Roger – that we should all do a solo ten minutes on the other record,' said Gilmour. 'So we all went in to try and do our things, whatever they were.'

Engineer Peter Mew remembers the decision-making process: 'My recollection is that everybody assembled in the studio on the first day with Norman Smith, who asked, "Have you got any songs?" To which Floyd replied, "No." After which, it was decided that each of them would have a quarter of the album. There was no grand plan. I think that was pretty much decided on the first day.'

Richard Wright's contribution was a four-part piano concerto entitled 'Sysyphus' [sic]. Later dismissed by its composer as 'pretentious', the heady piano rumblings identified Wright as the source of much of Pink Floyd's gothic musical tendencies. The title was taken from the

Greek myth of Sisyphus, a poor soul sent to Hades and condemned forever to push a giant rock up a hill only for it to roll back down again as soon as it reached the top. An analogy, some might suggest, for the browbeaten keyboard player.

'To annoy an audience beyond all reason is not my idea of a good night out,' said Nick Mason when asked about the perils of playing with Syd Barrett. With this in mind, perhaps, Mason lightened the percussive noodling on his own 'The Grand Vizier's Garden Party' with some soothing flute played by his new wife Lindy. Gilmour's composition, 'The Narrow Way', was a part acoustic, part electric guitar odyssey split into three segments on which he played all the instruments, including drums. Some of it had already been performed on John Peel's BBC show *Top Gear* under the title 'Baby Shuffle in D Major'. Yet Gilmour struggled with the lyrics. 'I remember ringing Roger to beg him to write me some words,' he admitted. 'And he just said, "No, do it yourself", and put the phone down, which was probably his way of helping me find my feet. It sort of makes me cringe now.'

Waters suffered no such insecurity, and managed two solo pieces, 'Several Species of Small Furry Animals Gathered Together in a Cave and Grooving with a Pict' and 'Grantchester Meadows'. The last was a gentle elegy to a picturesque stretch of the River Cam, and the album's most convincing track. The former has Waters spouting gibberish in a Scottish accent over various sound effects, as if The Goons had been allowed to run riot through Abbey Road.

What all of the pieces had in common was a section where each Floyd member sounds as if they've been left to fool around in the studio unsupervised.

'It would have been better if we'd gone away, done the things, come back together, discussed them, and people could have come in and made comments,' Waters admitted to *Disc and Music Echo*. 'I don't think it's good to work in total isolation.'

'All those tracks ended up being realised to their full potential,' believes Peter Mew. 'If you start from the point of view that you don't quite know what you're doing and you're making it up as you go along, it's difficult to know where it's going to end up. "Grantchester Meadows" is probably the most tuneful, but even that ends with a fly being swatted — so it's all rather tongue in cheek. I think they were exploring the boundaries of the technology on that album. There's lots of cute little sound effects – double speed, reverb – good stuff, bearing in mind the state of the technology at the time.'

Ummagumma was recorded on the hoof, with sessions fitted in around the band's gigging schedule. And, in hindsight, it shows. Nevertheless, two solid years of playing every hippie dive in the country had paid off. *Ummagumma* gave Floyd and EMI's Harvest label a number 5 album and the best reviews of their career so far: 'A truly great progressive rock album,' claimed *Record Mirror*.

The title itself prompted much speculation. Routinely described as 'Cambridge slang', Emo claims, 'It was a word I made up about shagging. As in, "I'm off home for some *Ummagumma*." Floyd thought I'd heard it somewhere before, but it was off the top of my head.'

The front cover shot was taken at the house of Libby January's parents, the scene of the Jokers Wild and Tea Set double-bill years earlier. It is the band's last attempt at traditional front cover pop star posing, with a barefoot Gilmour positioned at the front, alongside the images disappearing into infinity in the mirror to his right. Chief roadies, Alan Styles and Pete Watts, appeared on the back cover with the band's equipment arranged, at Nick Mason's suggestion, in the shape of a military aircraft carrier, a proper boys' toys collection of kit.

The inside sleeve contained the biggest surprise of all. While each band member had an individual portrait, Roger shared his with his new wife Judy, pictured cradling a glass of white wine, while Roger looked on dotingly.

In years to come, while remaining faithful to some of their earlier efforts, *Ummagumma* was rated less highly by the band themselves.

'My own view is that *A Saucerful of Secrets* had pointed the way ahead, but we studiously ignored the signposts and headed off making *Ummagumma*,' admitted Mason, 'which proved that we did rather better when everyone worked together rather than as individuals.'

'We were very good at jamming,' offered Gilmour. 'But we couldn't quite translate that onto a record.'

The next move, then, would be yet more jamming, not in London's Pye or Abbey Road Studios but in the more exotic locale of Rome. Italian director Michelangelo Antonioni had first seen Pink Floyd playing the launch party for *International Times* at the Roundhouse in 1966. In late 1969 he approached them to compose the music for his next film, *Zabriskie Point*. Reflecting the political mood of the time, the movie followed the exploits of a student rioter who steals a plane, flies it to Death Valley, California, and proceeds to have lots of sex with the obligatory hippie chick encountered along the way. He gets shot dead by the police; she blows up a mansion, as a protest, presumably, against 'straight' America's bourgeois values. So far, so good . . .

Antonioni paid for the band to stay at the opulent Hotel Massimo D'Azeglio in Rome, so the Floyd were at his beck and call. 'It was sheer hell,' claimed Waters. Work would begin at a nearby studio in the evening, after the band had consumed as much gratis food and wine as they could stomach, with Antonioni on hand but often nodding off in the studio as the night wore on. The next day, Roger would take the director the finished tapes for approval. 'It was always wrong, consistently,' explained Waters. 'There was always something that stopped it being perfect. You'd change whatever was wrong and he'd still be unhappy.'

The movie bombed, and the finished soundtrack, released the following year, included just three Floyd tracks, 'Heart Beat, Pig Meat' – which used the sound of a heartbeat, an idea later revisited on *Dark Side of the Moon* – a slight country-rock number called 'Crumbling Land', and a reworking of 'Careful With That Axe Eugene', entitled 'Come in Number 51, Your Time is Up'. The rest of the soundtrack was bumped up with contributions from The Grateful Dead and The Kaleidoscope, among others. Of the Floyd pieces overlooked by Antonioni for inclusion was Richard Wright's haunting piano-led 'Violent Sequence', recorded to accompany footage of real-life student riots, which would later reappear as 'Us and Them' on *Dark Side of the Moon*. As Nick Mason would ruefully admit, 'We were now following a band policy of never throwing anything away.'

CHAPTER FIVE THE SPACES BETWEEN FRIENDS

'I've always thought of going back to a place
where you can drink tea and sit on the carpet.'

Syd Barrett

Syd had painted the floorboards orange and blue. In his muddled state of mind, he'd started near the door and had, literally, painted himself into a corner. He had also neglected to clean the floor first, simply slapping the paint over discarded bus tickets, matchsticks and cigarette butts. But these were minor setbacks. Syd was waiting to be photographed for the cover of his first solo album by his friend Mick Rock. The two had taken an acid trip a fortnight before. They'd drawn pictures, listened to music and, as Rock recalls, spent most of the time laughing.

Syd had certainly made an effort. As well as a spot of interior decorating, he'd cleared the furniture out of his room at Wetherby Mansions, dressed himself in a yellow shirt and his polka dot Hung On

You trousers – changing later into his Granny Takes a Trip velvet pair – with flatmate Duggie Fields' 1940s demob coat for added vagrant chic, and positioned a vase of flowers on the bare boards beside him. As a finishing touch, he'd enlisted latest flatmate and sometime bed partner Iggy to smear his eyelids with kohl and appear naked behind him.

The Madcap Laughs was released in January 1970, with its snapshot of domestic life chez Barrett on the cover, and a glimpse of what Melody Maker deemed the 'mayhem and madness representing the Barrett mind spilling out of the music inside'.

For those used to the intergalactic rock of The Piper at the Gates of Dawn, this was an oddly earthbound experience: just Syd's sometimes faltering voice, his often desultory guitar-strumming and the sound of a drummer and bassist bluffing it out in the background. Barrett sounded familiar and whimsical on 'Terrapin' but psychologically wounded on 'Dark Globe'. On 'She Took a Long Cold Look', he could be heard turning the pages of his songbook halfway through, and on 'If It's In You' he even stopped the song and started it again.

Listening now, it all sounds as if it's held together with tape and string. Original producer Malcolm Jones winced at the finished album, especially those mistakes: 'I thought it was unnecessary and unkind to include those.' At first, Waters and Gilmour stuck by their decision to include everything. 'We wanted to inject some honesty into it,' explained the guitarist. 'We wanted to explain what was going on.' In truth, perhaps they'd wanted to shock both Syd and his audience after the experience of those tortuous recording sessions. As Gilmour said later, 'We got that very frustrated feeling of, "Look, it's your fucking career, mate. Why don't you get your finger out and do something?"'

By the time The Madcap Laughs was released, Syd's life at Wetherby Mansions was sometimes as deranged as his music suggested. The mysterious Iggy's bare behind would be for ever immortalised on the cover of the record. But for many years her identity and whereabouts would remain a mystery. Known as 'Iggy the Eskimo', the striking, dark-haired model had been photographed in a 1966 issue of New Musical Express with a gang of similarly hip, beautiful people demonstrating the dance craze 'The Bend'. She had previously been an acquaintance of Anthony Stern's before, according to Duggie Fields, she arrived penniless at Wetherby Mansions, needing somewhere to stay.

In March 2010, the elusive Iggy contacted the author, unaware that both her old friends from the 1960s and Syd Barrett fans were eager to know of her whereabouts. 'The "Eskimo" nickname was a joke,' says Iggy (real name: Evelyn). In reality, her father was British and her mother Nepalese. Iggy was briefly an art student before becoming a regular fixture on the London club scene, dancing on the reality TV show *Ready Steady Go!* and hanging out with Eric Clapton, Jimi Hendrix and Keith Richards.

In 1969, after bumping into Jenny Spires, she ended up briefly at Wetherby Mansions. 'I didn't know Syd had been a pop star,' Iggy insists. She had seen Pink Floyd at Alexandra Palace but didn't make the connection. The penny dropped when she heard an early tape recording of *The Madcap Laughs*. Not long after the album cover photo session, Iggy drifted out of Barrett's life as quickly as she'd arrived. 'I heard on the radio that Syd died,' she recalls, 'and I felt sad, but it was so long ago. It wasn't until I went online for the first time that I realised anyone remembered me.'

Some months after moving into Wetherby Mansions, and following on from his time with Quorum model Gilly Staples, Syd had begun a relationship with another would-be model, Gala Pinion. Gala had moved down to London with Aubrey 'Po' Powell, and landed a job at the Chelsea Drug Store. To complicate matters, she was one of Lindsay Corner's closest friends. When Syd and Duggie's original flatmate moved out, Gala moved in.

'I'd known Gala since she was fourteen,' says Po. 'Her and Lindsay were best friends, so I was surprised when that happened, and I suspect it caused a lot of upset. I think Gala thought she could take Syd on. Gala wanted to look after him, but Syd actually needed professional help.'

Like David Gale, Emo and others before him, Duggie witnessed Syd's violent mood swings. 'There was lots of melodrama,' he says. 'I had seen him being violent to Gilly, and it happened again with Gala. They would have these dramatic explosions and physical fights. Then, of course, Syd could change in an instant and be completely charming again.'

Over a period of a few months, Syd's behaviour began to deteriorate once more. To avoid him, Fields began staying in his room, painting. Left unsupervised, Syd's bedroom became increasingly fetid as he refused to open the windows or even the curtains. He allowed a couple of his friends, Greta and Rusty, to move into the flat's communal living room, having previously let them sleep in the hallway.

Sue Kingsford dropped by the flat regularly. 'At Duggie's, Syd just got odder and odder,' she recalls. 'He wouldn't speak for hours. We all watched the moon landings there [in July 1969]. I think we all thought it was a conspiracy by the Americans. Syd, of course, never said a word.'

Sue was among those that Syd routinely hustled for drugs. 'I'd found a chemist in Cambridge that would write me a prescription for sixty Mandrax a month,' she admits. 'Syd used to pester me for them. I'd say, "OK, I'll give you one", but he'd be like, "Come on, come on, I know you've got more than that." He was taking things so indiscriminately. He wasn't taking one of anything, he was doing six. It was like Syd was always trying to get out of it, to get out of himself.'

A trade name for the drug Methaqualone and prescribed as a sleeping tablet, Mandrax had become the favoured pill of London's hip set. After fighting off the initial temptation to fall asleep, usually by consuming mugfuls of tea or coffee, users that could stay conscious during the first thirty minutes would then find themselves slipping into a blissful, waking trance.

'Mandrax was everywhere,' admits Fields. 'Everyone was taking it. Dave Gilmour's flatmate fell off the balcony at Richmond Mansions because he was on it. Amazingly, he escaped unhurt.'

'There was,' Emo points out, 'a soft grass verge underneath.'

Jenny Fabian also visited Syd at the flat, and was shocked by his decline. She recalls him barely acknowledging her. She also took Mandrax with him. 'You enter this weird, fuzzy twilight world where everything's comfortable,' she recalled. 'It's a great place to be and you could see why Syd wanted to be there, because he'd obviously bombarded the old brain cells with acid.' However, like Duggie, she also witnessed plenty of moments of clarity amid all the drug-induced chaos. 'Every so often he'd make an incredibly pertinent remark that made you realise he was probably saner than the rest of us.'

'I knew people who took more drugs than Syd and were much bigger casualties than him,' insists Fields. 'Also, in the circles we moved in, madness was considered socially acceptable. There was almost a romance about mental disturbance, the same way there was about drugs. I still think that was part of it with Syd. It always felt to me as if he'd fallen into a depression more than anything. He was forever saying, "I have to get another band together . . ." but he just didn't have the drive. Without any schedule, he could lie in bed thinking he could do anything in the world he wanted. But when he made a decision that limited his possibilities.'

Syd even started painting again, or talking about painting. 'But he would never finish anything, never produced a final work,' says Duggie. It was during these quieter spells that Syd would reveal a painful awareness of his circumstances. 'I never had a conversation with Syd about being a pop star, when he *was* a pop star,' says Fields. 'But we had a significant conversation about it later. Syd would say to me, "I'm a failed pop star." Then he'd turn on me. "But what are you? You're twenty-three and you're not even famous. I'm already a has-been."'

Considering his frame of mind, EMI's decision to put Syd back in a recording studio seems like an incredible leap of faith. However, *The Madcap Laughs* had sold over 5,000 copies in just two months. Syd was recording again by February 1970, with David Gilmour producing and Jerry Shirley playing drums. The process would prove as arduous and disjointed as before. Gilmour tried recording the musicians first and getting Syd to sing along to the track later. When that proved difficult, he recorded Barrett first and put the other musicians on afterwards. The notion that Syd could work with musicians simultaneously seemed out of the question.

Pieced together over five months that year, some of the tracks to surface on the album, later titled *Barrett*, including 'Baby Lemonade', 'Dominoes' and 'Gigolo Aunt', showed traces of Syd's former sparkle. Others, such as 'Rats' and 'Wolfpack', were compelling in their sheer mania. Richard Wright added welcome keyboards to the record, helping Gilmour to coax their old friend through the recording process. 'By then, we were just trying to help Syd any way we could,' Wright recalls. 'We weren't worrying about getting the best guitar sound. You could forget about that.'

A curious Duggie Fields dropped in on the sessions. 'Syd was lost and having to be told what to do,' he recalls. 'He'd just zoned out. But you didn't know if he was deliberately messing up, because he did play mind games with people.'

'He rarely took any notice of what was said, or repeated what he'd done in the same way,' explained Gilmour. 'He never communicated whether he felt things were going well or badly.' One night, the guitarist offered Syd a lift back to his flat. Barrett was silent throughout the journey. Dropped off outside his front door, he turned to Gilmour and showed a tiny flicker of gratitude. 'He turned to me and said, "Thank you", very quietly,' recalled Gilmour. 'That was the only moment that anything like that happened.'

Backing up Duggie Fields's claims that Syd could be perfectly lucid at times, a BBC session for John Peel's *Top Gear* show recorded at the start of the sessions had found Barrett on unusually good form. A brief return to live performance later that summer at The Music and Fashion Festival at Kensington's Olympia found him stricken with nerves. 'I can't remember why we did it,' admitted Gilmour, who played bass with Jerry Shirley on drums. Promoted by Bryan Morrison, the six-day event also included Syd acolytes Tyrannosaurus Rex and Barrett's idol Bo Diddley. Syd acquitted himself well enough, but raced through his four-song set, dashing offstage as soon as the last chord was struck.

Sadly, for all Barrett's moments of clarity, there were still many instances of great confusion. One evening, Syd showed up at the Wrights' new home in Bayswater, thinking he was still in Pink Floyd and that they had a gig to play that night. One afternoon, bumping unexpectedly into Roger Waters in Harrods department store, Syd fled the shop, dropping his bag in a panic. Waters picked it up to discover it filled with children's sweets. On a whim, Syd swapped his red Austin Mini for a 1950s Pontiac Parisienne Convertible, which T.Rex's percussionist Mickey Finn had acquired in a raffle. The car would remain unused outside Wetherby Mansions, stickered with parking tickets, until Barrett gave it away to a passing stranger in exchange for a packet of cigarettes. In hindsight, it might have been for the best.

'When he became distracted from reality, you would not want to be in a car with Syd,' remembers Emo. 'He'd suddenly lose all concentration, stop driving and just get out. One time while driving he just stopped in the middle of the road and started messing around with his shoelaces. Or else he'd get out of the car, just disappear, and leave you to deal with all the irate drivers backed up behind. It was as if he just forgot he was driving.'

Despairing of Syd's behaviour, Duggie briefly moved out to stay with another friend, but came back when he found his new housemate's behaviour even more erratic. Within months, Syd had disappeared back to Cambridge. Gala followed suit, returning to her parents' home in Ely. It was left to Duggie to dismiss the various groupies and drug monkeys that had billeted themselves in the flat.

Barrett found himself back at 183 Hills Road. His mother had continued to let the vacant rooms to lodgers and Syd felt that his former practice space and dope-smoking retreat at the front of the house would bring him too close to the strangers occupying the family home. Instead, he moved into the cellar. Accessible only by a trap door positioned in the hallway, the L-shaped hidey-hole, with a tiny window that peeked out on the back garden lawn, was big enough for a mattress, Syd's record collection and books.

'Then Gala rang, to tell me the news,' laughs Duggie. 'She and Syd had gotten engaged and Syd was going to become a doctor.' Nothing would come of it. Gala began working as a housekeeper for drummer Jerry Shirley. A jealous Syd accused her of having an affair. The engagement was over. Though not before the couple had amassed a number of engagement presents from well-wishers. One day, a crestfallen Syd led Gala down the stairs to the cellar, where the presents were laid out. 'Gala told me it was like something out of *Great Expectations*,' recalls Sue Kingsford. 'Like Miss Havisham. I think it rather freaked her out.'

Libby Gausden, now married with a baby, visited Syd and Gala in the basement room. Libby's mother was still in close contact with Win, and he had asked to see her new son. 'Syd was gone, completely *gone*,' remembers Libby sadly. 'He even thought the baby was his. He was with this beautiful girl, Gala, and I remember the look on her face, as if to say, "Oh God"...'

Before long, Gala, too, would be gone.

When they weren't nursing their estranged frontman, Waters and Gilmour still had their day jobs to attend to. *Ummagumma*'s sales had reassured EMI that there was a market for, as the group called it, 'our weird shit'. In the meantime, the Morrison Agency had kept Floyd out on the road, plying their wares to the faithful, especially in Germany, France, The Netherlands and Belgium. Floyd's gig sheet included repeat visits to the likes of Amsterdam's Paradiso, a psychedelically painted theatre that modelled itself on America's hip Fillmore West. 'They seemed to pick up on what we were doing very quickly,' said Nick Mason. 'They made us feel very welcome.'

Back on home turf, they still played every university refectory, Top Rank ballroom and hippie hotspot that would take them. In September 1969, Floyd mucked in with Free, The Nice and Roy Harper at the Rugby Rag's Blues Festival in Warwickshire. The event had been organised by The Rolling Stones' old tour manager, Sam Jonas Cutler, who, a year earlier, had introduced Nick Mason to his friend, the musician, poet and composer Ron Geesin.

Born in Ayrshire, Scotland, Geesin learned to play the violin and the banjo, and began his musical career with a jazz band, The Downtown Syncopators, in 1961. Living in Notting Hill, he had recorded sessions for John Peel and had shared the bill with Pink Floyd at 'The 14-Hour Technicolor Dream' in 1967, by which time he'd made his own album, *A Raise of Eyebrows*. 'I'd barely heard any of the Floyd's music, though,' he says now, 'and when I did, I described it as "astral wandering".'

By 1969, Ron and his wife, Frankie, had become friends with Nick and Lindy Mason. Geesin was now recording incidental music for TV advertisements and documentaries. In October, Mason introduced Geesin to Roger Waters. The two later booked a game of golf, with Waters demonstrating his keenly competitive edge on the course, though, as Geesin noted later, 'I was slightly better than him at the time.' From here on, Ron was drawn into the Floyd's orbit, also spending time with Rick and Juliette. 'Rick was particularly interested in modern jazz, and I was into the vintage jazz,' recalls Ron. 'We spent many an evening with him and Juliette, eating dinner, listening to music, but whenever any pot-smoking started, we stayed out of it. I was always a pint-of-beer man.'

Waters and Geesin collaborated for the first time at the end of the year on the soundtrack to a documentary, *The Body*. Based on writer Anthony Smith's book of the same name, the film was a glorified biology lesson, narrated by actors Frank Finlay and Vanessa Redgrave. John Peel had recommended Geesin to the film's producer Tony Garrett. Realising that Garrett required specific songs as well as background music, Geesin asked Waters to help. 'Nicky Mason was a very nice chap and a good friend,' said Ron, 'but he didn't have that manic flair to do something crazy and make it a piece of art. You could tell Roger was the creative force in Pink Floyd.' The two worked on their music separately; Geesin in his 'padded cell box' in Notting Hill, Waters at home in Islington, and, later, in London's Island Studios.

Geesin's cello, violin and piano-led compositions shared space with four Waters-sung numbers and a couple of collaborative sound effects efforts. In the grand Floyd spirit of recycling, many ideas in *The Body* would reappear on their own albums, including the use of female backing vocalists and a repeat of the lyric 'breathe, breathe in the air . . .' on *Dark Side of the Moon*. Inevitably, the rest of Pink Floyd were bundled into the studio to give an uncredited performance on one track, 'Give Birth to a Smile'.

It came as little surprise then when Waters asked Geesin to collaborate on Pink Floyd's next studio album. After the previous year's *The Massed Gadgets of the Auximines*, the band were still taken with the idea of a single lengthy composition, split into individual movements. Early in 1970, they premiered a piece then titled 'The Amazing Pudding', for which Gilmour had been the original catalyst, devising a chord sequence on the guitar that reminded him of Elmer Bernstein's theme music to the 1960 Western movie *The Magnificent Seven*.

The presence of a choir and orchestral players during 'The Final Lunacy' at the Royal Albert Hall had triggered Waters' interest in using the same on a Pink Floyd album. By 1970 many rock groups coveted the highbrow status of classical musicians, making the idea of performing with orchestras a fashionable pursuit. The Nice, The Moody Blues and Deep Purple (EMI Harvest's other great white hopes) had all taken the plunge, with variable results. Now it would be Pink Floyd's turn.

Gilmour's movie theme intro now prefaced over twenty minutes of music. 'It sounded like the theme to some awful Western,' recalled Waters, interviewed in 1976. 'Almost like a pastiche. Which is why we thought it would be a good idea to cover it with horns and strings and voices.' Waters asked Ron Geesin to help out, before the band began another US tour.

'They went off to the States and left me to get on with it,' says Ron now. 'They handed me this backing track, and I wrote out a score for a choir and brass players, sat in my studio, stripped to my underpants in the unbelievably hot summer of 1970. All I had was a rough mix of what they'd put down and edited together, but one of the problems was that the speeds didn't always match up.' Waters and Mason, never the most virtuoso of musicians, had recorded the backing track in just one take, hampered by a new EMI ruling which rationed supplies of tape, thereby prohibiting too many takes. As the piece was over twenty minutes long, this resulted in a wavering tempo. As Mason dryly explained, 'It lacked the metronomic timekeeping that would have made life easier for everyone.'

Aside from Waters, the band had expressed only the sketchiest of ideas to Geesin before disappearing on tour. 'As far as I can remember,' says Geesin, 'Rick came round to my studio one morning and we went through a few phrases, but that was it. I still have all the scraps of paper from those meetings with the band, and there are no notes at all from my meeting with Rick. With Dave, I still have a scrap on which I jotted down his suggestions for a theme, and on the other side the theme I came up with.'

On returning from the US, the band were presented with the score and booked into Abbey Road. This time, Norman Smith would be listed on the finished album as executive producer only. 'A neat way of saying that he didn't actually do anything,' said Gilmour. 'I told them it was time they produced themselves,' insisted Smith, 'and that they should call me if they got stuck. I only received one phone call for that album, so it was clear they could look after themselves.' One of Norman's jobs, though, had been to book the classical session musicians. But there were problems. Mason revealed to Geesin that the first beat of the bar was absent from his score, rendering it virtually unplayable by the hired musicians.

'I was also not a conductor,' admits Ron. 'I made the mistake of giving the brass players more credit for thinking than they deserved. I'd been working with the top players from the New Philharmonic Orchestra on some TV commercials, and they would give you their ideas about a score. The EMI players were quality session musicians, but you'd ask them a question, and it was all: "You tell us"; "What do you want here?"; "I don't understand!" One of the horn players was being especially mouthy. I was getting distraught. I thought: Fucking hell, I've wrecked myself doing this work, and it deserves to be done properly. Eventually, when I went to hit him, they had me removed.'

Geesin's replacement was John Aldiss, a highly experienced conductor and King's College Cambridge alumnus, whose choir had already provided some ethereal vocals on the Floyd epic.

'That was fine by me,' says Ron. 'Except the way I'd envisaged the playing was a lot more percussive and punchy. I was very much into black jazz, like Mingus and Ellington, and my score reflected that. But John Aldiss hadn't a bloody clue about jazz, so the way he got them to play it was a bit wet.'

Considering its bungled score and uppity session musicians, *Atom Heart Mother*'s six-part title track hangs together better than might be expected. The orchestrated overture, 'Father's Shout', does, as Waters suggested, inspire images of cheroot-smoking high plains drifters, compounded by the sound of whinnying horses, but the whole thing plods rather than canters. The second section, 'Breast Milky', is better, with the choir complementing Wright's organ fills and Gilmour's sleepy guitar solo. It's Gilmour that saves 'Funky Dung' from living up to its title, his staccato fills and lazy riffs almost a dummy run for *Dark Side of the Moon*'s instrumental 'Any Colour You Like', before the choir return with some eerie Gregorian-style chanting. 'Mind Your Throats Please' suggests Waters, hank of hair hanging over his face, cigarette smouldering between his fingers, hunched over the console at Abbey Road, teasing out as many shivery sound effects as he can, including the noise of a crashing vehicle later reprised on *Dark Side of the Moon*. The closing 'Remergence' gathers together all the earlier strands in the fashion of a classical music coda, with frantic brass and strings and Nick Mason's plodding drums limping over the finishing line.

An inquisitive A&R man nosing around the sessions fell for Waters' sense of humour when the bass player and Geesin hid a record player under the desk and played a crackly 78rpm disc through the studio speakers, telling him it was 'the new stuff'. In truth, opinion on the real thing was divided.

'It wasn't how I envisaged it, but it was a good compromise,' says Geesin now. 'I wanted more punch, but then again the Floyd always seemed to need that pastel wash on their music, even on the punchy stuff.'

As early as the mid-1970s, Waters and Wright were publicly expressing dissatisfaction with the album, while in the nineties Gilmour would dismiss it as 'probably our lowest point artistically'. But, as Geesin suggests, 'that could be because Dave had the least to do with it.'

Tirelessly vilified by lazy music critics for being progressive rock at its worst, *Atom Heart Mother* is less self-indulgent than its reputation suggests. While Harvest's prog-rock pioneers The Moody Blues and Barclay James Harvest would forge entire careers out of orchestral rock, Floyd only flirted briefly with the genre. 'I think it's significant that I took all of the band, except for Roger, to see Wagner's *Parsifal* at Covent Garden,' says Ron, 'and they all fell asleep.'

The album's second half makes fewer demands on the listener, though, as Geesin says, 'they were just scraps that they scraped together.' Roger Waters' solo composition, 'If', seemed to pick up where his own 'Grantchester Meadows' had left off on *Ummagumma*. Waters' vocal sounds incredibly fey ('prissy and English' as he would later describe some of his own work) as he enunciates over the daintiest of melodies. The lyrics were less pastoral, addressing some soon-to-become-familiar issues, such as the threat of madness that would be explored in greater detail on *Dark Side of the Moon* and *The Wall*. Meanwhile, lyrics mourning the loss of a friendship and references to 'the spaces between friends' were construed by some to refer to Syd Barrett. Syd showed up at the studio unannounced during the album sessions, accompanied by old Cambridge pal Geoff Mottlow, but, according to Ron Geesin, 'he spun out again as quickly as he spun in'.

When asked in an interview in 2004 about Nick Mason's recent book about the band, Roger Waters expressed his surprise that 'there wasn't more sex in it'. What to make then of Richard Wright's 'Summer '68', a song about the band's second US tour in which its composer sings of the spiritual emptiness following an encounter with a groupie. Real or imaginary? 'In the summer of '68, there were groupies everywhere,' said Wright, years later. 'They'd come and look after you like a personal maid, do your washing, sleep with you and leave you with a dose of the clap.' The song was a welcome exploration of human emotions after four years of interplanetary musings and psychedelic whimsy.

Gilmour's contribution, 'Fat Old Sun', is similarly grounded, betraying the influence of hip new West Coast act Crosby, Stills and Nash, even if the vocalist's unmistakably English tones and the 'distant bells' and 'new-mown grass' in the lyrics suggest bucolic, summer evenings by the Mill Pond in Cambridge rather than on a hippie ranch in Laurel Canyon.

Only 'Alan's Psychedelic Breakfast', the group-credited closing contribution (in reality, the work of Nick Mason), seems tied to the old Floyd tradition of sound effects for their own sake. To a backdrop of gentle piano and guitar-led jamming, the piece unfolds with the mouth-watering sound of Floyd's chief roadie, Alan Styles, preparing a breakfast of cereal, toast, eggs, bacon and coffee, complete with amplified crunching, chewing, sizzling and gulping (tapes from the sessions typically began with the likes of 'Egg Frying Take One', followed by a startled 'Whoops!'). At various intervals, Styles's East Anglian tones drift across the stereo channels ('I like marmalade . . .') before the track closes with the sound of an hypnotically dripping tap recorded in Nick Mason's kitchen. Harmless fun, but the joke runs dry over thirteen minutes. Gilmour would later declare 'Alan's Psychedelic Breakfast' as 'the most thrown-together thing we've ever done'. Nevertheless, it was performed live, and made a minor star of the titular roadie.

Alan Styles was a Cantabrigian who'd once worked the punts on the River Cam. His long hair, moustache and fashionably tight jeans belied the fact that he was several years older than the band. Alan had been in the Merchant Navy and became a physical training instructor while doing his National Service in Germany. An accomplished musician in his own right, he had played sax in the Cambridge band Phuzz alongside Pink Floyd's future saxophonist Dick Parry.

'Alan was a real character,' recalled Nick Mason in 1973. 'But he got to be such a big star that we were afraid to ask him to do things like lifting gear. In the end, we had to fire him.'

Styles chose to remain in the United States while on a Pink Floyd tour. He quit the music industry and lived for many years on a houseboat in San Francisco. Sadly, Styles died in December 2011.

Pink Floyd's new composition had already made its way into the group's setlist by June that year, some four months before the album's release. Still called 'The Amazing Pudding', it was performed in full at the Bath Festival of Blues and Progressive Music in Shepton Mallet, a three-day shindig that also featured Led Zeppelin and Fairport Convention. The event was blighted by interminable traffic jams and a shortage of edible food. It's a testament to the hardiness of the seventies rock fan that any were still there when the band appeared on stage five hours late at around 3 a.m. Even more extraordinary is that the John Aldiss Choir and the Philip Jones Brass Ensemble lasted that long to join the group for the grand finale.

In the audience was BBC producer Jeff Griffin. When Blackhill staged its second free festival in Hyde Park in July, Floyd were announced on a bill with Kevin Ayers and the Edgar Broughton Band. Steve O'Rourke agreed to Griffin's request for a Floyd in-concert session, a few days before the Hyde Park gig, as it would also double up as a much-needed rehearsal for the show. 'When Steve told me they needed a twelve-piece brass section and a twenty-piece choir, I nearly fell over,' recalls Griffin now. 'First of all there was the cost, and, secondly, the technical feasibility of recording the whole lot at somewhere like the Paris Theatre.' Nevertheless, Jeff found the money and John Peel compered the show.

'But there was still the issue that the piece didn't have a title,' says Griffin. 'John wandered out to get an evening paper, and I think it was Roger who was looking over his shoulder. Peely was like, "Come on, what's the name of this piece? I bet you find something in the paper." And there in the *Evening Standard* was this story about a woman who'd been fitted with a nuclear-powered pacemaker. Roger was like, "That's it – Atom Heart Mother." Which had nothing whatsoever to do with the piece of music. We were saying, "Why?", but the band were like, "Why not?" '

At Hyde Park and the Paris Theatre, Floyd opened their set with 'Embryo', a track lasting more than ten minutes that has still never been officially released. At Hyde Park, the sound of children giggling and chattering echoed around the park, causing many looks of stoned confusion amid the crowd, until they realised that the sounds were actually coming from Richard Wright's keyboards. Their twenty-three-minute 'Atom Heart Mother' finale, complete with choir and brass, made a lasting impression on Ron Geesin. 'I left in tears,' he admits. 'The performance of the brass was terrible.' It was later discovered, in a possibly unconnected incident, that one of the tuba players had suffered the indignity of having a pint of beer upended into his instrument.

Floyd returned to America twice that year, running up against the customary setbacks that blighted their Stateside visits. In New Orleans, the band's rental truck, containing every piece of equipment, was stolen. Steve O'Rourke would have to bribe the local police to ensure its return. Separate choirs and orchestral players were hired for the

East and West Coast legs of the tour at enormous expense to help reproduce 'Atom Heart Mother' in its entirety. Not everyone was impressed. John Mendelsohn of the *LA Times* delivered a lacerating put-down of the band's gig at the Santa Monica Civic Center: 'Ultimately one can scarcely keep from wondering why the four human components of Pink Floyd bother to come out on stage at all when computers could hardly fail to make as interesting a use of their arsenal of gadgets.'

Composer Leonard Bernstein attended a show in New York, but was, David Gilmour revealed, bored stiff by the Floyd's latest composition. Still, the piece had some celebrity devotees. Director Stanley Kubrick would approach the group with a view to using 'Atom Heart Mother' in his upcoming movie, *A Clockwork Orange*. While the idea appealed to the Floyd's artier pretensions, Roger vetoed the plan when he discovered that Kubrick wanted the freedom to cut up the piece to fit his film.

Whatever misgivings some, including the band themselves, may have had about the album, which was released in October 1970, they would not impact on its success. *Sounds* applauded the record's 'rich, gentle atmosphere'; *Beat Instrumental* declared it an 'utterly fantastic record that moves Floyd into new ground'. But *Rolling Stone*, never easily pleased by Pink Floyd, canned the second half in particular as 'English folk at its deadly worst'. However, *Atom Heart Mother* outstripped *Ummagumma* and gave Floyd their first number 1 album in the UK, and a then respectable number 55 chart placing in the US.

With three Top 10 albums to their name, Floyd's financial situation had now improved. 'Our royalties cover us now,' Nick Mason told one journalist. 'For years previously we'd been paying off enormous debts. All our royalties and everything else were just being used to pay our running costs. The band still doesn't make any money but at least we're not fighting to pay back debts.'

For Gilmour, not before time. 'Nine months after I joined, we started to give ourselves £30 a week,' he recalled. 'For the first time we were earning more than our roadies. Money's the biggest single pressure on people. Even if you've got it, you have the pressure of not knowing whether you should have it. It can be a moral problem.'

Apart from the music, the album's appearance would become a major talking point for critics and fans. The Hipgnosis team had chosen the most obtuse and irrelevant image they could think of and something as far removed from psychedelia as possible: a cow. Lulubelle III, to give the beast its full name, was photographed in a field in Hertfordshire. It was, as Storm Thorgerson later elaborated, 'perfect, because it was just so *cow*'. The duo presented the image to Roger Waters, who, as Aubrey 'Po' Powell recalls, 'burst out laughing, and loved it'. The band insisted that the image remain unspoiled by the name of the group or the album's title.

'I wish I had a recording of my meeting with the managing director of EMI,' recalls Storm. 'He went absolutely apoplectic when he saw that cover.'

EMI may have balked, but on the morning of the album's release, they coaxed a herd of cows through the Mall for the benefit of the assembled press photographers.

Atom Heart Mother would be Ron Geesin's only collaboration with Pink Floyd. He shared a writing credit on its title track, but, to the surprise of some, wasn't given a co-credit on the album itself. 'It was never discussed with the group,' he insists now. 'Later, I considered the missing credit to be a typical example of the Great Mincing Machine and the little piece of meat.'

As one of the few outsiders to be invited to collaborate with Pink Floyd, Geesin was quick to spot the pressure the four bigger pieces of meat were under, and the emergent power struggles between them. 'By the time I worked with them, they were being pushed *all* the time by EMI and Steve O'Rourke. Steve was a heavy man. I knew him from before the Floyd because he handled a lot of jazz bands at the agency where he worked. My impression is that the Floyd were getting burnt out, which is probably why Roger wanted to work with someone else from the outside.

'Nick and Rick were very easy-going,' he continues. 'Rick wouldn't push anything and you could see how that might become a problem for him later on. Dave was a quiet fellow. I think he was a bit suspicious of me because he knew the least about me, so he could be cagey. I was closest to Roger, whom I liked a great deal, but he could still be very abrasive to those around him. But most artists of any worth create abrasion around them in some way or other. It's the abrasion necessary to create the heat for creativity. It's necessary but someone will always get damaged – wives, lovers, children, or the other people on the stage. I was close friends with Roger until he turned and bit just about everybody.'

In one interview that year, Waters was unusually candid about his threatening image. 'I'm frightened of other people,' he admitted. 'If you lower your defence, someone jumps on you. I find myself jumping on people all the time and regretting it afterwards.'

By now, the group were adapting to the fact that, as Nick Mason put it, 'Roger could be so frightening.' They followed Steve O'Rourke's suggestion of remaining slightly isolated from their record company, but ended up appearing even more standoffish in the process. By 1970, Malcolm Jones had relinquished his position at Harvest and been succeeded by Dave Croker, who soon realised that working with Pink Floyd meant waiting to be told what to do only when the group had decided. 'Steve and the Floyd planned everything in detail long before the event,' said Croker. 'Any conflicts they had were well over by the time the group got in touch with the outside world. They did all their arguing and sorting out in private.'

Yet Nick Mason seemed less convinced that the band's bickering was done behind closed doors. 'We frequently behaved appallingly,' he wrote in 2004. Attending dinners with record company staff and promoters, the band would commandeer the middle of the table and 'banish anyone we didn't know to the far ends. Group dinners were the focal point for all band fights, policy decisions and general jockeying for position.'

Years earlier, Mason had admitted to the press that relations within the band were akin to 'being in a small army unit or a prep school because you can oscillate so easily between love and hate'.

'It's never two against two, either. It's always three against one,' he told *Sounds* magazine's Steve Peacock. 'It really is amazing to watch sometimes. Jokes, and the way they become teasing and bullying. We can be incredibly spiteful.'

For Mason, though, there was less jockeying to be done. Aside from being Waters' closest friend in the band, he wrote very few songs on his own and therefore never had to fight Roger or the others to get his material on a Floyd album. For Gilmour and Wright, Waters presented more of a problem. Wright, who'd once been seen by Floyd's management as the strongest songwriter after Syd Barrett, was now completely overshadowed by the prolific bass player. Adding to the problem was the fact that the two had never got on in the first place. 'I had a personality clash with Roger even at Regent Street Poly,' says Wright. 'We would not have chosen to be friends, even at that time. Being the kind of person he is, Roger would try and rile you, try to make you crack.'

Gilmour could appear reserved, but he was also incredibly stubborn, a trait that would manifest itself fully when Waters strove to break up the band in the 1980s. In 1970, though, the guitarist was still shrugging off his 'new boy' status and struggling to establish himself as a songwriter. 'Roger doesn't do any more in the musical direction than the rest of us,' he insisted in an interview to accompany *Atom Heart Mother*. But years later Gilmour would concede that 'Roger was the ideas man and the motivator, and helped to push things forward.'

For Waters, himself, it was the others that were the problem. 'There was always a great battle between the musicians and the architects,' he admitted. 'Nick and I were relegated to this inferior position of being the architects who were looked down upon by Rick and Dave who were the musicians.'

Ron Geesin vividly recalls his old friend's struggles: 'Roger was grumbling most of the time I knew him. He frequently expressed dissatisfaction at the group's suitability as a mouthpiece for his ideas. I just said, "Leave!" but, of course, he was trapped. He knew where his bread was buttered. That's why Roger only left Pink Floyd when he could afford to.'

In August, during the recording of *Atom Heart Mother*, the band flew to the South of France to play some festival dates in the South of France. They set up camp in a large rented villa near St Tropez, joined by Steve O'Rourke, Pete Watts, Alan Styles and everybody's respective wives and children. Living in such close proximity to each other, though, meant that tensions soon ran high.

'The Floyd all had strong wives,' recalls Peter Jenner. 'Juliette Wright was a tough cookie, extremely sensible and grounded. Nick and Lindy Mason were probably the most straightforward couple. They'd almost been childhood sweethearts. She was musical herself, and, like Nick, she came from an impeccable middle-class background. Judy Trim was very nice but she was a screaming Trot. I always thought Roger was very influenced by his women, and Judy kept him left-wing and committed. She'd known him since before the Floyd, and she had her own life and her own career as a potter, which was good, because she didn't put up with any of his shit.'

There was another aspect to Roger and Judy's relationship that the bassist would later discuss in interviews, namely his mother's attitude. 'She thought it would be really bad for me to find a nice clean girl and get married when I was too young,' he revealed in 1980. 'I can remember her specifically encouraging me to go out and look for dirty girls.' Roger had instead married his childhood sweetheart.

It was in St Tropez that Mason and Waters clashed, when Lindy and Judy harangued the bassist after he admitted to being unfaithful a couple of years earlier after a gig in Texas. When Mason joined in, Waters took particular exception, largely on the grounds that the drummer was similarly guilty, but hadn't confessed to his own indiscretion.

Aside from the gigs and an ill-fated stab at communal living, there was another reason for the trip. Earlier that year Floyd had been approached by choreographer Roland Petit to write a piece for his dance company, Ballet de Marseille. Petit wanted to stage a production based around Marcel Proust's epic novel, *A la Recherche du Temps Perdu*. Lindy Mason was a ballet dancer, so Nick, for one, was well aware of Petit's credentials. The idea immediately appealed. 'The French have a more emotional, more intellectual edge to the arts,' he enthused in the press that year. After an initial meeting in Paris, Roger bought the entire twelve volumes of Proust and suggested the band start reading, before giving up himself after just one volume, with David Gilmour supposedly bailing out after just eighteen pages. The outcome would eventually be five performances in Marseilles in November 1972, and a further run in Paris a few months later.

In France, tensions also ran high outside the band's shared villa. Several of the proposed festival dates were cancelled due to run-ins with the local authorities over safety, or abandoned after rioters clashed with the police. When promoters pulled the plug on a planned open-air festival in Heidelberg, West Germany, at the end of August, Pink Floyd flew back home.

Gilmour took a detour via the Isle of Wight Festival, where Jimi

Hendrix was due to play what would turn out to be his final UK gig. Floyd's principal roadie and sound engineer Pete Watts had been hired to take care of the sound. But with Watts nervous and, arguably, too stoned to do the job properly, Gilmour took over instead, unknown to Hendrix as the young English guitar player from two years earlier that had squired him around Paris. Less than a month later Hendrix would be dead.

Pink Floyd's collaboration with Roland Petit would be just one of several non-album projects begun during the first year of the new decade. A proposed soundtrack for a new cartoon series, *Rollo* (by The Beatles' *Yellow Submarine* illustrator Alan Aldridge), was much talked about in the press, but floundered after a pilot was made and the money dried up. The group's next encounter with a film-maker would prove more rewarding than their earlier butting of heads with Michelangelo Antonioni on *Zabriskie Point*.

On tour in Australia in 1971, the band met film director and ardent surfer George Greenough. *Crystal Voyager*, his documentary film celebrating the national pastime, was crying out for a suitable soundtrack. The film's grand finale would feature footage of a surfer taken from a camera strapped to his body, and accompanied by a new piece of Floyd music: a 23-minute piece entitled 'Echoes'. These scenes would later be used by the band to provide a backdrop during parts of Floyd's live shows, but 'Echoes' itself would prove a landmark in the band's musical development.

'We were looking for something,' said Gilmour. 'During that whole period through *Ummagumma* and *Atom Heart Mother*, we were finding ourselves. "Echoes" was the point at which we found our focus.'

Yet the song's arrival was less a moment of epiphany than a series of moments, in which the band eventually managed to create something worthwhile from what Gilmour called 'the rubbish library'. Recording of the next Pink Floyd album, later christened *Meddle*, began at Abbey Road's Studio Two in January 1971. When they discovered that Beatles producer George Martin had installed sixteen-track machines at his own Air Studios in Hampstead. The Floyd took their eight-track tapes there and to north London's Morgan Studios. Tape operator John Leckie, who'd worked on some of the Barrett album sessions, was brought in alongside Pete Bown to engineer before the final mix at Air. The Floyd's initial ideas were far more avant-garde than the finished album might suggest.

'They spent days and days and days working on what people now call the *Household Objects* album,' recalls Leckie. *Household Objects* would never be released, but the group are said to have recorded around twenty minutes of music, utilising the sound of everyday objects: elastic bands, wine glasses, cigarette lighters. 'They were making chords up from the tapping of beer bottles, tearing newspaper to get a rhythm and letting off an aerosol can to get a hi-hat sound. It was very much Nick Mason's idea, but everyone was involved. The trouble was it didn't seem to be going anywhere.' The idea was abandoned after a week, and consigned to 'the rubbish library' from where it would, nevertheless, be retrieved three years later.

Household Objects wasn't the band's only indulgence. One idea from the time involved each of the four band members being invited to play whatever they liked as long as it was in the same key. The results were committed to tape, without any of the group hearing what their band-mates had previously recorded. 'Awful, absolutely awful,' said Gilmour. At least one Abbey Road engineer from the early seventies recalls how Pink Floyd sessions had a 'reputation for being rather long-winded. They could take for ever to do anything.' Allowed carte blanche by EMI, the group capitalised on the company's patience, deep pockets and the prevailing mood that rock 'n' roll bands should be taken as seriously as classical composers.

'Basically, we're the laziest group ever,' admitted Gilmour. 'Other groups would be quite horrified if they saw how we waste our recording time.'

Yet despite these inauspicious beginnings, there was some order being created out of the chaos.

'The tapes we took to Air were filled up with lots of little ideas — a bit of guitar jiggery-pokery, a bit of piano, some sound effects,' recalls Leckie. 'They were all called "Nothing" — "Nothing One", "Nothing Two" and so on. So the first couple of weeks was just putting down all these little bits. But they were often going off to play gigs, so you'd have to strip down the studio, they'd load the van and go off and play a gig, then come back and set it all up again.'

The only upside of this fractured process was that it gave the group a chance to test ideas on stage. 'Echoes', then still called 'Return of the Son of Nothing', was given a public airing.

'When they came back they'd got it into shape because they'd been playing it live,' recalls Leckie. 'It was conceived as one big thing, bits in various sections, so it was recorded that way.'

Salvaged from the various 'Nothings' was an idea from Richard Wright. A single note was played on a piano and then put through a Leslie cabinet, a gizmo normally used with a Hammond organ and containing a revolving horn that boosts the sound. The note – like the eerie ping of a sonar – would announce the beginning of 'Echoes'. From here on, the other 'Nothings' slotted together – a melancholy guitar figure, the eerie shriek of an incorrectly wired effects pedal, the final moody denouement – to arrive at the finished piece.

'We also did this thing with two tape recorders,' says John. 'You get two machines, one on each side of the room, run the tape through one, then thread it through the other and record on the first one and play back on the other. So there's this delay. The end of "Echoes" when the voices swell up is a snippet of that technique.'

'Echoes' had structure and a greater sense of purpose and a stronger melody than any of Floyd's earlier epics. Even if the process of putting it together was sometimes laboured.

'There could be periods of boredom and long silences,' admits Leckie. 'They were posh boys from Cambridge, after all, and they didn't suffer fools gladly. They wanted everything to be done properly. They were very critical of sound and tuning and what each other was playing. They were always fiddling about with the equipment, trying to make things sound better. Roger and Dave were undoubtedly the leaders. They were the ones who told you what they wanted. Rick Wright would sit at the back and not say anything for days, but his piano playing was always a highlight of any session.'

Speaking to the press before *Meddle* was released, Waters was visceral in his criticism of the band's current situation. 'I'm bored with most of the stuff we play,' he admitted. Above all, he was determined to rid Floyd's music of the loathed 'Space Rock' label. On tour in America, where the band's cult following got off on the music's cosmic imagery, Waters would berate those calling for old favourites such as 'Astronomy Domine' and even 'See Emily Play' with withering put-downs: 'You must be joking!'

Waters had been very taken with the rawness and grim candour of the previous year's John Lennon/Plastic Ono Band album, a record inspired by the primal scream therapy Lennon had submitted to in order to tackle issues from his childhood. Part of the Floyd's purge would involve Roger writing lyrics that connected the group with the real world, even if they couldn't mirror the abrasiveness of the Plastic Ono Band's music and still had to rely on what Ron Geesin called 'that pastel wash'.

Interviewed in 2004, Waters revealed that the inspiration for 'Echoes' lyrics came from the sense of disconnection he experienced during his early years living in London, and following Syd's turbulent departure from the band. Waters and future wife Judy Trim had moved to a flat in Shepherds Bush, West London. One window in the apartment afforded a clear view of the busy Goldhawk Road, down which the couple would observe an ant-like procession of commuters heading off for a day's toil in the morning and returning in the evening. The lyrics referring to strangers passing in the street were, he explained, 'all about making connections with other people. About the potential that human beings have for recognising each other's humanity.' Perversely, despite the icy distance that would develop between some of those writing and performing the music, the theme of communication, of reaching out, would be one the band would return to obsessively.

While 'Echoes' occupied the second half of the album, the first half contained five new songs. Tellingly, two of these, 'A Pillow of Winds' and 'Fearless', were credited to Waters and Gilmour, and signified their first co-writing partnership since 1968's flop single 'Point Me at the Sky'. Both songs seemed almost disarmingly lightweight and in stark contrast to all the *Sturm und Drang* acid rock of just three years earlier. 'A Pillow of Winds' was a lovely acoustic jangle (its title supposedly taken from the board game mah jong, of which the band were enthusiastic players), sung by a sleepy-sounding Gilmour, suggesting its protagonist drifting into a hemp-induced doze.

'Fearless' (according to John Leckie 'the highlight of that first side') made similar use of the acoustic guitars, but Roger's lyric of facing adversity despite the odds gave it more bite. The strumming guitars eventually fade to be replaced by the combined voices of Liverpool FC's 'Kop Choir' for a refrain of 'You'll Never Walk Alone'; an in-joke for the bassist, who was by then a committed Arsenal FC supporter.

Waters' solo composition 'San Tropez' was a lilting jazzy excursion, with Wright playing a supper-club piano solo after its writer saluted the joys of supping champagne and doing very little in the titular French hotspot.

If 'San Tropez' sounded slight, 'Seamus' was positively inconsequential. The songwriting blame was shared equally between all four. Here, Gilmour sings a corny blues and blows harmonica punctuated by the barks and howls of a collie called Seamus, who belonged to Humble Pie frontman Steve Marriott. (Gilmour was looking after the dog while Marriott was on tour.) As Leckie admits, 'It was very funny when Dave played the harmonica and that dog started howling, but I must admit I was surprised to hear it on the finished album.'

Most of *Meddle* invited comparisons not with Floyd's brain-box competitors Yes or King Crimson, but with the gentler sounds of The Band or Crosby, Stills, Nash and Young. Only the opening instrumental, 'One of These Days', seemed tied to the Floyd of old. With its ominous bass riff, BBC Radiophonic Workshop-style sound effects, and Nick Mason hissing the words, 'One of these days I'm going to cut you into little pieces', it sounded like a vamped-up, prog rock version of the Doctor Who theme tune spliced with The Tornados' 'Telstar'.

If, as Roger Waters once claimed, '*Atom Heart Mother* was the beginning of the end', then *Meddle* was the beginning of something completely new. Unlike *Ummagumma* or much of *Atom Heart Mother*, it sounded like the work of a band pulling together, rather than four individuals working alone and collectively battling to escape the shadow of their departed frontman. *Meddle* sounded like Pink Floyd's future.

Integral to this future, though, would be Roger Waters' desire for a grand show. While cannons, flower petals and roadies in gorilla suits had once accompanied Pink Floyd's live performances, their May 1971 performance at London's Crystal Palace Bowl was their most grandiose yet. Taking a break from the *Meddle* sessions, the band shook the crowd out of their stoned torpor with a quadraphonic sound system, exploding smoke bombs and a gigantic inflatable octopus hidden in the lake in front of the stage which reared up during the grand finale of 'A Saucerful of Secrets'. A spectacular end to the show, even if the effect was slightly spoilt by the sight of a roadie paddling into the water to untangle the beast's tentacles and coax it up into full view of the crowd.

While Waters would complain that 'the musicians in the band', namely Wright and Gilmour, were opposed to 'anything theatrical', there was a tacit understanding among all four that, in the absence of a sex-symbol frontman, such as Robert Plant or Mick Jagger, they'd better find other ways to hold an audience's visual attention. 'In the seventies people came to hear the music and see the show,' said Richard Wright. 'They didn't come to see me, Dave and Roger jumping around as individuals. We weren't standard rock 'n' roll people desperate to be personalities. We were happy not to be in the limelight.'

By 1971, fellow Brits Led Zeppelin had become notorious for their offstage activities, with astronomical hotel bills, Herculean drug habits and used-up groupies to show for it. For Pink Floyd, alcohol and narcotics were imbibed, and, like all English rock bands, they attracted the attention of groupies, although Waters claimed at the time, 'Unlike most other bands, we're not heavily into crumpet on the road.'

But like all touring rock bands, they had hours of crushing boredom to contend with. Games of backgammon, Monopoly and the afore-mentioned mah jong were among their favoured aftershow activities, appealing especially to Roger's competitive instincts. Yet there were still outbreaks of more traditional rock 'n' roll behaviour. Recalling the time Gilmour borrowed a fan's motorcycle and rode it through a restaurant in Phoenix, Arizona, to the complete disinterest of the diners present, Nick Mason said, 'It reminded us of why we didn't usually do that sort of thing in the first place.'

Back home, the communal crash-pads of some three years earlier were now a thing of the past. Each of the band had drifted into domesticity. In 1968, Roger and Judy had moved from Shepherds Bush and bought an £8,000 house in Islington's New North Road, a then rather dour main drag running from the Essex Road south towards Hoxton. It was considered an unusual place for an up-and-coming rock star to make his home. Syd's old flatmate David Gale, then starting his own theatre company, later moved in to a house just across the road.

Waters called on his architectural design skills and undertook some of the renovation work on the house himself. The décor was impeccably chosen, with plenty of sanded wooden floors and minimalist furnishings on which the couple's Burmese cats could roam freely. Roger and Judy's garden shed became their shared workspace. One half served as Waters' home studio, while the other was given over to Judy's potter's wheel and ceramics. Keen to assert her independence, Judy still taught full-time at the Dame Alice Owen School in Islington, whose pupils were apparently later stunned to discover that her husband was a member of Pink Floyd. Waters initially splashed out for an E-type Jaguar, until his Socialist principles got the better of him, and he traded it in for an Austin Mini.

Nick Mason shared none of his old friend's misgivings. A Lotus Elan would be among several sporty little numbers to end up parked outside the house he shared with Lindy in St Augustine's Road, Camden. Rick and Juliette Wright and their two young children, daughter Gala and son Jamie, had set up home a few miles west of Nick and Roger in Leinster Gardens, Bayswater.

David Gilmour was now the only unmarried member of Pink Floyd. Since joining the group, he'd relished his freedom in the bachelor pad flat at Richmond Mansions. During a rare break in the band's schedule, Gilmour dashed off to Morocco for a holiday with girlfriend and Quorum model Jenny Roff. Yet with the start of a new decade, his bachelor days would be numbered. By the end of the year, Gilmour had given up the flat at Richmond Mansions and bought his first property, an abandoned farmhouse, complete with barn and stables, near Roydon in Essex. Full of wood carvings, low beams and a wide sweeping staircase, it offered a welcome change of scene for the guitarist, who told one interviewer that year, 'I'm a country boy at heart.'

Disappearing on tour after first purchasing the house, Gilmour installed Emo to keep an eye on the place. Without electricity or heating, the early-morning din from a nearby chicken farm and the huge, curtain-less windows opening out on the deserted countryside, the house was not the best place to sleep off a hard night's excesses. But despite Gilmour's newly single status, the farmhouse would soon benefit from a woman's touch.

Midway through Floyd's 1970 American tour, the guitarist had encountered a striking blonde backstage at a gig in Ann Arbor, Michigan. Virginia Hasenbein, known to all as Ginger, was a twenty-one-year-old Philadelphian model, then the face of Leichner make-up, and also part of a troupe of roller-skating dancers. Ginger had been in a relationship with the same man ('a smooth entrepreneur', she recalled) since she was sixteen years old. Having met Gilmour after the Floyd gig, she ran into him again at a party later in the week. This time, she later claimed,

Gilmour enlisted Waters to distract her boyfriend, and introduced himself. By all accounts, the two were immediately smitten and Ginger flew to New York to hook up with the guitarist just days later.

'After every gig, he would set up a little chair by the amplifiers, and I'd sit there,' Ginger told the *Mail on Sunday* newspaper in 2004. 'David would leave the stage, and we'd be kissing. We never stopped kissing.'

'She looked like an angel and David fell in love with her,' recalls one confidant. 'Ginger was in this roller-skating show at the time, and they used to call her the "Dream On Wheels". I think there was talk that she was also going to be in a movie. It took something ridiculous like two weeks for her to give everything up – her career, her family, her home – and come to England to be with him. Steve O'Rourke put in an amazing amount of work to help make that happen.'

Back in England, the couple took Gilmour's E-type Jaguar and drove cross-country to Athens, before catching a boat to Rhodes, where they holidayed in a rented villa in Lindos.

When they arrived back in England, the couple set about renovating the Essex farmhouse. Over the next couple of years Gilmour would have a music room, home studio and swimming pool installed, while also acquiring a trials bike on which he could hare around the grounds. A retired brewer's dray horse set up home in the stables, while Gilmour's old car, a 1936 Buick Straight Eight, was put out to pasture in the barn. Later, an absent-minded Emo would leave the trials bike out in the rain only to find the horse eating its saddle. But, for now, life was good.

Strangely, Pink Floyd would manage two albums in 1971. In May, EMI put out *Relics*, an eleven-track compilation, on their low-budget Starline/Music For Pleasure imprint. Subtitled *A Bizarre Collection of Antiques and Curios*, it bracketed the hits 'Arnold Layne' and 'See Emily Play' alongside the non-hits 'Careful With That Axe Eugene', 'Interstellar Overdrive', and otherwise forgotten B-sides, including Richard Wright's charming 'Paintbox', a song he'd later dismiss as dreadful. *Relics* also included one previously unreleased composition, 'Biding My Time', a leftover from 1969's abandoned 'The Man, The Journey' suite, which had the rare distinction of including a trombone solo from Wright, a homage to his days as a bowler-hatted trad jazz fan in the early sixties.

The sketch of a Heath Robinson-style contraption on the cover of *Relics* would be Nick Mason's sole foray into album artwork, evidence that those three years hunched over a drawing board at Regent Street Poly had not been entirely wasted. Despite the fact that it was released as a contractual obligation, *Relics* would become a treasured item for the post-*Dark Side of the Moon* Floyd fan wanting to negotiate their way through the band's sixties era, without having to empty their wallet and buy all of the earlier albums.

Relics could be blamed for taking some of the wind out of the next Floyd album's sales. Nevertheless, *Meddle* was released some six months later in November. Its abstract sleeve shot, a close-up of a human ear under water, would remain Storm Thorgerson's least favourite Floyd album sleeve. Some of the blame for this could be attributed to the band phoning through the roughest of ideas while on tour in Japan. 'The band always say that *Atom Heart Mother* was a better cover than it was an album,' says Thorgerson, 'but I think *Meddle* is a much better album than its cover.' The band photograph in the inside gatefold sleeve would be the last group photo to appear on any original Floyd album until 1987's *A Momentary Lapse of Reason*. The parade of facial fungus, centre partings and scoop-neck T-shirts proved that the band were now utterly indistinguishable from their audience, which, of course, was just the way they liked it.

Despite completing their strongest album since *The Piper at the Gates of Dawn*, the band's restless nature ensured they were easily distracted by other projects. Adrian Maben, a young French film director, had made his approach to David Gilmour and Steve O'Rourke earlier in the year, proposing a film in which Pink Floyd provided the music to images of paintings by René Magritte, Jean Tinguely and Giorgio de Chirico, among others. 'I naively thought that it would be possible to combine good art with Pink Floyd music,' said Maben. The band politely turned him down.

That summer Maben, holidaying in Italy, took a sightseeing trip to the 2,000-year-old amphitheatre in Pompeii, at the foot of Mount Vesuvius. After losing his passport during the visit, Maben persuaded the security guards to let him back into the amphitheatre to look for it. Alone in the deserted arena in the dwindling light, he was struck by the ghostliness of the setting, and the fabulous natural acoustics amplifying the sound of buzzing insects and flying bats flitting among the ruins.

Maben secured some funding from a German producer, Reiner Moritz, and arranged another meeting with the band, this time proposing the idea of a rock movie that could be, in his words, an 'anti-Woodstock'; a reaction to director Michael Wadleigh's celebratory film of the 1969 rock festival. *Help!*, Richard Lester's film of The Beatles, and D.A. Pennebaker's Dylan vehicle, *Don't Look Back*, had followed in the same vein. Instead, Maben wanted Pink Floyd playing an empty amphitheatre to a film crew and a handful of roadies.

'There had to be a vast audience, the band had to be seen as being hugely successful – rock films had already become a cliché,' explained Maben. 'What was the point of doing the same kind of film with the Floyd?'

The band warmed to the idea, agreeing to pay 50 per cent of the costs, but leaving control of the final product to the producer, a decision they would come to rue.

At the beginning of October, Pink Floyd flew to Pompeii to commence filming, with a skeleton crew headed up by Pete Watts and Alan Styles. With more dates booked back in the UK, they were working to a tight schedule. There were, as Nick Mason later grumbled, 'No leisurely nights out sampling the local cuisine and wine list.' Instead, the band spent the first three days unable to do anything, due to the lack of electricity. When the power was finally switched on, it was insufficient to run both the band's sound equipment and lighting. Eventually a cable was connected to the town hall, snaking through the streets to the amphitheatre, with a roadie on guard to make sure it wasn't disconnected.

One of Floyd's stipulations was that Maben had to film and record them playing live. There would be no miming. The band performed live versions of their newest tracks 'Echoes' and 'One of These Days' alongside a resurrected 'A Saucerful of Secrets'.

Performing beneath the baking Mediterranean sun, and to an audience of cameramen, assorted roadies and a few local kids that had talked their way in, the footage offers a revealing glimpse of the post-Syd, pre-superstar Pink Floyd. The newborn 'Echoes' matches its surroundings perfectly: a languid, unhurried performance intercut with snaps of the surrounding sculptures and gargoyles for added drama. Later, as the song rumbles on, the band are shot loping across the bubbling lava pools and steaming, sulphurous rocks on Mount Vesuvius – all tie-dyed T-shirts and stovepipe hats – like four Kings Road hippies transplanted to a prehistoric landscape.

The band had played 'A Saucerful of Secrets' at Adrian Maben's request, as he wanted to film Waters reprising his old party trick of attacking a gong midway through the piece. Filmed in the morning sunlight, a barefoot Gilmour hunkers down in the sand, playing unearthly slides on his Stratocaster, while Mason beats a tribal pattern on the kit, and Wright plays cartwheeling figures on a keyboard in a homage to his late-sixties hero Stockhausen. Meanwhile, master of ceremonies Waters thrashes a rack of cymbals, before loping over to the gong and gleefully battering it with a mallet. He looks less like a musician and more like a sportsman, heading in for the final match point, wicket or goal. It remains the finest snapshot of each individual during the early 1970s.

After just three days of filming, the band returned to England for a gig at Bradford University. When the film's German producer Reiner Moritz was unable to settle their hotel bill, Maben remained a prisoner in the hotel until the funds could be sent to him. He also had another pressing worry: there were still gaps in the movie, which he hoped Floyd would agree to fill at a later date.

In December, the band joined Maben in Paris at the Studio Europasinor to mix the Pompeii film and shoot some more footage. They were filmed on an empty soundstage in Paris, performing 'Set the Controls for the Heart of the Sun', 'Careful With That Axe Eugene' and a version of Meddle's novelty track, 'Seamus', this time named 'Mademoiselle Nobs' in homage to the Afghan hound, Nobs, coaxed into howling along to Gilmour's harmonica.

Maben also shot fly-on-the-wall interview footage in Paris, which was left out of the original edit but surfaced on the director's cut in 2002. The group's knockabout humour is in full flow, as an off-camera Maben attempts to conduct an interview. The Floyd, scooping out oysters and swigging from bottles of beer, deflect each enquiry. Waters, his eyes little beads of mischief, is the most evasive of the lot.

'Are you happy with the filming?' asks Maben at one point.

'What do you mean, *happy*?' hisses the bass player, blowing smoke rings.

'Well, do you think it's interesting?'

There's an excruciatingly long pause.

'What do you mean, *interesting*?' replies Roger, almost sneering.

'They took the mickey out of me all the time of course,' admitted Maben. 'Roger was perhaps the most unsettling of the four. Although Peter Watts, the roadie, mentioned to me that Syd Barrett was a hundred times worse.'

Watching now, it offers a candid glimpse of the band dynamic. The group had developed a telepathic sense of humour and penchant for in-jokes and one-upmanship, as would any gang of young males who had spent far too much time in each other's company over the last three years. Nevertheless, their respective roles are neatly encapsulated. Waters is the ringleader and chief tormentor; Gilmour backs him up without rising to his levels of outright sarcasm; Mason makes some attempt at conciliation ('Adrian . . . Adrian . . . this attempt to elicit conversation out of the chaps is doomed to failure') but can't help goading Waters on; Wright grins wearily and tries to give straight answers to the questions. In the background, a laughing Floyd roadie, Chris Adamson, enjoys the all-too-familiar display of feathers. When Maben attempts to involve Adamson in the interview, Mason jumps in, quick as a flash: 'He's not very important; don't waste any film on him. What's the French for "He is only a roadie"?' Beneath loud guffaws, it sounds as if Gilmour attempts to answer.

A sixty-minute version of *Live At Pompeii* would eventually premiere at the 1972 Edinburgh Film Festival to mixed reviews. Yet it was not quite the finished article. Maben would meet up with the band again the following year to shoot some more footage, which, unbeknown to all of them, would give the film even greater importance.

In the meantime, while not matching *Atom Heart Mother*'s number 1 placing, *Meddle* still reached a healthy number 3. Frustratingly, it fared less well in the US at number 70, later prompting a serious review of the band's relationship with their American label, Capitol.

Despite its poorer showing in the US, *Meddle*'s streamlined approach won over the group's toughest critics, with *Rolling Stone* applauding 'David Gilmour's emergence as a real shaping force in the group'. On home turf, the music press were divided. *Sounds* praised 'Echoes' as 'one of the most complete pieces of music Pink Floyd have ever done'. The magazine's rival, *Melody Maker*, was less impressed. Deputy editor Michael Watts, a long-time fan of the band, berated 'Pink's Muddled *Meddle*' and 'vocals that verged on the drippy and instrumental workouts that are decidedly old hat'.

A month later, Watts took delivery of a parcel at the *Melody Maker* offices. Unwrapping what he presumed was a Christmas gift from some grateful record company PR, he found himself confronted with a bright red hardwood box, the lid held in place with a catch. Watts flipped the catch and jumped back as a spring-loaded boxing glove shot out, narrowly missing his face. It was a Yuletide present from Pink Floyd.

For Syd Barrett, the start of a new decade would mark the beginning of his slow withdrawal from the music business. His second solo album, *Barrett*, appeared at the tail end of 1970, in a sleeve drawing of insects that Syd himself had created during his art school days. 'Syd Barrett is capable of much greater things than this,' carped *Disc and Music Echo*. Syd half-heartedly agreed to promote the album, appearing in photographs in the *Melody Maker* sporting a drastic crop. He made for a reluctant, distracted interviewee: 'I've never really proved myself wrong, I just need to prove myself right.'

In the summer of 1971, Mick Rock was granted an audience, taking photographs and interviewing Syd in the garden at Hills Road for *Rolling Stone* magazine, while Syd's doting mother kept them fuelled with tea and cakes. In the pictures, Barrett appeared smiling and relaxed, looking closer to his previous pop star self with his hair grown out again. Yet the interview is loaded with telling phrases, betraying both his muddled mind ('I've got a very irregular head') and a sense of uncertainty about what the future might hold. 'I'm treading the backwards path,' he admitted ruefully. 'Mostly, I just waste my time.'

Syd would show up in London that summer to visit Mick and his then wife Sheila at their flat in Shepherds Bush. He would appear on the doorstep unannounced, smoke a joint and then disappear again, re-appearing months later.

In January that year, Syd had been among the guests at his old flatmate Seamus O'Connell's wedding in Cambridge. He turned up with

Roger Waters, behaved impeccably and even disappeared to the pub after the ceremony with Seamus's mother. Back in Cambridge, Peter Wynne-Willson, who had now become a *satsangi*, picked Syd up at his mother's house and took him to a local Sant Mat meeting. 'There were going to be a few people there that he knew, and we thought that he might like it,' remembers Peter. 'But he became edgy very quickly and left. That was the last time I ever saw Syd. I rather got the impression that he really wasn't very keen on seeing people that reminded him of *those* days.'

While Barrett may have been keen to distance himself from his contemporaries in Pink Floyd, by the end of the year he'd made a welcome reacquaintance with an old girlfriend. Jenny Spires was now back in Cambridge and living with her new partner, a musician named Jack Monck. Syd felt safe around Jenny, and, in January 1972, she brought him to watch a gig at the local King's College Cellars. Monck was playing bass for American bluesman Eddie 'Guitar' Burns. Playing drums was John Alder, aka Twink, who'd previously drummed for UFO club regulars Tomorrow. He and Barrett had met before on numerous occasions in London. 'I thought he was very together,' recalled Twink. 'It was a warm relationship, no bad vibes at all.'

That night at the King's College Cellars, Barrett borrowed a guitar, climbed on stage with Monck and Twink, and ran through a handful of improvised twelve-bar numbers as a warm-up to the headliner's set.

Later, Barrett joined the pair for an ad-hoc support slot to Hawkwind at the Cambridge Corn Exchange. They used the name The Last Minute Put Together Boogie Band, and had even rehearsed a handful of Syd's own songs earlier in the day. The trio were joined that night by American guitarist Bruce Paine and Fred Frith, guitarist with English jazz-rockers Henry Cow. Unfortunately, Barrett was unable to remember the chord changes to his old songs, choosing instead to repeatedly thrash out the riff to the Yardbirds' version of 'Smokestack Lightnin'.

Undeterred, Twink and Monck persevered, showing up at Hills Road a few days later to talk to Syd about playing together. Barrett agreed and the three began rehearsing, even working up his own songs 'Octopus' and 'Golden Hair', before being offered a gig at the Cambridge Corn Exchange, supported by MC5, the late-sixties protest rockers of 'Kick Out the Jams' fame.

On 5 February 1972, Barrett, Twink and Monck adopted the name Stars and made their debut, an off-the-cuff afternoon gig at the local health food eaterie, the Dandelion. Some eyewitnesses recalled the show as being a little chaotic and that Barrett's musicianship trailed behind that of his bandmates, but the group were pleased with their performance.

Stars played again at the Dandelion, and also performed a similarly spur-of-the-moment open-air gig just off the Market Square in Cambridge. The only known photograph of Barrett at these gigs shows his hair grown out to shoulder length and his face obscured by a heavy, dark beard; unrecognisable from the pop star of five years earlier, and indistinguishable from any of the bearded, long-haired 'heads' for whom he was performing. Drugs, however, were noticeable by their absence. None of his bandmates even recall Syd smoking a joint, never mind taking anything stronger. While his general manner was distracted and he appeared a little fragile, he was, in the words of one eyewitness, 'no more peculiar than a lot of people around, but you had to be on your toes to keep up with the odd tangents he would hit in conversation.'

It was an impression shared by the rock critic Nick Kent, who'd first seen Barrett unravelling on stage in 1967. Kent was then writing for the underground newspaper *Frendz*. The paper's offices in Notting Hill's Portobello Road were above a rehearsal space, where he encountered Syd and some of the Stars entourage. 'This was early 1972, the hippie dream was dying and there were an awful lot of acid casualties like Syd, so he fitted right in,' explains Kent. 'Every day you'd encounter people who'd had a bad acid experience coming into the office and trying to tell us their vision of the world. Syd actually wasn't as bad as most of those people.' However, Kent also experienced Barrett's odd conversational tangents. 'There was a young hippie kid there that day that asked him, "Written any new songs, Syd?"' laughs Nick. 'And Barrett replied, "I'm sorry, I don't speak French."'

Back in Cambridge, the boomy, shed-like ambience of the Corn Exchange was unsuited to Syd's new band. As word spread that Barrett was performing live again, tickets for the 24 February show sold quickly and the venue was packed, with bus-loads of Syd devotees making the trip to Cambridge. Unfortunately, as precursors to punk rock, the incendiary MC5 were bound to make it difficult for any act that had to follow them. Barrett had initially shown willing. He'd shaved off his beard and bought a new pair of velvet trousers. Eyewitnesses recall a set that included Syd's solo pieces, 'Golden Hair' and 'Octopus' and Pink Floyd's 'Lucifer Sam'. On stage, though, Stars were beset with sound problems, as Barrett sliced a finger on one of his strings and began bleeding, and Jack Monck's bass amp cut out midway through the show. Syd began to visibly retreat on stage, looking and sounding, once again, as if he'd rather be anywhere else.

Still undeterred, Stars played the Corn Exchange again, just two days later, alongside the progressive rock band Nektar. Mick Brockett was then working as a lighting engineer for Nektar and had previously seen Pink Floyd while working at the Roundhouse. Brockett, who kept a diary at the time, described the gig in one word: 'pathetic'.

'I was very disappointed,' he recalls now. 'Syd and Twink bombarded our ears, even backstage, with disjointed chord sequences, screaming and yelling, with almost no musical content.'

It would be the last time Stars performed. Just days later, *Melody Maker* appeared with a poor review of the first Corn Exchange show by writer and Syd aficionado Roy Hollingsworth. 'He changed time almost by the minute, the keys and chords made little sense,' he wrote. 'The fingers on his left hand met the frets like strangers. They formed chords, re-formed them and then wandered away again. It was like watching somebody piece together a memory that had suffered the most severe shellshock . . .'

Also in the audience that first night at the Corn Exchange was Clive Welham, the drummer in Barrett's very first band. 'Syd just seemed to stand there, doing nothing, looking around, as if to say, "What's happening?"' remembers Clive. 'I left the gig early. I was almost close to tears. I couldn't stand to see him like that.'

'It was a disastrous gig,' conceded Twink. Barrett showed up on his doorstep, holding a copy of the *Melody Maker* review the morning it came out. 'Syd was really hung up about it. He said he didn't want to play any more.' Stars was over.

Barrett contained his anger until he was back at Hills Road. Ranting and raving, he smashed furniture, before retreating to his bedroom in the cellar. Once down there, he began smashing his head repeatedly against the ceiling.

CHAPTER SIX **NEW CAR, CAVIAR**

'You've got to be competitive, aggressive and egocentric – all the things that go to make a real star.'

Roger Waters

In London's cavernous Earls Court exhibition hall it is the favourite topic of conversation as showtime draws near. While the human traffic buzzes between the overpriced food stands, merchandise stalls stacked high with Floyd designer Storm Thorgerson's latest artistic creations, and bars dispensing warm beer in flimsy plastic cups, the question gets tossed back and forth: Will they or won't they do *Dark Side of the Moon*?

It is October 1994 and Pink Floyd have been on tour since April. Sometime in July, somewhere in the American Midwest, Pink Floyd had begun performing their 35-million-selling album in its entirety during the second half of the show. Since then, it has been played again randomly as the tour passed through Rotterdam, Basel, Hanover and Rome. London will strike it lucky. Six of Pink Floyd's fourteen completed gigs at Earls Court will feature the complete *Dark Side of the Moon*. Roger Waters' dissertation on the human condition is now twenty-one years old. Waters is gone, but his former colleagues and a team of hired hands will reproduce his finest forty-one minutes tonight, rolling back the years for those in the audience old enough to remember it first time around, and those younger who've discovered it since. It begins and ends with the sound of a human heartbeat, in between pinwheeling through the gamut of emotions and experience, exploring fear, failure, greed and insanity, beautifully played and packaged for a stadium audience.

It was all very different in 1972.

'Due to severe mechanical and electric horror we can't do any more of that bit, so we'll do something else . . .'

Roger Waters made his announcement about twenty minutes into the first performance of Pink Floyd's new piece at The Dome, Brighton on 20 January. The plan had been to open the show with their latest work in progress, still unrecorded, but supposedly entitled *Dark Side of the Moon*. Struggling to play in time to a tape of sound effects, their equipment began misbehaving and the band ran aground, just a few bars into a song that in a year's time would be known as 'Money', and which would help turn Pink Floyd into one of the biggest bands on the planet. In reality, it wasn't the taxing nature of the band's new music that was the problem. Just as in Pompeii, Floyd's mammoth sound and lighting rigs were being run from the same power source. Something had to give.

Frustrated, Waters and Gilmour stalked off stage. After a brief respite, they returned to strike up the opening bars to 'Atom Heart Mother'. Unfortunately, as Nick Mason later admitted when discussing the band's general frame of mind, 'We were in acute danger of dying of boredom.' That night, the cod orchestral rock concerto, albeit minus the orchestra, from 1969, sounded lacklustre and old hat. In a strange way, the band had run out of steam and lost their way yet again.

On the same night in Cambridge, Syd Barrett was jamming on stage at the King's College Cellars with the musicians that would make up his new band Stars. Yet his old group's planned musical venture couldn't have been further from Barrett's frayed twelve-bar blues.

Nick Mason's frustration with much of the group's existing material was shared by his bandmates. Roger Waters, especially, was keen to explore the direction the group had taken with 'Echoes', and to create another so-called 'epic sound poem' driven by a similar lyrical theme. Despite the red herring of the *Dark Side of the Moon* title, there was still an overwhelming desire to shake off the 'Space Rock' image, to write about real people, real emotions and real life.

Dark Side of the Moon (the definitive article would appear with the 2003 reissue) began the way most Pink Floyd albums began: with the band messing about in a studio for hours and seeing if they could come up with anything worthwhile. On 29 November 1971, having just completed a run of North American dates, the group booked five days at Decca Studios in West Hampstead, the same venue in which David Gilmour had once auditioned with Jokers Wild. Prior to this, they had held a band meeting at Nick Mason's house in Camden, where Roger Waters pitched an idea.

'I remember sitting in his [Mason's] kitchen, looking out at the garden and saying, "Hey, boys, I think I've got the answer,"' he recalled. Waters described his vision for a piece of music 'all about the pressures and difficulties and questions that crop up in one's life and create anxiety'.

'I remember Roger saying that he wanted to write it absolutely straight, clear and direct,' remembered Gilmour. 'To say exactly what he wanted to say for the first time and get away from psychedelic patter and strange and mysterious warblings.'

'That was always my big fight in Pink Floyd,' said Waters. 'To try and drag it kicking and screaming back from the borders of space, from the whimsy that Syd was into, to my concerns, which were much more political and philosophical.'

Now a twenty-nine-year-old married man, the bassist was still grappling with many of the same issues that had troubled him since adolescence. At the root of it all was his mother Mary's staunch belief, drummed into him from an early age, that he needed 'to get a decent education, a decent job, because you're going to want to have a family, so you need to prepare . . .' Roger had, he admitted, believed that he was still in the preparation stage when reality struck: 'I wasn't preparing for anything – I was right in the middle of it, and always had been. Fucking hell – this is it!'

With Waters' encouragement, the four effectively compiled a list of the things that troubled them at this stage in their lives. These ranged from the tedium and danger of air travel to a fear of growing old, the problems of organised religion, violence, greed and, most poignant in the light of their former singer's situation, insanity.

Further ideas would find their way into the lyrical mix as the work progressed, but for now, they needed some music. At Decca Studios, the band riffled through leftover ideas and snippets discarded from their previous albums. They revisited a gentle piano piece composed by Richard Wright, which had, bafflingly, been rejected by director Michelangelo Antonioni from the *Zabriskie Point* soundtrack two years earlier. It would take shape over the next few months and become 'Us and Them'. Another of the keyboard player's downbeat offerings would wind up as 'The Great Gig in the Sky'. Waters brought a couple of ragged home demos – just his voice and an acoustic guitar – that would form the basis of 'Money' and 'Time'. The band's magpie tendencies reappeared, with the bassist recycling the lyric 'breathe, breathe in the air . . .' from 'Give Birth to a Smile', a track on *The Body* soundtrack, as a starting point for the song that would eventually become 'Breathe'.

Progress on the new material stalled in December when Floyd flew to Paris to be filmed again for *Live At Pompeii*. Yet they began recording at Abbey Road Studios throughout January and February 1972, the sessions broken up by further writing stints and rehearsals at The Rolling Stones' warehouse studios in Bermondsey, South London. With further concert dates booked throughout the UK in February, the band were determined to have something new to play, if only to assuage their own boredom.

Although the Brighton Dome gig had ended badly, Floyd had at least had the chance to premiere some of their new material. Some of the taped special effects that would enhance the finished album were already being used. The opening song 'Breathe' was still in a formative stage, yet to acquire the sweet, distinctive pedal steel used on the final version. 'On the Run', then still called 'Travel Sequence', was seven minutes of jazz-rock noodling between Gilmour and Wright, and nothing like the urgent synthesiser-driven version on the record. Elsewhere, Wright fluffed his lines on a hesitant version of 'Time', and a prototype of 'The Great Gig in the Sky', then entitled 'Mortality Sequence', included a spoken-word section splicing extracts from St Paul's Epistle to the Corinthians with a monologue by Malcolm Muggeridge, the journalist and Christian scholar, then newsworthy for his involvement with the Festival of Light organisation, a pressure group dedicated to upholding Christian values. Muggeridge's colleague in the Festival of Light, the Christian campaigner Mary Whitehouse, would also feel the full brunt of Roger Waters' ire on a later Pink Floyd song.

Roadtesting up to forty minutes of new material live on stage offered a challenge to both the band and their audience. But at a time when rock music was desperate to be taken seriously as an artform, it was far less of a leap than it might be now. Floyd gigs had often been largely sedentary affairs, with some of the audience positively horizontal and shrouded in the sweet fug of any number of illegal cigarettes. Furthermore, as Waters explained, 'We wanted the audience to actually *listen*. And later on I'm afraid I used to get terribly annoyed when they didn't.'

February's run of gigs continued across the country, with *Dark Side of the Moon* being played in its entirety, such as it was, for the first time at Portsmouth Guildhall. There were still hurdles to be overcome: Coventry's Locarno Ballroom saw them unveiling their magnum opus at midnight after a set from crowd-pleasing showman Chuck Berry, while a gig at the Manchester Free Trade Hall was abandoned after just one and a half songs following a power cut. The real test of the band's mettle would be a four-night stand at the Rainbow Theatre at the end of the month; the London premiere of what was being touted as 'Dark Side of the Moon: A Piece for Assorted Lunatics'.

The band had also made a greater effort to ensure they sounded and looked their best. At the beginning of the year, they had taken delivery of a new, custom-built PA, complete with four-channel, 360-degree quadraphonic sound; a far cry from the 1967-era Azimuth Coordinator, with which Richard Wright panned their sound around the four corners of a venue from a gizmo on top of his Hammond organ. In this instance, looking their best didn't mean abandoning the ubiquitous Floyd uniform of T-shirts and jeans (usually the same jeans but a different T-shirt come showtime), but the deployment of a state-of-the art lighting rig, manned by new crew member Arthur Max, an outspoken

American whiz-kid whom the band had first met two years earlier as lighting engineer at San Francisco's Fillmore West. Max's greatest claim to fame had been that he'd worked a spotlight at the Woodstock Festival for three days straight.

Playing to full houses each night, the band opened the Rainbow shows with *Dark Side of the Moon*, followed by 'One of These Days' from *Meddle*, and closed with an encore of 'Echoes'. In between, they obliged only with the crowd-pleasing 'Set the Controls for the Heart of the Sun' and 'Careful With That Axe Eugene'. The message was explicit: the old Floyd was dead; long live the new Floyd. Although, a ghost from the past, an apparently gaunt-looking Syd Barrett, had been spotted in the audience at one of the shows. *Melody Maker*, seemingly back on message after the boxing glove incident of Christmas 1971, raved over 'burning flashlights, wind-blown sparkle dust and a trip to the dark side of the moon'. Derek Jewell of the *Sunday Times*, one of a new breed of Fleet Street critics determined to take rock music ever so seriously, slipped into a reverie about 'music overlaid with a maze of extra tapes which titillate the ears' before finally declaring, 'Floyd are dramatists supreme'.

Somewhere between the disastrous Brighton Dome gigs and the victorious Rainbow shows, Roger Waters had written a crucial part of the new piece, a dramatic grand finale entitled 'Eclipse'. 'I think I arrived at a gig with the song in my pocket,' Waters told writer John Harris. 'I said something like, "Here, lads, I've written an ending." '

Eclipse would briefly take over as the title of the album. The band changed the name under duress when it was discovered that folk rockers Medicine Head had released an album called *Dark Side of the Moon*. When the dust had settled and the album's sales turned out to be modest, Floyd reverted to the original title. As Gilmour explained at the time, 'It didn't sell well, so we thought what the hell . . .'

The only fly in the ointment was the news that a bootleg from the Rainbow Theatre was now on sale in the nation's less scrupulous record shops. According to some sources, it would go on to shift over 100,000 copies, with the band's new *pièce de résistance* still a year away from an official release.

In hindsight, then, the decision to temporarily abandon the making of the record and record a whole other album of new material seems astonishing. Barbet Schroeder, the French movie director for whom

Floyd had recorded the soundtrack for *More*, had placed another call. Schroeder's latest celluloid creation, *La Vallée*, needed some music. Floyd agreed and flew out to Strawberry Studios at Château d'Hérouville on the outskirts of Paris. The studio would be immortalised in the title of Elton John's album that year, *Honky Chateau*.

In another, unusually focused two-week recording session, Floyd broke with their usual tradition of interminable jamming. Armed with stopwatches, pens, paper and a rough cut of the film, they knuckled down and scored the individual sequences. They managed ten songs in fourteen days, despite flying off for a whistle-stop tour of Japan in the middle of it all. As Nick Mason would admit later, 'We had no scope for self-indulgence.'

Gilmour, who would later claim, in an uncharacteristic burst of enthusiasm, that he loved the resultant album, also warmed to the discipline. 'It was rapid stuff,' he said. 'We sat in a room, wrote, recorded, like a production line. It's good to work like that under extreme constraints of time and trying to meet someone else's needs.'

La Vallée itself was another spiritual quest in the style of *More*. The female lead, Viviane (played by Schroeder's wife Bulle Ogier), is married to a French diplomat, and visits the island of Papua New Guinea in search of rare birds' feathers to sell in her Paris boutique. She becomes distracted by hippie explorer Olivier and joins him to search for a mystical valley (marked on a map with the words 'obscured by clouds'). They encounter the indigenous people, she ditches her materialistic obsessions, and most of her clothes, and is somehow reborn. The Mapuga tribe of New Guinea, featured in the film, also made a vocal appearance on 'Absolutely Curtains', the closing track on the Floyd's soundtrack album. The film's preoccupations may seem rooted in a different era, but are really no different from the 2000 Hollywood blockbuster *The Beach*: essentially, it's all about the plight of shallow Westerners in search of Shangri-La.

The focus and excitement generated by the *Dark Side of the Moon* work-in-progress rubbed off on the soundtrack, which was eventually called *Obscured by Clouds*. The group were clearly no longer 'dying of boredom'. Firstly, the album made full use of Richard Wright's recently purchased VCS3 synthesiser, a piece of kit from the team behind the BBC Radiophonic Workshop, which would also be put to use on *Dark Side of the Moon*. Secondly, most of the tracks were credited to two or more band members (an unusually democratic move, in the light of future rows over songwriting credits). Finally, with no track longer than five and a half minutes, there was a rare sense of musical economy.

The instrumental title cut was an ominous synth-driven fanfare that suggested gathering storm clouds and was adopted as an intro during the next run of live dates. The following track, 'When You're In', built around an heroic-sounding guitar and keyboard figure, was another instrumental also worked into the set. The title was taken from a catchphrase used by the Floyd's roadie Chris Adamson.

Adamson, perhaps reviving Paul Newman's egg-eating stunt from the 1967 prison movie *Cool Hand Luke*, had livened up one day at the Honky Chateau by betting everyone that he could eat a stone of raw potatoes in one sitting. Bets were taken, and Adamson began slicing the vegetables and dousing them in salt. 'To give him his due, he got through about two and a half pounds before he said, "Fuck it," ' recalled Roger Waters. 'They're full of starch so it would definitely have killed him if he'd managed to get them all down.' Adamson would show up later on *Dark Side of the Moon*, uttering the now famous line: 'I've been mad for fucking years.'

Of the vocal tracks on *Obscured by Clouds*, 'Burning Bridges' arrived first, a gentle Waters and Wright creation in a similar vein to *Meddle*'s 'Pillow of Winds', and 'Breathe' from *Dark Side of the Moon*. Elsewhere, Wright's reflective piano and voice on 'Stay' suggested the languid, roach-in-the-ashtray feel of Steely Dan's debut album, *Can't Buy a Thrill*, released the same year. In an interview with *New Musical Express* that summer, the keyboard player named *Your Saving Grace*, a 1969 album by the Californian guitarist Steve Miller, as one of his favourite records. Aptly, then, four of the other vocal tracks, 'Childhood's End', 'The Gold It's in the . . .', 'Wot's . . . Uh the Deal' and 'Free Four', were all steeped in country, blues and folk-rock influences. For a band that three years before had sounded quintessentially English, Pink Floyd had acquired a disarmingly American lilt. 'Wot's . . . Uh the Deal' was reprised by David Gilmour for his 2006 solo tour, acknowledging its status as one of Pink Floyd's great lost songs. The acoustic guitars suggest a front-porch jamming session in Topanga Canyon, with Neil Young and Stephen Stills looking on, blowing dope smoke rings. Wright also plays a wonderful, understated piano solo that gives added credibility to producer John Leckie's observation that his piano playing was often a highlight of any Floyd recording session.

In contrast, Gilmour's electric guitar honks and chugs on 'The Gold It's in the . . .' rattling away behind a simplistic lyric before running away into a long, whinnying guitar solo of which the similarly honking and chugging Steve Miller would be proud.

Roger Waters' solo composition 'Free Four' remains the album's biggest surprise. The lyric explored what would quickly become familiar terrain for the bass player including a stark reference to his father's death in the Second World War. ' "Free Four" has got all that stuff,' said Gilmour, years later. 'Which is where *The Wall* and *The Final Cut* came from.' Yet whatever the gravitas of its subject, the lyrics were yoked to a nursery-rhyme guitar riff that in part sounds like David Gilmour spoofing Marc Bolan.

Despite its black lyrics, the gonzo riff of 'Free Four' was perfect for American FM radio. Floyd still stoically refused to release singles in the UK, but made an exception for America. 'Free Four' garnered enough airplay in the States to engender a minor breakthrough. *Obscured by Clouds* was released worldwide in June 1972, and reached number 46 in the US, the first time a Pink Floyd album had cracked the American Top 50.

Despite some striking cinematography, *La Vallée*, the movie, didn't fare quite so well (even garnering an entry in the 1986 compendium *The World's Worst Movies*). But for its director Barbet Schroeder, the soundtrack proved a point to the band. 'I liked the album very much,' he says now. 'I do think it surprised the Pink Floyd that they could make such a good album in just two weeks. Perhaps they shouldn't have taken so long in the studio on all those other records.'

'It's one of the annoying things, that the difference between something we spent a week on and something that takes nine months isn't that great,' admitted Nick Mason. 'I mean, the thing that takes nine months isn't thirty-six times as good.'

The front cover design was also not so good. Courtesy of Hipgnosis, it featured a heavily blurred image from the movie, of one of the characters, obscured by foliage, reaching out to pick fruit from the branches of a tree. Storm Thorgerson and Aubrey 'Po' Powell had settled on the image after sifting through numerous 35mm slides from the film in search of something, anything, to stick on the cover. When one particular slide was jammed into their film projector, the image became blurred.

'Suddenly, in front of our very eyes, the out-of-focus quality imbued an ordinary image with more transcendental qualities,' wrote Thorgerson in his book *Mind Over Matter*. 'Or so we told Barbet.'

'They [the band] knew they had another Pink Floyd album coming out soon and didn't want *Obscured by Clouds* stealing the show,' laughs Schroeder. 'So they made sure the cover wasn't too appealing. I thought it was very funny.' A claim Thorgerson now rigorously denies.

Although the band made some muddled comments about *Obscured by Clouds* not being a 'proper Pink Floyd record', and 'just a collection of songs', it quickly secured a number 6 placing in the UK. In America, *Circus* magazine applauded their latest efforts: 'Pink Floyd can rocket bizarrely from one end of the musical spectrum to the other and come back with songs in their pockets.' In the UK, the ever-faithful *Disc and Music Echo* was still making do with the same science fiction metaphors: 'Blasts through your head with aural sunbursts synthesized from some dark, sinister corner of the solar system.'

Yet in the week that *Obscured by Clouds* was released, Floyd were busy with another month-long stint at Abbey Road, recording more of the 'aural sunbursts' that would make up their next album. Abbey Road had finally installed the sixteen-track machines they hadn't installed in time for *Meddle*. Floyd would produce themselves, but were joined by studio engineer Alan Parsons. The twenty-three-year-old had worked as assistant engineer on The Beatles' *Abbey Road*, which had led to a similar role on Paul McCartney's debut solo album. Now a staff engineer on a £35-a-week salary, Parsons had cut his teeth with Pink Floyd as a tape operator on some of the *Ummagumma* sessions and as a mixing engineer on *Atom Heart Mother*. He was used to the Floyd way of working.

'They would come into the studio and have no idea of what they were going to do, and just start improvising,' says Alan now. 'But the improvisation period had definitely become a lot more structured by the time of *Dark Side of the Moon*. Mainly because they'd been playing it live. They didn't have to mess around with the compositions. It was an excellent piece of music to see coming together.'

Basic tracks for 'Us and Them', 'Money', 'Time' and 'The Great Gig in the Sky' would be completed over the next eight weeks. According to Parsons, the band's work ethic also depended on the distractions around them, primarily BBC2's surreal comedy show *Monty Python's Flying Circus* and televised football matches, of which Arsenal FC fan Waters was particularly keen.

With the band distracted, Parsons was free to produce a rough mix of whatever they'd just been working on, and add his own ideas. 'I was one of a new breed of engineers that didn't mind making criticisms or suggestions that would normally be made by a producer . . . You could have argued that I should have kept my big mouth shut. And sometimes I did, and sometimes I didn't.'

One of the engineer's suggestions related to Richard Wright's composition, 'The Great Gig in the Sky', then still being referred to as 'The Religious Section' or 'The Mortality Sequence'. Live, it was performed on the Hammond, and augmented with spoken-word taped effects. Wright played it instead on a grand piano in Abbey Road's Studio One, thinking the rest of the group were playing along next door in Studio Two. Instead, they'd played him a tape of themselves doing so from an earlier take, taking great delight in surprising him in the doorway when the take was finished. Despite the prank, when the group listened back to Wright's piano version, they realised it was far superior to what they'd been playing live, and was, as Parsons later claimed, 'one of the best things Rick Wright ever did'. Yet the engineer still had a nagging feeling that the song needed some extra element, and, on a whim, dubbed on some dialogue of astronauts in space, taken from the NASA recording archives. 'I think I did it while they were off watching a football game,' says Parsons. But he quickly met with the Floyd's disapproval. 'I thought it worked very well . . . They didn't think so.'

'Us and Them' had already been knocked into shape on the road, but it would be another few months before the band included its now distinctive saxophone solo. This time, the song's dream-like quality and snail's pace was heightened by the slow delay running through the piece and feeding back and forth through the sound. Without modern-day flangers or samplers to do the job for them, the band and Parsons relied on their own sense of timing and expertise. When played live, 'Time' had previously sounded unfinished and too slow. In the studio, Gilmour weighed in with a far more assertive vocal and what would prove to be one of the most exciting guitar solos on the album.

'Money' also presented a challenge. In the live show, the song had been accompanied by a tape loop, created by Waters in his garden shed/studio. Roger had commandeered one of wife Judy's potter's bowls and, with a hand-held tape recorder, captured the sound of coins thrown into the bowl. To produce the same sound on record, the loop had to be re-recorded. The band had now decided that the album should be released in quadraphonic, as well as stereo; an added complication which would backfire when the album was released, as few record buyers owned quadraphonic sound systems on which to play it. The aim, then, was for the sound effects to essentially 'circle' the room. This meant that each of the sounds they wanted to include – the coins, the ringing cash register, the sound of money (in reality, just paper) being torn up – all had to be recorded on different tracks.

Five individual lengths of tape ended up circling the studio, held tight by carefully positioned microphone stands to prevent them becoming chewed up in the machines. 'It was,' as Nick Mason later recalled, 'all *very* Heath Robinson.' It was also something that can now be achieved in a studio in a matter of a few seconds with the press of a button.

Musically, 'Money' was an even greater break from the Floyd tradition. The tricksy, 7/4 riff proved a challenge for Nick Mason ('It was incredibly difficult to play along with'), and the tempo varies even on the finished album. The unusually funky feel also made it the 'blackest' Pink Floyd song to date. 'Nice white English architecture students getting funky,' was Gilmour's description of the song later. As well as delivering a fiery guitar solo, Gilmour was also free to squeeze in some of his R&B and soul influences from the Jokers Wild days, notably Booker T & The MGs.

Like his predecessor John Leckie, who'd engineered the *Meddle* album, Parsons quickly discovered that the band were rarely given to expressions of outright enthusiasm, even when things were going well. 'It was always very low-key, very calm. After an amazing guitar solo, Roger would turn around and say something like, "Oh, I think we might be able to get away with that one."'

With yet another American tour pending, the group took most of the summer off, but decided to spend it together. A vacationing party of

Gilmour, Waters, Wright (Nick Mason stayed behind, as Lindy was now pregnant with the couple's first child), Steve O'Rourke, girlfriends, wives, drug buddies and sparring partners decamped to Lindos. Here, they hired a boat, rented a villa, sunbathed, drank, smoked, played endless games of backgammon and locked conversational swords with fellow guests Germaine Greer, author of the recent feminist tome, *The Female Eunuch*, and the artist Caroline Coon, a contemporary from the UFO club days, who had set up the drugs charity Release in the early sixties.

'I was in ecstasy about finally having a few weeks off that summer,' says Caroline. 'But I found myself in the Pink Floyd stronghold of Lindos. I'd come from a very upper-class background but had been thrown out of home when I was eighteen and was now absolutely poor. I got into this terrible argument with Roger Waters. I was talking about how there was a need for the wealthy to give money to the poor and for rock groups to do more free gigs. Roger said something terribly cutting, about how the reason the country was falling apart – with the unions on strike – was due to the slackness of the working classes. I contradicted him, and he came back with some suitably smug comment.'

Unknown at the time, Roger Waters' personal wealth was about to increase immeasurably. Despite the balmy surroundings of Lindos, there was business to attend to. Floyd's lack of progress in the US had long been a source of discontent. The band were signed to EMI's partner and subsidiary Capitol in America, but were languishing on Tower Records, an offshoot that dealt mostly with jazz and folk acts, but had none of the cachet of Harvest Records in the UK. Floyd had one more album, *Dark Side of the Moon*, left on their Capitol contract, and, by the summer of 1972, were in the market for a new deal.

Jeff Dexter, the former Middle Earth DJ, was now managing the folk-rock duo America and sharing an office with Steve O'Rourke. He had also joined the Floyd and friends in Lindos. America's debut album had been released that year on Warners, and Jeff Dexter's closeness to Pink Floyd's management was such that he helped bring the company's new president, Joe Smith, into the running. Atlantic Records' head honcho Ahmet Ertegün, who'd previously signed Led Zeppelin to the label, was also circling. Both parties were aware of the band's success outside of America, and, with Atlantic and Warners merging to become the WEA group, believed they could break them properly in the States. Meanwhile, Capitol had appointed a new president, former Delhi and Oxford Universities graduate Bhaskar Menon, who was determined to halt the company's poor track record with the Floyd.

'Steve O'Rourke was playing the game,' says Dexter now. 'He wanted to let everyone know that things were up for sale. So between Joe and Ahmet and Bhaskar Menon, he had a sort of auction going over a period of a few months . . . There was one telephone in the whole village, and it was half a mile from the beach. We had a nickname for the guy that ran the phone office. We called him Yani Ring Ring. Every time we had a call, Yani would stand at the top of the square and call out over the village to where we were all lying around on the beach . . . Of course, I was running back and forth all day taking their phone calls as well as my own. One day we were on the beach, and a call came in for Steve from Ertegün. Steve said, "Look Jeff, you've got to talk to them for me. Talk to Ahmet and tell him to fuck off." Ahmet and Joe Smith both thought they were going to get the Floyd.'

It was a prime example of the bombastic O'Rourke's unstinting defence of the band. But his attitude did have its drawbacks.

'I sometimes wondered what made the Floyd keep Steve,' offers Storm Thorgerson. 'Roger later denounced him. But he was very useful to the band. Unfortunately, the bullishness that was useful against record companies, or anyone else that might abuse the Floyd, was not that useful when turned on those nearest and dearest. He didn't need to bully me, but he did. Steve had his qualities otherwise they wouldn't have kept him, but those qualities didn't always need to be utilised among the inner circle.'

In the end, neither Ahmet Ertegün nor Joe Smith would sign Pink Floyd.

With fourteen dates booked in North America, there was further opportunity to hone the new album in front of the public. Alan Parsons had now been recruited to look after the front-of-house sound, beginning a trend for Floyd's studio engineers joining them on the road. Buoyed by the success of *Obscured by Clouds*, the band's popularity as a live act in America was starting to grow. In September they booked into the open-air Hollywood Bowl. Far bigger than the 12,000-seater venues they usually played, the gig failed to sell out, but was a spectacular showcase for both their new work and their most striking light show to date.

'We hired four of those searchlights that they use at film premieres,' said Gilmour. 'We fanned them out backstage and pointed them at the sky, creating a pyramid over the stage.' Within two years, the band would take the pyramid of light idea to another level completely.

Back in the UK in October, they sold out the Wembley Empire Pool at a benefit gig for the charities War on Want and Save the Children, filling the stage with dry ice, letting off flash bombs and setting Roger Waters' beloved gong on fire for a grand finale of 'Set the Controls for the Heart of the Sun'. Reviewing the show, *Sounds* praised 'a faultless demonstration of what psychedelic music is all about'.

The Wembley show interrupted another burst of activity at Abbey Road, as the band made progress on the songs they hadn't tackled in the summer. Two instrumental pieces, 'The Travel Section' (originally called 'The Travel Sequence' and later titled 'On the Run') and 'Any Colour You Like', were recorded. The first was still a conventional jam, and would undergo a further radical transformation before the album was finished. 'Any Colour You Like' provided a necessary bridge between 'Us and Them' and the penultimate 'Brain Damage', but was not crucial to the narrative of the album. 'We used to do very long, extended jamming on stage,' said Gilmour. 'Interminable, many people would say, and probably rightly . . . and that's what that one came out of.' A two-chord jam dominated by Gilmour and Wright, the guitarist played through a pair of Leslie speakers with the express purpose of capturing the same sound Eric Clapton had achieved on Cream's 'Badge'.

On 'Brain Damage', Waters took his first lead vocal of the album ('He was very shy about singing,' said Gilmour, 'so I tried to encourage him'). If Waters' voice wasn't as strong as his bandmate's, he had the benefit of being joined by four female backing vocalists hired for the sessions. English singer-songwriter Lesley Duncan had previously sung for the Dave Clark Five and Donovan, and had seen her own songs covered by Elton John and Olivia Newton-John. Liza Strike was another prolific English session singer who'd appeared on Elton John's 1971 album *Madman Across the Water*. Barry St John was another of Elton's backing singers. An American, then living in London, she'd also sung on the first solo album of Daevid Allen, founder member of Soft Machine.

Completing the quartet was Doris Troy, a New York-born soul singer, who'd been recording since the early sixties after being discovered by James Brown. She'd released a solo album on The Beatles' Apple label in 1970, and had sung back-up on The Rolling Stones' *Let It Bleed*. A formidable talent with the presence to match, Doris was an Abbey Road regular, and was given to disguising her inability to sight-read by tossing aside any sheet music put in front of her during a session, declaring, 'Get that outta here. I don't need that!'

As well as 'Brain Damage', the quartet made their presence felt on 'Us And Them', 'Time' and the album's dramatic closing moment, 'Eclipse', which contained a compelling gospel-style ad-lib from Strike and Troy. 'Dave Gilmour was running the session,' Liza Strike told writer John Harris. 'He knew exactly what he wanted. Even when we were ad-libbing, he told me what to sing.'

Gilmour was also instrumental in hiring saxophonist Dick Parry for the June sessions. Dick was a jazz musician and mainstay of the Cambridge club circuit ('Part of the Cambridge Mafia', according to Nick Mason). He and Gilmour had often played together during Sunday night sessions at the Dorothy Ballroom in the sixties. Yet Parry's recruitment was based on something else besides his musical talent. 'We didn't know anyone,' admitted Gilmour. 'We were so insular in some ways. We really didn't know how to get hold of a sax player. And it can be tedious bringing in these brisk, professional session men. A bit intimidating.'

Parry delivered a gentle solo on 'Us and Them', punctuating the verses and choruses while never intruding on the rest of the instrumentation. On 'Money' he came in harder, matching Gilmour's raucous solo with a brassy outburst that fulfilled his loose instruction from the band to play something like the cartoon saxophonist that appeared alongside the theme music for the Pearl and Dean ads screened in cinemas at the time.

Undeterred by his rejected idea for the early version of 'The Great Gig in the Sky', Alan Parsons found his next brainwave met with a more positive response. Shortly before starting work on *Dark Side of the Moon*, Parsons had made a recording designed to demonstrate the effects of quadraphonic sound, comprising various clock sounds. 'I made the recordings in an antique clock shop not far from the studio,' said Parsons. 'I went out with a portable tape machine and got the owner to stop all the other clocks in the shop, and record each one at a time. I then comped them together at Abbey Road.'

The assembled ticks, chimes and alarm bells would then be spliced onto the beginning of 'Time'. Following the explosive din, guaranteed to shake any stoned listener out of their torpor, came another new sound. Just as the band had featured instruments left in the studio at Abbey Road on *The Piper at the Gates of Dawn*, a set of rototoms discovered in the studio found their way onto the intro to 'Time'. These were single drumheads stretched over a frame, which could be tuned to a specific pitch. Against Gilmour's guitar and Wright's piano, Mason delivered measured beats on the tuned drums, ramping up the tension for over two minutes before the first verse began.

By the end of the month, with more work on the album still to be done, the band were back on tour. There was, after all, a ballet to be performed.

Pink Floyd's collaboration with Ballet de Marseille had finally come to fruition, after twelve months of toing and froing. Floyd performed five shows at Salle Valliers in Marseilles in November 1972, before taking the show to the Palais de Sports in Paris in January the following year.

The programme included three pieces: 'Allumez Les Etoiles' (Light the Stars), a ballet based around the Russian Revolution, with music by Mussorgsky and Prokofiev; 'La Rose Malade' (The Sick Rose), based on the William Blake poem of the same name; and, finally, the prosaically titled 'The Pink Floyd Ballet', during which the band performed 'Echoes', 'One of These Days', 'Careful With That Axe Eugene', 'Obscured by Clouds' and 'When You're In'. Roland Petit's choreographed routines included performances from Ballet de Marseille stars Rudy Bryans and Danièle Jossi; the latter apparently dragged across the stage in the full splits position, much to the dismay of the assembled rock press, unused to such athleticism.

There were the inevitable cock-ups. In Marseilles, an elongated version of 'One of These Days' meant the dancers had completed their routine some minutes before the song ended, making for a hesitant exit from the stage with the Floyd still pounding away. As a precaution, Floyd ordered one of their hangers-on to sit beneath Richard Wright's piano and hold up cards with the number of bars written down on them.

He was instructed to hold up a new card after every four beats, effectively letting the band know where they were in the piece they were playing. On most nights, though, the assembled rock fans were in no mood to sit through two ballets before the main attraction, and began heckling and shouting for the Floyd during the first act.

'It was fantastically offensive,' complained Nick Mason at the time. 'Roland [Petit] did what is an old Floyd routine – he just went out and harangued the audience, told them to go and have a drink until there was something they did want to see.' Like *Atom Heart Mother*'s collaboration between group and orchestra, the mutual love-in between hairy, heavy rock and classical ballet made sense for the times, and, as Nick Mason later confessed, 'appealed to a certain intellectual snobbery among us'.

Roland Petit would try to get the band to commit to similar projects. Plans to take the show to Canada stalled when the government refused to allow the use of Communist red flags in 'Allumez Les Etoiles'. Later, the ballet star Rudolf Nureyev and film director Roman Polanski both became involved in Petit's schemes. There was a boozy lunch meeting at Polanski's house in Richmond with Mason, Waters and Steve O'Rourke. Various themes were mooted – Proust (again), Frankenstein, the Arabian Nights. Roger Waters subsequently recalled Polanski and Nureyev sunbathing in the garden in their underpants. As Waters later griped, 'It was a complete joke, because nobody had any idea what they wanted to do.'

'In the end,' offered Gilmour, 'the reality of all these people prancing around in tights in front of us didn't feel like what we wanted to do in the long term.'

By the second week of January 1973, Floyd were back at Abbey Road for the final push on *Dark Side of the Moon*. One of the first songs they went back to tackle was 'Travel Sequence'. In concert it had been a formless guitar jam, sometimes lasting up to seven minutes. The band turned to their new toy, the VCS3 synthesisers for inspiration. Peter Zinovieff, who'd previously worked at the BBC Radiophonic Workshop, had built the machine, and kept the first model in his garden shed in South London. 'I visited his home and he had this machine all around the wall, floor to ceiling, hundreds of components, masses of wires,' remembered David Gilmour.

The band had bought a scaled-down version of the synthesiser and taken it to France for the *Obscured by Clouds* sessions. By their own admission they couldn't work out how to get any actual notes out of it or use it properly as a keyboard. 'No one had told us how to,' said Gilmour. As such, its presence can be heard on the album, if largely confined to a sequence of gothic-sounding drones.

A few months later, and a compact version of the VCS3, the Synthi A, found its way to Abbey Road. The original VCS3 was used on 'Breathe', while the Synthi A found its way into 'Brain Damage', 'Time', 'Any Colour You Like' and, most importantly, 'Travel Sequence'. Waters and Gilmour programmed an eight-note sequence into the machine, against which the band added a mêlée of backwards-recorded cymbals, slide guitar, a Farfisa organ, and the ghostly sounding footsteps of Alan Parsons' assistant Peter James. An explosion taken from the Abbey Road library of special effects completed the piece. The maddening synth rhythm became the standout feature of the track, which would now be retitled 'On the Run'. It was unlike anything Pink Floyd had recorded before.

In the meantime, Adrian Maben had made yet another approach to the group. 'I had been fly-fishing with Roger Waters,' said Maben, 'and we vaguely discussed the idea of doing an extended version of *Live At Pompeii*. The band was about to embark on a new recording. Roger somehow managed to persuade the other members of the group, and, after a few months of telephone calls, hesitations and cancellations, I was invited to film certain parts of the recording of *Dark Side of the Moon*.'

Maben's specially shot footage from January 1973 would become as compelling as the scenes filmed in Pompeii itself. In the space of just over twelve months, Pink Floyd had undergone a significant change. The footage of the band at work in Abbey Road retains a certain time-capsule charm. Spot the countless smouldering cigarettes, a reminder of when smoking was still permitted in the workplace, or Richard Wright's patterned jumper, straight out of a Christmas 1972 stocking, not to mention the spaghetti junction of cables and leads around the pre-digital studio. Wright plays the haunting piano sequence for 'Us and Them', Gilmour is seen tearing off a guitar solo for 'Brain Damage' ('Where would rock 'n' roll be without feedback?' he quips to the control room), while Waters is filmed manhandling the Synthi A for 'On the Run'.

Yet the most enduring scenes were those filmed in the archaic-looking Abbey Road canteen. The four are seen seated at what could conceivably have been a boarding school dining table, preparing for a classic mid-1970s carbohydrate overload. Nick Mason's order, 'Can I have egg, sausage, chips and beans . . . and a tea?' date-stamps the footage as much as his Zapata moustache ever could.

Amid much slurping and gnawing, Roger Waters clambers onto his high horse to challenge the claim – made off camera by a person unknown – that a broad knowledge of music is not an essential qualification for a record producer. Floyd manager Steve O'Rourke is mentioned. Waters' tone becomes fabulously haughty: 'Steve knows what rock 'n' roll's about, but he's got no idea what the equipment's about and he's got very little idea – in terms of technicalities – what the music's about.' At some point, the same unknown voice pipes up, 'We all know you're God Almighty, Roger.'

Just as in Paris a year earlier, it is the bass player that dominates proceedings. At the far end of the table, Wright chews away, largely ignoring the argument, Mason asks a minion to fetch him a slice of apple pie ('no crust'), and Gilmour concentrates on his own meal, offering a knowing, ruminative smile to the camera.

The band, minus Wright, are interviewed individually and are all slightly more forthcoming than they were in Paris, though Gilmour manages to evade a question about drugs. 'I still think that most people see us as a drug-oriented group . . . Of course, we're not . . .' He smirks. 'You can trust us.'

'I'm a bit embarrassed by that young chap in *Live At Pompeii*,' said Gilmour in 2006. 'I find it excruciating, because he was pretentious and naive.'

For a record that subsequently acquired a reputation as a classic 'stoner' album, none of those involved in *Dark Side of the Moon* recall, or admit to, any significant use during its making. Alcohol was officially banned at Abbey Road, but that didn't stop Pink Floyd having a bar and an ice bucket, and keeping a fridge stocked with Southern Comfort. Cocaine would find its way onto the subsequent tour, but there was, by all accounts, none of it in the studio – only the occasional joint.

'Some of the interview bits done in the canteen at EMI are really funny,' said Waters later. 'You can see we were fucking stoned. Dave and

I were completely out of our brains. I was going through a stage where I was giving up nicotine, so I'd roll a joint every morning. I was out of my brain for a couple of years, pretending not to smoke cigarettes.'

Of the three interviews it is the resolutely un-stoned Nick Mason that offers the most honest comment. 'Unfortunately, we mark a sort of era,' he admits. 'We're in danger of becoming a relic of the past. For some people we represent their childhood: 1967, Underground London, the free concert in Hyde Park . . .'

As the new songs developed, so too did the themes behind them, broadening out from Waters' initial abstract ponderings on the pressures of modern life. The pressures had now become more specific. The damning lyric of wartime cannon fodder in 'Us and Them' seems inextricably linked to the Vietnam War then still occupying the headlines, and infiltrating American politics via the Watergate scandal of 1972. The song also, inevitably, touched on the fate of his father.

'Time' was even more explicit in its handwringing, fretting over unfulfilled hopes and dreams, as well as containing another outright reference to Waters' childhood and not knowing when real life was about to begin. The song's denunciation of the rat race was also a nod to the human worker ants that Waters and Judy Trim used to watch day after day from their Shepherds Bush flat, and which had so inspired the song 'Echoes'. Similar inspiration had come from a message spray-painted on a wall near their local tube station in the late sixties.

'If you got the tube at Goldhawk Road, there was this inspired bit of graffiti,' recalled Waters. 'It said: "Get up, go to work, do your job, come home, go to bed, get up, go to work . . ." It was on this wall and seemed to go on for ever, and as the train sped up, it would go by quicker and quicker until – bang! – you suddenly went into a tunnel.'

While Waters couldn't have made his preoccupations – fear, death, violence – more topical and more removed from the old cosmic flights of fancy, there was still one pressing theme that linked the new music to the past. One day Waters had been seated in the Abbey Road canteen when he suddenly felt himself, in his words, 'recede'. The sound of the people next to him talking became indistinct, and everything he saw seemed to diminish in size. He was not, he insisted, stoned. Getting up from the table, he went back into the studio and waited for the feelings to subside. He would later claim that he thought he was going mad and had been on the verge of a nervous breakdown. The parallels with Syd Barrett were unavoidable.

The theme of madness had now become central to the new album, most explicit on its closing 'Brain Damage' and 'Eclipse'. 'When I say, "I'll see you on the dark side of the moon", what I mean is, "If you feel that you're the only one . . . that you seem crazy cos you think everything is crazy, you're not alone,"' explained Waters. 'There's a camaraderie involved in the idea of people who are prepared to walk the dark places alone. A number of us are willing to open ourselves up to all those possibilities. You're not alone!'

'Syd's mother blamed me entirely for his illness,' said Waters years after the event. 'I was supposed to have taken him off to the fleshpots of London and destroyed his brain with drugs' (a suggestion refuted by Libby Gausden: 'I don't think Win blamed him for anything. I think Syd would have gone off the rails an awful lot sooner if it hadn't been for Roger Waters'). While trying to shake off the ghost of Barrett in public, and distance themselves from his era, 'Brain Damage' seemed to be about Barrett's experience, and the 'Is he or isn't he mad?' dilemma that had so frustrated the group. This time, though, Waters had written a happier ending to the story. The exultant gospel vocals of 'Eclipse' and the penultimate line of 'everything under the sun is in tune' suggested that we may *all* be mad, but there is still hope.

During the final sessions for the album, Waters had another brain-wave. While the songs were now almost complete, he suggested recording snippets of speech to be woven into the songs, linking the narrative and tapping into the lyrics. He compiled a series of questions relating to death, violence and insanity, and wrote them down on separate pieces of card. These were turned face down on a music stand in Studio Three. Each would-be speaker would then be invited to turn up a card, answer the question, then turn up the second card and answer the next question which would be linked to the first, for example: 'When was the last time you were violent?' followed by 'Were you in the right?'

Potential interviewees were rounded up at Abbey Road. From the band's immediate circle of roadies came potato-eating champion Chris Adamson, Peter Watts and his then wife Patricia (nicknamed Puddie), roadie Bobby Richardson, aka 'Liverpool Bobby', and another occasional Floyd road crew member, Roger 'the Hat' Manifold.

Scouring the building, Waters also collared Gerry O'Driscoll, a middle-aged Irishman employed as a handyman and caretaker, alongside Paul and Linda McCartney and guitarist Henry McCulloch, who, as Wings, were recording the album *Red Rose Speedway* at the same studio. Alan Parsons was also invited to take part, but on being asked, 'What do you think *Dark Side of the Moon* is all about?' confessed to not being able to come up with an interesting answer, and found his contribution cut. Strangely, the same fate would befall Paul and Linda. Waters was looking for spontaneity and candid, off-the-cuff remarks. The former Beatle and his wife were both too guarded, too keen to put on an act. As Waters would complain later, 'He was trying to be *funny*, which wasn't what we wanted at all.'

Replying to questions such as 'Are you afraid of dying?' and 'Do you ever think you're going mad?', the other contributions proved far more revealing and, in the context of the finished album, atmospheric. The opening track, 'Speak to Me', collaged sounds lifted from elsewhere on the album – ticking clocks, jangling coins – set against an eerie, booming heartbeat. But its most striking elements were Peter Watts' deranged laughter, and Chris Adamson and Gerry O'Driscoll's pronouncements: 'I've been mad for fucking years – absolutely years' and 'I've always been mad, I know I've been mad, like most of us have . . .'

Similar snippets of speech now peppered the rest of the album. Waters had lost the question cards by the time he'd tracked down Roger the Hat, and was forced to bluff it. The roadie's answers were funny, candid and among the most memorable on the record, as he can be heard recalling a road rage incident with a motorist in North London, in response to the question, 'When was the last time you were violent?'

'If you give 'em a quick, short, sharp shock, they won't do it again,' he explains. 'I mean, he got off lightly, cos I would've give him a thrashing . . .'

The speech was slipped in alongside Wright's gentle keyboards on 'Us and Them'. Elsewhere, on the fade-out groove of 'Money', Puddie and Henry McCulloch were among those justifying the last time they'd hit someone. Puddie, the only female interviewee, is emphatic: 'That geezer was cruising for a bruising.' McCulloch offers an even simpler explanation: 'Why does anyone do anything? Who knows? I was really drunk at the time.' Gerry O'Driscoll's would be the last voice heard on the album, his soft Irish accent punctuating the last few bars of 'Eclipse': 'There is no dark side of the moon. Matter of fact, it's all dark.'

Waters' quest for 'honest, human voices' had worked perfectly.

In Adrian Maben's footage from Paris six months earlier, the band had, in a rare moment of candour, admitted to conflict. 'We understand each other very well,' explains a rather earnest Richard Wright. 'We're very tolerant of each other, but there are a lot of things unsaid . . . I feel . . . sometimes . . .' At which point the keyboard player looks rather dolefully at the camera. 'How do you get over the difficult times?' asks Maben. 'I don't know how,' answers Wright, 'but we do.'

'Our working relationship was still good during the making of *Dark Side*,' Gilmour later told *Mojo* magazine. 'On *Dark Side*, as on all the records, we had massive rows about the way it should be, but they were about passionate beliefs in what we were doing.' In this case, Gilmour and Waters' passionate but conflicting beliefs were about how the album should actually *sound*. As Nick Mason later recalled, 'At times, three separate mixes were done by different individuals – a system which, in the past, had tended to resolve matters, as a consensus normally developed towards a particular mix. But even this was not working.'

'We argued so much that it was suggested we get a third opinion,' explained Gilmour. The guitarist favoured a warmer sound ('I wanted it to be big and swampy') and preferred the spoken-word segments to appear more subtly in the mix. This was also largely Wright's preferred choice. Roger was still in thrall to the sound of John Lennon's Plastic Ono Band record, and favoured a cleaner, drier mix, with the spoken word segments more dominant. Nick Mason also favoured this approach.

The band took the decision to bring in an outside mediator, or 'umpire' as David Gilmour later called the role. 'Chris Thomas came in for the mixes,' he said. 'His role was essentially to stop the arguments between me and Roger.' Thomas was a friend of Steve O'Rourke's, had worked as producer George Martin's assistant on The Beatles' *White Album*, and had just produced John Cale's *Paris 1919* album.

'The band felt they needed a fresh pair of ears,' said Thomas in 2003.

'Someone who could say, "Can we put some more compression on the guitars?" or "Can we have more echo on that?"'

Time may have healed some wounds, but when Parsons talks about the decision to bring in Thomas at this late stage in the album, he chooses his words carefully. 'I'm not sure there *was* a huge conflict on the way the album should be mixed. As the engineer I would have preferred it if my voice had been as loud as anyone else. But Chris made his voice heard. At the end of the day, we were dealing with subtleties by now. Chris didn't turn the album from being one thing into another.'

During these final weeks, though, Thomas would become involved in the decision to add extra guitars to 'Money', reduce the number of guitars in 'Us and Them', and apply the finishing touches to the album's sixty-second fanfare, 'Speak to Me'. 'The Great Gig in the Sky' also came under scrutiny. While the band had now opted for a piano, rather than an organ-led version, there was still something missing. Parsons's NASA archive sound effects may have been rejected, but a voice of some sort was needed. Parsons decided to call session singer Clare Torry.

'There was a chap who worked at Abbey Road called Dennis,' says Clare now. 'Dennis paid all the musicians. He gave Alan my number. But when he rang me, I said I couldn't do it. I didn't even know what the job was. It was a Friday evening and I told them I was working. But that was a lie because I was going with my then boyfriend to see Chuck Berry at the Hammersmith Odeon, and I didn't want to miss that. I suggested Sunday evening. They agreed. I asked who it was and Alan said, Pink Floyd. I was like, "Oh." I wasn't really a big fan.'

Torry, a session singer and songwriter, was a regular at Abbey Road, and had sung on numerous albums of cover versions, in which the popular hits of the day were re-recorded by unnamed sessioners. Parsons had heard one such album, and had decided to call her rather than one of the other backing singers already used on the album.

On Sunday, 21 January, Clare showed up at Abbey Road. 'They explained the album was about birth, and all the shit you go through in your life and then death. I did think it was rather pretentious. Of course, I didn't tell them that, and I've since eaten my words. I think it's a marvellous album. They played me the track, but when I asked what they wanted me to do on it, they didn't seem to know.'

Gilmour was in charge of the session, and, after rejecting her original improvised vocals – 'a lot of "oooh, aaah babys" ' – Torry began going for longer notes, no specific words, just general wailing, or, as she describes it now, 'caterwauling'.

'We told her to sing flat out, then quiet,' recalled Gilmour. 'I think we mixed it down from about four versions into the orgasmic version we know and love.'

'We said, "Just busk it," ' said Richard Wright. 'We told her, "Just go in and improvise." Think about death, think about horror, which she did, and out came this wonderful vocal.'

'In the past, Rick has said, "Clare was really embarrassed after doing the vocal," ' says Torry. 'He's right, I *was* embarrassed, but that was because when I walked back into the control room after singing, there was no feedback at all. I thought they hated it. On any other session you'd have got some feedback, even if it was, "My God, that was awful." '

It wasn't until years later, when Clare read an interview with fellow *Dark Side of the Moon* backing singer Lesley Duncan, that she realised she wasn't alone in her feelings. 'I knew exactly what Lesley was talking about. Nobody spoke to her, either. There was a sense of, "I can't wait to get out of here." I suddenly realised Pink Floyd were like that with *everyone*.'

The end result that evening was a dramatic, striking vocal performance, conjuring sex, fear, death; all the component parts of the album. For Clare, though, it had been just another studio session. Not entirely convinced that her 'caterwauling' would make it onto the finished album, she collected her £30 fee from Dennis and was back home in time to go to dinner with her boyfriend.

Chris Thomas's final credit on the album would read 'Mix Supervised By . . .'. Like Alan Parsons' engineer's credit, the roles between engineer, mixer and producer would become blurred, sometimes to the chagrin of those involved. 'I worked ridiculously long hours,' said Parsons, 'making sure I never missed a session. I wanted my contribution to be special. I wanted everything to be right.' To this day, he has never made any more money out of *Dark Side of the Moon* than what he was paid at the time. 'I'm sometimes bitter that I earned little or no money from the album. But that's offset by the fact that it did wonders for my career.' Parsons would eventually receive a Grammy Award for his engineering on *Dark Side of the Moon*.

'Alan Parsons, without doubt, would have done more than simply engineer the record,' said Nick Mason. 'We were extremely lucky to have him. Alan was definitely an engineer/producer.'

'Alan was a very good engineer,' concurred David Gilmour. 'But we would have got there with any good engineer operating the knobs and buttons.'

While the band initially agreed to let Chris Thomas mix the album alone, Waters, unable to help himself, snuck into the studio on the first day of mixing. When Gilmour found out, he snuck in on the second day. From then on, the two would sit either side of Thomas, making their feelings known. As Gilmour would later insist, 'Luckily, Chris was more sympathetic to my point of view than he was to Roger's.'

Diplomatically, Chris Thomas would later state, 'There was no difference of opinion between them. There were never any hints that they were going to fall out later.'

Yet, whatever musical tug of war may or may not have been raging between the bassist and the guitarist, Roger Waters was convinced of the album's worth. 'I had a very strong feeling when we finished the record that we had come up with something very, very special.' He played a copy of the just-finished album to his wife Judy. She listened in silence. Then as soon as it ended, she burst into tears. 'I took that as a very good sign.' A month after completing the recording, EMI hosted a press reception at the London Planetarium in Baker Street. As EMI's staff engineer, Alan Parsons was entrusted to produce the event. When the company were unable or unwilling to install a quadraphonic sound system in time, the band tried to stop the event. When that proved impossible, they chose to boycott it. The assembled writers and liggers gathered for cocktails at 8 p.m., to be confronted by life-size cut-outs of Gilmour, Waters and Mason in the Planetarium reception. According to press reports from the time, Richard Wright was the only Floyd to show up in the flesh, though he subsequently claims to have no memory of the event: 'Did I go or didn't I? . . . I'm not sure. I guess I did.'

'I thought the fact that they didn't show up was rather churlish,' says Parsons. 'But it was a case of, "We are Pink Floyd and we want to do it *our* way."' *Melody Maker*'s subsequent assessment of the album, on first hearing, described some of the music on the first side of the record as 'diabolically uninteresting', while describing how various guests made comedy shadows on the wall of the Planetarium as soon as the lights dimmed.

There was, however, another underlying factor to the Floyd's non-attendance: their relationship, or rather lack of, with the music press. The cosy bond that existed between many rock groups and writers in the mid-1970s did not extend to Pink Floyd. By 1973, the band would submit to interviews, but only rarely and sometimes, it seemed, under duress. 'We weren't a favourite with the music journalists, since none of us had worked that hard to cultivate a relationship with them,' admitted Nick Mason, who would, nevertheless, prove more press-friendly than some of his bandmates at the time.

'Roger once told me that when they were touring the States they hired a person specifically to reply no to any requests for interviews or talk shows,' remembered Adrian Maben. 'This was the Pol Pot quality of the Floyd. Remain unseen, enigmatic; don't let anyone know who we are.'

The same enigmatic quality would find its way into the artwork for *Dark Side of the Moon*. The original idea for what is now one of the most instantly recognisable album covers of all time was conjured up by Storm and Po at Hipgnosis during one of their weekly nocturnal brain-storming sessions. 'We'd stay up until, say, 4 a.m., working up ideas and then sell them to a band,' says Po. However, their creations for the last two Floyd albums, *Obscured by Clouds* and *Meddle*, had not been among their best. The pair had heard some of the new album and had been shown some of the lyrics. 'So we had some understanding of where Roger's head was at,' says Po.

'Rick Wright suggested we do something clean, elegant and graphic, not photographic,' explained Thorgerson. At one late-night session, Storm showed his partner a photograph of a prism sat on top of some sheet music, which he'd found in a second-hand photography book. 'It was a black and white photo,' remembers Po, 'but it had a colour beam projected through it to give it a rainbow effect.' Thorgerson also saw a similar picture in a physics textbook. Their graphic designer, George Hardie, created a line drawing of a prism, but in white on a black back-ground, which was then airbrushed, so EMI's printers could reproduce it.

In contrast to *Ummagumma* and *Atom Heart Mother*, the design for *Dark Side of the Moon* was clinical and almost cold. According to the band, several other alternative ideas were also proposed, but the only one anyone can remember was a design based on the Marvel Comics character the Silver Surfer. All the ideas were pitched to the band at Abbey Road, during the final recording sessions, but there was no contest.

'As soon as we saw it, I think everyone said, "That's the one!"' said Waters.

'I think it took about two minutes,' laughs Po. 'They were like, "That's it!" And went back to finishing the record.'

When EMI agreed to produce a gatefold sleeve, Waters suggested that the colours continue across the inside, augmented by an image of a heartbeat, akin to the blip seen on a hospital oscillator. Thorgerson then decided to add a second prism to the back cover. There would, of course, be no mention of the band's name or the album's title anywhere on the outside cover. Clearly on a roll, Hipgnosis then proposed some additional artwork: a sticker featuring a cartoon drawing of the Egyptian pyramids at Giza, and two posters: one featured an infrared image of the pyramids; the other individual photographs of the band members playing live, superimposed over a pink-lit, almost abstract group shot of the band on stage. There were, however, two shots of Roger, though perhaps only for design purposes.

Hipgnosis' original suggestion of putting everything – posters, stickers and album – in a box was refused by EMI as being too expensive. Nevertheless, in a tribute to the record company's largesse and Hipgnosis' admirable blagging skills, Storm and Po were given a budget to fly to Egypt and shoot the pyramids themselves. Unfortunately, Po was struck down by, in his own words, 'the worst runs you could ever have in your life', and had to stay back at the hotel, leaving Storm to complete the shoot.

'I scared myself shitless doing it, too,' Thorgerson recalled. 'I hired a taxi at 2 a.m. to take me out to the pyramids. It was a wonderful, clear night and the moon was fantastic. So I'm doing it, and then, at 4 a.m., these figures come walking across – soldiers with guns. I thought: This is it – young photographer dies a strange death in a foreign land. Of course, they were really friendly, and just wanted a bit of *bakshish*, a little bit of money, to go away.'

Hipgnosis' eye-catching cover design was a gift for record shop window displays. With the gatefold covers opened and the front and back covers matched up, the prism and spectrum continued into infinity. 'It was such a brilliant concept,' said Gilmour. 'I remember the first time I saw it pinned up in the window of a record shop. I thought it looked amazing.'

A window display in a record shop alerted Clare Torry to the possibility that her vocal, from some two months earlier, might have found its way onto vinyl.

'There was a record shop next door to the Chelsea Potter pub on Kings Road, and there was this display in the window with the prism,' says Clare. 'I remember thinking: Is that the thing I did? I went in, took the cover out of the plastic sleeve and opened up the record. Sure enough, it was. My name was on it. And they'd spelt it right, too . . . I bought a copy and took it home and played it to my boyfriend when I got in. I was astonished when I heard "The Great Gig in the Sky". I thought they'd just use a few bars of my singing. I didn't expect them to use the whole thing.'

Reviews for *Dark Side of the Moon* disproved the belief that all critics were opposed to the band. Despite some sniffiness at the Planetarium playback, *Melody Maker* now insisted that it was 'the best Pink Floyd album since *Ummagumma*' and that 'side two is perfect'. *New Musical Express* was even more effusive: 'Floyd's most artistic musical venture.' In America, where the band were already touring when the album was released, *Rolling Stone* writer Loyd Grossman (who would go on to a high-profile career in the UK as a TV chef and presenter) applauded 'a grandeur that exceeds mere musical melodramatics and is rarely attempted in rock. *Dark Side of the Moon* has flash.' Elsewhere in the review, though, Grossman suggested that 'The Great Gig in the Sky' should have been canned. It was the one song on the album that most polarised opinion. 'Some people love it, some people hate it. It's *that* kind of song,' admits Clare. *Q* magazine once asked David Gilmour if, when listening to 'The Great Gig in the Sky', he'd ever thought, 'Oh, put a sock in it.' He replied, 'Sometimes. Sometimes no. Sometimes yes.'

Played out against a domestic situation in 1973 in which Britain was stricken with its highest unemployment levels in years, and with the IRA soon bringing its conflict with the British government on to English soil, *Dark Side of the Moon* also seemed to mirror the troubled world around it.

'A grim record for a grim time,' as one observer put it, albeit with the promise of something better over the next horizon. Like so much of Roger Waters' future work, it bleated and moaned and harangued the listener, while also grabbing hold of them and reassuring them that all would be OK in the end. It was a sad but uplifting experience.

Waters' philosophical message was also making its way through to the critics, with *New Musical Express* picking up on its themes of 'madness, death from overwork, and the separation of the classes'. Even now, though, when questioned about the album on its various anniversary reissues, each of the band members has expressed slightly different interpretations of what it all means. 'But it expressed emotions that I think we all felt at the time,' said Wright.

What Wright and Gilmour, especially, brought to Waters' personal vision was a musicality. However bitter the pill, these two sweetened it with some inspired arrangements and musicianship. There was none of the freeform wig-outs heard in *A Saucerful of Secrets*; even the album's instrumental jams showed a rare economy and focus. This was highbrow rock music with a broader, low-brow appeal.

For Floyd's ex-managers Andrew King and Peter Jenner, hearing the album was a strange experience. 'I played it and immediately picked up on certain influences,' says King. 'One of Rick's favourite composers had always been Stockhausen, and you could still hear that in there. The whole album contains a lot of study and awareness of what was happening in the avant-garde in Europe, especially on things like "On the Run". But Roger synthesised it in a way that made sense in a pop group. They made it palatable for a mass audience.'

'After Syd left, they never had the musical excitement for me,' admits Jenner. 'And I remember really pouring piss on *Dark Side* when it came out, because I was still comparing it to what they'd done with Syd. I had what you might call cultural sour grapes. Why? Because I'd backed the wrong horse. Once I got over that, I came to appreciate what they were doing. I just needed to adjust my view and accept what Pink Floyd had become. That it was now Roger's baby.'

For the first time on a Pink Floyd album, Roger Waters had, at his own behest, written all the lyrics, a decision that had not gone unchallenged, but which would have repercussions later on.

Richard Wright's single or co-writing credit on five of the ten tracks hints at a greater musical contribution than history sometimes allows. His co-written composition with Waters, 'Us and Them', would remain both parties' favourite song on the record, long after their personal relationship had soured. '*Dark Side of the Moon* contains the best songs the Floyd have ever written,' Wright told writer Carol Clerk. 'Even though I wasn't great friends with Roger, there was a great working relationship. To this day, I think it's sad we lost it.'

Nick Mason scooped two credits, a co-writer's credit alongside Waters and Gilmour for the space-filling instrumental 'Any Colour You Like', and a sole writer's credit for the opening fanfare 'Speak to Me'. Oddly, Gilmour's name was listed on just four of the songs, and only ever in conjunction with one or more of his bandmates. Yet his presence is all over the album: taking the lion's share of the lead vocals; maintaining a dominant presence on the guitar; and, finally, acquiring a close approximation of the warm sound he'd pushed for on the final mix.

'I didn't pull my weight when we were writing *Dark Side of the Moon*, though,' Gilmour told writer Phil Sutcliffe. 'I went through a bad patch. I don't think I contributed to the writing in the way that I would have liked, hence the credits.' Gilmour would blame his lack of songs on 'laziness'.

Roger Waters would take a more sanguine view: 'He doesn't have very many ideas. He's a great guitar player, but he's not really a writer. However conscientious or hard-working Dave was, he would never actually write anything.'

For Waters, the decision to allocate some writing credits in the spirit of band democracy would come back to haunt him.

However good it may have been, there was still the issue of selling the new album. Not least in America. In 1971, Bhaskar Menon had moved to Los Angeles to take up the position of president of Capitol Records. Menon had been appointed to address the issue of the label's under-performance, immediately cutting back their roster and focusing on those acts he believed to have a future.

Menon was a Pink Floyd fan, but also understood why America didn't quite get it. 'Extremely long tracks, philosophical ruminations and some very English themes – these were all outside the radar of American Top

40 radio,' says Menon now. 'America was still coming out of the Eisenhower period of pop music. FM radio was still evolving, and was almost regarded like an underground society, like a "head shop".'

Bhaskar realised that Capitol's marketing and promotional departments were as unfamiliar with the band's music as the public, and, in some cases, intimidated by their overseas success. 'The label was struggling to adjust to the post-Glen Campbell and Beach Boys markets,' he says. 'They just didn't understand it.'

Dark Side of the Moon was Pink Floyd's last album under contract to Capitol. Despite the concerted wooing by Warners and Atlantic, which Steve O'Rourke had been fending off in Lindos, the band had agreed to sign to Columbia in the US, for a rumoured £1 million advance. The label's president, Clive Davis, was a huge presence in the industry, had signed Janis Joplin and Santana, and would later sign Bruce Springsteen. (In the event, Davis would drop out of the picture almost as soon as Pink Floyd signed the deal, when he was relieved of his position after it was discovered that he'd paid for his son's bar mitzvah out of the Columbia coffers.) Nevertheless, Bhaskar Menon flew to France in November 1972 to watch Pink Floyd perform with the Ballet de Marseille, and talk business with Steve O'Rourke.

The group and their manager had neglected to tell Menon that Pink Floyd would not be renewing their contract with Capitol. 'In our usual, non-confrontational way we just forgot to mention it,' wrote Nick Mason later. However, Bhaskar insists that he knew all along. 'I was aware of what was happening with Columbia, but could see no great value in sharing that information with Pink Floyd.'

Adding to Menon's problems, Steve O'Rourke was also angling to have the band released from their contract, meaning that Pink Floyd now effectively owned *Dark Side of the Moon*, and could shop it to Columbia. O'Rourke believed that Capitol would agree to this in exchange for a long-term deal with the band for territories outside North America.

Menon proposed a bet. 'I wagered him my Casio watch against his bejewelled Rolex that he would never succeed in dividing the EMI empire,' he laughs. 'I wanted to ensure that the momentum we'd got going on *Obscured by Clouds* continued. Some people might have said, "Why waste your energies on this?" But it wasn't in my interests or Capitol's shareholders' not to keep going. I *wanted* this album.' An all-night meeting ensued in a seedy Algerian bar and restaurant near to the band's Marseilles hotel. 'I finally concluded a deal for the album just after sunrise,' says Menon, 'rescuing Steve from the loss of his very valuable watch and me from having to pick up another Casio at the Duty Free counter.'

Having culled several acts from the roster, Menon was free to put the weight of Capitol's promotional department behind the new Floyd album. His diligence and belief in a record that he claims 'was as important as *Sgt Pepper*' paid off. *Dark Side of the Moon* made it to number 1 in the US. America had finally come round to Pink Floyd. The album reached number 2 in Britain, number 1 in France and Belgium, and number 3 in Australia, with similar Top 5 placings in Brazil, Germany and Spain.

Back on tour in America in March, the band were now joined by saxophonist Dick Parry, and three female backing singers − sisters Phylliss and Mary Ann Lindsey, and Nawasa Crowder, all fresh off the road with American songwriter and pianist Leon Russell. DJ Jeff Dexter joined the touring party in New York, and found the band and their entourage in high spirits. While the wives shopped for antiques, Gilmour and Waters were engaged in high-stakes games of backgammon. In between, they attended a lunch reception in their honour at the exquisitely upmarket Four Seasons Restaurant.

'It was a buffet affair,' recalls Jeff Dexter. 'One of the servers put a spoonful of caviar on Dave Gilmour's plate. He asked if he could have some more, and was told, "I don't think so, sir." At which point someone from the record company stepped in: "If the gentleman would like more, then give him as much as he would like." Dave took the ladle and helped himself. Then he turned to me and said, "If I can afford it, *they* can afford it, too."'

At New York's Radio City Music Hall that night, Pink Floyd's entrance on stage at 1 a.m. was as portentous and dramatic as their new album demanded. An elevated platform transported them upwards to stage level, where they materialised, like scruffy, hippie deities, coloured smoke billowing around their feet, lights blazing, and a twenty-speaker quad system relaying the throbbing heartbeat and chiming clocks of *Dark Side of the Moon* to the rapt audience. 'It was,' says Jeff Dexter, 'one of the best shows ever.'

A late-night soirée back at the group's hotel would culminate in Jeff and Floyd lighting wizard Arthur Max riding the elevator, 'dressed in matching Chinese Communist suits, reading out loud from Chairman Mao's *Little Red Book*'.

Back in England, the conquering heroes sold out two nights at London's Earls Court. Just as in America, they bombarded their audience with blinding lights, blazing gongs and more industrial quantities of dry ice, prompting one critic to compare the stage to a 'Macbethian blasted heath'. This time, *Dark Side of the Moon* backing vocalist Liza Strike and fellow session singer Vicki Brown provided the back-ups. Clare Torry had been sent two complimentary tickets for the show, but found it an emotional experience: 'I'm afraid I cried when they did "The Great Gig in the Sky". I thought it was mine and I should have been up there doing it. It's hurt me a lot over the years.'

Torry would perform the song again with Pink Floyd, including a headlining performance at Knebworth Park in 1990. Later, she would launch a claim to songwriting royalties from the album, believing her contribution to the song justified it. In 2005, the case was finally settled out of court in her favour, although she is prohibited from revealing any details about the settlement. From then on, 'The Great Gig in the Sky' would be credited to Richard Wright *and* Clare Torry.

Floyd's home visit would be brief. There were more US dates booked throughout June. While having a number 1 album in America had raised their profile, having a hit single in America would take them into a different league altogether. While 'Free Four' from *Obscured by Clouds* had been issued in the US as a single, the band had no desire to do the same with any of the songs on *Dark Side of the Moon*. Bhaskar Menon thought otherwise. The album's success had made them a *cause célèbre* with America's serious rock audience, but a Top 40 hit would enable them to reach the heartland and a different audience of record-buyers altogether.

'"Money" was the song,' says Menon. 'That was the obvious choice. Though I did have to work very hard to persuade the group and Steve O'Rourke that we should put it out.'

'At first they didn't agree because they said the time signature was too unusual,' remembers Jeff Dexter. 'I played it at the Roundhouse and could see how well it worked. You knew it was going to be a monster hit. But I think at the time Pink Floyd were taking a leaf out of Led Zeppelin's book, who were shifting shitloads of albums without having to go through all that radio bullshit.'

For the band themselves, the memory of their last single, 1968's disastrous 'Point Me at the Sky', was still too raw.

'We decided that if the public didn't want to buy our singles we didn't want to put any out,' says Nick Mason.

'We didn't think anything would happen with "Money",' admitted Richard Wright. 'And, suddenly, it just did.'

A shorter version of the song, with the word 'bullshit' edited out to appease prudish radio programmers, was released in America on 7 May. By the end of the following month, it had crept to number 26. With blanket airplay on US Top 40 radio, taking it into the homes of non-album buyers and non-Floyd fans, it finally peaked at number 13. The provocative lyrics, in which a soon to be very rich rock 'n' roll band sang of greed and selfishness, Gilmour's squalling guitar, Dick Parry's similarly squalling sax, and that clubfooted but compelling funk rhythm all helped to make it a song that sounded fantastic when played on the radio.

It didn't take long for the band to feel the ripples. In June, Pink Floyd returned to America for eleven dates, running from New Jersey down to Florida. On the opening night at the Union City Roosevelt Stadium, they broke all box office records. Through Detroit, Ohio and Kentucky, most of the shows were sold out, and the audience's reaction was the same wherever they played. Where once the Floyd faithful would sit, rapt, contemplating the twenty-minute mind trip of 'Echoes', they were now louder, more animated and, as Gilmour grudgingly explained, 'ready to boogie'.

'Everywhere we played, we suddenly found ourselves confronted with an audience that just wanted to hear the big hit,' said the guitarist. They wanted to dance, drink beer and have a good time. And they wanted to hear 'Money'. 'That's all you'd hear, throughout the show, until we finally played it: "Money" . . . play "Money" . . .'

The unthinkable had happened; Pink Floyd were now pop stars. It could only go downhill from there.

CHAPTER SEVEN **RIDING THE GRAVY TRAIN**

'That's why I stay in the group. I'm worried about the others – what's going to become of them.'

Roger Waters

In a private room at London's exclusive members' club, The Groucho, Richard Wright conveys the genteel manner of a retired public school teacher. He has that rather absent air you'd expect to find in one who has spent their adult lifetime in a higher seat of learning. You half expect to see chalk dust on his elbows. It is 1996 and Pink Floyd's keyboard player is now fifty-four. The paisley-shirted psychedelic poster boy of 1967, second only in the ranks to Syd Barrett, is gone, as is the bearded hipster of 1972's *Live At Pompeii*. Wright's hair is now completely white, and, while his jeans and brogues are high street issue, you suspect that the overcoat hanging on the back of a nearby chair is from somewhere a little more up-market and outside your price range.

In conversation, he is nervous, obliging, reticent and precise. Wright is here to talk about his new solo album, a record that will disappear off the radar of all but the most dedicated of Pink Floyd fans within a few months. It is, nevertheless, an album full of aural tics and moments of familiarity that make you scrabble around in the back of your mind, trying to remember which Pink Floyd song it now reminds you of.

When you ask Wright about the Floyd albums he rates the most highly, you already know the answer. Now back in the group as a full-time member, he doesn't bother subscribing to David Gilmour's party line: that the new Floyd is on a par with the old Floyd. Wright's tastes are strictly old school.

'*Dark Side of the Moon* and *Wish You Were Here*,' he answers. 'But if I was forced to name one, *Wish You Were Here*.'

'Or *Wish You* Weren't *Here*,' as Roger Waters once called it, balefully recalling the mood in the studio during its making. Pink Floyd had ended 1973 playing a benefit concert for Soft Machine drummer Robert Wyatt, who had broken his back after falling from a window, but before Christmas, they reconvened at Abbey Road, and began messing around again with the *Household Objects* project, on hold since 1971. *Dark Side of the Moon*'s number 1 chart position and the hit single 'Money' had been the start of what Nick Mason would later describe as 'Floyd's scorched earth policy', but, contrarily, they had gone back to trying to make music with wine glasses, saws, rolls of sticky tape and buckets of water.

'I remember a rubber band being stretched between two objects to make a bass sound, with matchsticks as frets,' says engineer Alan Parsons. 'Actually, I was always rather disappointed it never came to anything.'

In truth, it was a delaying tactic, a ruse to make the band feel they were doing something without actually having to write any new songs. Yet something was salvaged out of the aborted sessions: the high-pitched sound produced by a finger on the rim of a wine glass became a starting point for one of Pink Floyd's most enduring songs.

As 1974 rolled in, the group dispersed to spend time with their families or to sample a musical life outside the Floyd bubble. Nick Mason produced an album for folk rockers Principal Edwards Magic Theatre, before doing the same for Robert Wyatt's *Rock Bottom* album and its spin-off hit single, a cover of The Monkees' 'I'm a Believer'. David Gilmour produced the Cambridge band Unicorn, in between occasional stints playing guitar for Tim Renwick's and Willie Wilson's band Sutherland Brothers and Quiver. It was through Unicorn that Gilmour was also introduced to an unknown teenage singer-songwriter, Kate Bush, who would record her demos at his home studio.

In the meantime, Gilmour splashed out on a town house in Notting Hill, Mason moved a few miles up the road from Camden to Highgate, and Wright bought himself a country manor house in Royston, near Cambridge, installing his own studio, The Old Rectory, which would become a popular haunt for many local bands. The Floyd's keyboard player even found himself participating in a Parents and Teachers Association benefit gig for neighbouring Therfield village. It was an event that saw *Atom Heart Mother* co-writer Ron Geesin performing an improvised act with a folding chair and a length of drainpipe. 'The villagers in attendance were totally bemused,' recalled one of his fellow performers.

Wright's house parties were lavish, hedonistic affairs. 'There was a time when going to Rick and Juliette's place was fantastic fun,' recalls Jeff Dexter. 'I think it was Rick's thirtieth birthday party, when I had a real Kesey-type trip. There was also a beauty contest that night, with a few cross-dressers, too, all dressed up sparkly, taking it quite seriously. One fellow traveller thought it would be a good idea to have all the "sparklers" in the pool, so we pushed many of them off the catwalk into the water.'

The Floyd's property portfolios would expand even further over the next two years: Wright and Gilmour purchased villas on Rhodes, and Mason bought a place in the South of France. Meanwhile, Waters acquired a villa in Volos on the Greek coast, which quickly became his wife Judy's pet project.

'I have to accept that, at that point, I became a capitalist,' admitted Waters in 2004. 'I could no longer pretend that I was a true Socialist.' He salved his left-wing conscience by eventually siphoning a percentage of his earnings into a charitable trust.

Gilmour and Floyd roadie Peter Watts both bought flats in McGregor Road, Ladbroke Grove. Iain 'Emo' Moore would also frequent those flats during the seventies. 'The Floyd let people they knew who were on hard times live in those flats for very little money. They were often rented or lent to people,' recalls one visitor. 'They had these scrupulous Socialist principles, and they really believed this was the right thing to do. Waters was instrumental in this.'

Peter Watts had been the longest-serving member of the Floyd's crew, having joined six months before David Gilmour. Unfortunately, his drug use had now made him a liability. Watts was repeatedly sacked, for such misdemeanours as nodding off on Mandrax while driving the band's car, but would always end up being re-hired. The group would pay for a drug treatment course, but to no long-term avail. Watts was fired in 1974, and died in August 1976 in his flat on McGregor Road. His daughter, Naomi, would go on to become a world-famous model and actress.

Pink Floyd spent the first half of the year in a state of general inertia. 'We were all rather badly mentally ill,' joked Waters at the time. 'We were all completely exhausted for one reason or another.' Having achieved the success they'd longed for with *Dark Side of the Moon*, the band were pondering the inevitable question: What do we do now? As Waters would later explain, 'All the things you wished for when you started a band had now happened. It had all come true.' Away from the music, there were also wives and girlfriends to be appeased. Ginger had been living with David Gilmour for four years, and wanted to get married. Meanwhile, Waters' relationship with Judy was in terminal decline.

Nobody was feeling particularly inspired when the band met up again in a grim, windowless rehearsal studio in London's Kings Cross. They would begin work on three new pieces. The first, 'Shine On', would later incorporate the wine glass sound from *Household Objects*, but came together from a distinctive four-note guitar figure cooked up by Gilmour. The second, 'Raving and Drooling', had a harder edge and a throbbing riff similar to the one that had driven 'One of These Days'. The third, 'Gotta Be Crazy', was bleaker still. These were not pop songs for those fans who'd bought into the band through the hit single 'Money'.

Waters had written the lyrics for all three. The first was at least in part inspired by Syd Barrett. The other two found him at his most misanthropic yet, spitting venom at the corporate machinations of the music industry and the lemming-like mentality of the band's new mainstream audience. 'Gotta Be Crazy' even contained the line, 'You've got to keep everyone buying this shit'.

'Raving and Drooling' and 'Shine On' (which would acquire its full title of 'Shine On You Crazy Diamond') would be introduced into the

Floyd's set during a tour of France that summer. On the Continent, the band ran into further problems. Two years earlier they'd struck a deal with Gini, a French drinks company, to appear in a photograph advertising a soft drink. The picture had been taken in Morocco, for use only in France, for which the band had been paid handsomely. 'In a fit of madness we all agreed that we'd do it,' said Nick Mason. 'We thought we'd rip them off for loads of cash, and of course that didn't happen. We'd intended them to subsidise the tour, so we could make the tickets cheaper, and in the end no one could work out whether the tickets were cheaper.' Again, wrestling with his principles, Waters insisted the band donate the money to charity. On tour in France, though, the group discovered that a clause in their contract meant being tailed by a gaggle of models hired by Gini to promote what Gilmour later called 'that fucking drink'. With tour sponsorship unheard of at the time, the Floyd's promotional stunt was greeted with suspicion. Waters would write a song, the still unreleased 'Bitter Love', lamenting the whole sorry affair.

The French dates also served as rehearsal for a larger UK tour planned for later in the year. The band had now acquired a 40ft circular screen to be positioned at the back of the stage, onto which they could project films and images. Footage from surfer George Greenough's *Crystal Voyager* movie had been used previously for 'The Great Gig in the Sky', along with Ian Eames's animated sequence for 'Time'. Eames had been discovered by the band when he created a similar animated sequence, in the pre-promo video age, to accompany 'One of These Days' for the BBC's music show *The Old Grey Whistle Test*. The band now wanted a complete library of images. Roger Waters and Arthur Max busied themselves in an editing suite in Soho, London, working out a running order and identifying where the 'dead periods' were going to fall in the show, and how to fill them.

One of the first people they contacted was cartoonist and film-maker Gerald Scarfe. 'Nick Mason had phoned me years before, and said the group had seen a film I'd made for the BBC called *Long Drawn-Out Trip*,' says Scarfe now. He had made the animated film in Los Angeles in 1971, 'a stream-of-consciousness drawing' that included as many images as he could think of relating to the United States. This collage of Jimi Hendrix, John Wayne and Mickey Mouse had fascinated Waters and Mason. 'I was invited to do something for them back then, but for whatever reason it never happened. Nick called me again, and I went and had a meeting at his house. They wanted me to come up with some images to show on tour. They gave me a pile of Floyd albums to listen to.'

Scarfe's animations would include a human figure that dissolves into sand and a robotic monster for the song that would become 'Welcome to the Machine' and would be unveiled on their 1975 dates. In the meantime, his cartoon drawings would be used in the Hipgnosis-designed programme for the 1974 tour. Billed a 'Super, All-Action Official Music Programme for Boys and Girls', the programme was an expert pastiche of an American pulp comic, with each of the group recreated as action heroes, including Gilmour as a fearless biker named 'Dave Derring'.

Hearing *Dark Side of the Moon* for the first time had also inspired another film-maker, the band's old Cambridge confederate Anthony Stern. Since 1967, Stern had returned repeatedly to the film ideas he and Syd Barrett had devised under the title of 'The Rose-Tinted Monocle'. 'I dug out all this footage and it worked perfectly with *Dark Side of the Moon*,' says Anthony. Having borrowed a film projector from David Gilmour, he arranged to visit each member of the band and show them his film, with a view to using *Dark Side of the Moon* as its soundtrack.

'They knew that Syd had been involved with the roots of the film, and on a purely aesthetic and creative level they all gave it the thumbs up. They all said, "Of *course* you can use *Dark Side of the Moon* for this",' laughs Anthony. 'I came home elated. It had taken me about two weeks to get to see them all. Roger, despite his immense ego, was incredibly friendly, warm and enthusiastic about the idea of me using this music in such an abstract, non-commercial way. I think that appealed to him.'

Before long, though, the project would hit the buffers. 'The thing collapsed when I went to see Steve O'Rourke. I showed him the film. He looked at it completely impassively and finally said, "Anthony, I just don't *get* it. This is not the sort of imagery I see associated with Pink Floyd . . . I see jets taking off . . . I see New York skyscrapers . . ."'

Interviewed two years earlier, Richard Wright had expressed a fear that the Floyd were 'in danger of becoming slaves to our equipment . . . Sometimes I look at our huge truck and tons of equipment and think:

Christ, all I'm doing is playing an organ.' Pink Floyd's entourage had grown even more since then.

Maintaining the arsenal of sound and light equipment required an army of stagehands and technicians. By 1974 the key roles now fell to Mick Kluczynski, a stocky Scotsman of Polish origins, who had joined his old friend Chris Adamson to help take care of the sound as part of the so-called 'Quad Squad'. Like Adamson, and his potato-eating stunt, Roger Waters later recalled Kluczynski consuming twenty-eight fried eggs as a bet before having to throw up. The bassist also challenged Kluczynski to drink a pint of whiskey during a day off on tour in America. Elsewhere, Robbie Williams was now on board as stage technician. Williams was noted for having, in the words of a fellow crew member, 'a very deep voice from right down in his boots', which had prohibited him from being one of the interviewees on *Dark Side of the Moon*. Elsewhere, the numbers were made up with new recruit, Phil Taylor, who would go on to become David Gilmour's long-serving guitar technician. Kluczynski and Williams would later head up their own production companies, and continue to work with Pink Floyd in the 1990s.

Alongside Dick Parry, Floyd were now joined by backing singers Venetta Fields and Carlena Williams, collectively known as The Blackberries.

The tour opened on 4 November with two dates at Edinburgh's Usher Hall. The set would comprise just five pieces: 'Shine On You Crazy Diamond', 'Raving and Drooling', 'You Gotta Be Crazy', *Dark Side of the Moon* and an encore of 'Echoes'. The visual extravaganza would begin with *Dark Side of the Moon*. For 'Speak to Me', an image of the moon was projected on the huge circular screen, growing bigger and bigger with each heartbeat, until it filled the entire screen. 'On the Run' would be illustrated with aircraft landing lights and flashing police lights before switching to swooping bird's-eye footage of a city landscape and various explosions. Airborne clocks accompanied 'Time', George Greenough's magnificent surfer appeared for 'The Great Gig in the Sky', and a quick-fire display of Lear jets and banknotes flashed up on the screen during 'Money'.

The logistics of such a big production brought with it another set of problems. 'The equipment was pretty unreliable,' recalled Wright. 'The film would break or the projector would break. There were a lot of missing cues and trying to get back in time. We were always getting snappy with the technicians.' A review in *New Musical Express* of the opening night complained about the malfunctioning sound system, too much feedback and 'David Gilmour's dreadful singing on the new material'.

Floyd's refusal to play the media game is best summed up by Gilmour's recent explanation: 'Once we realised we could sell records and tickets without having to talk to the press, we chose not to.' *Melody Maker*'s Chris Charlesworth sidestepped the band's refusal to give him a ticket for the Edinburgh show by buying one from a tout and talking his way into a post-gig supper with the band. The day after, he managed to get an interview with Richard Wright, much to the displeasure of the rest of the group, especially Roger Waters, who was still smarting from a comment made by the keyboard player in a previous interview, suggesting that the Floyd's lyrics weren't that important.

Wright's remarks in the subsequent *Melody Maker* article suggested a very insular attitude, even by Floyd standards: 'I don't listen to what is being played on the radio. I don't watch *Top of the Pops*. I don't watch *The Old Grey Whistle Test*. I don't even know how the rock business is going . . .'

An even greater shock to Charlesworth was the news that the band were choosing their hotels on the basis of how near they were to decent golf courses. 'I recall being astonished that Waters played golf,' he later wrote. 'It seemed the unlikeliest of pastimes for a man whose lyrical pre-occupations were space flight, insanity and death.' As well as golf, Waters was also a keen squash player, with Gilmour his closest challenger in the band.

In his own memoir, Nick Mason (the band's worst squash player, according to some) was admirably frank about the problems now besetting the Floyd. 'We seemed to be more interested in booking squash courts than perfecting the set,' he wrote. 'We were demonstrating a distinct lack of commitment to the necessary input required.'

After the glamour and glitz of New York's Radio City Hall, a trawl through Great Britain's provincial theatres in a cold, wintry November must have seemed less enticing. Meanwhile, in the real world, the IRA blew up a pub in Birmingham a couple of weeks before the band were due in town, ramping up the paranoia and general unease. Inside the

Floyd bubble, there was uncertainty about the new material, frustrations with their own or others' performances, and a sense that the visual rather than musical aspect of the show was now becoming too important.

In early 1974, cinema projectionist Pete Revell answered an ad in *Melody Maker*, and found himself being interviewed by Arthur Max for the job of projectionist in the Floyd's road crew. ('I was shocked to discover it was for Pink Floyd, as it was the smallest, cheapest ad you could possibly buy.')

'There was always a vibe around Roger,' says Revell now. 'Everybody felt it on that tour, even, I think, the band. David was a real gentleman and Rick was away in his own quiet world, but Roger was so bloody aloof, so far up his own arse.' Nick Mason was also well liked, though Revell recalls that the drummer's request to a crew member to buy him a half-inch drive socket set during an afternoon off in Bristol went ignored. The crew spent the day in the pub, wondering why Mason needed a half-inch drive socket set for his drum kit. Later, the penny dropped, when the drummer screeched up to the band's hotel in his new toy, a second-hand Ferrari.

Problems within the crew were also having an impact. The band's newly acquired mixing desk proved a temperamental beast, and front-of-house sound engineer Rufus Cartwright was let go after just a few dates. Order was restored by his replacement, Brian Humphries, who had worked at Pye Studios and engineered the *More* soundtrack. But Arthur Max, the band's brilliant, if fiery-tempered lighting wizard, would also find his days numbered, as the fractious atmosphere took its toll.

Day after day they would be confronted with new stories about Max's run-ins with crew members and venue officials. 'I walked out twice – told him to shove the job,' recalls Pete Revell of the friction amongst the crew (often involving Arthur). 'They sent Steve O'Rourke round to my house to talk me into coming back.'

Max's last Pink Floyd gig would be at the Sophia Gardens Pavilion in Cardiff. His deputy, the more emollient Graeme Fleming, would take his place. After Fleming's debut at the Liverpool Empire, Waters would inform the crowd that this had been the best gig of the tour. 'The Liverpudlians thought it was something to do with them,' says Revell,

Publicity shot for
*The Piper at the Gates
of Dawn*, Ruskin Park,
Denmark Hill, London,
summer 1967.
From front: Syd Barrett,
Nick Mason, Richard
Wright and Roger
Waters.   *Colin Prime*

Obscured by clouds: Syd Barrett in the back garden at 183 Hills Road, Cambridge, circa 1964. *Courtesy of Iain Moore*

Syd Barrett (second, right) with Cambridge friends (from left) Iain 'Emo' Moore, Ian 'Pip' Carter, girlfriend Lindsay Corner, Emo's girlfriend Frances 'Fizz' Fitzgerald and occasional

David Gilmour entertains family friends, Waterbeach, Cambridge, Christmas Day 1965. *Courtesy of Christine Smith*

David Gilmour (top left) and college friend John Watkins (bottom, pointing), on board the Cambridge School of Art's rag week float, 1965. *Courtesy of John Watkins*

Jokers Wild, from left: David Gilmour, Dave Altham, John Gordon and Tony Sainty, Cambridge, early 1965. *Courtesy of Christine Smith*

Any colour you like: Pink Floyd on stage at UFO, London, early 1967.
Adam Ritchie, Redferns

Syd and girlfriend Jenny Spires at 101
Cromwell Road, London, spring 1967.
Phil Smee/Strange Things

Syd's Cambridge friends and flatmates, Nigel
and Jenny Lesmoir-Gordon, autumn 1967.
Courtesy of Nigel Lesmoir-Gordon

Pink Floyd at their hotel in Sausalito, California, during their debut US tour, November 1967. Syd fusses with his new Vidal Sassoon perm.
Baron Wolman

The short-lived five-piece line-up, with new recruit David Gilmour (back row, second left), January 1968.
Phil Smee/Strange Things

Syd Barrett, after recording *The Madcap Laughs*, with Cambridge friend Mary Wing and her partner Marc Tessier, Ibiza, August 1969.
Courtesy of Iain Moore

DJ Jeff Dexter flanked by ex-Floyd managers Peter Jenner (left) and Andrew King, Midsummer High Weekend, Hyde Park, London, 29 June 1968.   *Rex Features*

Pink Floyd's inflatable
octopus comes up
for air, Crystal Palace
Garden Party,
15 May 1971.
Robert Ellis, Repfoto

Hipgnosis' Aubrey
'Po' Powell,
David Gilmour
and first wife
Ginger relaxing
backstage,
Empire Pool,
Wembley, 15
November 1974.
*Jill Furmanovsky/
rockarchive.com*

Richard Wright
watches David
Gilmour and
Hipgnosis' Storm
Thorgerson at
the backgammon
board, British
winter tour,
November 1974.
*Jill Furmanovsky/
rockarchive.com*

Pink Floyd performing *Dark Side of the Moon*, Usher Hall, Edinburgh, 4 November 1974. *Robert Ellis, Repfoto*

Pink Floyd's manager Steve O'Rourke (centre) holding forth backstage during the British winter tour, November 1974. *Mick Gold, Redferns*

David Gilmour and Iain 'Emo' Moore (with brand new teeth, paid for by Gilmour!), at home, Royden, Essex, Christmas Day 1973. *Courtesy of Iain Moore*

The pig at rest before Pink Floyd's show at the Sportspaleis, Ahoy, Rotterdam, the Netherlands, 19 February 1977.
Rob Verhorst, Redferns

Roger Waters, with girlfriend Carolyne Christie, enjoying the support acts before Pink Floyd's headline appearance at Knebworth Park, 5 July 1975.
Robert Ellis, Repfoto

Residents of Battersea are startled to see a pink pig rising between the towers of the famous Power Station one day in December 1976 during the photo shoot for the cover of *Animals*.
Mirrorpix

Syd Barrett outside his house during his encounter with journalists from the French magazine *Actuel* in 1982. *Retna*

Spare bricks: assembling the stage and the wall before one of Pink Floyd's performances at Earl's Court exhibition centre, August 1980. *Corbis*

The show must go on: performing *The Wall* at Earls Court, August 1980. *Rex Features*

Nick Mason and toys, circa 1987. Mason founded the company Ten Tenths in 1985 to hire out vehicles to TV and film companies.   *Rex Features*

Shine on: the *Momentary Lapse Of Reason* stage set in full effect, Stadion Feyenoord, Rotterdam, The Netherlands, 13 June 1988.   *Rob Verhorst, Redferns*

A great day for freedom: Roger Waters and guests performing The Wall, Potsdamer Platz, Berlin, 21 July 1990. *Retna*

Coming back to life: Pink Floyd on the *Division Bell* tour at the British Columbia Palace Stadium in Vancouver, Canada, 25 June 1994. *Mick Hutson, Redferns*

David Gilmour CBE, with daughter Alice, wife Polly Samson and son Charlie, outside Buckingham Palace, November 2003. *Rex Features*

Roger Waters addresses members of the 'ignoble profession' backstage at Live 8 in Hyde Park, 2 July 2005. *Retna*

David Gilmour and Roger Waters performing 'Wish You Were Here' at Live 8. *Getty Images*

Group hug, anyone? David Gilmour, Roger Waters, Nick Mason and Richard Wright at the end of their Live 8 set. *PA Photos*

Nick Mason and David Gilmour enjoy a Big Brother moment with Roger Waters during the UK Music Hall of Fame induction ceremony at Alexandra Palace, London, 16 November 2005. *Getty Images*

David Bowie singing guest vocals on 'Arnold Layne' with David Gilmour at the Royal Albert Hall, May 2006. *Rex Features*

One of the last sightings of Syd Barrett: doorstepped at 6 St Margaret's Square in Cambridge in January 2006. *Mirrorpix*

Flowers outside Syd Barrett's house following his death in July 2006. *Rex Features*

Syd Barrett's home-made speakers and his guitar on display at Cheffins auction house in Cambridge, November 2006. Barrett left an estate worth over £1.25 million. *Rex Features*

It's time to go? Nick Mason and Roger Waters backstage at the Barbican Theatre for Madcap's Last Laugh, the Syd Barrett tribute concert on 10 May 2007. *Danny Clifford*

The Final Cut? Richard Wright, Nick Mason, David Gilmour and Oasis's Andy Bell (but no Roger Waters) performing 'Arnold Layne' at the Syd Barrett tribute concert. *Danny Clifford*

'but really it was because they had all stopped rowing.' The Floyd's outspoken lighting designer would eventually go on to a glittering career in Hollywood as a movie art director, winning an Oscar nomination for his work on Ridley Scott's blockbuster *Gladiator*.

While some equilibrium had been restored by the time of the Liverpool Empire show, the band had still received their fiercest dressing down yet in the music press. The 23 November issue of *New Musical Express* included a detailed critique of the band's Wembley Empire Pool gig a week earlier, written by their star writer Nick Kent. In it, Kent castigated Pink Floyd for their musical lethargy ('Floyd, as always, let the song sprawl out to last twice as long as it should'), their indifference towards the audience ('they wander on like four navvies who've just finished their tea break') and the perceived hypocrisy of Waters' latest lyrics ('I cannot think of another rock group who live a more desperately bourgeois existence in the privacy of their own homes'). Its opening salvo was especially cutting about David Gilmour: 'His hair looked filthy there on stage, seemingly anchored down by a surfeit of scalp grease and tapering off below the shoulders with a spectacular festooning of split ends.' A comment that caused some amusement with laid-back, American backing singers Venetta Fields and Carlena Williams who rather enjoyed challenging the band's painfully English reserve. 'I was overly sensitive about my split ends,' Gilmour jokingly told this writer in 2011. 'Nick Kent has every right to say what the fuck he likes.'

'The hair thing was a low blow on my part,' admits Kent now. 'But I still stand by what I wrote. The Floyd's whole attitude that night was like, "Oh fuck, I suppose we better do this now", as if it was all too much trouble. They really did remind me of workmen, wandering on to dig up the road. Like it was a job that had to be done. I saw Rick Wright after that piece came out and he actually *thanked* me for it. He said he didn't like what I'd written, but at the same time it stimulated some kind of intra-group discussion, because as a group they had become so detached from each other. He said it actually brought them together.'

Kent's colleague Pete Erskine interviewed a furious David Gilmour a few weeks later. Naturally, Gilmour defended the band's position to the hilt. Kent had taken umbrage at a line in the new song 'Gotta Be Crazy' – 'Gotta keep everyone buying this shit' – believing that it was sneering at the band's fans. But Gilmour claimed that Waters' lyrics were directed as much at the band as their audience. 'I'm cynical of our position,' he said. 'I don't think anyone on our level feels deserving of the superhuman adulation number.' Gilmour explained that *Sunday Times* writer Derek Jewell's gushing appraisal of the same Wembley show had irritated them also, as it was 'probably the worst [show] we've done on the whole tour'. Yet the guitarist couldn't maintain a united front against all of the charges, admitting that there was laziness in the group and confessing that *Dark Side of the Moon* had 'trapped us creatively'. Privately, Roger Waters found himself acknowledging more than a little truth in some of Nick Kent's observations. Always fearful of complacency, he had a nagging sense that something needed to change.

By the end of the tour in December, Waters was dedicating some of the performances of 'Shine On You Crazy Diamond' to 'Sydney Barrett'. Meanwhile, EMI/Capitol had reissued the group's first two albums, *The Piper at the Gates of Dawn* and *A Saucerful of Secrets*, as a double LP package entitled *A Nice Pair*. Hipgnosis' packaging included various images relating to the album's title and similar catchphrases, including 'a nip in the air' and 'a kettle of fish'. However, an attempt to run a photograph of the boxer Floyd Patterson ran aground when he demanded $5,000. Patterson was substituted by a picture of the Pink Floyd football team, in which all four members, plus Steve O'Rourke, the now departed Arthur Max and Hipgnosis's own Storm Thorgerson could be seen posing. Gilmour later recalled a particularly bloody defeat at the hands of the North London Marxists in which the guitarist nearly bit off part of his tongue. For the title, *A Nice Pair*, Hipgnosis went for the very literal, including a pair of naked breasts and a photograph of court jester Emo wearing a nice pair of Peter Wynne-Willson's cosmonocles. The gaps in Emo's teeth, visible in the picture, would soon be rectified, thanks to the generosity of his old friend Gilmour.

'Dave sent me to his dentist four times,' admits Emo. 'The first new set of teeth I had done, I got beaten up about a day later in a pub on the Kings Road, and Dave had to pay to have them done again.' Gilmour's largesse would extend to others in the Cambridge fraternity, paying for ex-roadie Pip Carter's drug rehabilitation, and, over the years, quietly helping out with mortgage payments and tax bills for those friends finding themselves in dire financial straits.

In 1974 Syd Barrett emerged again from his Cambridge hidey-hole. A year before, several months after the Stars débâcle, Barrett had been seen playing guitar alongside former Cream bassist Jack Bruce in a Cambridge church hall. Royalties from the Pink Floyd compilation *Relics* had started coming in, and Barrett again moved to London. After a spell at the Park Lane Hilton he took out a lease on two flats in Chelsea Cloisters, near to Sloane Square. He filled the first sixth-floor apartment with guitars, amplifiers and other possessions, while living in a two-room flat on the ninth.

In April 1974, Nick Kent had written an article about Barrett in *New Musical Express*, interviewing former associates, including David Gilmour, and drawing together the wealth of anecdotes about the former Floyd singer, many of which subsequently passed into legend: the Mandrax-in-the-hair tale; the meltdown on American TV . . .

'Tony Secunda, who used to manage The Move, told me the story about Syd rubbing Mandrax into his hair,' says Kent. 'Then someone else told me the same story. As is the case with after-the-fact gossiping, it seemed to me that maybe 70 per cent of these stories were actually true.' These stories also included the claims that 'Barrett may or may not have worked in a factory, as a gardener, tried to enrol as an architecture student, grown mushrooms in his basement, been a tramp, spent two weeks in New York busking, tried to become a Pink Floyd roadie . . .'

Seven months before his scathing live review in *NME*, Kent found David Gilmour an obliging interviewee: 'We met in a pub in Covent Garden and he was totally candid about the Syd situation and didn't try and whitewash it. Gilmour had this everyman quality about him. Totally unpretentious. He was with an American girl then, Ginger, who kept bugging him throughout the interview to go to a restaurant with her. She kept fidgeting and saying, "How *long* is this going to go on, Dave?" And he was only there for forty-five minutes.'

As well as suggesting that some of Syd's problems were attributable to his father's death and that 'his mother always pampered him – and made him out to be a genius of sorts', Gilmour also wisely pinpricked the mystical aura already surrounding Barrett: 'He functions on a totally different plane of logic, and some people will claim, "Well, yeah, man, he's on a higher cosmic level", but basically there's something drastically wrong.'

In his article, Kent mentioned that Barrett was now living in Chelsea, and frequently visited the Morrison Agency. Bryan Morrison owned Lupus Music, Barrett's publishing company, who took care of his royalties. Kent also mentioned that EMI were keen to get Barrett back into the studio. Between July and August that year, Syd returned on several occasions to Abbey Road, at Bryan Morrison's behest.

Engineer John Leckie, then working with singer-songwriter Roy Harper, was present when Pete Jenner brought Syd in. 'The plan was that Syd was going to make another album by himself,' says Leckie. 'He was going to make the album by doing different things every day – piano one day, drums the next, bass the next. I remember he came in with a load of new guitars. But we never got that far. I don't think we made it to the piano.'

The idea was for Barrett to be recorded playing whatever he wanted, and for Jenner to listen through the tapes, and take anything worthwhile, onto which a bass and drums could be overdubbed. A handful of scraps emerged. But the sessions were a disaster. Syd hadn't written any new songs, and, according to one observer, turned up one day without any strings on his guitar.

'Bryan Morrison was there,' continues Leckie. 'Bryan always smoked a cigar and was in evening wear. He was a big guy who went on to play polo with Prince Charles. Morrison kept pushing Syd – "Come on, Syd, come on, Syd, get it together" – but it was no use. He didn't have anything.'

Morrison's anxiety may have been exacerbated by another incident involving Syd from around the same time. Barrett had turned up at Lupus Music and demanded a royalty cheque. When he was told that he'd been in a day before and had signed for his cheque then, Syd began shouting. Morrison came out of his office to reprimand him and Barrett bit Bryan's outstretched finger, drawing blood.

At Chelsea Cloisters, Barrett installed a huge colour TV set, and splashed out on expensive hi-fi equipment and clothes, most of which were stashed in the sixth-floor apartment and rarely touched again. His frequent haunt became the neighbouring Marlborough Arms, where he'd sit alone, polishing off pints of Guinness. Over the course of a few months, he retreated back into himself, cutting off all his hair again, gaining a vast amount of weight, and donating his possessions randomly to the porters at Chelsea Cloisters. At least one eyewitness from the time remembered seeing Barrett in Sloane Square wearing a woman's dress underneath his overcoat.

'After my article came out, I kept encountering people who knew Syd from the Cambridge days,' says Nick Kent. 'There was always someone saying, "Oh, I was his girlfriend for two months" or "I used to roadie for one of his groups", and they all spoke about how much he'd changed physically.'

John Whiteley, Syd's occasional flatmate from Earlham Street nearly ten years before, was among those who spotted him in London that year. 'I saw him on the Kings Road,' says Whiteley. 'It was shocking, because he'd been such a handsome boy. Now he was so overweight, and he'd shaved his head, but he was *still* walking on his tip-toes, in the way that he did. I stayed on the other side of the road. I couldn't speak to him.'

Whiteley's impressions were echoed by others. The sightings soon had a depressing familiarity: the bloated, bald man incongruously dressed in a Hawaiian shirt or huge overcoat, hanging around Earls Court or South Kensington, walking the same way, up on his toes.

Storm Thorgerson and Aubrey Powell would also encounter Syd that year. A few weeks after the *NME* article, EMI reissued Barrett's two solo LPs as a double album package. Storm and Po went to Chelsea Cloisters to try and take a new photograph of Syd for the album sleeve. They knocked on the door of his flat. 'Finally, he called to us through the door, "Who's there?"' remembers Po. 'I said, "It's Storm and Po. Can we come in and have a chat?" And he just said, "Go away!" That was the last time I ever spoke to him.'

'Part of me was angry,' admits Storm. 'I thought: Screw you, I'll be off. Here I was knocking on the door of someone I'd known since I was fourteen and he wouldn't let me in.'

David Gilmour's confession in *NME* that *Dark Side of the Moon* had left the band 'creatively trapped', was still pertinent when Pink Floyd gathered at Abbey Road in January 1975.

'After *Dark Side* we were really floundering around,' said Gilmour years later. 'I wanted to make the next album more musical. I always thought that Roger's emergence as a great lyric writer on the last album was such that he came to overshadow the music.'

Waters wanted to make another themed album, this time dealing with the idea of emotional absence; the concept of people being there but not *really* there, into which Waters' reflections on the music industry and the band's general state of mind could also be filtered. Gilmour simply wanted to record the tracks they'd already written and steer clear of another grand concept. Meanwhile Wright struggled with Waters' ideas, as he simply didn't share the bassist's preoccupation with the evils of the music industry. 'Roger's view wasn't necessarily my view,' he said.

Nick Mason later summed up the group's collective mindset: 'Roger was getting crosser. We were all getting older, there was much more drama between us, people turning up at the studio late. There was more pressure on me to make the drumming more accurate and less flowery.' At the time, he was more candid, telling Capital Radio DJ Nicky Horne, 'I really did wish I wasn't there. But it wasn't specifically to do with what was going on in the band, as much as what was going on outside the band. I am very bad at closing off my mind to whatever is bothering me. But my alarm and despondency manifested itself in a complete rigor mortis.' With marital problems, Mason's mind simply wasn't on the job.

'Some of the lads needed to be jollied along a bit,' joked Waters at the time. In reality, it was the closest Pink Floyd had yet come to splitting up. Later, Mason would claim that each of his bandmates had approached Steve O'Rourke individually to discuss leaving.

Despite the air of unease, some progress was made. Between January and the beginning of March, the album that would become *Wish You Were Here* began to take shape. 'Shine On You Crazy Diamond' had now been expanded to around twenty minutes, and would incorporate longer instrumental passages, backing vocals from The Blackberries and a saxophone solo from Dick Parry. John Leckie ended up overseeing the first sessions on the song, until Floyd's front-of-house engineer Brian Humphries took over. (Abbey Road agreed to the use of an outside engineer 'but only because it was the Pink Floyd'.) Humphries' job had originally been offered to Alan Parsons. 'They offered me £10,000 a year to become their permanent sound engineer,' says Parsons. 'But I also wanted a royalty on the next album, and Steve O'Rourke said no.' Parsons was also about to start work on his own music, as The Alan Parsons Project. 'So I also had that going on. I still think that if they'd offered me the job a few months earlier I would have taken it.'

'Shine On You Crazy Diamond' had been inspired in some part by Waters' frustration with the endless speculation about Barrett in the music press. 'I've never read an intelligent piece on Syd Barrett in any magazine, never,' he complained in 1976. 'I wrote and rewrote and rewrote and rewrote that lyric because I wanted it to be as close as possible to what I felt. There's a truthful feeling in that piece. That sort of indefinable, inevitable melancholy about the disappearance of Syd. He's withdrawn so far away that he's no longer there.'

The initial plan had been to put the piece on one whole side of the album, like 'Echoes' on *Meddle*, with 'Raving and Drooling' and 'Gotta Be Crazy' on the other. This was Gilmour's preferred option. But that would have been the easy option, and Waters was in no mood to make things easy. Instead, he suggested splitting 'Shine On . . .' into two and having it bookend the album. 'Raving and Drooling' and 'Gotta Be Crazy' would now be put aside for a future Floyd album, with the bassist deciding to write songs more in keeping with the same theme of absence that had so inspired 'Shine On . . .' He only had to look at some of his bandmates for subject matter. 'No one was really looking anyone in the eye,' he recalled. 'It was all very mechanical.'

Waters wrote two new songs on his own, 'Welcome to the Machine', 'Have a Cigar' and, in partnership with Gilmour, 'Wish You Were Here'. The songs would be worked up in stages now and later in a second burst of activity at Abbey Road that summer. 'Welcome to the Machine' was a unyieldingly bleak dissertation on the human condition, and, more personally, those – a rock 'n' roll band, maybe – who spent their lives in search of a dream, only to find that the machine runs on dreams and very little else. 'People are very vulnerable to their own blindness, their own greed, their own need to be loved,' explained Waters. 'Success has to be a real need. And the dream is that when you are successful, when you're a star, you'll be fine, everything will go wonderfully well. That's the dream and everybody knows it's an empty one. The song is about the business situation which I find myself in. One's encouraged to be absent because one's not encouraged to pay any attention to reality.' The lyrics hardly disguised the autobiographical nature of the song. Making Gilmour take the lead vocal somehow accentuated rather than softened the message. But it is Wright's VCS3 synth lines that now dominate, giving the song an unremitting bleakness.

'Have a Cigar' continued the theme, offering another sarcastic jibe against the air-headed nature of the music industry. Lighter than 'Welcome to the Machine', its jazzy lilt was broken up with plenty of spluttering guitar fills and an extended guitar solo. One lyric referred to the time the band had been asked by a record company minion: which of them was Pink? The only problem was that Gilmour felt uncomfortable singing Waters' words, while Waters struggled with taking the lead vocal. The problem would be rectified in the summer recording sessions.

Finally, the Gilmour/Waters co-written title track assumed the same uplifting quality that had typified the best of *Dark Side of the Moon*. Its subject matter, though, was as self-questioning as the rest of the album. The line 'two lost souls swimming in a fishbowl year after year' could have referred to the sense of dislocation among the band members at the time, as much as to Waters' crumbling relationship with his wife, which was at least part of its inspiration. 'It's about the sensations that accompany the state of not being *there*,' offered Waters. 'To work and to be with people whom you know aren't there any more.'

Further sessions on the album throughout June were slipped in between a sold-out US tour. In keeping with their press-unfriendly image, the band's sole advertising for the tour was a syndicated live Pink Floyd show, which was broadcast in each of the major cities in advance of the tour. Demand was such that the Los Angeles Sports Arena shifted all 67,000 tickets in a single day. 'Raving and Drooling' and 'Gotta Be Crazy' were still in the set, joined by the extended 'Shine On You Crazy Diamond', 'Have a Cigar', 'Echoes' and *Dark Side of the Moon*. The band's special effects had been extended even further and now included an arsenal of pyrotechnics, as well as a model aircraft, which zoomed over the audience and 'crashed' during *Dark Side of the Moon*, and which, without fail, would make soundman Brian Humphries duck as it hurtled overhead.

Meanwhile, the Floyd's trademark circular screen flashed Gerald Scarfe's images, created in many cases before he or his team of animators had heard any of the Floyd's new music.

'I said to Roger, "We can't get them to do anything as there are no tracks,"' recalls Scarfe. 'Roger was like, "Just get them to do *anything*; I'll make it fit later on." Sure enough, what we did do fitted in alongside certain passages. What was frustrating for the animators is that they knew it could have been better if they could have picked up an accent in the music now and again. But that gave it a disjointed feel that somehow complemented the music by not following it precisely.'

This flying-by-the seat-of-the-pants quality had been the norm since Scarfe began his relationship with Pink Floyd on the 1974 tour. 'I'd produce new bits of film as and when I could, and just turn up at the gig with a can under my arm. Sometimes, because of the traffic, I wouldn't get there until twenty minutes before showtime, and I'd find Roger in the dressing room, going, "Where the fuck have you *been*?" They'd lace up the film there and then and put it in anywhere.'

As an outsider coming into the Floyd's closed circle, Scarfe observed the band members' individual roles: 'Nick was the organiser, the ambassador. He approached me at first, but I remember him saying, "Just wait, once you get started you'll suddenly find you're dealing with Roger." Rick was always off to the side somewhere, in his own world. Dave was always very easy-going, but I had the impression he thought it should just be about the music.'

The planned *pièce de résistance* of the 1975 US tour was an inflatable pyramid designed to float above the stage, anchored by cables, recreating the prism on the sleeve of *Dark Side of the Moon*. Waters sketched out the design, but, at a height of 60ft when inflated, and powered by a considerable amount of helium, the pyramid would prove to be an unwieldy beast.

At the Three Rivers Stadium, Pittsburgh on 20 June, projectionist Pete Revell witnessed the pyramid's last, ill-fated stand. 'It used to go up on a pair of hydraulic winches, but at Three Rivers one of them came off, but the other one just kept pumping, so the whole thing flipped upside down. The bottom was like a soft skin, but there was this aluminium framework in the corners, pumped up with helium. All the buoyancy was now pointing at the bottom. This thing shot out into the night sky, like a giant jellyfish.'

The weight of the pyramid sent it over the side of the stadium wall, dragging the ropes behind it. 'It then started bouncing around the car park,' says Revell, 'and as there was this aluminium frame inside, it started busting up cars, lamp-posts. I remember we were trying to get everyone out of the car park, but it was no good. There were about two hundred kids out there with knives and bottles, hacking bits off to keep as souvenirs, inhaling the helium and rabbiting away like Donald Duck. I think what was left of the balloon eventually came down in a river near Pittsburgh.'

While marital and musical angst was rife within the band, the crew were having a rather better time of it. 'We were very well looked after,' says Revell. 'But in the end, we were told we were costing them too much money and were told not to order anything more on room service. In America it was getting silly – you'd phone up at 2 a.m.: "Can I have four gin and tonics and 400 cigarettes, please." They put a stop to all that.'

Nevertheless, Revell would feel the wrath of his paymasters on the final date of Floyd's US tour. The band's increasing use of pyrotechnics had led to run-ins with local fire marshals, and the crew began hiding their flash bombs from the snooping officials, before letting them off at the last possible moment. The decision was taken to mark the end of the North American tour with a gig at the Ivor Wynne Stadium in Hamilton, Ontario, with, to quote the projectionist, 'the biggest, loudest, fuck-off explosion ever' to accompany the Floyd's 'crashing plane'. The explosion was suitably dramatic, and, with the gig over, the crew began stripping down the stage. 'That was when I realised a couple of the bins hadn't gone off,' says Pete Revell. 'We had four sticks of dynamite, flash powder and detonators left over, all out of their tins, that we had to get rid of somehow. I said, "Stand back, I'll set this lot off." What we didn't realise is there was more in these bins than had gone off during the gig.' The resulting explosion blew out half the stadium's back wall and windows in some of the nearby houses. 'One bin went up in the air and we never saw it again. Above us was one of those scoreboards surrounded by light bulbs. The explosion went through the bottom and blew the front out, sending glass and aluminium everywhere. I was in shock for two hours.'

Once he'd sufficiently recovered, Revell was sent for, back at the band's hotel. 'They'd pulled a table round and set up four chairs behind it, as if they were a board of directors. I felt like a schoolboy being sent to see the headmaster. They were like, "I think we need to have words." '

The band were especially sensitive after a previous mishap with pyrotechnics in France.

'One of them said, "After Paris, we said this would never happen again." I replied, "I didn't do Paris", to which they said, "No, but you've just *done* Canada."'

Revell kept his job, but a final show in the UK at Knebworth Park was a dispiriting experience for the band. The 40,000-capacity open-air arena ended up holding nearer to 100,000, when the perimeter fence was removed. Floyd were due to headline over Captain Beefheart, The Steve Miller Band and their old friend Roy Harper, all of whom would be using the band's PA during the day. The jet-lagged road crew arrived late to set up the equipment, only to discover that the backstage generators were liable to voltage fluctuation. This meant that Richard Wright's state-of-the-art keyboards kept slipping in and out of tune. A decision to buzz the crowd at the start of the gig with two Second World War Spitfires failed to have quite the desired effect, as the road crew were still feverishly preparing the stage at the time. At one point during the gig, half of the PA failed completely. Backstage, in a fit of pique after having his stage clothes stolen, support act Roy Harper smashed up his trailer. Roger Waters witnessed the incident and filed it away for use in a future Pink Floyd song.

Harper's connection with Pink Floyd would grow stronger during 1975. At Knebworth, he sang lead vocals on 'Have a Cigar', reprising his performance on a recorded version of the song from a few weeks earlier. Midway through the US dates, when the band had returned to the UK for a second burst of activity at Abbey Road, they had found Harper in a neighbouring studio, recording his next album, *HQ*, with producer John Leckie. He had known Pink Floyd since the late sixties, when the two acts had appeared on the same bill at the free festival in Hyde Park. A singular, eccentric talent, Harper also shared some of Roger Waters' concerns and worldviews.

Waters had been struggling with the lead vocal on 'Have a Cigar' for some time. Gilmour had refused to sing it, claiming not to feel sufficient empathy with the lyrics. 'Roy was in and out of the studio all the time,' said Waters. 'I can't remember who suggested he sing it – maybe I did, probably hoping everyone would go, "Oh no, Rog, *you* do it." But they didn't. They all went, "Oh yeah, that's a good idea."'

'Roger can write songs but he's never going to be in the top one hundred as a rock singer,' said Harper. 'He tries hard, he's a good lad. Anyway, neither of them could get up there. I just stood at the back, leaning against a machine and laughing. I said, "I'll sing it for you", and someone said, "OK", and I said, "For a price." '

Harper delivered the necessary degree of incredulous sarcasm on lyrics that referenced the music biz hysteria that had greeted the band after *Dark Side of the Moon* – lyrics that referred to riding the gravy train. In years to come, when working with producer Bob Ezrin on *The Wall*, Waters would tell him, 'You can write anything you want, just don't expect a credit.' Harper's name would appear on the finished album. But that was all.

'Roger said, "We must make sure you get a payment for this," ' says John Leckie, 'and Roy said, "Just get me a life season ticket to Lord's [cricket ground]." He kept prompting Roger, but it never came. About ten years later Roy wrote a letter to Roger, and decided that, due to the success of *Wish You Were Here,* £10,000 would be adequate. And heard nothing at all.' Though Gilmour claimed it was unlikely that Waters would have agreed to such a thing.

'I think it was a bad idea now,' said Waters. 'Roy did it very well, but it's just not *us* any more.'

Roy Harper wasn't the only special guest, or old friend to drop by the sessions. When it was discovered that classical violinists Yehudi Menuhin and Stephane Grappelli were recording a duet at Abbey Road, Gilmour suggested Grappelli come in and play a final violin coda to the song 'Wish You Were Here'. Grappelli haggled over his fee but finally settled at £300. In the end, his playing is virtually inaudible on the final mix. 'It was terrific fun, though,' recalled Gilmour. 'Avoiding his wandering hands.'

One addition to the final mix was a snippet from a radio programme that linked the end of 'Shine On . . . Part One' to the beginning of 'Wish You Were Here'. The opening lines of the song were mixed in such a way as to sound as if they were coming out of the radio. As Gilmour explained, 'It's all meant to sound like the first track getting sucked into the radio with one person sitting in the room playing guitar along to the radio.' The radio programme and interference was recorded on Gilmour's own car radio, while someone turned the dial. The tiny sample of Tchaikovsky's Fourth Symphony fitted the beginning of 'Wish You Were Here' perfectly.

On 5 June, as the band busied themselves for another day at the coalface, each of them in turn wondered who the bald, overweight man fussing around at the back of the studio was. Most assumed that, as he'd made it past the reception desk into the confines of the studio, he must be, to quote Nick Mason, 'something to do with one of the engineers'. Hardly ones for confrontation at the best of times, his presence went unchallenged. In the grand tradition of hearsay, nobody present that day can quite agree on the exact circumstances of Syd Barrett's arrival in the studio.

'Everyone has a different version of that story,' says Mason. 'I talked to at least one person who thought that Syd had been in the studio on at least three or four days, I thought he was only there for an hour, and someone else says he was there for the whole afternoon . . .' The drummer remembers a 'large, fat bloke with a shaven head, wearing a decrepit old tan mac and carrying a plastic shopping bag'. The only known photograph of Barrett at the sessions shows him shaven-headed and wearing a tight-fitting, white, short-sleeved shirt, with the waistband of his trousers hiked up over his stomach. He is certainly unrecognisable as the Syd Barrett of four years earlier.

For Roger Waters, the physical transformation was shocking. 'I was in fucking tears,' he said later. It was Waters that pointed Barrett out to Richard Wright. 'Roger said, "You don't know who that guy is, do you? It's Syd,"' recalled Wright. 'It was a huge shock. He kept standing up and brushing his teeth, then putting his toothbrush away and sitting down.'

According to Mason, Wright and Waters, Barrett's arrival coincided with a playback of 'Shine On You Crazy Diamond'. Gilmour, whose memory of the event is sketchier than the others, claims not to remember which song they were working on, but claimed in one interview that Syd 'turned up for two or three days and then didn't come any more'.

According to Richard Wright, at one point, 'Syd stood up and said, "Right, when do I put the guitar on?" And, of course, he didn't have a guitar with him, and we said, "Sorry, Syd, the guitar's all done."'

On 7 July, during a break in the *Wish You Were Here* sessions, Gilmour married girlfriend Ginger at Epping Forest Register Office, and the Syd tale takes on another curious twist. In conversation with *Mojo* magazine in 2006, Gilmour disputed any stories that Syd had attended his wedding. Yet at least three of the guests claim they saw Syd at a post-wedding meal at Abbey Road. Ex-manager Andrew King recalled Barrett looking 'like the type of bloke who serves you in a hamburger bar in Kansas City'. Humble Pie drummer Jerry Shirley referred to him as 'an overweight Hare Krishna-type chap'. But whatever the frequency of his visits, there could be no possible reconciliation. Barrett was clearly very sick. The band moved on, and he moved back to Chelsea, where he would remain on and off for the next six years.

'He doesn't want to be bothered,' Bryan Morrison told one inquisitive reporter. 'He just sits there on his own, watching television all day and getting fat.'

Towards the end of the *Wish You Were Here* sessions, Hipgnosis presented the band with ideas for the album cover. Aware of the theme of emotional absence running through the music and, in some cases, the personal lives of the band, Storm Thorgerson hit on the idea of an 'absent' (read: 'hidden') cover. He proposed concealing the cover in a black opaque cellophane wrap. The idea was mooted during a meal in the Abbey Road canteen, with the band, Steve O'Rourke and anyone else that happened to be eating alongside them, listening in. The band agreed, with the only record company proviso being that the cellophane wrap included a sticker identifying the name of the band and the album. The hidden sleeve featured another enduring Floyd image: two business-suited men shaking hands, one of them on fire.

Thorgerson explained his thinking in a radio interview at the time: 'The handshake was a symbol of the whole notion of how you may get hold of somebody, shake them by the hand, and they're trying to tell you how much they're really there when they gripped you, but in fact they're miles away.' For most, the burning man was taken as a very literal reference to the notion of 'getting burnt' in business. Photographed on an empty Hollywood film lot, the flaming stuntman, Ronnie Rondell, was frequently seen risking life and limb in such TV shows as *Charlie's Angels*. In what would become a familiar artistic approach of layers within layers for Pink Floyd album covers, Hipgnosis included separate designs along the same theme for the back and inside covers. Of these an image of an upturned diver, the top half of his body concealed beneath motionless water, was the most striking. 'A dive without a splash? An action without its trace? Is it present or absent?' offered Thorgerson later.

The photograph had been taken at Lake Mono in California. The yoga-trained diver had assumed a handstand position, and held his breath underwater while waiting for the ripples in the lake to subside and the photograph to be taken. Designer George Hardie's creation for the sticker and the record label itself repeated the theme of the insincere handshake, with two robotic hands clasped together.

Wish You Were Here was released worldwide in September 1975. But that summer's appearance at Knebworth would be the last Pink Floyd live show until 1977. In an interview conducted for the *Wish You Were Here Songbook*, published a month after the album's release, Roger Waters made little attempt to disguise the unrest and dissatisfaction he felt. 'I'm sorry, I wanted to do this interview, but my mind's scrambled . . .' he protests at one point. Instead, Waters ran through the difficulties experienced while making the album, refusing to present the kind of united front David Gilmour had worked so hard to maintain during his encounter with *NME* at the beginning of the year.

The bass player's willingness to admit to problems within the band had manifested itself in a suggestion during the making of the album to include segments of dialogue, in the style of the 'interviews' on *Dark Side of the Moon*. 'I'd like to have heard us argue and talk things over on this record,' he said. 'I'd like to have heard extracts of the conversations that took place during the recording.'

Waters' idea may not have been that far-fetched. Throughout some dates on the tour, Storm Thorgerson and Waters' friend Nick Sedgwick had accompanied the band. Also from Cambridge, Sedgwick had moved in the same circles since his teenage years. By the mid-1970s, he was working as a freelance writer. Nick played golf with Waters and had previously spent time with Roger and Judy in Greece. Waters had invited him and Storm to accompany the band on tour and write, as Roger would later describe it, 'the definitive book on the experience in Pink Floyd'.

Photographer Jill Furmanovsky, one of the few music press personnel allowed access to the Floyd's inner sanctum, also joined them on some dates. 'Storm got me to take pictures of *everything*,' said Jill. 'He would ring me up and say, "Quick, come to Room 253 as Dave's playing backgammon" or "Roger's playing golf".' Yet as the photographer would also admit, 'You never knew with the Floyd if you were persona grata or non grata. Even some of the individual members of the band weren't always sure if they were in the band or not, let alone if a photographer was welcome.'

The vibe around the tour was what Jill Furmanovsky describes as a 'dark soap opera'. It also filtered beyond the bands to their wives and girlfriends. After a Floyd gig in the US, Waters called his now estranged wife Judy back home in England. Another man answered the phone. The couple would divorce that year.

Sedgwick and Thorgerson had chronicled the band's 1974 UK dates, and written up their impressions. Early chapters were distributed to the band. 'We all sat down and read it, and it was fascinating,' said Waters. 'Dave read it and said, "Yeah", and then, a couple of days later, he just *exploded*. He started saying things like, "If this is true, then I might as well not be in the band", because it didn't fit with how he thought of himself and his role in the band. It described me as the leader. So the whole book was suppressed.'

'I don't think it's strictly true to say that David stopped it,' says Storm Thorgerson. 'I think it was circumstantial that the book didn't come out. They had to go and make *Wish You Were Here*, Roger was getting divorced, and I was busy. We didn't follow it through, either. But it does display the dynamic in the group at that time. I had tapes of certain discussions, some arguments. At times, people perhaps said things they wished they hadn't.'

There was, perhaps, a further complication. Thorgerson had also joined Pink Floyd on tour in the US, without Sedgwick. 'There were various indiscretions that occur more on foreign tours than on domestic tours,' he admits. 'And I think we would have been very likely to report them in the book.'

It was Sedgwick that would conduct the interview with Waters for the subsequent *Wish You Were Here Songbook*. He would remain one of Waters' closest confidants, and golf partner, long after the bassist's split from Pink Floyd. 'Nick was the only one of us that Roger didn't cut out of his life,' says another of his Cambridge contemporaries. The book remains unpublished.

Whatever turmoil the band were experiencing made little difference to the public's reaction to *Wish You Were Here*. The album debuted at number 1 in both the UK and US, despite the lack of any tour dates to promote it. *Sounds* was effusive in its praise ('light years better than *Dark Side of the Moon*'), but others were less impressed. Pete Erskine's review in

New Musical Express arrived at the conclusion that 'as a last, desperate, uninspired measure they've finally succumbed to recycling the more obvious musical bits of [*Dark Side of the*] *Moon*'. No great fan of the previous album, though, Erskine admitted that 'where *Moon* seemed aimless and sometimes positively numbskull, *Wish You Were Here* is concise, highly melodic and very well played'. *Melody Maker*'s Allan Jones came in much harder: 'It forces one to the conclusion that, for the last two years (possibly longer), Floyd have existed in a state of suspended animation ... *Wish You Were Here* sucks. It's as simple as that.'

The criticism extended across the water. *Rolling Stone*'s Ben Edmonds berated the band for gimmickry over music and cited 'Shine On You Crazy Diamond' as a fumbled opportunity for Waters really to sing about Syd Barrett. There was a recurring theme in the complaints: that Floyd were too insular, disconnected from reality, and that Waters' lyrics were below par and too quick to bite the hand that feeds. Yet with 900,000 advance orders for the album in the US (the largest for any Columbia release), Floyd's new American paymasters hardly needed to worry. *Wish You Were Here* would go on to sell 6 million copies in its first year alone.

The record's subsequent reputation as the serious Pink Floyd fan's album *du jour* lies in the fact that it distills the very essence of the band's sound at the time: that sense of dislocation and of emotions struggling to get out, anchored to music that sounds similarly cold and melancholy. 'I'm glad people have copped the sadness,' said Waters. 'It's a very sad record.' Much of the credit for this sound lies at Richard Wright's door. His ghostly synthesiser seems to dominate *Wish You Were Here*, especially on the second half of 'Shine On You Crazy Diamond'. Of the song's nine parts, Wright takes a songwriting credit on eight of them. No wonder it's his favourite Pink Floyd album. For the others, opinion was predictably divided. In 1995, Gilmour told *Guitarist* magazine: 'I think it's [*Wish You Were Here*] better in some ways than *Dark Side of the Moon*. There were moments when we didn't concentrate hard enough on the music side of it as we should have done. That was absorbed into an effort to try and make the balance between the music and the words a better one on *Wish You Were Here.* I thought that some place between the two was the ideal place where we should be heading.'

Waters felt differently: 'Some of it goes on and on and on ... I think we made a basic error in not arranging it in a different way so that some of the ideas were expanded lyrically before they were developed musically.' Interviewed barely a year after the album came out, Nick Mason expressed surprise at how good he thought it was. He'd been largely absent in mind, if not in body, and *Wish You Were Here* would be the first Pink Floyd album on which he didn't receive a writing credit. For the first time, Mason's name didn't appear anywhere on a Pink Floyd record.

Number 35 Britannia Row was an imposing-looking, three-storey converted chapel just off Islington's Essex Road. 1976 would be the first year since Pink Floyd began in which they didn't play live. Freed up to concentrate on how best, or not, to spend their money, the band had purchased the building with a view to turning it into a recording studio and warehouse facility. With the group off the road, their arsenal of PA and lighting systems was finally located under one roof and available for hire by other bands. Two companies were formed. Road crew members Mick Kluczynski and Robbie Williams were entrusted with the job of running Britannia Row Audio, while Graeme Fleming headed up Britannia Row Lighting. In truth, it was also a way to provide jobs for all three while the band weren't touring.

For Pink Floyd, the prospect of owning their own studio was both good for the ego and, so they thought, their bank balances. The original terms of their deal with EMI Records involved them receiving unlimited studio time at Abbey Road, in exchange for a cut in their percentage. But now the deal had lapsed, the band were conscious that any lengthy trawls through the 'rubbish library' might be hampered by the sound of a ticking studio clock.

The top floor of number 35 was converted into an office, complete with billiards table. The middle floor became the storage facility, while the ground floor was turned into a studio. Unfortunately, few of the Floyd's contemporaries required the band's quadraphonic mixing desk or space-age lighting effects, and the companies were only allowed to hire out existing Floyd equipment and not purchase anything new. The rental side of the business eventually floundered, until Robbie Williams and his business partner moved in, bought the equipment from the band, and set up an independent production company in the 1980s.

In the meantime, the Floyd's new studio fared rather better. Designed by Waters, Mason and another of their Regent Street Poly classmates, Jon

Corpe, it was, claimed Mason, 'fashionably austere', or, according to Waters, 'a fucking prison'. The dour interior design may have been rather forbidding, but it was, at least, theirs. With Brian Humphries and new in-house engineer Nick Griffiths installed, and with their road crew on call on the floor above, Britannia Row became Pink Floyd's centre of operations and their very own bunker. But it needed to pay for itself, and required a steady stream of bands booking studio time, while still leaving the place free for whenever Pink Floyd wanted to use it. In the meantime, the studio's accounting system wasn't quite as stringent as it might have been. The members of the band were earning huge sums, but spending the same. 'It was a bit like the Apple situation with The Beatles,' according to one insider.

With the group off the road, Nick Mason spent the first part of the year producing albums for Robert Wyatt and French jazz rockers Gong. Yet the drummer would also spend time in 1976 reprising his role as Pink Floyd's resident ambassador. Nicky Horne, DJ on London's independent station, Capital Radio, had an evening show, *Your Mother Wouldn't Like It*, which was the station's rival to the BBC's John Peel show. Horne played the heavyweight, album-oriented bands of the era, and was an unashamed Pink Floyd fan.

'Nick Mason introduced himself to me after a gig at the Hammersmith Odeon,' says Nicky Horne now. 'I have no idea whose gig it was, but I was upstairs in the green room when he came over. He said, "Hello, I'm with Pink Floyd, and I know you play us a lot on your programme, so thank you, we appreciate it." I was rather taken aback.' Mason gave Horne his telephone number and invited him round for tea.

'He had this place in Highgate, and I remember he had a miniature Bugatti that he drove around the garden in. So we were very much like boys with their toys – buzzing around the garden. Then we had tea, all very English, and Nick talked about Pink Floyd's image. It seemed so incongruous that he was being this hospitable, when the band had such a reputation for not giving interviews and not being approachable. He asked me if I had any ideas about how they might go about improving that. I hadn't been on air for very long and I was still a bit naive, so I thought, Sod it, and said, "I'd really like to do the definitive Pink Floyd interview for my show." Amazingly, he agreed.'

Capital Radio's *The Pink Floyd Story* would be broadcast in six parts over six consecutive weeks beginning in December 1976. In the months preceding this, Horne had unlimited access to all four of the band, but on the proviso that they would have pre-approval of each of the programmes before broadcast ('We'd never normally do that, but we thought: Fuck it, it's Pink Floyd'). It was an unprecedented PR exercise from a band usually so wary of publicity.

Nicky Horne amassed hours of interviews with each of the Floyd, but found Waters the most fascinating. Now separated from Judy, Roger had moved out of Islington to a house in Broxash Road, near Clapham Common, South London. Horne spent a day there.

'I was surprised because I expected him to be reticent and difficult and guarded, but with Roger it was all quite close to the surface. He was disarmingly honest about the problems they'd had making *Wish You Were Here* and his feelings about Syd Barrett. Those feelings were very raw. One of the sessions was almost like therapy. I said, "Tell me about guilt", and he would talk for twenty minutes.'

Among the exclusive material made available for the programme was the unedited interview between Waters and Roger 'The Hat' Manifold, the roadie whose voice could be heard on *Dark Side of the Moon*. Manifold's stoned ruminations on violence, death and the problems of working with musicians ('They should be more like normal people') were both sharp and funny. At one point the two could be heard puffing on a joint.

'Nick gave me that tape as he wanted me to hear it,' says Horne. 'I think because it showed Roger in a different light. You could tell that when he'd had a couple of joints you could delve anywhere, deep into his psyche. He wasn't guarded at all.'

Midway into the project, Horne realised that there was one important interviewee missing. 'I wanted Syd, and Dave Gilmour told me he was living at the Playboy Apartments in Park Lane. They knew where he was because they were sending him his royalty cheques. So I went there and they said, "No, he's now staying at the Hilton."'

Horne found out the room number at the Hilton and made his approach. 'The door was opened by this huge guy with no hair and no eyebrows – just completely bald. I thought he must be a bouncer or a bodyguard. I said, "Dave Gilmour's sent me to talk to Syd." And this guy looked at me and, with immense difficulty, sort of contorting his face, said, "Syd. Can't. Talk." And closed the door. I went downstairs and rang

Dave and told him about this guy I'd just met and what he'd said, and Gilmour replied, "That wasn't a bouncer, that was Syd." It was tragic to see him like that.'

The broadcast of *The Pink Floyd Story* was due to coincide with the release of Pink Floyd's next album. In April 1976, Floyd began an eight-month stint at Britannia Row to record the follow-up to *Wish You Were Here*. They went back to the two songs rejected from the last album, 'Raving and Drooling' and 'Gotta Be Crazy'. Re-examining the lyrics he'd written almost two years earlier, Waters found himself eventually sketching out another concept. If *Wish You Were Here* had been dominated by Waters' disillusionment, then the next Floyd album would find him in a an even spikier, and more confrontational mood.

The world around him would hardly improve his frame of mind. During one of the longest, hottest summers on record, violence erupted at the Notting Hill Carnival, the now annual celebration of West Indian culture of which the Floyd's former manager Peter Jenner had been the first treasurer. Police officers arrested a pickpocket near Portobello Road, prompting a group of black youths to come to his defence. Riot police were met with a hail of bricks, bottles and traffic cones. The incident would be eulogised in the song 'White Riot' by an angry new rock band called The Clash.

The economic and social environment influenced a musical sea change of which The Clash were not the only proponents. By the mid-1970s, there was a growing unease among some critics and fans with what they saw as the complacent attitude of rock's super-league bands. Pink Floyd's financial status, general aloofness and age (each of the band members was now in his thirties) made them a target for critics who believed that rock music should be made by younger, hungrier bands.

By 1974, groups had sprung up on both sides of the Atlantic championing a return to short songs and the death of the concept album. In New York, The Ramones shambled on stage looking like a sixties motorcycle gang, playing tracks that sometimes barely lasted two minutes. In Essex's Canvey Island, Dr Feelgood – all short hair and tight suits – peddled their own revved-up brand of dirty rhythm and blues.

Before long, others had arrived, and the music press had begun championing the likes of The Clash, The Damned and The Sex Pistols, 'punk rock' groups whose confrontational songs didn't require a quadraphonic PA system to be heard properly, and seemed a world away from Pink Floyd's studied introspection. Floyd were hardly the worst offenders, or the most maligned. With their gatefold album sleeves, musical virtuosity and arty conceits, Yes, Jethro Tull, Supertramp, Emerson Lake & Palmer and Genesis found themselves even more in the firing line.

Like The Ramones and Dr Feelgood, punk bands shunned the laid-back hippie fashion sense of the old guard. Beards and flares were out; their drug of choice was speed, not marijuana. Their musical brevity and anti-everything stance made them an attractive proposition to those fans bored of watching millionaire rock stars the size of matchstick men playing at the far end of football stadiums.

The Hipgnosis design team had enjoyed an early encounter with punk rock. Aubrey 'Po' Powell was photographing pop singer Olivia Newton-John behind the company's Denmark Street studios when he heard someone coughing up phlegm and spitting out of a nearby window. It was The Sex Pistols' singer Johnny Rotten (in real life, a twenty-year-old Hawkwind fan called John Lydon). The band and their manager Malcolm McLaren had moved into a rehearsal space in the same building. Over the coming months, Storm and Po would regularly pass the aspiring punk rockers in the communal hallway.

One day, Lydon appeared wearing a customised Pink Floyd T-shirt. Above the Floyd's logo, he'd added the words 'I Hate'. Po recalls: 'I said, "Are you having a fucking go at me?" He said, "Yes, you and all that other *shit* you're always playing." Mind you, they were terribly nice and polite most of the time.'

The accusations of complacency were hardly unfounded. The young guard of 1966 was now the old guard of 1976. A year before The Who had released *The Who By Numbers*, a highly confessional album in which Pete Townshend bemoaned his own band's slide from hungry young mods to corporate rock monsters. Townshend's lyrics from another Who song, 'New Song', created in 1977 about writing the same old song with some new lines, which everybody wanted to cheer – could have related to Roger Waters, who'd been voicing similar concerns since the success of *Dark Side of the Moon*. Yet while Townshend strived to engage with these young upstarts, and found himself riding on a degree of goodwill from those punk bands that had grown up listening to The Who, Pink Floyd remained indifferent. The growing distance between them and their audience may have troubled Waters, but, unlike Townshend, he was not given to drunken nights at the Roxy club in the company of various Sex Pistols. He remained resolutely aloof.

'When was punk?' quipped Waters in 1992. 'I didn't notice it.'

Gilmour was more accommodating, just. 'I don't think we felt alienated by punk, we just didn't feel it was particularly relevant to us,' he later told *NME*. 'I'm always amazed when I meet young English musicians who were big in the punk era, and they say they loved everything we did – and that includes one of The Sex Pistols! No, I'm not going to tell you which one.'

Nick Mason would end up producing The Damned's second album, *Music for Pleasure*, at Britannia Row in 1977: 'But that's only because they wanted Syd Barrett to do it. Obviously, he wasn't available, and I think they were rather disappointed to get me.' The Damned's desire to create, in their words, a 'psychedelic punk masterpiece' was thwarted, as their bass guitarist Captain Sensible soon realised. 'Nick Mason was not an unpleasant bloke,' said the Captain. 'But, here we were, bunking the Tube everyday and saying, "Fuckin' hell, Nick, I nearly got caught by the ticket collector this morning", and all he could say was, "I came in my Ferrari." There just wasn't a meeting of minds.'

Yet while his age, wealth and reputation may have been against him, Roger Waters' concerns – with inequality, prejudice, rampant monetarism, the numbing of the human spirit – weren't so far removed from those being expressed by some of these young bands. Pink Floyd's next album, *Animals*, would chime with the times rather more than anyone might have expected.

In a concerted burst of activity throughout the last half of 1976, Waters pieced together a new concept: a nightmarish future world in which the human race had been reduced to three sub-species: dogs, pigs and sheep. Each had different traits designed to reflect the foibles and pre-occupations of human beings: the clawing, fighting dogs; the tyrannical, despotic pigs; and, inevitably, the mindless sheep. The concept was borrowed from George Orwell's 1945 satirical novel *Animal Farm*, in which the animal society is an allegory for the Soviet Union under Stalin's regime. In Pink Floyd's version the sheep ultimately rise up to conquer their oppressors. A happy ending of sorts to a concept that never quite hung together as well as *Dark Side of the Moon* or Floyd's next concept album, *The Wall*.

'Sometime during the middle of recording it, it seemed like the right thing to do, to tie it all together,' explained Waters. 'Raving and Drooling' and 'Gotta Be Crazy' would now be reworked at Britannia Row to fit the theme of the new album. The former would become the song 'Sheep', while the second would become 'Dogs'. Waters would contribute two further songs, 'Pigs (Three Different Ones)' and 'Pigs On the Wing'. Once again, Waters was the dominant songwriter and ideas man.

Subsequently, some band members have claimed that the mood around the band was better than it had been during *Wish You Were Here*. Though Nick Mason later recalled that 'Roger was in full flow with the ideas, but he was really keeping Dave down, and frustrating him deliberately.' Part of the subsequent problem between the two would lie in the allocation of royalties. These were allocated per song, and Gilmour had a co-writing credit on only one track, 'Dogs', which was, nevertheless, the longest song on the album, taking up most of the first side.

At the eleventh hour, Waters appeared with 'Pigs on the Wing', which he promptly split into two, so that one verse opened the album and the second one closed the album, making it two separate pieces of music and bumping up his royalties even further. But while the others may have felt aggrieved by this situation, none of them was bringing very much to the table. Gilmour, by his own admission, was never the quickest or most prolific of songwriters, and he now had another distraction: Ginger had just given birth to the couple's first child, a daughter named Alice. In the meantime, neither Mason nor Wright was contributing new songs. In the drummer's case this was less unusual, but considering how many songwriting credits the keyboard player had on *Wish You Were Here*, something had clearly changed.

'It was partly my fault, because I didn't push my material,' says Wright. 'Or I was too lazy to write anything. But Dave *did* have something to offer, and only managed to get a couple of things on there.'

In truth, Wright was distracted by problems in his marriage to Juliette. But for him, the *Animals* sessions also marked the beginning of a swift decline in his relationship with Waters: '*Animals* was a slog. It wasn't a fun record to make, but this was when Roger *really* started to believe that he was the sole writer for the band. He believed that it was only because of him that the band was still going, and obviously, when he started to develop his ego trips, the person he would have his conflicts with would be me.'

Most of the songs that made up *Animals* would be among Waters' most forthright and vitriolic to date. But if Gilmour was, as Mason maintained, being 'kept down' by the bassist when it came to songwriting credits, he makes up for it in his explosive playing. Gilmour does some of his best work on *Animals*. He takes just one lead vocal on the Gilmour/Waters-written 'Dogs', giving the bassist's sour lyrics the same sweetening makeover they received on 'Welcome to the Machine', only to make them even more affecting in the process. While the guitarist would freely admit to not sharing Waters' bitter worldview, he never lets the mask slip on this caustic dismissal of money-hungry corporate climbers. There's something almost unbearable about Gilmour's unflinching delivery on the line 'Just another sad old man, all alone and dying of cancer . . .' Partway through, the song slows down to a funereal pace, allowing Wright to reprise the weeping synthesiser sounds used on *Wish You Were Here*. Waters assumes the lead vocal on the final verses, reeling off repeated statements in a high-pitched, slightly strangulated tone ('Who was fitted with collar and chain'). The nature of these final lyrics prompted some comparisons to the beatniks' set-text of some ten years earlier, the Allen Ginsberg poem 'Howl' ('Who walked all night with their shoes full of blood'). For all those music press accusations of complacency, these were not the lyrics or sentiments you would find expressed on an album by any of Floyd's contemporaries.

'Pigs (Three Different Ones)' was briefer, simpler but no less unpleasant. The metronomic, funky rhythm and repetitive cowbell almost puts the listener in mind of Free's 'Alright Now', especially when Gilmour starts playing some bluesy fills around the beat. In reality, the song was a close relative to *Wish You Were Here*'s 'Have a Cigar'. Then comes a barrage of grotesque honking noises, as Waters starts singing about the tyrannical pigs, while name-checking the pro-censorship campaigner Mary Whitehouse. 'I kept throwing that verse about Mary Whitehouse away,' said Waters. 'But I kept coming back to it.' The lyrics 'bus stop rat bag' and 'fucked-up old hag' also find their way into the song. The combination of lyrical spite and pristine musicianship makes the song sound even nastier.

While 'Sheep' is again credited to Waters alone, it's difficult to imagine the song without Gilmour's contribution. The group's savage humour finds a way in with the inclusion of the 23rd Psalm, albeit modified to celebrate a Lord who maketh me to hang on hooks in high places and converteth me to lamb cutlets, in which the unquestioning sheep – a metaphor for unquestioning Pink Floyd fans, maybe? – rise up and savage their masters. The song fell victim to what Waters had complained about on *Wish You Were Here*, by 'going on and on and on', but Gilmour's closing guitar solo, a moment of pure heavy metal riffing, justifies the wait. 'Sheep' was the only song from *Animals* to be considered for the band's setlist when they reconvened in 1987. While Gilmour may have loved the guitar solo, he declined to play it on the grounds that he could never sing it with the same amount of venom as Waters did.

'Pigs on the Wing Part One' and 'Part Two', the bassist's last-minute additions to *Animals*, offered a tiny ray of hope amid all the ranting and raving. The sentiments behind the song were inspired by events in Waters' life outside the band. 'I'm in love,' he said at the time. 'The first verse poses the question, "Where would I be without you?", and the second says, "In the face of all this other shit, I know you care about me and that makes it possible to survive." '

It marked the first time an outright love song had found its way on to any Pink Floyd album. Waters' new romantic interest was Carolyne Anne Christie. The daughter of a military captain, she was the niece of the Marquis of Zetland, part of the Zetland-Dundas lineage of landowners, with estates in Scotland and Yorkshire. Her involvement in the music business extended much further than her relationship with Pink Floyd's bassist. Carolyne had previously worked for Atlantic Records and was employed by Canadian record producer Bob Ezrin when she met Waters. She was also still married to her second husband, Robert 'Rock' Scully, manager of The Grateful Dead. According to Scully, in his autobiography *Living with the Dead*, their 1974 marriage took place purely so Carolyne could obtain a green card and join Led Zeppelin on a US tour. Carolyne's background and outlook – she was a member of the British aristocracy and a rock 'n' roll fan – couldn't have been more different from those of Waters' first wife, Judy. Roger and Judy had not had any children together, but in November 1976, Carolyne gave birth to her and Roger's first child, a son called Harry.

Animals was completed by Christmas. Taking a break from new fatherhood, Waters turned his attention to the pressing matter of the album's front cover. In an unprecedented turn of events, Hipgnosis had found their initial ideas for the sleeve rejected. Among several ideas presented was a drawing of a small child in his pyjamas stumbling into his parents' bedroom and seeing them having sex ('Copulating . . . like animals!' explains Storm Thorgerson).

Waters was unimpressed. 'I don't think the rest of the boys thought those ideas were that brilliant, either,' he said. 'So there was this feeling of, "Well, if you don't like it, do something better." So I said, "OK, I will." And I pedalled around South London on my bicycle with my camera and took some photos of Battersea Power Station.'

The South London power station was then already partially closed, and would cease operation completely by 1980. Drawn to what Waters described as 'the doomy, inhuman' image of the building, he proposed the idea of flying a pig between its four towers. 'It's a symbol of hope,' he explained, the ideas inspired by the more optimistic message contained in 'Pigs on the Wing'.

Hipgnosis agreed to help stage the photoshoot. Waters had already devised the idea of including a huge, inflatable pig as part of the stage show for the band's next tour. The same company that had produced the original Zeppelin airships had made the pig in Germany. The band took possession of a 30ft model, which, according to Nick Mason, was quickly nicknamed 'Algie'. The deflated pig was brought to the site, where various members of the Floyd's road crew and employees of the inflatable company set about trying to inflate it with large quantities of helium. Hipgnosis had hired a team of some fourteen photographers for the day, while Steve O'Rourke had cannily employed a marksman to shoot down the pig should it break free of its moorings, aware that its size and buoyancy could make it hazardous to any airline traffic. But technical problems meant that the pig couldn't be fully inflated. A second attempt the following day was more successful. The pig became airborne, and, with the aid of mooring ropes, was coaxed up alongside the building.

Suddenly, a gust of wind caused the inflatable to slip its moorings. O'Rourke had neglected to book the marksman for the second day, and the helium-filled porker broke free. By the afternoon it had been spotted at some 18,000ft above the coastal town of Chatham in Kent.

'All hell broke loose,' remembers Po. 'The RAF and air traffic control at Heathrow all started reporting this flying pig. We even had a mention on the evening news.' It was a perfect publicity stunt, and the best possible advertising for the new Pink Floyd album. Finally, at 10 p.m., the band had word that the beast had landed in a farmer's field in Godmersham, Kent. 'He was furious,' says Po, 'as it had apparently scared his cows.' Surprisingly, the pig was still in one piece. Roadies were sent to Kent to retrieve it. A third day of shooting went off without a hitch, although this time O'Rourke employed two marksmen, just in case.

But the problems weren't yet over. 'When we got the photographs back, the shots from the third day looked rather dull,' says Po. 'Whereas the pictures from the first day had this fantastic doomy sky and these wonderful cloud formations. So we used the sky from the first day and dropped in the picture of the pig from the third day. If we'd done that at the beginning, we could have saved thousands of pounds.'

The image of an airborne 'Algie' drifting between two pillars at Battersea Power Station made for an eye-catching motif on the cover of *Animals*. The forbidding clouds overhead made the sky look as if it had been lifted from a turbulent landscape painting by J.M.W. Turner, and were as striking as the pig itself. Inside, some downbeat black and white photographs of the partially derelict station's outhouses added to the grim atmosphere.

Animals was released on 23 January 1977. The final part of Capital Radio's *The Pink Floyd Story* aired two days earlier, completing six weeks of build-up to the 'New Floyd'. But there would be a twist in the 'tail', in keeping with the album's spirit of conniving one-upmanship. 'We made a very big deal of how we had the exclusive on *Animals*,' says Nicky Horne, 'and how we were going to broadcast it first. And the night before, I was driving home, listening to John Peel's show on the radio, when he said, in John's inimitable style, "We play tomorrow's hits today". . . and he played side one of *Animals*. I think Gilmour had given him a copy of the album. I was absolutely beside myself. After six weeks of us going on and on about our exclusive, we had, of course, got our comeuppance.'

Animals debuted in the UK at number 2 and at number 3 in the US, just failing to match either of its predecessors. 'I never expected *Animals* to sell as many as *Wish You Were Here* and *Dark Side of the Moon*,' said Gilmour. 'There's not a lot of sweet, singalong stuff on it.'

'It's a very violent album,' admitted Waters at the time. 'Violence tempered with sadness.' The music press agreed. Angus Mackinnon in *New Musical Express* applauded *Animals* as 'one of the most extreme, relentless, harrowing and downright iconoclastic hunks of music to have been made available this side of the sun'. Mackinnon pinpointed Waters' reluctance to 'toe the line taken by most rock names in positions similar to his own'. There was, the review claimed, something surprisingly compassionate about Waters' 'supremely agnostic fatalism' even if he comes across as vitriolic or embittered.

In *Melody Maker*, Karl Dallas earmarked the same lyrics as an 'uncomfortable taste of reality in a medium ("progressive" rock) that has become in recent years, increasingly soporific'. While the review's closing line seems rather glib – 'Perhaps they should re-name themselves Punk Floyd' – there's truth in the statement. Since the early seventies Pink Floyd had been lumped with other album-oriented bands under the convenient 'progressive rock' banner. Although, as Gilmour cautioned years later, 'I was never a big fan of most of what you'd call progressive rock. I'm like Groucho Marx – I don't want to belong to any club that will have me as a member.'

Animals hardly sat well alongside 1977's punk calling cards, The Clash's first album and The Sex Pistols' *Never Mind the Bollocks*, but nor did it fit with the music being made by Floyd's beardy contemporaries. Yes released *Going for the One* in 1977, an album full of fairytale lyricism and whimsy, while Emerson Lake & Palmer's *Works Volume I* from the same year contained an entire vinyl side given over to Keith Emerson's *Piano Concerto* (a similar idea had been explored by Pink Floyd eight years earlier on *Ummagumma*). These bands were not wringing their hands over corporate greed, man's inhumanity to man, or railing at the 'fucked-up old hags' that tried to censor what we watched on TV.

As well as the unprecedented PR exercise of Capital Radio's *The Pink Floyd Story*, the band also found a music critic that they deemed worthy of their attention. A year earlier Waters had given a revealing interview to Philippe Constantin, a friend who worked at the band's record label in France. But although he continued to treat most critics with suspicion or outright contempt, *Melody Maker*'s Karl Dallas would suddenly find himself persona grata in a way that few had managed before. Dallas was a musician in his own right and a long-time contributor to *Melody Maker*. He had seen Pink Floyd at the UFO club but had never been a fan. 'I used to talk to Syd and Roger in the refreshment bar,' he says. 'I thought the concept of Pink Floyd was interesting but the music was a bit boring.'

Dallas attended the press conference to launch the *Animals* album at Battersea Power Station. Steve O'Rourke was the sole representative of the Floyd camp, informing one writer that David Gilmour's non-appearance was because he was having trouble getting a babysitter. The writers were informed that they would not be allowed to take notes. Dallas enterprisingly bootlegged the record on his tape recorder, so that he could listen to it again later at his leisure. His favourable write-up was published a week before the album came out. Floyd's next tour was due to open in Dortmund, West Germany, at the end of the month, and Dallas found himself invited by EMI to attend a later show at Frankfurt.

'They were taking a load of journalists out there, and I agreed to go,' says Dallas. 'So we went along and had dinner with the band. Dave and Nick were always, "Hail fellow, well met", but they wouldn't usually give interviews, so the game was to try and get something quotable out of them, but they were usually one step ahead of us. Unfortunately, Roger was a complete arsehole. He sat at one of the tables and refused to speak to anyone. We were on the same plane back to England, and he completely ignored me. Then, out of the blue, a few days later, I received a letter which began something like, "I don't usually communicate with members of your ignoble profession, *but* . . ." Typical Roger Waters. But, in short, since coming back from Frankfurt, he'd read my review of *Animals* and liked it.' The two met again by coincidence at a gig, and Dallas challenged Waters to give him an interview. For the next two years, Dallas would find himself becoming one of the few journalists granted an audience with the band whenever they wished to communicate with the world at large.

Pink Floyd's latest excursion would take them through the next seven months, visiting Europe, Britain, North America and Canada. The female backing vocalists were gone, but Dick Parry was re-hired to play saxophone, alongside a second guitarist and bassist, Terence 'Snowy' White. A friend and confidant of Fleetwood Mac's Peter Green, White had a similar musical background in the blues to Gilmour. He had recorded an unreleased album for EMI with his own band Heavy Heart, but had busied himself lately with sessions for songwriter Joan Armatrading, as well as just turning down a gig with Steve Harley and Cockney Rebel. White's name was passed on to David Gilmour through a mutual friend, Kate Bush's then manager.

The guitarist had been summoned to Britannia Row during the final sessions for *Animals*. One of David Gilmour's solos had been accidentally erased, and White walked in to encounter a tense atmosphere and a similarly tense Gilmour. Asked if he wanted the gig, White said yes, but asked if he could at least have a jam while he was here. Gilmour's reply was a rather blunt: 'Well, you wouldn't be here if you couldn't play, would you?' At which point Waters suggested White play something. Snowy's sole contribution to the *Animals* album was a spur-of-the-moment guitar solo used to link the final 'Pigs on the Wing Part Two' back to the opening track, 'Pigs on the Wing Part One', but only for the eight-track cartridge release of the album. On tour, White would play both bass and rhythm guitar.

The *Animals* tour was a prime example of bigger and louder, though not always better. Promoters found themselves presented with a list of requirements before each gig, specifying the exact amount of space required for the stage, the PA and the lighting towers, and exactly how much power was required to run the show. The sheer scale of it meant that a theatre tour would be impossible. Only sports arenas or football stadiums could accommodate the PA, lighting rig and a whole series of inflatable props. The pig was now either suspended on steel cables to travel the length of the arena, or floated above the stage on cables, where it would explode at some suitably climactic moment in the show. Set designers Mark Fisher and Jonathan Park were also commissioned to create an inflatable 'nuclear family', comprising a father, mother and 2.4 children, which would make its debut at the Wembley Empire Pool. The helium-filled family would be pumped up backstage with the help of an industrial fan, and unleashed on the audience during the song 'Dogs'. In America, the props were extended to include a blow-up car, fridge and TV set. Meanwhile, Nick Mason's new party piece involved scanning through the airwaves on a transistor radio, picking up random noises for the introduction to 'Wish You Were Here'.

Gerald Scarfe's animations were also employed on 'Shine On You Crazy Diamond' and 'Welcome to the Machine'. 'Now that we finally had the music to work with, the animators were able to do even better than they had on the last tour,' recalls Scarfe. The visual extravaganza of severed heads, robotic reptiles and seas of blood matched the brutal mood of the music. Pink Floyd's set was now split into two halves. The first consisted of the whole of *Animals*, but rearranged to open with the album's closing track, 'Sheep'. The second set was the whole of *Wish You Were Here*, with encores of 'Money' and, occasionally, 'Us and Them'.

Richard Wright's prediction that Pink Floyd were in 'danger of becoming slaves to our equipment' seemed to have been realised. In Frankfurt, the stage filled with so much dry ice that the band were almost completely obscured. Disgruntled fans threw bottles and drink cans, one of them smashing on Nick Mason's drum kit. Ensuring that the props and film footage were always in sync with the music increased the pressure. Meanwhile, to aid his concentration, Roger Waters took to wearing headphones at every gig. While helping him stay in time, it gave the impression that the bassist was somehow isolating himself from both his fans and the band. Hired hand Snowy White's presence on the tour was another source of confusion for the audience. He would be the first member of the band to appear on stage, thudding out the bass guitar introduction to 'Sheep', while most of the bemused crowd wondered who he was.

The show arrived in England from Europe, with a five-night stand booked at London's Wembley Empire Pool. They ran straight into red tape. Officials from the Greater London Council descended on the venue to check that the band's inflatable pig had been equipped with a safety line as instructed. Roger Waters oversaw the inspection, barking orders to the pig's operators ('Halt pig! Revolve pig!'). Further GLC restrictions led to serious sound problems on the opening show at Wembley, with the band's crew working through the night to rectify the trouble. 'In a band like this, everyone's got to be working at full efficiency on stage, technically and emotionally,' Gilmour told Karl Dallas. 'I can get over things like that, but Roger can't. He gets very hung up about it.'

The warm reception *Animals* had received in the press was not repeated for the live show. Only the ever-gushing Derek Jewell in the *Sunday Times* seemed won over ('Their presentation is the ultimate in brilliantly staged theatre of despair'). UFO club regular Mick Farren, writing in *New Musical Express,* was less convinced by a 'depressingly hopeless journey through a menacingly sterile cosmos'. Just like the 1974 tour, there was a wearying familiarity to the complaints: that the show was in danger of over-powering the music.

Hugh Fielder, who'd once hired Gilmour to play guitar in his own band in Cambridge, was now writing for *Sounds.* 'The trouble was, the whole show ran to a click track,' says Fielder now. 'You could hear it start before the show began. There were no computers at the time, so if you wanted that pig to fly out at exactly the right time, you had to be synchronised. And that meant the band, with their heads down, headphones on, hardly looking at each other.' A week after the Wembley shows, *Melody Maker* printed a letter from an aggrieved Pink Floyd fan, claiming they'd seen David Gilmour yawn during the show.

The North American leg of the tour – now called *In the Flesh* – began at the Miami Baseball Stadium on 22 April. Everything was about to get even bigger. Chief technician Mick Kluczynski later recalled checking the venue for the first open-air American gig and panicking. 'I walked down on to the field and started looking upwards . . . and up . . . and up,' he said. 'I got on the phone to London and told them to double what we'd ordered.'

Once again, lack of rehearsal time brought with it the same problems that had hampered their last tour. 'The shows varied in quality,' wrote Nick Mason later. 'We were not spending enough time on key aspects like segueing from one number to the next. My memory is that some of the staging was as erratic as the music.'

Outdoor shows presented further problems. Playing sports stadia designed to hold as many as 80,000 people, the band found themselves confronted with an audience that had been herded into the venue hours before the show was due to start, many of whom had killed time since by consuming as much booze and drugs as they could get their hands on. The gigs became a godsend for local police officers looking for an easy marijuana bust. The audience was in no frame of mind to concentrate on the nuances and subtleties of the Floyd's new music, and were still, as Gilmour had complained before, determined 'to boogie'.

Despite the added pressures, recordings from the *In the Flesh* tour suggest that Gilmour, for one, seemed to spark off having another musician in the band, and both he and Snowy White shook up some of the material, producing some dynamic twin-guitar readings of 'Shine On You Crazy Diamond'. At California's Oakland Coliseum, White even found himself bundled back on stage for a spur-of-the-moment encore of 'Careful With That Axe Eugene', a song he had never heard, let alone played before.

Offstage, though, the mood was sometimes fraught. Roger Waters preferred to isolate himself from the rest of the group, arriving at the venue alone, and shunning any post-gig parties or meals. In Montreal, he was on the local golf course within minutes of checking into his hotel. The bass player's attitude was, as ever, a particular problem for Richard Wright, who jumped on a plane after one of the gigs and flew back to England. 'I was threatening to leave, and I remember saying, "I don't want any more of it." Steve [O'Rourke] said, "You can't, you mustn't."'

At the Oakland Coliseum, promoter Bill Graham filled a backstage pen with pigs in honour of the band's new mascot. Ginger Gilmour, who was accompanying David on the tour along with baby daughter Alice, was a staunch vegetarian. She demanded the animals be released. 'I think Ginger eventually went vegan,' says Emo. 'Of course, Dave was the complete opposite. He'd be off sneaking steak sandwiches and hamburgers.'

Ginger also found herself clashing with Waters' new girlfriend, Carolyne Christie. Both came from wildly different backgrounds and, as one associate from the time recalls, 'they did not see eye to eye. Carolyne was landed gentry, and had all the attitudes associated with her class, and she seemed to have this huge effect on Waters. He went through a massive change in the seventies. Firstly, he had this devout Socialist wife of whom he was very enamoured intellectually, and then he was with this very aristocratic woman, and he seemed to change completely.'

For Richard Wright, Waters' recent decision to buy a country house had been a prime example of his bandmate's hypocrisy. 'I was the first of the band to buy a country house, after *Dark Side of the Moon*,' said Wright, 'and Roger sat me down and said, "I can't believe you've done this, you've sold out, you're doing what every other rock star does." It took him, I think, a year and a half to buy his own country seat. I said, "Roger you're a hypocrite", and he said, "Oh, I didn't want it, my wife wanted it." Absolute bullshit.' Water's country seat was near Horsham in Sussex. Though his next property would be grander still: a Georgian mansion in the beautiful Hampshire village of Kimbridge, right on the River Test, a stretch of water renowned for some of the best trout fishing in the country.

The 1942 Oscar-nominated movie *Orchestra Wives* – 'It's hep! It's hot! It's hilarious!' – was a fictional account of a swing-era big band and the bitching and cat-fighting that went on between the musicians' wives. 'If you've ever seen that film, it will tell you what it was like between the Floyd and their other halves,' says Jeff Dexter. 'Let's just say that two of the band members had extremely influential wives.'

As the tour drew on, Waters' mood became even darker. He was frustrated by playing cavernous, impersonal arenas to audiences that he believed were only there to get stoned or drunk and hear 'Money'. At Soldier Field, the Superbowl stadium in Chicago, Steve O'Rourke took Waters up to the top of the bleachers behind the stage to look at the crowd. The promoters claimed to have sold out the 67,000-capacity stadium, but Waters was suspicious. 'I looked down and said, "No, there's at least 80,000 people there." I'd done enough big shows to know what 60,000 people looked like.' When the promoters insisted they'd only sold 67,000 tickets, O'Rourke hired a helicopter, a photographer and an attorney. The crowd was photographed from the air. 'There were 95,000 people there, and we were due another $640,000.'

On stage, Waters began shouting out random numbers, usually while the band ploughed through 'Pigs (Three Different Ones)'. It was only after a few gigs that the others realised that the numbers related to how many shows the band had played on the tour so far, so that he could identify any future bootlegs. His health was also suffering. Backstage before a show at the Philadelphia Spectrum, Waters collapsed with stomach cramps. A physician injected him with a muscle relaxant, which enabled him to perform, albeit without any feeling in his hands. The experience would inspire the lyrics in Floyd's 'Comfortably Numb'. Waters was later diagnosed as suffering from hepatitis.

Playing two nights at New York's Madison Square Garden, Waters lost his temper with the audience. 'Pigs on the Wing', his acoustic love song to Carolyne, was marred by the noise of exploding fireworks being thrown by members of the audience, a hazardous but frequent occurrence at American stadium shows. Waters was in no mood for interruptions. 'You stupid motherfucker!' he shouted. 'Just fuck off and let us get on with it!'

The final night of the tour was at Montreal's newly built Olympic Stadium. The construction team had only just moved out, leaving behind a giant crane, which did little to dispel the impersonal atmosphere of the arena. Just a couple of lines into 'Pigs on the Wing', the air was rent by a couple of loud explosions: more firecrackers. 'Oh, for *fuck's* sake!' Waters seethed. 'I'm trying to sing a song up here that some people want to listen to.' Further firecrackers went off at the start of 'Wish You Were Here'. By the end of the show, Waters was furious. Accounts vary as to what exactly happened. The bassist has since claimed to have been infuriated by one particularly raucous fan, who was tirelessly screaming his devotion to the band. Others claimed that Waters encouraged the behaviour; some that he was sick of hearing the fan calling for 'Careful With That Axe Eugene'. Waters eventually walked to the lip of the stage, leaned over and spat in the fan's face.

The band returned to the stage for a final encore, a slow blues jam, while the crew slowly dismantled the equipment around them. But Gilmour was nowhere to be seen. Refusing to join in, he walked out of the dressing room area and into the crowd, just another anonymous long-haired guy in a T-shirt, and made his way to the sound desk to watch the rest of the band playing on without him. 'I thought it was a great shame to end a six-month tour with a rotten show,' he said. The guitarist was now pondering whether Pink Floyd still had a future.

CHAPTER EIGHT WHY ARE YOU RUNNING AWAY?

'I'd have to say that Roger Waters is one of the world's most difficult men.'

Nick Mason

'Oh, dear, do we have to?' There is a note of distress in Nick Mason's voice.

And it had all been going so well.

Pink Floyd's drummer is on the campaign trail for an updated version of his memoirs, carefully subtitled 'A *Personal* History of Pink Floyd'. It is winter 2005, and the group's Live 8 reunion is still foremost in people's minds. Mason is droll and self-effacing, appearing to have an endless supply of 'I'm only the drummer' quips. But he's clearly proud of the reunited band's performance in Hyde Park. He painstakingly points out that this thaw in relations between David Gilmour and Roger Waters does not signify a long-term reunion for Pink Floyd, but, unable to help himself, admits that *should* they decide to 'do something again, my bag is packed and ready to go'. Mason is, after all, as David Gilmour once damned with the faintest of praise, 'the best drummer for Pink Floyd'.

Mason is conducting interviews from an office/warehouse in a tucked-away little street in Islington, North London. It is the centre of operations for his company, Ten Tenths, which has been hiring out cars, motorcycles, aeroplanes, in fact, every conceivable mode of transport, to film and television companies since 1985. Mason's own collection of sporty little numbers are among those available for the likes of pop singer Robbie Williams to tear around in for his next video.

After merrily recalling watching jazz pianist Thelonious Monk playing a New York club in 1966, the conversation has moved on through the years and we have arrived, somehow, at *The Wall*: Pink Floyd's 1979 album, stage show and movie. All of a sudden, Mason's earlier enthusiasm for his subject seems to have drained away.

'It's just that it was such an awful time,' he explains. 'I've tried to put it out of my mind.'

Roger Waters' desire to build a wall between himself and Pink Floyd's audience had been festering for some years before the 'awful time' of *The Wall*. But the moment it came closer to becoming a reality had been the final date on the *In the Flesh* tour in July 1977. Waters was mortified by his behaviour ('Oh my God, what have I been reduced to?'). Backstage, he began a play fight with manager Steve O'Rourke, and a misjudged karate kick led to him cutting his foot.

Carolyne Christie had been at the show with the Canadian producer Bob Ezrin, for whom she'd worked as a secretary. The twenty-eight-year-old Ezrin had overseen albums by Lou Reed, Kiss and the Floyd's old support band, Alice Cooper. Ezrin, Carolyne and a bleeding Roger Waters piled into a limousine for the drive back to the band's hotel via a hospital. Also in the car was a psychiatrist friend of Ezrin's.

'I always thought it was a wonderful coincidence that I had a psychiatrist with me that night,' says Ezrin. 'So we drove Roger to the emergency room to get his foot looked at, and then, as we're heading onto the hotel, he starts talking about his sense of alienation on the tour, and how he sometimes felt like building a wall between himself and the audience. My friend, the shrink, is fascinated. And, for me, there was a moment's spark. I don't know whether it was me or Roger or the shrink that said it first, but one of us went, "Wow! You know that might be a really good idea." '

'I loathed playing in stadiums,' explained Waters later. 'I kept saying to people on that tour, "I'm not really enjoying this, you know. There is something very wrong with this." And the answer to that was, "Oh really? Yeah, well, do you know we grossed over 4 million dollars today", and this went on more and more. And so, at a certain point, something in my brain snapped, and I developed the idea of doing a concert where we built a wall across the front of the stage that divided the audience from the performers.'

With the tour over, the band returned to England. Gilmour and Wright, encouraged by their wives, planned solo albums. In years to come, Waters would challenge the accusation that he had turned down their compositions and discouraged them from writing: 'How on earth could I possibly stop Dave Gilmour writing?' In truth, nobody was entirely sure whether Pink Floyd would even make another album. Solo projects afforded them all some much-needed time apart. Through the end of 1977 and the beginning of 1978, Gilmour would help produce Unicorn's third album and, to greater commercial success, protégée Kate Bush's second single, 'The Man with the Child in his Eyes'.

Despite his lack of songwriting credits on *Animals*, Gilmour also had enough material to start an album of his own. 'I think Dave was a bit bored and had some time on his hands,' says Rick Wills, who played bass alongside drummer Willie Wilson. It was the first time the three of them had worked together since their trip to Spain and France over ten years before. Jamming sessions at Gilmour's home studio led to sessions at Britannia Row and, for tax purposes, a recording stint at Super Bear Studios near Nice in January 1978. The album, entitled simply *David Gilmour*, appeared four months later. Roy Harper and Unicorn's Ken Baker were among those that contributed lyrics. 'There's No Way Out of Here' and 'So Far Away' could have referred to Gilmour's fraught situation in Pink Floyd, while the 'oohs' and 'aahs' of the female backing vocalists, the resolute mid-tempos and smouldering guitar solos were straight out of the Floyd songbook. Gilmour would later claim, though, that much of the album had a 'mortality theme'.

On the front cover the guitarist posed outside his Essex barn studio looking less like the lord of the manor and more like he'd come to muck out the stables. Gilmour promoted the album, but was guarded in most interviews, though he did make a point of telling *Sounds*, 'One of the nice things about recording in France is that I don't have to give quite as much to the taxman.' Aptly, then, one of the songs on the album was titled 'Mihalis', named after his new boat, bought to go with his new villa in Lindos. The album crept into the UK Top 20.

No sooner had Gilmour vacated Super Bear than Richard Wright moved in to make his record. *Wet Dream* would be released in September 1978. It featured Floyd's hired-help guitarist Snowy White, and was full of Wright's calling-card Hammond and synthesiser. The songs themselves were rather slight, with the main inspiration being Wright's holiday home in Lindos ('Holiday' and 'Waves') and the gloomy state of his marriage. 'Against the Odds' alluded to the turmoil in his personal life, while his wife Juliette's lyrics to 'Pink's Song' seemed to be an open letter asking for forgiveness from the couple's housekeeper. *Wet Dream* failed to chart. 'It was rather amateurish,' says Wright. 'The lyrics weren't very strong, but I think there's something rather quaint about it.'

For hardcore Pink Floyd fans, though, both records contained some worthwhile moments. Waters would later air his frustration about Wright's approach to songwriting: 'Rick would write these odd bits. But he secreted them away and put them on those solo albums that were never heard. He never shared them. It was unbelievably stupid.'

Back in England, both Mason and Waters had been busy. While the drummer produced ex-Gong guitarist Steve Hillage's *Green* album, Waters' girlfriend Carolyne had produced the couple's second child, a daughter, India. Roger had also been busy, writing and demoing songs for another *two* albums. His productivity would prove a blessing in disguise, as Pink Floyd were about to discover.

In 1976 the group had hired a firm of financial advisers, Norton Warburg, to oversee their financial affairs. Under Prime Minister James Callaghan's Labour government, earners in the Pink Floyd bracket could pay as much as 83 per cent in tax. Norton Warburg suggested the band put a percentage of their gross earnings into various venture capital enterprises to save giving it to the taxman. Floyd's money was subsequently invested in pizza restaurants, skateboards, a security firm, a money and chequebook printing venture . . . With the exception of a property deal in Knightsbridge, most of these enterprises under-performed or failed dismally. When a financial adviser from Norton Warburg was appointed to run the band's affairs at Britannia Row, he discovered that those higher up in the firm had been skimming off funds from the investment company to offset against their disastrous enterprises. (Norton Warburg subsequently collapsed.) This meant a loss to the band of, in their estimation, £3.3 million. Additional skulduggery meant that the band's tax planning for the next financial year was in chaos, making them liable for tax on money they'd actually lost. The nature of the arrangement also meant that any decision taken by one band member regarding their investments affected the others. 'It was,' as Gilmour later understated, 'very tricky.'

In July, with the extent of the financial fiasco slowly unfolding around them, the band met at Britannia Row where Waters presented them with his two ideas: a ninety-minute demo provisionally entitled *Bricks in the Wall* and a demo of what would become his first solo album, *The Pros and Cons of Hitch-hiking*. The band voted for *Bricks in the Wall* over *The Pros and Cons* . . . (with only Steve O'Rourke apparently in favour of the second). Yet each of them still had reservations about what they'd heard.

'It was like a skeleton with lots of bones missing,' offered Nick Mason, 'Roger made the most appalling demos, but what an idea!'

Gilmour was more cautious. 'It was too depressing, and boring in places, but I liked the basic idea.'

By September, the full extent of the Norton Warburg problem had become even more apparent. The band withdrew from the deal and demanded the return of all their uninvested money. They eventually began legal proceedings to sue the company for £1 million on the grounds of fraud and negligence. 'The whole experience cast an enormous cloud over us,' wrote Mason. 'We always prided ourselves on being smart enough not to be caught out like this. We had been utterly wrong.'

There was now an even greater need to earn money, and quickly.

Realising that *Bricks in the Wall* would only work as a double album, and would present a greater challenge than anything the band had attempted before, Waters decided to bring in an outside producer and collaborator. On past experience, Gilmour also understood the importance of a mediator and agreed.

'I needed a collaborator who was musically and intellectually in a similar place to where I was,' said Waters later, claiming that Gilmour and Mason weren't sufficiently interested and that Wright was 'pretty closed down at that point'. Carolyne Christie suggested her old boss, Bob Ezrin, who'd just given an ultra-modern sound to ex-Genesis frontman Peter Gabriel's first solo album.

Ezrin flew to England and spent the weekend at the bassist's country house. 'The demo he played me needed a lot of work,' says Ezrin, 'but it was obvious that there was something very exciting there.' Ezrin agreed to take on the role of co-producer.

In an all-night session in London – 'not chemically unassisted' – Ezrin wrote a script for what he then believed to be an imaginary movie, plotting out Waters' story, working out where the music would fit, what was working, what wasn't working, and what else was needed. 'So I ended up producing like a forty-page book that night . . . The next day at the studio, we had a table read, like you would with a play, but with the whole of the band, and their eyes all twinkled, because then they could see the album.'

Roger Waters' story was divided into two parts, with its chief character, later to be known as Pink, effectively flashing back on his life. The first part was inspired by Waters' own life, beginning with the death of his father in the Second World War (effectively, the first 'brick in the wall'), before moving through further 'bricks' in his relationships with an over-protective mother and bullying schoolteachers. 'Whenever something bad happens, he isolates himself a bit more,' explained Waters.

Ezrin suggested broadening out the story. 'We went out of our way to take it away from being a completely autobiographical work. Roger was thirty-six at the time, and it *was* "The Roger Waters Story". My sense, though, was that our audience probably wasn't that interested in a 36-year-old rocker that was complaining! But that they *might* be interested in a *Gestalt* character, Pink, that was a composite of all the dissipated rockers we have known and loved. And that allowed us to get into some really crazy stuff.'

The second half of the story was inspired by both Waters' experience of the music business and the demise of Syd Barrett. Pink becomes that dissipated rocker, pumped full of drugs and forced to perform on stage, where he starts hallucinating and transforms into a Hitlerian megalomaniac.

'If you looked at the original lyrics, Roger was being very honest about his fear and pain and isolation,' says Ezrin. 'But when we turned him into Pink, we were able to give him even more fear, pain and isolation.'

In the last dramatic chapter of the story and album, a deranged Pink finds his audience becoming increasingly fascist, and the concert becomes less of a rock show and more of a political rally. The dramatic coda to the piece finds Pink tearing down 'the wall', and becoming a caring, vulnerable human being once more. Another happy ending, then?

Ezrin believed that by creating a third-person character, Waters could 'express levels of fear, alienation and isolation that otherwise would have been unacceptable – and just wrong'. Yet it was difficult to separate the character of Pink from the notion of this complaining, yet very rich rock star. As Richard Wright admitted, after first hearing the demos, 'There were some things where I thought: Oh, here we go again – it's all about the war, about his mother, about his father being lost . . .'

The scale of Waters' vision was larger than any of his bandmates might have imagined. 'He came round to my place in Chelsea, and played me the demos,' says artist Gerald Scarfe. 'It was all very rough, but he told me *The Wall* was going to be a record, a show and a movie. He obviously had the whole thing mapped out in his head. We used to play a lot of snooker and drink Carlsberg Special Brew together round at his house, and I do remember him saying, "I'll never be in this position again, Gerry . . ." Presumably having his hand on the steering wheel to this extent.'

Over the coming months, Scarfe worked through the songs and ideas, sketching out the characters and creating storyboards for the individual scenes. 'I envisaged Pink as a vulnerable creature,' he explained, going on to render Pink's schoolteachers, his wife and his mother; creating the grotesque images that would become the defining look of the album, the stage show and the movie. With the songs still being worked on, Scarfe's images would influence Waters' lyrics, while new lyrics would be passed on to the artist and could inspire a new drawing.

Back at Britannia Row, there was another new addition to the team. Soundman Brian Humphries was now, in the words of one band member, 'burnt out' by five years of working with Pink Floyd. The decision was taken to bring in another engineer, but one with more experience than Britannia Row's in-house soundman Nick Griffiths.

Alan Parsons recommended twenty-five-year-old James Guthrie to the group. 'Brian Humphries was great, but real old school,' said Nick Mason. 'James brought a young ear.' After being interviewed by Steve O'Rourke and Roger Waters, it was carefully pointed out to Guthrie that he was being hired as a *co*-producer.

'I saw myself as a hot young *producer*,' Guthrie later told writer Sylvie Simmons. Regrettably, Floyd failed to tell Guthrie about Bob Ezrin, and vice versa. 'When we arrived, I think we both felt we'd been booked to do the same job.'

'There was confusion, when we first began,' agrees Ezrin. 'As you can imagine, there were three of us – myself, James and Roger – all with these very strong ideas about how this album should be made.' For Ezrin, though, there was also the hurdle of Waters' attitude to be overcome. 'There was what you might call a public school atmosphere to the sessions,' he says. 'And Roger was very much the head boy and some-times he could be a bully. I was the new kid, so, sure, I got tortured. But I came to London with a New York punk attitude. So very early on, there was a moment when Roger was pushing me and I turned around and said, "Read my lips, motherfucker, you cannot talk to me like that!" And the rest of the band were instantly on side, going, "Yessss!" And I think that held me in good stead from that point onwards.'

Ezrin's role quickly extended to helping 'broker a collaboration' between Waters and the rest of the band. 'Roger's initial concept was that these were his songs, his stuff, and I was brought in to handle "the muffins" – that was literally how he referred to them. But this needed to be a Pink Floyd project. So I wanted to get the other guys involved, and we had to meet with Roger's natural resistance, because he had a very clear vision in his head of what the album ought to be.'

Sessions at Britannia Row continued until March 1979, and, as an accomplished keyboard player and songwriter himself (he'd co-written Alice Cooper's 1975 hit 'Elected'), Ezrin was able to translate his ideas into music in the studio.

'Ezrin is the sort of guy who's thinking about all the angles,' said Gilmour. 'How to make a shorter storyline that's told properly, constantly worried about moving rhythms up and down, all that stuff which we've never really thought about.'

By March, another set of demos had been completed. But the

full extent of the band's financial situation was about to impact on their lives.

'We were going bankrupt,' said Waters. 'We'd gone from fourteen-year-olds with ten quid guitars and fantasies of being rich and famous, and made the dream come true with *Dark Side of the Moon*. And then, being greedy and trying to protect it, we'd lost it all.'

Under the tax laws of the time, the only solution to avoid losing everything was for the band to leave the UK by 6 April 1979 and make sure they didn't return until at least 365 days later. They were advised to earn as much money as possible during their time away, which, due to their non-residency, they would not be taxed on.

Within a month of being given this advice, all four had packed up their families and moved out of the UK. While they already had second homes abroad, it was still the beginning of what David Gilmour would describe as twelve months of 'a rather nomadic existence'. With the new tax year looming, the band quickly decided to hire the Super Bear Studios near Nice, bringing over as much of their own equipment from Britannia Row as they could. Also, to improve the general ambience at Super Bear, the band arranged to rip out the existing carpet to reveal the original marble floor underneath. Once work was underway, Ezrin proposed a then radical method of recording, in which drum and bass tracks were recorded on a sixteen-track machine and then copied to a mixed-down version on twenty-four-track, after which the drums were reduced to a few tracks and other instruments and overdubs were added. The intention was to sync up both the sixteen- and twenty-four-tracks, with everything on the sixteen-track coming through louder and clearer, as the tapes had been stashed away and not played repeatedly and worn out in the meantime. This contributed to the full, dense sound of the finished album, though Ezrin found his English counterparts alarmed by this process of working, especially when it came to erasing anything on the twenty-four-track: 'It was like witchcraft.'

Mason and Wright stayed in accommodation at the studio. Waters and Gilmour rented houses nearby. Mason, finding his lodgings rather wanting, eventually moved into Waters' upmarket villa near the town of Vence. Bob Ezrin, meanwhile, booked himself into the exclusive Negresco Hotel in Nice.

Despite the lavish surroundings, the pressure to deliver an album ensured that they worked to a tight schedule ('very un-Floydlike,' said Nick Mason). Waters instigated a strict 10 a.m. to 6 p.m. working day, to ensure that he was able to spend his evenings with Carolyne and their two children. He became particularly angry when Ezrin repeatedly showed up late.

Clearly, at some point during the French recording sessions, the producer's New York punk attitude started to crumble under Waters' singular English disdain. Ezrin was on a lower royalty rate than the band, which delighted Waters no end. So much so that he made badges for the band that read NOPE (No Points Ezrin). In 2004, Ezrin would inform *Mojo* writer Phil Sutcliffe that the bassist's behaviour reminded him of being bullied as a child at school in Toronto.

'It took me back to that time, when I was a gangly kid,' he said darkly. 'It started off playful but what was playful to Roger was very painful to me.' Ezrin would also claim that his late arrival at the studio was because he dreaded going in, as the 'atmosphere, especially around Roger, was so tense. It was this horrible, passive-aggressive, English-style conflict, where so much was just unsaid. Roger is a tough guy, and he's tougher on himself than anyone. But he takes the harshness and perfectionism that he applies to himself and applies it to other people, which is sometimes not the right thing to do.'

The band would subsequently deflect Ezrin's complaints by claiming that Bob was, in the words of Nick Mason, 'going through an unreliable phase of his life', with the implied suggestion being that the producer was enjoying far too many late nights out in Nice. Ezrin would subsequently admit to not being 'in the best shape emotionally', not least because of problems in his marriage. However, the producer's run-ins with Roger Waters would comprise just a small part of the overall conflict. Tensions were also running high between the respective wives. Meanwhile, the relationship between Waters and Richard Wright had all but broken down.

The recording process at Super Bear rarely involved all four band members being in the studio at the same time. While this had the liberating effect of allowing each one enough time to record their parts, it ran the risk of isolation and of separate camps within the group. At Super Bear, Nick Mason, who had, much to Waters' surprise, learned to read sheet music for the drums, recorded most of his parts during the early sessions, which were then left for Ezrin and James Guthrie to edit together. Having effectively laid down the foundations for the others to build on, this had the added benefit to Mason of allowing him to duck out of the later sessions and race his Ferrari at Le Mans. (He came second in his class.)

Guthrie's long working day would involve engineering the 10 a.m. to 6 p.m. shift with Waters and Gilmour, before returning to the studio until the small hours with Richard Wright. As ever, each of the band and their collaborators would have a different take on the 'Rick Wright situation'.

For Waters, part of his ongoing issues with Wright during *The Wall* sessions stemmed from the keyboard player's desire for a producer's credit on the album.

'Up until *The Wall*, we'd always had "Produced By Pink Floyd" on our records,' said Waters. 'Although most of the production work had been done by me and Dave. So I put it to Nick and Rick that Bob Ezrin would be producing the record with me and Dave, and you won't because you never have. Nick went, "Fine, no problem." But Rick went, "But I *can* produce the record, I can help." I said, "I don't think you can, Rick, you never have in the past."' Waters agreed to give Wright a 1 per cent point and producer's credit on the album, but only after a trial period in which he was 'seen to be producing the album'.

'I did have reservations when Bob Ezrin was brought in,' admitted Wright. 'But it was not a financial thing about losing production points, but because I thought the band was losing one of its strengths, which was that even if we would fight each other we were all hands together as a group. I think our best work came out of that, and I thought that we ran the risk of losing that if we brought in an outside producer. Now I think bringing Bob in was the right decision.'

'We'd been working on the record for a few weeks, and Rick, unusually, would be in the studio for the whole time, from the moment we started in the morning to the moment we finished at night,' said Waters. 'One day Bob Ezrin asked me why Rick was always sitting in the studio. And I said, "Don't you get it? He thinks he's producing the record . . . Have you noticed occasionally how he goes, 'Uh, uh, uh, I don't like that.'" And Ezrin says, "Yes, it's rather irritating." And I said, "He thinks that's record producing."'

According to Waters, Ezrin challenged Wright, after which he claims the keyboard player stopped coming into the studio, and only showed up when he was requested to, preferring to work on his own at night.

'I went in at night because the whole album had been mapped out, and I could just go in and do a piano part,' said Wright. 'But it *was* very hard if Roger or Bob wasn't there to say, "That's good" or "That's not so good." But this idea that I was sitting around wasting my time is not really fair.'

'Rick's relationship with all of us, but certainly Roger, did become impossible during the making of *The Wall*,' said Gilmour. 'He had been asked if he had any ideas or anything that he wanted to do. We would leave the studio in the evening and he would have the whole night to come up with stuff, but he didn't contribute anything. He just sat there and it was driving us all mad.'

Bob Ezrin offers a gentler assessment of Wright's problems: 'Rick is not a guy who performs well under pressure, and it sometimes felt that Roger was setting him up to fail. Rick gets performance anxiety. You have to leave him alone to freeform, to create . . .'

Outside the band, the marital difficulties that had beset Wright during the making of *Animals* had escalated. 'At the time of *The Wall* I think I was depressed,' he said. 'For whatever reason – the divorce, a terrible relationship with my first wife – and I wasn't offering anything because I wasn't feeling very good within myself. But I'm pretty sure the others interpreted it as, "He doesn't care", "He's not interested".'

Halfway through the sessions, Columbia offered a deal increasing the percentage points the band could earn if they could deliver a finished album in time for the Christmas market. Further sessions were booked at jazz pianist Jacques Loussier's Miraval Studios in Provence to run parallel with the recordings at Super Bear. As well as saving time, the studio's location was helpful to Waters, who, determined to sing as much of the album as possible, used it to record many of his vocal parts. 'Super Bear was quite high in the mountains and it's notorious for being quite difficult to sing there,' recalled Gilmour. 'And Roger had a lot of difficulty singing in tune.' Bob Ezrin meanwhile was entrusted to flit between the two studios, appeasing Waters in one and Gilmour in another.

With holidays booked for August, the original plan was to reconvene in Los Angeles, where they were booked into Cherokee Studios and the

Producers' Workshop, in the first week of September. Waters devised a schedule for what still needed to be done, 'and I realised it was impossible'. With many of the keyboard parts still unrecorded, he proposed starting ten days earlier, and suggested Ezrin hire an additional keyboard player – 'because you're going to need it' – to work alongside Wright.

However, Wright was in no mood to cut short his family visit to Rhodes. 'The rest of the band's children were young enough to stay with them in France but mine [Gala aged nine and Jamie aged seven] were older and had to go to school. I was missing my children terribly.'

The exact circumstances of quite how and why Wright was ousted from Pink Floyd now depend on which of the protagonists is telling the story.

'I got Steve O'Rourke to call Rick and tell him the new plan,' said Waters. The Floyd's manager was enjoying a cruise on the *QE2* at the time. 'A couple of days later I got a call from Steve and he said, "I've found Rick, he's in Greece." I said, "Oh, is that OK, then?" and he said, "No, he said, 'Tell Roger to fuck off.'" And that was the straw that broke the camel's back.'

'I didn't say, "Tell Roger to fuck off,"' insisted Wright. 'I said, "No, I'm coming on the agreed date." We'd all agreed, and I had specific time with my children, and there was no indication to me that we were that far behind schedule. Steve said, "Fair enough, I understand." And that was the last I heard of it, until I arrived in LA and Steve said, "Roger wants you out of the band."'

David Gilmour's quiet holiday in Dublin was rudely interrupted by the news of Waters' ultimatum. As the flat he was renting didn't have a telephone, the guitarist was forced to ring his bandmate from a public call box. 'I remember saying, "Roger, you can't do that. Rick's been in the band all along. If you don't like it, your choice is to leave, it isn't to throw someone out." I said, "You're letting this get very personal, aren't you?" and I won't quote what he said.'

However much Gilmour may have objected to Waters' railroading behaviour, he couldn't ignore the fact that the two of them were still capable of producing some brilliant work together. Renting villas near to each other, Gilmour and Waters would often drive to Super Bear together each morning. 'We had some pretty major arguments during *The Wall*, but they were artistic disagreements,' Gilmour insisted later.

'The intention behind *The Wall* was to make the best record we could. I can remember driving with Roger one morning and he said, "God, we must never stop working together, we make a great team." '

When work resumed in Los Angeles, Wright approached Gilmour and asked him to go out for a drink to discuss Waters' ultimatum. Sitting in a restaurant, Gilmour told the keyboard player that he would defend his right to remain in the band, despite agreeing with Waters that he wasn't contributing as much as he should. 'I said, "You have to make your own mind up about this, Rick, but you haven't really pulled your finger out, have you?" '

Waters' position was clear: either Wright agreed to leave quietly at the end of the album or Waters would refuse to release *The Wall* as a Pink Floyd album.

'Roger's attitude was, "It's my record, and I've let the rest of you play on it," ' says Bob Ezrin. 'With everything that was going on financially with the band, he was the one standing there holding what he saw as a satchel full of pound notes.'

Wright agonised for days before agreeing to quit. 'I was terrified of the financial situation, and I felt the whole band was falling apart anyway,' he said. 'But I made the decision to finish recording the album and I told them I wanted to do the live shows.' Clearly, whatever reservations Waters may have had about Wright's musicianship didn't impinge on him wanting to present a united Pink Floyd for publicity purposes, once the album came out. The news of Wright's departure was also kept out of the music press.

In the 1990s, when relations between Waters and the re-formed Pink Floyd were still poor, the bassist would tell interviewers that, while they were in France making *The Wall*, Gilmour had suggested they fire Mason as well as Wright. This would tally with Wright's suspicion that Waters wanted sole control of Pink Floyd, with Gilmour as his guitarist, and any other roles fulfilled by session musicians. Gilmour later refuted any suggestion of firing the drummer. Mason said at the time that he felt 'like the ship's cook. I see various commanders come and go, and, when things get really bad, I just go back down to the galley.' Nick now favours the traditional Pink Floyd stance of ignoring the problem in the hope that it will just go away. Which, in this case, it has. 'I am happy to say that everyone denies even considering getting me out of the band,' he says.

'But I'm certainly not going to undertake a forensic investigation into the matter.' Unsurprisingly, Wright's name was not included anywhere on the original *Wall* album. Yet neither was Nick Mason's, until he insisted, and it was added to later pressings.

Wright, however, never shared Mason's bluff exterior or innate sense of self-preservation. He also believed that his forced departure was a personal more than musical issue: 'I annoyed Roger and he annoyed me.' He had always been an easy target for Waters since their days at Regent Street Poly. 'Roger used Rick as a punchbag,' said Jenny Lesmoir-Gordon, recalling their trip to Greece in 1966, and Pink Floyd's ex-manager Andrew King once said, 'Roger thought *everybody* needed toughening up.'

Subsequently, persistent rumours would circulate that cocaine use was also to blame for Wright's departure. 'There *were* people who were doing a lot of drugs,' Waters told writer Sylvie Simmons. 'Some of us had big, big problems. Though I wasn't taking drugs at that point.'

Wright has always disputed any rumours that he had a cocaine problem. 'I can honestly say that it really was not a drug problem,' he said in 1999, while admitting that cocaine was taken socially by all band members during the time in which the band was making *The Wall*.

'Rick's such a sweetheart, but he's suffered rather badly from everything that's happened,' said one associate. In Wright's own rather sad words from 2000: 'Since I've been talking to a therapist, I've realised I was probably depressed. He thinks I'm still angry about the whole thing.'

Amid all this drama, somehow an album was still being made. By August 1979, the running order of songs for *The Wall* was largely finalised. What would become known as 'Comfortably Numb' was still being called 'The Doctor', while the opening song had yet to acquire the title 'In the Flesh' and was still known as 'The Show'. At Cherokee Studios, Richard Wright fulfilled his duties, with additional keyboards played by session men Peter Woods and Freddie Mandel. When Nick Mason failed to nail the unusual rhythm on the song 'Mother', Jeff Porcaro, drummer with session band extraordinaire Toto, stepped in. 'Nick, to his credit, had no great pretence about it,' remembered Waters. 'He just said, "I can't play that."'

Meanwhile, at the Producers' Workshop on Hollywood Boulevard,

Bob Ezrin oversaw the editing of various tape loops (including Waters' maniacal schoolteacher's voice used on 'Another Brick in the Wall'), and more session players. Pink Floyd's former closed-shop policy had been completely abandoned. Hired gun guitarist Lee Ritenour was brought in to beef up one of *The Wall*'s heaviest rock numbers, 'One of My Turns'. Clarinets, concertinas and a mandolin were added to the closing track, 'Outside the Wall'. Backing vocals were supplied by, among others, Beach Boy Bruce Johnston and Toni Tennille of the MOR pop duo The Captain and Tennille, both of whom contributed to the thunderous heavy metal pastiche 'In the Flesh', as well as 'The Show Must Go On' and 'Waiting for the Worms', in the last of which Pink fantasises about leading a Fascist rally through the streets of London.

Toni Tennille was highly conscious of just how different her music was from Pink Floyd's, and arrived at the sessions expecting to encounter a stereotypical, dope-smoking hard rock band. She was immediately disarmed when the ultra-professional and very un-stoned Gilmour told her that he'd watched her singing on a children's TV show that very morning.

Bruce Johnston's involvement had come about when Floyd had been unable to co-ordinate a recording session with all of the Beach Boys. He too found his preconceptions quashed after arriving at Roger Waters' rented tax shelter house in Beverly Hills. 'I thought: God! Pink Floyd. They're ultra-civilised people making this bizarre album,' recalled Johnston. 'Roger's got a staff that work for him, beautiful furniture, a nice wife, a couple of little babies . . . We even talked about getting together and playing tennis.'

Also at the Producers' Workshop, Waters and Ezrin set about recording the countless sound effects needed for the album. Waters taped the sound of Hollywood Boulevard at night by simply hanging a microphone out of the studio window. Gilmour's guitar tech Phil Taylor was sent out into the studio car park to create the sound of screaming tyres on his station wagon for 'Run Like Hell'. Taylor was also entrusted with finding a television set to be smashed with a sledgehammer for 'One of My Turns', in which Pink freaks out in his hotel room in front of a groupie. Back at Britannia Row, engineer Nick Griffiths was told to record the sound of smashing crockery for the same song. The groupie's voice belonged to actress Trudy Young, whom Ezrin had recorded in

Toronto earlier that year. Her exaggerated Valley Girl accent – 'Oh my *God*! What a fabulous room . . . are all these your *guitars*?' – would become one of the most enduring non-musical moments on *The Wall*. The song began with the sound of Pink attempting to place a collect call to his wife, and hearing another man answering the phone; a direct reference to the incident on the last American tour when Waters had telephoned his ex-wife Judy.

Earlier that summer, while the band stayed at Super Bear, Ezrin had also overseen extra sessions at Columbia's own studios in New York. Waters had agreed to Ezrin's suggestion to add orchestral arrangements to various songs, including 'Nobody Home', 'The Trial' and what would become 'Comfortably Numb'. Musicians from the New York Philharmonic and New York Symphony Orchestras were hired. 'Bring the Boys Back Home' was also bolstered by a choir from the New York City Opera and thirty-five hired snare drummers.

Native New Yorker Michael Kamen was brought in to help score the orchestral arrangements. Kamen was a musician, arranger and acolyte of composer Leonard Bernstein. His rock 'n' roll experience had been acquired as musical director of David Bowie's 1974 US tour. Like Toni Tennille and Bruce Johnston, Kamen was baffled by his new employers. With none of Pink Floyd present at the sessions, he could only speculate about his latest clients. 'I'd wondered how they functioned,' he told *Circus* magazine. 'Were they a band or a fucking board meeting?' While in New York, Ezrin had been producing guitarist Nils Lofgren at the Power Station studios. Also recording there were the funk band Chic, making their third album, *Risqué*, containing the future dancefloor hit 'Good Times'. 'I stood out in the hallway listening to [Chic's] Nile Rodgers and Bernard Edwards play, and hearing this whole other approach to rhythm,' recalls Ezrin now. 'And I kept going out to listen because what they were doing was so funky, and there I was, working with white people, who weren't very funky at all, and thinking: Damn! Maybe we can do some of that!'

Back at Super Bear, Ezrin's idea would find a home on 'Another Brick in the Wall Part 2', *The Wall*'s stinging condemnation of the education system, in which Pink is bullied by tyrannical schoolmasters, before standing up to his oppressors. The song contained a winning chorus that denounced the need for education, and refused to bow to 'thought control'. By the spring of 1979, only Gilmour's clipped guitar figure gave any hint of the disco rhythm of the finished version. 'There was all that delayed guitar and the synthesiser melody and Roger's voice on top,' remembers Ezrin. 'It was a funereal, gloomy thing,' recalls Nick Mason. 'Dirge-like might be a little too disparaging.'

Ezrin suggested adding a disco beat to the track, telling David Gilmour to go to a nightclub and actually *listen* to some of the music he was talking about. The guitarist grudgingly obliged. Waters and Mason had no such reservations. 'I thought the disco drums were great,' says Mason. 'But then I did have a slightly more simplistic approach anyway.' Another song on the album, 'Run Like Hell', would have a similar drum beat in the end.

Listening to the new version of the song, Ezrin had another brain-wave. 'The minute I heard the song with the beat on, I said, "This is a smash." But the problem was it was only one verse and one chorus long.'

Despite a couple of ventures into the US singles market in recent years, Floyd were still resistant to the idea of chasing hits. 'Roger said, "Fuck it, we don't want a single,"' says Ezrin. 'So I started pleading, but he was like, "No, I'm not going to be told what to do." So we waited until they'd gone home, and copied the track. I found a small disco break that we picked out of a verse, stuck it into the middle to link it and stuck the first verse back in and tacked the ending on. Now we had a single. James [Guthrie] and I played the song to Roger and he liked it.'

But with two verses exactly the same, the song needed some extra input. 'There's some controversy over who said, "Let's put some kids on it,"' admits Ezrin. The producer had used children's voices on albums for Alice Cooper and Lou Reed, so has largely been credited as suggesting the same for *The Wall*. 'I'm known as "the kid guy", but James recalls that it was Roger's idea. Whoever said it, it was a great idea.'

Guthrie and Ezrin made a twenty-four-track reel of the song, leaving twenty tracks open. They sent the tape from France to Nick Griffiths at Britannia Row in London. 'We said to Nick, "Please find us some kids, and just fill up the tracks. Have them do it every way possible – cockney, posh, nasty, angelic . . ."'

Griffiths contacted Islington Green school in nearby Prebend Street and enlisted the help of the school's head of music, Alun Renshaw. Described as an 'anarchic teacher' in what was then a struggling inner-city comprehensive, Renshaw had previously written his own socially conscious musical, *Requiem for a Sinking Block of Flats*, which had been staged at the school. He had a poster for the Sex Pistols' *Never Mind the Bollocks* on the wall of the music room, and took what might be described as a highly individual approach to teaching. As one of his former pupils recalls, 'We'd go outside in Alun's music lesson, sit on the side of the road, listen to the cars and then be told to *draw* the sound.'

Griffiths asked Renshaw if he could round up some children to sing at Britannia Row. 'I thought: Great, yes!' says Renshaw, who was enticed by the promise of free recording time for the school orchestra. 'I wanted to make music relevant to the kids – not just sitting around listening to Tchaikovsky. I thought the lyrics were great – "We don't need no education, we don't need no thought control . . ." I just thought it would be a wonderful experience for the kids.' Unfortunately, Renshaw forgot to ask permission from the school's headmistress; an oversight that would have a serious impact in the months to come.

Alun rounded up those children he could find, not all from the school choir. As one of them recalls, 'I think it was more of a case of, "What are you doing?" "Nothing?" "Come with me." ' Caroline Greeves (formerly Woods) was among the twenty or so pupils who found themselves at Britannia Row. To start with, Griffiths recorded just three pupils on their own before inviting the rest to join, conducting them as best he could. 'We sang in our best school choir voices, but then we were told to shout and make it a lot more cockney,' says Caroline. 'They'd played us a tape of the song first and I remember it ran on to the next track. I went home that night and told my brother, who was a big Pink Floyd fan, that not only had I sung on their next album, I'd also heard some of their unreleased material.'

Not all of the ad-hoc choir were so easily impressed. 'I was a mod wannabe and not interested in Pink Floyd at the time,' says pupil Tabitha Mellor, who was more impressed by the 'Space Age sound desk' but baffled by the bales of straw placed behind them at Britannia Row during the recording. 'The engineers told us it was to absorb the sound and improve the acoustics.'

With the session complete, Griffiths multi-tracked the voices to make it sound like the work of a full choir and then Federal Expressed the tape back to the band in Los Angeles. 'We threw it up on the console and I opened all the faders,' says Ezrin, 'and when that *gang* came back at us, it sounded just spectacular. Roger was beaming. From the moment we heard it, we knew we had a hit record.' While the group agreed to release the song as a single, none of them knew it would give them a Christmas number 1 hit.

The artistic disagreements between David Gilmour and Roger Waters during *The Wall* would, in many cases, have a positive result on the songs. As James Guthrie recalled, 'Roger was always willing to edit, to throw away something that wasn't working, no matter how much time he might have put it into it.' The song 'Nobody Home' was a late addition to the album, recorded in October at the Producers' Workshop. Challenged to write something by Gilmour, Waters left the studio 'in a sulk', according to the guitarist, before coming back the next morning with 'something fantastic'. Waters' temper had yielded one of the most atmospheric and moving songs on the record. In 'Nobody Home', Pink sits in his LA hotel room, spaced out in front of the television, unable or unwilling to do anything else. The lyrics were loaded with references to Syd Barrett; 'the wild, staring eyes', 'the obligatory Hendrix perm' and 'elastic bands keeping my shoes on' all referred to his appearance and disconnected behaviour during Pink Floyd's first US tour in 1967.

For some of Syd's other friends, certain moments on *The Wall* took them right back in time. 'There's a moment on the album where you hear this voice, and it's meant to be Pink's manager, saying, "It's time to go . . . It's time to go,"' says Matthew Scurfield, of the spoken words leading into the song 'Comfortably Numb'. 'That reminds me of being with Syd in Earlham Street, and the band were downstairs waiting to take him to the gig: "Come on, let's get him away from sitting on the floor or at the table, painting and being in his own fairytale world."'

For 'Comfortably Numb', Waters would also write about his own experience during Floyd's 1977 US tour, when he was struck down with what transpired to be hepatitis and was injected with a muscle relaxant which enabled him to go on stage and perform. In the song, Pink undergoes the same experience, slipping into a state of delirium before playing the show. But what would become one of the defining songs of Pink Floyd's career was blighted with arguments.

'"Comfortably Numb" was *the* song we argued about the most,' remembers Bob Ezrin. Gilmour originally presented Waters with a chord sequence left over from his solo album sessions ('I never used it then, but thought: I'll store that and come back to it later'). Yet, as Ezrin explains, Waters was resistant to using it as 'this was Roger's record, about Roger, for Roger'. Ezrin insisted, as the existing song needed filling out. Waters went away and begrudgingly wrote what started out as a spoken-word verse and additional lyrics for the chorus. 'And what he came back with just gave me goosebumps,' says Ezrin.

Nevertheless, by the time they reached Los Angeles they had two versions of the song. One was stripped-down and harder, with very little of Michael Kamen's orchestral arrangements; the other was what Ezrin describes as 'the grander Technicolor, orchestral version'. Gilmour wanted the harder arrangement; both Waters and Ezrin favoured the wide-screen orchestral version. 'So that turned into a real arm-wrestle,' says Ezrin. Having repaired to an Italian restaurant in North Hollywood to thrash out a compromise, a full-scale argument erupted. 'But at least this time there were only *two* sides to the argument: Dave on one side; Roger and I on the other.' Finally, the deal was struck. The body of the song would comprise the orchestral arrangement; the outro, including that final, incendiary guitar solo, would be taken from the Gilmour-favoured, harder version. 'I'm so glad we did that,' raves Ezrin, who clearly adores the song. '"Comfortably Numb" still makes me think of being in bed with a comforter pulled up around your ears, and a pillow over your head, saying, "Leave me alone. I want to be alone in this cocoon." And then, at the end, Dave breaks out and declares himself, and a whole measure of beauty and anger has to be expressed.'

As Gilmour ruefully admitted, 'I think things like "Comfortably Numb" were the last embers of mine and Roger's ability to work collaboratively together.'

'This is terrible. It's rubbish. What are we going to do?'

Not everyone was impressed by *The Wall*.

The first official playback took place at Columbia's headquarters in Century City, California. According to the band, more than one of the executives in attendance balked at what they heard. Those hoping for *Dark Side of the Moon Part Two*, or even another instalment of *Wish You Were Here*, were instead bombarded with some ninety minutes of Kurt Weill-style opera, military marching bands, dissonant heavy metal, disco, divebombing aeroplanes . . . all washed down with lyrics that suggested an existential cry for help. Waters had also engaged in another battle of wills with the company. After being told that, as *The Wall* was a double album, he would receive a reduced percentage per track, he threatened to withhold the record. Columbia backed down. It was not an auspicious start.

Then the unthinkable happened. On 16 November 1979, with the album still two weeks away from being issued in the UK, 'Another Brick in the Wall Part 2' was released as a single. Gerald Scarfe was badgered into producing a promotional video in time for an airing on the BBC's *Top of the Pops*. 'I said to Roger, "How on earth can I do a video in time for next Tuesday? Today is Wednesday!" He said, "Just find some kids!"' Scarfe hastily assembled a group of stage school children to be filmed singing, intercut with footage already produced for the upcoming stage show. The video brought to life the images record buyers would first encounter on the artwork for the album.

Three weeks later, Pink Floyd, a band who hadn't released a single in the UK since 1968, had a number 1 hit, usurping 'Walking on the Moon' by The Police; one of the new wave groups that had emerged as an antidote to Pink Floyd and their ilk. 'We were astonished,' admits Nick Mason.

'Another Brick in the Wall Part 2' reached number 1 in the US, Norway, Portugal, Israel, West Germany and South Africa, where it was later banned after being adopted as a protest song by black school-children against apartheid. Who knows how widespread the so-called public outcry about the song really was, but it was sufficient for the *Daily Mail*, one of Britain's most staunchly right-wing newspapers, to pounce on the story. It reported that Patricia Kirwan, a member of the Inner London Education Authority, had voiced her disapproval: 'It seems very ironical that these words should be sung by children from a school with such a bad academic record . . . the grammar is appalling, too.' Islington Green was an easy target. Headmistress Margaret Maden defended her position by claiming that music teacher Alun Renshaw 'wasn't clear about the lyrics, but we decided it wasn't as bad as all that'. As damage limitation, she banned the children from appearing on television or having their photographs taken in connection with the record. 'I remember being cross that there were different kids singing it in the video,' says Caroline Greeves. 'But we were told we couldn't do it as we didn't have Equity cards. Some of the kids at our school were in [the children's school drama] *Grange Hill*, so we knew about Equity cards and thought that was a good explanation. Really the school didn't want any more adverse publicity.'

'The parents didn't have a problem with it,' insists Alun Renshaw. 'They couldn't understand what all the fuss was about.' Within a month, with the uproar still going on around him, Renshaw emigrated to Australia, where he still lives today. 'The forces of Conservatism had come in by then,' he laughs. 'I never saw the song as a big political statement, but Margaret Thatcher had become Prime Minister, and I expect she did . . . Although who gives a shit about her?'

With the band still in Los Angeles when the scandal broke, Britannia Row engineer Nick Griffiths found himself doorstepped by news reporters and, on one occasion, forced to escape the studio via a window. The press were also quick to point out that the children hadn't been paid for their performances on the record and had therefore been ripped off by an unscrupulous multi-millionaire rock band. In the end, each child was given a free copy of *The Wall*, while the school received a £1,000 donation. In 1996, a music business lawyer traced a number of the pupils that had sung on the record and began pursuing a claim for additional royalties on their behalf. By 2007 four of the pupils had been paid.

Released on 30 November in the UK and a week later in the US, Floyd's new work prompted both confusion and vitriol among the music press. *New Musical Express* had embraced punk rock and was now a tough nut to crack for bands of Pink Floyd's vintage, especially with an album the magazine viewed as a 'monument of self-centred pessimism'. *Melody Maker* was more sympathetic: 'I'm not sure whether it's brilliant or terrible but I find it utterly compelling.' In America, the band's old nemesis *Rolling Stone* magazine offered cautious praise, with writer Kurt Loder applauding the grandeur of the exercise but warning that Roger Waters' worldview was 'so unremittingly dismal and acidulous that it makes contemporary gloom-mongers such as Randy Newman or, say, Nico seem like Peter Pan and Tinker Bell'.

Behind the scenes, the suspicion that some members of Pink Floyd might agree with such criticisms is borne out by their comments about *The Wall* since. Wright, understandably perhaps, is said not to like all of the music on the album, while Gilmour has admitted to not quite sharing Waters' views about the music industry and their audience, particularly the bassist's desire to build a wall between themselves and their fans. *The Wall* was also, said Gilmour, 'a year of very hard work by Roger and all of us, turning a good idea that can only be described as a pig's ear into a silk purse.'

There was also the small matter of credits to dampen the enthusiasm. With Mason and Wright not named anywhere on the record, Gilmour eked out just three co-writer credits for 'Run Like Hell', 'Young Lust' and 'Comfortably Numb'. 'If anyone was not given sufficient credit it was Dave,' said Mason.

'I think *The Wall* is stupefyingly good,' claims Waters. 'Christ! What a brilliant idea that was. It holds together so well.'

The album now seems to encapsulate everything that both repels some and attracts others: its bombast, pretension and unstinting melodrama. While the narrative was inspired by Waters' disgust at playing stadiums, perversely, much of *The Wall*'s music was perfect for being played in such large amphitheatres. The opening fanfare, 'In the Flesh', with its dive-bombing sound effects and grinding riff, was a pastiche of the heavy metal bands then filling stadiums across America. But for fans of the genre, Floyd had simply written a sterling heavy rock song to match similar efforts by Black Sabbath or megalomaniac guitar hero Ted Nugent. Any intended parody was likely to go over the heads of many of those listening.

Meanwhile, 'Comfortably Numb', 'Run Like Hell' and 'Hey You' were a gift to FM radio DJs. This was grown-up rock with a message, but the message would never encroach on David Gilmour's next guitar solo. Listening over twenty-five years later, *The Wall*'s hidden treasures include those often overlooked moments bridging the gaps in the story: Waters' painful vocals on 'Don't Leave Me Now' where he sounds as if he might be drawing his last breath; the ugly, amateurish-sounding synthesiser at the start of 'One of My Turns', both of which go against the musical grain but are perfect for the songs. These snippets give you a glimpse of how *The Wall* might have sounded had it been a Roger Waters solo album. Graceless and uncompromising on their own, they make perfect sense alongside Gilmour's warmer, welcoming contributions. To paraphrase Waters, what a great team they made.

To coincide with the album's release, Roger granted BBC Radio 1 DJ Tommy Vance an interview. Vance played the whole of *The Wall*, inter-cut with Waters' comments about each track, while Floyd fans sat by their radios taping the programme. Not that it made a jot of difference to the sales. *The Wall* cleared a million copies in its first two months, and is now believed to have sold somewhere in the region of 23 million copies worldwide.

Gerald Scarfe's marching hammers, bug-eyed schoolmaster and thunder-thighed mother were among the cartoon images splashed across the inside cover. The outside of the album stuck to the usual Floyd pack drill of 'no band name, no album title', but was their most minimal design ever: a simple, white brick wall. It was also the first Pink Floyd album design since *The Piper at the Gates of Dawn* not created by Hipgnosis.

'Roger didn't want to use me on *The Wall*, which is understandable, as he was already using Gerry Scarfe,' said Thorgerson. 'But he was also supposedly cross with me for a credit I'd given him in a book I'd done.'

The book, *Walk Away Rene*, featuring Hipgnosis' artwork, had been published a couple of years earlier, and had included the sleeve for *Animals*. 'I rather fell out with Storm when he included that sleeve in a book, because it had nothing to do with them,' protested Waters. The disagreement would mark the end of Waters and Thorgerson's working relationship, despite a friendship that had stretched back to their teenage years.

'We didn't speak for twenty-five years,' says Thorgerson. 'That's a long time for someone I'd known since I was fourteen and used to pass the ball to on our rugby team. I was upset about it for the first three or four years, and then I had to get on.'

It would be the first in a series of estrangements that would find the Floyd songwriter backing away from many of his oldest friends and collaborators.

For newcomer Gerald Scarfe, any feuding between the band and their other collaborators was of little concern. 'I think Roger realised the benefits of having something fresh. But I came in very naive to this whole set-up, so I wasn't really aware of Storm. I remember someone saying to me, "Oh, the thing about you, Gerald, is you're like Walter Raleigh to the court of Queen Elizabeth I. You're this social being that can just walk in and out of the court." I must admit, I rather liked the idea of that.'

'I do recall Roger once saying that he wanted the flying pig to defecate on the audience.' Cambridge contemporary and guitarist Tim Renwick remembers the genesis of *The Wall* stage show. Renwick had previously seen Pink Floyd sawing pieces of wood on stage, and inflating a sea monster in the lake at Crystal Palace as part of their mission to dazzle the audience. By the end of the seventies, Waters' ideas were becoming increasingly extreme. 'I think by then Roger was looking for ways to intimidate the audience. *The Wall* was all about giving the audience a hard time.'

The notion of constructing a barrier between Pink Floyd and their audience had been in Waters' mind for some ten years. Appalled by the impersonal atmosphere at the 60,000-seater venues they had played on the 1977 US tour, and by audiences 'screaming and shouting and throwing things and hitting each other', Waters declared that *The Wall* would be staged in smaller, 16,000-seater venues, despite a financial loss to the band. Initial plans to transport their own mobile tent-like venue, nicknamed 'The Slug', were nixed when they realised they would never be granted a licence for it by any local authority.

The problem was that, while attempting to convey *The Wall*'s important message to the audience, Waters still had an obligation to entertain that audience. Though, at first, that seemed not to be the case.

'Roger's very purist idea at the beginning was there should be no let-up,' recalls Gerald Scarfe. 'He wanted a wall between the band and the audience, and everything would be sung from inside the wall. I think David vetoed that. After which they agreed to open holes in the wall, through which they would be seen performing.'

Pink Floyd's 40ft-high wall would be constructed from around four hundred heavy-duty cardboard bricks, spanning the width of the auditorium and completely obscuring the stage. Designers Jonathan Park and Mark Fisher originally wanted to use plywood panels for the wall. When they realised how heavy they were and difficult to transport, they came up with the idea of flat-packed cardboard boxes that could then be opened and turned into 'bricks'. 'The solution came to us in a pub,' said Park.

As the show progressed, individual bricks would be removed to reveal the band and scenes from the story, most memorably Waters as Pink (or Syd Barrett?), sitting in front of a TV in a motel room scene for 'Nobody Home', audibly flicking the channels on his remote control. Extra speaker cabinets were also installed under the tiered seating in the venues, to be fired up during the wall's eventual collapse.

A circular screen above the stage and the wall itself would act as a backdrop for Gerald Scarfe's animations. These would include the corpulent judge during 'The Trial', in which Pink imagines himself 'in the dock' for past misdemeanours, and the infamous 'marching hammers' for 'Waiting for the Worms', where Pink transforms from rock star to fascist dictator. 'Roger talked a lot about the forces of oppression,' says Scarfe, 'and I thought of the most unforgiving instrument of oppression I could, and it was a hammer.' One of Scarfe's personal favourites was the animation for 'Goodbye Blue Sky'. A song inspired by the fear of war, it featured the 'frightened ones', tiny child-like creatures with heads shaped like gas masks, an image triggered by Scarfe's own memories of growing up in the Second World War.

A new pig was also designed. Tattooed with Scarfe's crossed hammers insignia, it made its appearance on stage during the opening song 'In the Flesh', reappearing above the audience for 'Run Like Hell'. Fisher and Park also rendered four of Scarfe's characters as puppets. The 49ft-high schoolmaster would make its debut during 'Another Brick in the Wall Part 2'; the pinch-faced mother appeared as a 500lb, 35ft-high monstrosity during the song 'Mother', while a snake and a praying mantis inspired Pink's estranged wife. 'I had no idea what Roger's ex-wife looked like,' said Scarfe. 'So it wasn't based on her.' The character of Pink was also created as a human-sized puppet: toothless, distressed and very, very pink, it would be propped up on stage or on top of the Wall at key moments during the show.

On every night of the tour, a radio DJ was hired to act as master of ceremonies, egging on the audience before the gig and during the intervals, but also lampooning the role of the traditional MC. Four backing singers were hired for the tour, but, as an added twist, each show would open with the appearance of a 'surrogate band', which the audience believed to be Pink Floyd, rising from underneath the stage.

'Roger once told me his dream was to have a surrogate Pink Floyd so he could go to the Bahamas and they could play at Earls Court,' says Gerald Scarfe. As the first song, 'In the Flesh', drew to a close, complete with exploding fireworks and a crashing Stuka aeroplane, the fake Floyd would freeze, revealing the real Floyd behind them. The surrogate band would include drummer Willie Wilson, guitarist Snowy White, keyboard player Peter Wood and bassist Andy Bown, and would also play alongside the real group during parts of the show. Each surrogate band member would also wear a prosthetic mask of their respective counterpart's faces, specially moulded by a Hollywood make-up artist.

The band and crew were also required to wear a *Wall* uniform – black shirts, with the hammer insignia stitched on to the breast – though the group abandoned the shirts for some dates, Waters wearing a white T-shirt with, tellingly, the number 1 emblazoned across his chest.

Rehearsals commenced at the MGM film lot in Culver City, Los Angeles in January 1980. Rick Wills, who'd turned down the surrogate band, as he'd landed a big-money gig with Foreigner, had recommended bassist Andy Bown in his place. A multi-talented musician who'd played alongside Peter Frampton in The Herd, Bown took a leave of absence from his regular day job of playing keyboards for Status Quo. He was by no means a Pink Floyd fan.

'I didn't know anything about them,' Bown admits now. 'It wasn't until I got sent cassettes of the album that I realised it was called *The Wall*. I thought it was called *The War*. I'd misheard on the telephone, you see.' Andy also listened to *Animals*, and was pleasantly surprised. 'I thought: Cor, that's a bit heavy, but also quite simple. I hadn't realised that Pink Floyd was mainly three chords. One of them is A minor, that's the only difference.'

Gilmour was in charge of rehearsals, and, for the first week, the surrogate band ran through the set without Roger Waters. As the days went by, Andy became increasingly curious about the absent bass player. 'All I kept hearing was, "Oh, Roger's coming tomorrow . . . Oh no, not tomorrow, the day after." Everyone seemed to think he was God. I was like, "Who *is* this Roger?"'

When he finally arrived, Waters and Bown rehearsed side by side, both playing bass. 'And then Roger made a fucking awful mistake, and I turned to him and said, "If you're going to play like that I want smaller billing." And I rather think that broke the ice.'

Three further weeks of rehearsals at the venue preceded the opening night at the Los Angeles Memorial Sports Arena on 7 February. With barely twenty-four hours to go, Floyd's long-serving lighting technician Graeme Fleming was removed from the job. His replacement was Bruce

Springsteen's lighting designer Marc Brickman, who answered a call from Steve O'Rourke, believing it was an invitation to watch the show. Instead, Brickman found himself put in charge of the lights for the whole tour, despite never having heard the album. He would later tell *Q* magazine that it was 'the most terrifying experience of my life'.

For Waters it was the realisation of a dream. With the wall in place, Waters roamed the empty arena, climbing up to the furthest seats in the venue. 'My heart was beating furiously and I was getting shivers up and down my spine,' he remembered. 'And I thought it was fantastic that people could actually see and hear something from everywhere they were seated.'

For the surrogate band members, the opening of the show was an exhilarating, if bizarre moment. 'We had the masks on, but you could still see the first five or six rows,' remembers Willie Wilson. 'But the look on their faces when we stopped playing and the real band appeared was very amusing.'

A quarter of the way into the opening night gig, sparks from the crashing Stuka set one of the stage curtains alight. Waters began shouting, 'Stop, stop', but some of the band believed this was part of his performance and carried on playing. They only stopped when pieces of the burning curtain started landing on the stage. 'Half the fans panicked and began running for the exits,' said James Guthrie, who was now in charge of the front-of-house sound. 'The other half were all stoned and thought it was a pretty far-out part of the act.' The Stuka was grounded for the next few shows under orders from the LA fire department. Movie director Barbet Schroeder, for whom Floyd had recorded the *More* and *Obscured by Clouds* soundtracks, attended a show at the Sports Arena. 'I will remember it for the rest of my life,' he says. 'The sheer noise and the sensation when the wall fell down at the end of the show was especially impressive . . . particularly in a city with a well-known earthquake problem.'

On stage, the meticulous timing and choreography left little room for manoeuvre. 'You could never risk having a drink before the show,' explained Gilmour. 'I had great piles of cue sheets hanging over my amps, because every song needed four different settings for four different people. At the beginning and end of every number, everyone was looking at me, waiting for the next cue.'

Los Angeles was followed by five sold-out nights at the Nassau Veteran Memorial Coliseum on New York's Long Island. Andy Warhol showed up one night, as did Bob Ezrin, who was now persona non grata with Roger Waters.

'I did a stupid, stupid thing,' says Ezrin. 'But I had no idea the lengths some people will go to for a story.' Ezrin had been involved in the development of *The Wall* stage show since the beginning, when a tabletop model of the set had been built, complete with tiny figurines and miniature inflatables. Asked by Waters to help stage the tour, he declined, as he was in the middle of a divorce and custody battle. Waters was determined to keep all details about the upcoming shows a secret, and made Ezrin sign a non-disclosure agreement. 'I had a friend who was a big Floyd fan and was living in LA,' explains Ezrin. 'I arranged tickets for him to see *The Wall* at the Sports Arena. A week or so before, he rings me up, saying he couldn't get the time off work to go to the gig and begging me to tell him what it was like. Then, one week before the opening night, there's this article in *Billboard* magazine, giving a detailed account of the show, "as described over dinner with Bob Ezrin"! Once he saw that, Roger went nuclear. He shut me down, looking for breaches of contract so he didn't have to pay my expenses. I screwed up, sure, but it didn't call for that violent a reaction.'

Ezrin was banned from attending any of the shows: 'Not that that stopped me.' Undeterred, he bought his tickets, hired a limousine and turned up backstage at the Memorial Coliseum. Pink Floyd's security team refused to let him in, but the staff security had previously been employed by Ezrin's old clients Kiss and immediately ushered him through.

'It was the best rock show I ever saw,' says Ezrin. Not for the last time at a Pink Floyd gig, the producer was moved to tears. The source of his emotion was the final epic denouement of 'Comfortably Numb', in which Gilmour appeared on top of the wall, lit by brilliant blue and white lights.

While Waters sang the opening verse, the guitarist would wait in the darkness for his cue to begin singing: 'I'd be up there in the pitch-black looking down at the audience. When I opened my mouth to start singing and the lights hit, the whole audience would look upwards, gasping. It was a fantastic moment.'

Behind the scenes, Gilmour was actually standing on a flight case on casters, on top of the hydraulic lift platform to give him the extra height to appear above the Wall. The makeshift and potentially life-threatening platform was held in place behind him by guitar tech Phil Taylor, clinging on in the darkness for dear life.

The closing moments of the show, after which the wall came down, found the real and fake Floyds and their backing singers joining together at the front of the stage. The final song, 'Outside the Wall', was performed amid the discarded bricks, by the makeshift band on acoustic guitars, mandolins, clarinets and tambourines. It was a rare moment of outright human contact with the audience, and with each other.

There was no such contact going on backstage. The VIP area was carpeted in Astroturf, and scattered with café-style tables and parasols and even pinball machines. Ezrin found himself welcomed by Gilmour and Mason, but noticed that Waters stayed in his separate dressing room. 'We'd have four Winnebagos parked in a circle,' admitted Waters years later, 'with all the doors facing away from the circle.'

'Roger wanted it that way,' said Wright. 'Dave and Nick and I didn't. Roger would travel in his own car to the gig, stay in different hotels from anyone else. He created the isolation.'

Quite how Wright coped with performing in a band from which he had just been fired is a testament to his terribly English stiff upper lip. As one former associate bluntly put it, 'Had Pink Floyd been an American group, they'd have punched each other's lights out long ago.'

'It wasn't that bad,' insisted Wright. 'Basically I shut myself off from the whole idea that I was leaving the band. I actually fooled myself into thinking that, maybe if I play as well as I can, Roger will admit that he was wrong.'

There would be no such change of heart, yet the browbeaten keyboard player would end up having the last laugh. Andy Bown recalls having a conversation with Steve O'Rourke during the rehearsals. 'It was costing the band an incredible amount of money just to set up those shows. Steve said, "Guess how much we're in the hole for?", and it was some phenomenal figure. I won't tell you as it's a personal matter, but I thought: Fucking hell!'

Despite sold-out shows, the cost of production was overwhelming. Waters has since told interviewers that the band lost around $600,000 staging *The Wall*. All except Wright. Under the terms of his new deal, the band he had co-founded were paying him as a hired hand. Any losses were made by the other three.

Witnessing the sold-out run in New York, concert promoter Larry Magid approached the band at the end of February, offering them a $2 million guarantee (plus all their expenses) to bring the show to Philadelphia's JFK Stadium for two nights. There were no further *Wall* shows planned until London in August, but Waters flatly refused.

'I said to the others, "You've all read my explanation of what *The Wall* is about,"' Waters told writer Chris Salewicz. 'It's three years since we did that last stadium and I saw then that I would never do one again. *The Wall* was entirely sparked off by how awful that was and how I didn't feel that the public or the band or anyone got anything out of it that was worthwhile. And that's why we've produced this show strictly for arenas. And I ain't fuckin' going.'

Considering the financial pressure of the Norton Warburg situation, Waters' decision to turn down the money seems extraordinary. The rest of the band disagreed, and immediately approached Andy Bown to see if he would stand in for Waters.

'I immediately said yes,' says Bown. 'I would have been delighted.'

'In the end they bottled out,' said Waters. 'They didn't have the balls to go through with it at that point.' Although Gilmour insists that the idea was never seriously considered.

Back in the UK by the end of April (their year of tax exiledom now over) rehearsals began at Shepperton film studios for the forthcoming six nights at Earls Court. Thirty of Gerald Scarfe's original paintings for *The Wall* were put on display in the lobby of the venue, and ten of them were promptly stolen. On stage, Gilmour modelled a fashionably short haircut, while Waters sported his number 1 T-shirt and berated *Melody Maker*'s Alan Jones for being 'a stupid shit' (Jones hadn't liked *The Wall*). Waters' cutting tone was employed for some of the between-song announcements: 'This one's for all you disco fans,' he declared before 'Run Like Hell'. 'As if to say, "What I am doing is high art. Now, get this, you peasants,"' grumbles Nick Kent, who slated the Earls Court shows in *New Musical Express*, suggesting the group should offer the audience refunds on their tickets.

While Richard Wright's departure was still being kept a secret, Waters was forthcoming in a rare interview with *Newsweek*: 'We have been pretending that we are jolly good chaps together, but that hasn't been true in seven years. I make the decisions. We pretended it was a democracy for a long time, but this album was the big own-up.'

Backstage visitors were often surprised by the understated normality of the band members, despite the melodramatic performance being staged out front every night. One Earls Court visitor was struck by the sight of David Gilmour eating sushi and toying with a Rubik's Cube during the interval, completely unfazed by the fact that, just minutes later, he would be perched on top of the wall playing a guitar solo in front of nearly 20,000 fans: 'David doesn't *do* "freak out".'

Cambridge associate Nigel Lesmoir-Gordon went backstage at the same shows, but offered a gloomier verdict. 'They *all* had separate caravans,' he grumbles. 'I told Dave the music was too loud, and he said I should take more drugs. Alcohol and cocaine, presumably.'

Come July, the band went their separate ways for the rest of the year. Norton Warburg finally crashed, and its founder Andrew Warburg disappeared to Spain. He returned a year later, and would end up serving three years in prison for fraudulent trading and false accounting. As well as rich rock stars, it transpired that Warburg's activities had also resulted in considerable losses to ordinary members of the public.

David and Ginger now had a second child, Clare, and would soon have a new home to replace the Essex farmstead. Hookend Manor, in Oxfordshire, was once a fourteenth-century Tudor monastery, and was owned by Alvin Lee, guitarist with Ten Years After. Lee had built his own studio in the property, and installed waterbeds in each of the eleven bedrooms. The property was supposedly haunted, and Lee decided to sell when he realised he didn't need somewhere with quite so many rooms; a decision taken after he discovered a friend living in one of them without him even knowing about it.

'Alvin never opened the curtains in his playroom. He was like a vampire,' recalls Emo, who moved in with the Gilmours. 'We found a secret hiding place in one of the floorboards. We unscrewed it, and there was somebody's hash and grass. No cocaine, unfortunately.'

Meanwhile, Nick Mason and James Guthrie applied the finishing touches to the drummer's first solo album, *Nick Mason's Fictitious Sports*, which had been recorded at the end of *The Wall* sessions, but would not be released until May 1981. The album was a collection of songs written by Mason's recent discovery, jazz vocalist Carla Bley, with contributions from her husband, the trumpeter Michael Mantler, and old pal Robert Wyatt. The album's most intriguing song was 'Hot River', which, promised Mason, 'contains all my favourite Pink Floyd clichés of the last fourteen years'. To nobody's great surprise, though, the album failed to chart. In November, EMI put out *A Collection of Great Dance Songs*, the first Pink Floyd compilation since 1971's *Relics*, which tapped into material from *Meddle* onwards. Roger Waters was sufficiently disinterested in the project to permit Storm Thorgerson to design the cover.

Waters was preoccupied with other matters. The third stage of *The Wall* campaign was the movie. Plans for it were already afoot when Floyd returned to play the final *Wall* shows in the New Year: eight nights at Westfalenhalle in Dortmund, Germany, and a further six at Earls Court.

'When I watched that show in LA, I kept thinking how you could turn this into a film,' says Barbet Schroeder, 'and I eventually realised that there was no way you could.' Not everyone felt the same way, though. Alan Parker was a 36-year-old English film-maker, whose CV had included *Bugsy Malone*, *Fame* and his 1978 breakthrough, *Midnight Express*, a savage drama set in a Turkish prison, which received several Oscar nominations. Parker approached EMI about the possibility of making a movie of *The Wall*. He and his director of photography, Michael Seresin, flew to Dortmund to watch one of the live shows. Parker was astounded by what he saw: 'Coming from the slow, archaic film process, to see *everything* – every hoist, every light, every cue – hit on time, was wonderfully impressive.'

Waters had intended *The Wall* movie to be a combination of live concert footage and additional animated scenes. EMI were reluctant to commit, however, and MGM eventually agreed to fund the project, to the relief of the band, who had put up some of the initial start-up costs. Parker was tied up completing his latest film, *Shoot the Moon*, and suggested Michael Seresin should co-direct along with Gerald Scarfe. The pair arranged to shoot five of the six final nights at Earls Court, but it proved a disaster. The band was unable to compromise any aspect of the meticulously precise stage show to suit the filming. Instead, as Gerald Scarfe recalls, 'Every time I put my lights on, fans would start shouting that I was spoiling the show.' None of the footage would make it into the final film, and, to date, none has been made available to the public.

With Waters' original plan scrapped, Parker agreed to commit as director and began taking a radically different approach to the project: no live footage, no actual dialogue, the story portrayed by actors and animated sequences, with the Floyd's music from *The Wall* moving the narrative on.

Tellingly, in Gerald Scarfe's original storybook for the film, the animated version of the main character was known as Pink, whereas the human version was called Roger. However, as Parker quickly discovered, after a couple of screen tests, Waters was not cut out for acting. Parker recalled being impressed by videos he had seen of Bob Geldof, the outspoken lead singer with the Irish rock band Boomtown Rats. Despite a run of hits, it had been some six months since the band had troubled the Top 10, and their lead guitarist had just walked out. At least a decade younger than anyone in Pink Floyd and a product of the punk revolution, Geldof was disdainful of anything Floyd had done since the Syd Barrett days. Having condemned *The Wall* storyline as 'bollocks', he was enticed by the prospect of acting in a major film, and receiving a hefty pay cheque.

With Michael Seresin replaced by producer Alan Marshall, and with Alan Parker now on board as director, Gerald Scarfe found himself moved sideways. His title would now be 'designer'.

'Alan could get the money from Hollywood as he had the clout,' says Scarfe. 'If he directed it, they would put the money in; they wouldn't if I was directing it. I was an unknown. I stepped aside, and I was relieved, as I had enough to do with the animation sequences.'

Recalling the process of making the film would elicit some dramatic reactions from all parties involved. Roger Waters would tell *Rolling Stone* that it was 'the most unnerving, neurotic period of my life with the possible exception of my divorce'. (Coincidentally, Waters would begin his first course of psychotherapy sessions in the same year.) Alan Parker would liken the experience to 'going over Victoria Falls in a barrel'. Gerald Scarfe recalls driving to Pinewood film studios at 9 a.m. with a bottle of Jack Daniels on the passenger seat beside him. 'I'm not a heavy drinker,' he insists, 'but I had to have a quick slug before I went in.' As he explains, 'Someone said to me, "Well, what do you expect if you put three megalomaniacs in a room together?" '

Showing considerable foresight, Parker persuaded Waters to take a six-week holiday during the actual filming. With one of the megalomaniacs out of the picture, he began a frantic, sixty-day shoot. British character actors including Bob Hoskins (Pink's manager) and Joanne Whalley (playing a groupie) joined Bob Geldof as the adult Pink and thirteen-year-old Kevin McKeon as the young Pink. Familiar vignettes from the album and stage show were recreated. While initially sceptical, Geldof seemed drawn to the role of the damaged rock star, recognising parallels with his own misadventures in the music business.

'I'm not going to waste my time on Geldof, trying to explain *The Wall* to him,' said Waters. 'But he *understands*. He just doesn't realise that he understands.'

Geldof's bravado compensated for his lack of acting experience. He refused to stop filming after cutting his hand during the hotel-wrecking scene; overcame his inability to swim to float in a swimming pool of fake blood; and achieved the right haunted stare for a scene in which Pink shaves off his body hair (something Syd Barrett had done to himself in 1967).

By the time Pink mutated into a political tyrant, Geldof was afraid he was turning the same way himself. Decked out in a military uniform, complete with the crossed hammers motif, he presided over a scene filmed at London's New Horticultural Hall, featuring a rally of real-life skinheads, recruited from the East End of London. Subsequent scenes of a riot between the skins and the police found the action continuing with great gusto after the cameras had stopped rolling. In between the human action scenes, Gerald Scarfe had organised a team of up to fifty artists to produce nearly fifteen thousand hand-coloured drawings, bringing back to life the characters that had graced the album and the stage show.

When Waters returned from his vacation he was incensed by the artistic licence Parker had taken with what he perceived as his film. 'I think he was fearful I wouldn't let him back in,' Parker told writer Karl Dallas, 'and I was just as paranoid about the cut being tampered with.'

'The trouble is Roger and I had lived this thing together for about three years,' says Gerald Scarfe. 'So when it came to the film, Roger didn't want to relinquish control. So there was me and Roger on one side and Parker on the other – and that's when the war started.'

After one row, Parker threatened to walk out. 'That's when Roger's and my relationship became unworkable,' said Gilmour. 'We had to persuade Alan Parker to come back to it, because there was very big money invested, and the entire film company at Pinewood were going to remain loyal to Alan, because he's a film-maker, not Roger Waters. So I had to go to Roger and say to him, "Give him what it says in his contract . . . I'm sorry, otherwise we'll have to have a meeting of the shareholders and directors" – which is me, Nick and Roger – "and we'll out-vote you." There was nothing he could do.'

Waters could at least distract himself with the film soundtrack. Holed up with James Guthrie, he oversaw the transfer of the music from the original *Wall* master tapes. New versions of 'Bring the Boys Back Home', 'Mother' and 'Outside the Wall', among others, would be recorded, with Tim Renwick providing additional guitar on one track. Bob Geldof also recorded his own vocals for a version of 'In the Flesh' under Gilmour's guidance. One new song was recorded. In the movie, 'When the Tigers Broke Free' soundtracked a flashback to Pink's father in the Second World War and the young Pink discovering some of his dead father's personal effects, including a letter of condolence to Pink's mother, rubber-stamped by King George VI. The song had not been included on *The Wall*, as it was felt to be too autobiographical. It was released as a single in July 1982 to coincide with the film's release. With Waters offering more of a spoken-word soliloquy about his father's death than a conventional vocal, and with the notable absence of any guitar solos, the song scraped into the Top 40 in the UK, but disappeared completely in America.

The Wall opened at London's Leicester Square in May, and cleared nearly £50,000 at the box office in its first week. David Gilmour would subsequently consider the film to be 'the least successful of the three ways of telling that particular story'. Alan Parker would protest that it was a struggle between his own interest in delivering cinematic action and Waters' desire to 'delve into his psyche to find personal truths'.

'I once had a very heated conversation with Alan Parker where he said to me that the perfect film is made up of one hundred perfect minutes,' said Waters. 'That, to me, seems to be wrong. There's got to be lots and lots of imperfect minutes to make a perfect hundred. And that's the feeling I got from watching the movie – that every minute was trying to be full of action. I found it a bit difficult to watch in a sitting. I've become kind of numbed by it.'

With the absence of conventional dialogue, *The Wall* asked a lot of its creators, actors and, ultimately, its audience. Bob Geldof acquits himself well, having sufficient charisma (not to mention an endless supply of haunted stares) to compensate for his lack of proper lines. In Alan Parker's quest for cinematic action, there are also some powerful set pieces. The opening scenes, in which soldiers under fire are spliced with footage of rock fans stampeding into an arena, is a literal interpretation of Waters' hatred of playing what he saw to be violent stadium gigs. The scenes outside the arena, in which the fans are roughed up by the police, were directly inspired by events at one of Pink Floyd's Los Angeles concerts in 1975. Similarly, the film contains poignant moments from Roger Waters' own childhood. In an early scene, the young, fatherless Pink is seen tagging along behind another child's father at a children's playground, and being brushed aside.

'As soon as I could talk, I was asking where my daddy was,' said Waters in 2004. 'In 1946 everybody got demobbed, and, suddenly, all these men appeared. Now they were picking their kids up from nursery school, and I became extremely agitated.'

Like the album and stage show before it, Gerald Scarfe's animations are now so crucial to *The Wall* movie that it is impossible to imagine it without them. There are only fifteen minutes of animated sequences in the whole film, but Scarfe's garish parade of malevolent worms, blood, guts and copulating flowers seem to dominate. Ostensibly, the same nagging doubt remains about the movie as it does about the album: that, at times, it's hard to care or sympathise with the central character of Pink, with his self-pity, his pretensions, his narcissism . . .

It's tempting to think that at least some of the band felt the same way. When the film opened in New York, Nick Mason excused himself from attending, as he simply couldn't face watching it again. Richard Wright's non-appearance was excused with the party line 'Rick is on holiday'. But by the summer, they could hardly keep up the pretence any longer, and the band made public the news of his departure. Yet these days, even *The Wall*'s creator has little empathy with the monster he created. 'The one disappointment I had – and it's my fault – is that it gave me the chance to introduce my sense of humour to the piece,' said Waters. 'And I signally failed to do that. It's extremely dour.'

Back then, life in Pink Floyd was about to become even more dour.

CHAPTER NINE INCURABLE TYRANTS AND KINGS

'When you've been in a pop group for fifteen years, things that made you laugh about someone when you started can irritate the shit out of you later.'

David Gilmour

On 2 May 1982, the British submarine HMS *Conqueror* torpedoed the Argentine cruiser, *General Belgrano,* killing 368 men on board. The sinking was the latest act of aggression in the Falklands War, a conflict that had begun a month before when Argentine forces attempted to claim the islands in the South Atlantic Ocean. Argentina and the United Kingdom both believed the islands to be their territory, but it was the UK that had claimed sovereignty since the nineteenth century.

For a generation that had grown up in Britain after the Second World

War and the Korean War, the Falklands conflict would be the first taste of military action. Confusion over the precise whereabouts and the intention of the cruiser, and political misinformation between the British military and cabinet ministers would spark controversy. But to the then serving Conservative government, under Prime Minister Margaret Thatcher, there was political capital to be made: a marauding foreign force had invaded a British dependency; retribution had been swift and decisive.

For Roger Waters, a songwriter informed by the shadow of war on his own life, this latest conflict was yet more grist to the mill. By the time Pink Floyd began work on a follow-up album to *The Wall* in July 1982, the war in the South Atlantic was foremost in his mind. The futile loss of lives on both sides was one factor, but there was also the belief that the conflict was being manipulated as a potential vote-winner in a country puffed up with nationalist pride.

'I'm not a pacifist,' said Waters. 'I think there are wars that have to be fought, unfortunately. I just don't happen to think that the Falklands was one of them.'

The death of Pink Floyd Mark II came not with a bang, nor a whimper, but with a sort of bark. *The Final Cut*, the last Pink Floyd album to feature both Roger Waters and David Gilmour, is, as Gilmour tactfully pointed out at the time, 'very much Roger's baby'. With all that this implies. Gilmour was sidelined, and sang lead vocals on just one song. Waters performed the remainder of the album in that heartfelt, hysterical, affecting, and occasionally rather affected, strangulated bark. It would be impossible to imagine these songs being sung by anyone else.

The final credits of *The Wall* movie promised that the soundtrack was now available. Having re-recorded some songs from the original album for the film, the band had planned to piece together enough for another full-length record, *Spare Bricks*. When the Falklands conflict began, Waters became distracted, and started writing the piece that would eventually be subtitled 'Requiem for a Post-War Dream'. Inevitably, this new work would be dedicated to his father, Eric Fletcher Waters. *Spare Bricks* was immediately forgotten.

'*The Final Cut* was about how, with the introduction of the Welfare State, we felt we were moving forward into something resembling a liberal country where we would all look after one another,' explained

Waters. 'But I'd seen all that chiselled away, and I'd seen a return to an almost Dickensian society under Margaret Thatcher. I felt then, as now, that the British government should have pursued diplomatic avenues, rather than steaming in the moment that task force arrived in the South Atlantic.'

However left-leaning his views may have been in private, David Gilmour was less enamoured of Waters' overt politicising. With wearying inevitability, the two butted heads the moment Waters proposed the album.

'There were all sorts of arguments over political issues, and I didn't share his political views,' explained Gilmour in 2000. 'But I never, never wanted to stand in the way of him expressing the story of *The Final Cut*. I just didn't think some of the music was up to it.'

Gilmour's bugbear was that four of the pieces making up the 'new' song cycle, 'Your Possible Pasts', 'One of the Few', 'The Final Cut' and 'The Hero's Return', were scraps from *The Wall* which had been earmarked for the *Spare Bricks* album. Although the band had frequently recycled from their 'rubbish library' in the past, Gilmour was adamant that these particular items just weren't good enough. Waters again seemed to be operating a closed-shop policy when it came to writing songs for Pink Floyd. But he had his reasons.

'Dave wanted me to wait until he had written some more material,' said Waters, 'but given that he'd written maybe three songs in the previous five years I couldn't see when that was going to happen.'

Gilmour has since admitted as much. 'I'm certainly guilty at times of being lazy, and moments have arrived when Roger might say, "Well, what have you got?" And I'd be like, "Well, I haven't got anything right now. I need a bit of time to put some ideas on tape." There are elements of all this stuff that, years later, you can look back on and say, "Well, he had a point there." But he wasn't right about wanting to put some duff tracks on *The Final Cut*. I said to Roger, "If these songs weren't good enough for *The Wall*, why are they good enough now?"'

As Bob Ezrin recalled from *The Wall* sessions, 'David was a little more taciturn back then. He did a lot of smiling, and rarely went toe to toe, but when he did he was completely unmoveable.'

Unfortunately, Ezrin, the great mediator, was not available to help. He was still banished to Pink Floyd's personal Siberia after accidentally revealing secret information about *The Wall* stage show, and had been busy producing new albums for his old sparring partners Alice Cooper and Kiss. Instead, Michael Kamen, who had helped score the orchestral arrangements for *The Wall*, was brought in. Kamen, James Guthrie and Waters, naturally, would share the final production credits; the absence of Gilmour's name the result of a later disagreement during the final sessions for the album.

The musicians' credits for *The Final Cut* read like an entry from the 1982 *Who's Who* guide to session players. In Richard Wright's absence, the classically trained Kamen played piano and harmonium and conducted the National Philharmonic Orchestra. Andy Bown, *The Wall*'s surrogate band member – and now Waters' neighbour in East Sheen – was hired to play Hammond organ. Nick Mason found his role augmented by Elton John's percussionist Ray Cooper and, when Mason struggled to master the necessary timekeeping on the song 'Two Suns in the Sunset', Andy Newmark, fresh from drumming on Roxy Music's *Avalon* album. Veteran Floyd associate Dick Parry was now replaced by saxophonist Raphael Ravenscroft, previously heard on Gerry Rafferty's 1978 hit single 'Baker Street'. For a band once so insular and self-preserved, this was a very different way of working. Similarly, instead of barricading themselves in their own studio at Britannia Row, work was undertaken at no less than eight studios, including Mayfair in Primrose Hill, Gilmour's home studio at Hookend Manor, and the 'Billiard Room' at Waters' new house in East Sheen, where the bassist had installed a twenty-four-track recorder alongside the obligatory green baize table. Waters was, by all accounts, a formidable snooker player. 'Roger would give you a ten or fifteen-point start and *still* beat you,' explains Andy Bown. 'At one point I thought he was even going to put a blindfold on to give me a fighting chance.'

Initially, Gilmour and Waters worked together in the studio. Waters would later recall that the pair preoccupied themselves with *Donkey Kong*, the recently launched Nintendo computer game, when not recording. But as time wore on, and the tension mounted, they chose to work separately.

'James [Guthrie] and I would literally have one each,' said Andy Jackson, who co-engineered *The Final Cut*. 'I tended to go to Roger's and work with him on the vocals, and James would go to Dave's and work on the guitars. And we'd occasionally meet up again and swap what we'd done.' While Jackson insists that this was not a particularly unusual way of working, it also had its benefits: 'The time that Dave and Roger were in the studio together was definitely frosty.'

Andy Bown, a man who, to date, has survived nearly thirty-five years as keyboard player to Status Quo, takes a more unusual view. 'There was quite a lot of friction,' he admits. 'But the difference between Pink Floyd and every other band I've worked with is that they are gentlemen. No outsider would be able to tell there was friction. Pink Floyd are the only band I've encountered who know how to behave properly.'

Yet even the quietly smiling Gilmour couldn't keep smiling quietly for ever, as he found himself increasingly shut out of the project: 'I lost my temper on more than one occasion. There were no fisticuffs. But it was close on a couple of occasions.'

Even Waters' new collaborators felt the strain. Michael Kamen's work on *The Wall* had taken place in New York, away from the band. When he finally came to work with them, face to face, he wisely chose to keep his distance from intra-band politics. But even his professional reserve was challenged during one particularly punishing session in the Billiard Room. Waters had never found singing particularly easy, but he was having an especially difficult day pitching. Kamen sat patiently in the control room, and eventually began writing on a pad of paper. Waters finally lost his patience, ripped off his headphones and demanded to know what Michael was writing. Kamen had become so worn down by the tortuous vocal takes that he started to believe that it was some kind of payback for misdemeanours in his past life. In his traumatised state he had begun writing 'I Must Not Fuck Sheep' over and over again on the pad of paper in front of him . . .

The involvement of 'ship's cook' Nick Mason in the album was, in his own words, 'pretty minimal'. The band's passion for newfangled sound technology had first been indulged with a quadraphonic version of *Dark Side of the Moon*. The craze for quad sound had never quite caught on, as most conventional hi-fi set-ups couldn't really do it justice. For *The Final Cut*, the group had been sold on the promise of 'Holophonic' or 'Total Sound', a process devised by an Italian scientist. This process worked on conventional stereo tape but when played back through headphones could effectively 'move' the sound around, to give the impression that it was being heard above, beside or behind the listener's head.

A sucker for such special effects, Waters entrusted Nick Mason with overseeing the recording of various holophonic sound effects needed for the album. Mason would keep himself busy taping the sound of warplanes at an RAF base in Warwickshire and screaming car tyres at a police driving school. Away from his musical duties, though, he was also free to indulge his passion for motor racing. By the time he returned for the final sessions, relations between Gilmour and Waters had broken down completely.

'Sometimes I drove home from the recording studio and screamed and swore, although I was alone in the car,' Gilmour admitted. 'That was Roger's fault. He didn't want my music, he didn't want my ideas. It got to the point where I just had to say, "If you want a guitar player, give me a call and I'll play some."'

The upshot of the final argument was that Gilmour's name as producer was removed from the final credits, although it was agreed that he would still be paid.

'Dave's attitudes and beliefs were very different from mine, and a lot of niggling developed,' explained Waters. 'But if you want to be in a band and go on making the money you have to have songs. Gilmour didn't like *The Final Cut*'s politics. He didn't like the attacks on Margaret Thatcher.'

'Not true,' said Gilmour in 2008. 'I am completely against war if it can possibly be avoided, and I was not in favour of Thatcher going into the Falklands.'

For all his tenacity and willingness to fight to the death, even Waters was feeling the strain. 'I was in a pretty sorry state. There was so much conflict in my professional life. By the time we had gotten a quarter of the way into making *The Final Cut*, I knew that I would never make another record with Dave Gilmour and Nick Mason.' The drummer, for so long Waters' closest ally in Pink Floyd, also found himself siding with Gilmour over the musical arguments.

Argentine forces surrendered the Falklands in June 1982, by which time the total death count for both sides had almost reached 1,000. Come December 1982, Gilmour and Mason had been forced to accede to Waters' wishes, effectively relinquishing any control they might have had over *The Final Cut*. Waters has since hinted that he threatened to put it out as a solo record, but, as the band were contracted to EMI to make a Pink Floyd album, it seems unlikely that the company would have permitted this.

While the process of making the record was clearly a harrowing experience, *The Final Cut* has suffered rather badly by association. History now views it as so bound up with the demise of Pink Floyd Mark II that it's difficult to appraise the music independently. Roger Waters' dominant vocals ensure that it's not an entry-level album for the curious. However, his occasional madman ranting and, yes, strangulated bark suits most of the material. 'A lot of the aggravation came through in the vocal performance, which, looking back, really was quite tortured,' he admits.

If nothing else, he always sounds utterly committed to his deeply personal lyrics: calling Prime Minister Thatcher to task on 'The Post-War Dream' ('Oh, Maggie, Maggie what have we done? . . .'), and berating her for the sinking of the *General Belgrano* on 'Get Your Filthy Hands Off My Desert'. The thoughtful 'Southampton Dock', a lament to returning war heroes and those heading off to face almost certain death, taps again into Waters' own story of an absent father, missing in action. On 'Your Possible Pasts' and 'Two Suns in the Sunset', there's even something of Bob Dylan during his gnarly, late-seventies period, in Waters' voice. It would have been pushing even Gilmour's stoic professionalism to sing these songs with anywhere near as much conviction. Yet, however sidelined he may have been, his guitar solos on 'Your Possible Pasts' and 'The Fletcher Memorial Home' are almost the measure of anything on *The Wall*.

Despite Waters' universal despair at the state of Great Britain, *The Final Cut* still managed a traditional Pink Floyd happy(ish) ending. The theme of impending nuclear Armageddon in 'Two Suns in the Sunset' found Waters pondering his character's last few minutes alive. 'It says, "Don't be scared to live your life," ' Waters told writer Carol Clerk. ' "Don't be scared to take risks. Don't be scared to take the risk of touching people or being vulnerable." '

Released in March 1983 in the UK, *The Final Cut* appeared in a sleeve designed by Waters, with photographs taken by his brother-in-law, Willie Christie. The detail on the front, of various Second World War service medals, including the Distinguished Flying Cross, was rather more subtle than a back cover photograph of a soldier, holding a film canister under one arm, with a knife protruding from his back. *The Final Cut* gave Pink Floyd another number 1 album, though this was clearly off the back of *The Wall*'s popularity, rather than on the commercial appeal of the material. In America, it managed a similarly impressive number 6 placing.

The opening sounds of several perfectly enunciating British newscasters, including one discussing the Falklands War, gives the whole record an identifiably English flavour, which must have baffled American audiences not traditionally inclined to take notice of wars in parts of the world they had never heard of. 'Not Now John', the one song on which Gilmour sang lead vocals, was released as a single in the UK and US, after Steve O'Rourke persuaded the band that American radio stations were keen to play it. One of the album's few up-tempo tracks, its chorus line of 'fuck all that' was hastily substituted by a new line of 'stuff all that'. Gilmour's rasping vocal and squalling guitar were still red herrings. A song about the unquestioning, 'fuck all that' mentality of the jingoistic Brit, 'Not Now John' was still a punchy, cynical number. For British listeners there also seemed something prickly and snobbish about its closing lines of 'Where's the bar?' repeated in French, Italian, Greek, Spanish and, finally, English: 'Oi, where's the fucking bar?' The song made it into the UK Top 30, but failed to do anything in America.

Critical reaction veered from *Melody Maker*'s blunt assessment that *The Final Cut* was 'a milestone in the history of awfulness' to *Rolling Stone*'s belief that it was 'art-rock's crowning masterpiece'. In *NME*, Richard Cook claimed that Waters' songwriting was 'blown to hell. Like the poor damned Tommies that haunt his mind.'

Waters granted an interview to Karl Dallas, in which he admitted that 'communication in the band isn't too good' while insisting that his comments in an earlier interview did not suggest 'the end of the band, which is nonsense', only that he was now toying with the idea of making a solo album.

David Gilmour stuck to the party line in an interview from the same year. 'We did have an argument about the production credits,' he explained carefully, 'because my ideas of production weren't the way that Roger saw it being [sic]. [*The Final Cut*] is very good but it's not personally how I would see a Pink Floyd record going.'

In years to come, Gilmour would become increasingly bullish in his dismissal of the record, trotting out a standard response that there are only three good songs on the album: '"The Fletcher Memorial Home",

"The Final Cut" and, umm, I can't remember right now . . . there's two of them anyway.'

However disliked it may now be among some of their audience and the band themselves (even Waters would later admit that 'not everything can be a fucking masterpiece'), *The Final Cut* could never find Pink Floyd accused of complacency. The musical offerings from many of their sixties and seventies contemporaries at the time prove how difficult some of their peers found it to stay relevant in the new decade. The Rolling Stones' *Dirty Work* album saw the beleaguered Jagger/Richards partnership hitting an all-time low, and The Who's *It's Hard* suggested that even their old firebrand Pete Townshend was all out of puff. In such lacklustre company, *The Final Cut*, however heavy-going, sounded as if Pink Floyd still gave a shit about *something*.

Without a tour or any serious promotional campaign to support the album, the band seemed to have fallen into professional limbo by 1983. Meanwhile, their one-time frontman, Syd Barrett, had left London and returned to Cambridge. His excessive spending had left him penniless and his poor diet had given him stomach ulcers. Syd's old management company, Blackhill, was now looking after Ian Dury and The Clash, when a ghost from their past appeared in the office.

'I think he wanted us to sign a passport form,' recalls Peter Jenner. 'He could barely talk, and he looked like a bouncer. He'd put on an enormous amount of weight and was wearing this overcoat that looked more like a tent. We were like, "*Who* is that?" A whisper went round the office. "My God, it's Syd."'

By now, Barrett's mother had sold the house in Hills Road and moved, with her son, to nearby St Margaret's Square. Barrett agreed to an operation to alleviate his stomach problems. According to Tim Willis's superlative biography, *Madcap*, Roger Waters' mother Mary helped him find a gardening job, but it didn't last long. In 1982, as his former band released their challenging new album, Barrett drifted back to London and booked himself into his old haunt, the Chelsea Cloisters. Within weeks he was gone again. According to Barrett myth, walking back to Cambridge. 'I have no idea if he really did *walk* back,' ventures old friend David Gale, 'but that's the story.'

Two journalists from a French magazine, *Actuel*, trailed Barrett to

Cambridge, bringing with them a bag of laundry he'd left behind at Chelsea Cloisters. Barrett answered the door, politely offering to pay them for his clothes. Asked if he played guitar while living in London, he replied, 'No, I watch TV, that's all.' He allowed the pair to take a photograph before scuttling back into the house.

Old friends would run into him from time to time, but they didn't encounter the same Syd they'd known before. Sue Kingsford was driving to her parents' house on the outskirts of Cambridge when she saw Barrett standing by the side of the road, looking as if he were trying to hitch a lift.

'So we stopped the car and told him to get in,' says Sue. '"Where are you going, Syd?" "I'm not going anywhere." We took him to a pub, the Tickell Arms. He had a pint of Guinness, but didn't say a single word. In the end, I said, "Great to see you, Syd, I have to go home now." He said, "Yes, great to see you, too." And we drove him back to Cambridge.'

In interviews, Roger Waters would often state that Syd was suffering from schizophrenia, though his family never confirmed this. 'I think Syd was just terribly unlucky with one trip,' offers Libby Gausden. 'Syd's mother, Win, always thought somebody had slipped something into his drink. That really was what she believed. I don't think she knew anything about drugs.'

However, throughout the first half of the 1980s, he voluntarily spent time in nearby Fulbourn psychiatric hospital ('That was awfully ironic,' says Libby Gausden. 'Syd loved that area, and we often used to sit and look at the hospital') and, according to some, Greenwoods Therapeutic Community near Billericay in Essex. Once again, though, he is said to have ended up walking back to Cambridge.

'We'd get reports back about Syd during this time,' says Storm Thorgerson. 'He seemed very protected by his family, and I think Pink Floyd were supporting him financially. But I don't think he was happy. One wishes it could have all been better.'

With Pink Floyd's future uncertain, David Gilmour seemed determined to keep busy. The Gilmours now had a new addition to the family, a third daughter, Sara. The guitarist also spent his time demoing songs at his home studio, and singing backing vocals on Kate Bush's brilliantly bizarre new album, *The Dreaming*.

For Gilmour's second solo album, 1984's *About Face*, he rounded up an

A-list roster of session players, including drummer Jeff Porcaro and bassist Pino Palladino. By the time sessions began at Pathé-Marconi Studios in Paris, Gilmour had also called in the cavalry.

'David had got himself into a certain depth and decided he needed some help, so he rang me,' explains Bob Ezrin, who was swiftly recruited to co-produce the record. 'I think David felt liberated doing something outside of the Floyd, and had a good time making the record.' Ezrin's abiding memory of the sessions is Gilmour's breakneck dashes around the Champs-Elysées in his new Porsche 928. 'He had right-hand drive in a left-drive country, so I'm in the seat where I think the driver is supposed to be. Terrifying.'

About Face was released in March 1984. Gilmour gamely signed up for a promotional campaign unlike any he had undertaken with Pink Floyd. The album's first single, 'Blue Light', was a funky pop song, which matched Earth, Wind and Fire-style horns to the guitar riff from The Eagles' 'Life in the Fast Lane'. Aware of how important it now was for rock stars to make videos, Storm Thorgerson directed a promo, in which a freshly shorn, spruced-up Gilmour played guitar alongside a troupe of dancing girls before falling to his knees on a helipad – complete with helicopter – to play the final guitar solo.

The rest of the album was more convincing. Pete Townshend con- tributed lyrics to the wistfully romantic 'Love on the Air' and a scabrous 'All Lovers are Deranged', while Gilmour forced himself out of his comfort zone to write about his feelings; expressing anger and confusion at the killing of John Lennon ('Murder'), his opposition to having American Pershing-2 missiles on British soil ('Cruise'), and even his troubled relationship with Roger Waters ('You Know I'm Right'). 'It wasn't initially about that,' he said, 'but when I wrote the first verse, people all assumed it was about that and it coloured the rest of the writing.' If writing the words still proved to be Gilmour's Achilles' heel, there was enough of his signature guitar bluster and breathily English vocals to mask any lyrical shortcomings.

Nowadays, the album's use of then cutting-edge studio technology and celebrity session-men marks it down as a typical mid-eighties solo album from a superstar rocker on day release. Critical response was polite but lukewarm, and the album peaked just outside the UK Top 20 and US Top 30.

'I thought too much about the album,' says Gilmour now. 'I tried too hard to get away from Pink Floyd. It was very rocky, and I think, in some ways, I was being less true to myself than I was on my first solo record.'

The real issue was that 'the great unwashed', as Roger Waters would later describe the general public, didn't really know who anyone in Pink Floyd was. Gilmour willingly addressed the issue at the time: 'The fact is, our individual names mean virtually nothing in terms of the great record- and ticket-buying public.'

After an uncomfortable appearance on the hip new UK TV show, *The Tube*, Gilmour set off on a European and North American tour of 24,000-seater theatres, rather than arenas. His touring party included bassist Mickey Feat and former Bad Company guitarist Mick Ralphs. With his own multi-platinum rock band in dry dock, Ralphs, who lived near Hookend Manor, asked if he could join the tour. No slouch as a lead guitarist, Ralphs was content to play back-up to Gilmour in a set that included the whole of *About Face*, some extracts from the first solo album and just two Pink Floyd numbers.

On stage, without the distraction of flying pigs, a cardboard brick wall or a scowling Roger Waters, Gilmour seemed to relish just playing and singing. As Gerald Scarfe explains, 'When we were doing *The Wall*, while Dave never said it that straightforwardly, I think he would have been happy to give a concert without *any* visual effects. For him, it's all about the music.'

Also on the tour were support band The Television Personalities, a punk-era group whose sound now borrowed from the psychedelic era. Their cover of 'Arnold Layne' and their own song, 'I Know Where Syd Barrett Lives', both impressed Gilmour. But by the time they rolled into Birmingham, The Television Personalities had fallen from favour and been removed from the tour.

Nick Mason and Richard Wright attended one of the three nights at London's Hammersmith Odeon, with Mason playing drums on an encore of 'Comfortably Numb'. Poor ticket sales for some dates led to cancellations, but the tour eventually turned a profit. No sooner had Gilmour flown home from the final date in New York on 16 July, than Roger Waters began the American leg of his own solo tour a day later in Connecticut. Waters, it seemed, was almost shadowing Gilmour, with his new solo album, *The Pros and Cons of Hitch-hiking*, released just six weeks after *About Face*.

Waters' new offering was the song cycle, which had been passed over by Pink Floyd in favour of *The Wall* five years before. *The Pros and Cons . . .* told the story of one man's night of dreaming and waking, counted down in real time, with each song title preceded by a time, beginning at 4.30 a.m. and ending at 5.11 a.m. The front cover picture of a naked female hitch-hiker from behind, belonging to porn model Linzi Drew (a black band obscured the offending rear in some sensitive countries), was the starting point for the story.

In the course of his forty-minute sleep pattern, Waters' hero juggles the positives and negatives of monogamous family life over meaningless sexual encounters. As well as some more random scenarios, the hero picks up a hitch-hiker with whom he has a fumbled sexual encounter, before being interrupted mid-coitus by knife-wielding Arabs; a metaphor, perhaps, for his conscience. Waters' rather unique vocal style – plenty of madman shrieks and Dylan-ish whining – was perfect for a lot of the material. His lyrics, too, were darkly witty and sometimes wonderfully politically incorrect. This was Waters rummaging around in another corner of his psyche, exploring the sexual neuroses of a post-war, middle-class Englishman. Adhering to Roger's customary love of a happy ending, the hero finally wakes up in his own bed, overjoyed to discover his wife lying beside him. 'It's a complicated piece of work,' said Waters in an understatement. 'Although it's quite clear to me what was going on, the narrative is by no means linear.'

Waters also shared musical resources with Gilmour. Engineer Andy Jackson and musicians Michael Kamen and Ray Cooper worked on both *The Pros and Cons . . .* and *About Face*. Waters' trump card, though, was his choice of guitarist. Through girlfriend Carolyne Christie's friendship with Patti Boyd, Waters bagged himself Patti's husband, Eric Clapton.

Musically, Clapton's presence made sense. Aside from bonding over a mutual love of fly-fishing, Waters shared the guitarist's passion for the blues (bonding over a mutual love of Nashville pianist Floyd Cramer), and, for all the lyrical and thematic complexity, the music rarely deviated from the genre. Furthermore, having Eric Clapton play on his record was an obvious snub to guitar hero David Gilmour.

The problem with *The Pros and Cons . . .* is that it suffocates some interesting ideas with too many lyrics, and there are simply not enough tunes. Those tunes, scant as they are, are also used once too often. The title track and first single is one of the few moments of balance, with Clapton's signature riffing yoked to a deranged lyric in which, at one point, the hero dreams that Yoko Ono is telling him to leap to his death from the wing of an aeroplane. The second single, '5.06 a.m. (Every Stranger's Eyes)', was a booming power ballad, made less chart-friendly but more interesting by Waters' vocals, which suggested an asylum inmate muttering to himself in the dark.

A number 13 chart placing in the UK showed that Waters was the least anonymous member of Pink Floyd. Critics, however, were less enamoured, especially *Rolling Stone* writer Kurt Loder, who'd praised *The Final Cut*, but denounced Waters' latest offering as 'a strangely static, faintly hideous record'. Even Waters' ally, *Melody Maker*'s Karl Dallas, found it a struggle, but ended on an upbeat note: 'His second album, I predict, will blow your wig off.'

'*The Pros and Cons* . . . wasn't a wham, bam, thank you, ma'am, far-out rock 'n' roll album,' offered Waters in its defence later. 'It was a very introspective piece about how I felt about my failed marriage [to Judy], my feelings about sex and all kinds of difficult areas.'

To the astonishment of his record company, management and fans, Eric Clapton also announced that he would now be joining Waters' band on tour. A year earlier, Clapton had made a comeback with his *Money and Cigarettes* album, explaining to all that this was his first record since giving up alcohol. Yet his willingness to play in Waters' band may have had more to do with his own fanciful desire for anonymity; the same impetus behind him forming Derek and The Dominoes in the early seventies, and attempting to convince fans and critics that he was 'just one of the band'.

The rest of Waters' group included, among others, *The Final Cut*'s session drummer Andy Newmark, keyboard players Michael Kamen and Chris Stainton, and additional guitarist Tim Renwick, from Waters' old alma mater the Cambridge County.

Waters' show would be split into two sets: the first made up of Pink Floyd songs, including less obvious choices 'If' (from *Atom Heart Mother*) and 'The Gunner's Dream' (from *The Final Cut*), along with the likes of 'Money', 'Wish You Were Here' and 'Hey You'. The second set would be

The Pros and Cons . . . in its entirety with the reward of an encore of 'Brain Damage' and 'Eclipse' from *Dark Side of the Moon*.

Tim Renwick joined Waters a couple of months before the rehearsals officially began: 'I went round to Roger's once a week, going through all the old Pink Floyd stuff as he couldn't be bothered to work out the chords. He was absolutely charming . . . until we went on the road.'

The grand unveiling of Waters' new band and stage show took place in Stockholm on 16 June. Gerald Scarfe and film director Nicolas Roeg had created new animations and films to be projected on to 30ft-high screens covering the back width of the stage. In front of these screens hung three gauzes painted with scenery: a motel window, a motel room wall and a huge television set, designed to recreate the hero's bedroom. Scarfe's latest creation was a comically lazy cartoon dog named Reg, who acted out the hero's neuroses on screen. Nicolas Roeg, whose directorial film credits included *The Man Who Fell to Earth* and *Performance*, delivered film footage of, among others, rolling American highways and free-wheeling trucks. *The Wall* set designer Mark Fisher was on the payroll to co-ordinate the project, later estimating that the film footage alone cost in the region of $400,000.

However, as David Gilmour had already discovered, an individual name didn't carry the same weight as Pink Floyd. Poor sales led to cancellations in Frankfurt and Nice. On the first of two nights at London's Earls Court, the performance was below-par and a disgruntled Waters refused to play an encore. The rearranged Pink Floyd songs had an oddly brisk tempo, and many fans found it odd hearing and seeing Eric Clapton playing Gilmour's guitar parts. Nick Mason, watching from the audience at Earls Court, found it disconcerting to see someone else playing the drums on old Floyd songs. In charge of *everything* now, Waters was feeling the strain. 'One of Roger's problems is that he has great trouble delegating,' explains Tim Renwick. 'He took it all on: the music, the production, the lot. So he was constantly walking around with his head in his hands, and you'd have great trouble communicating with him. He was also very, very serious about it all, and he didn't like anyone else having a laugh. He'd soon stamp on that.'

Adding to Waters' woes was the issue of sharing the stage with a superstar guitarist. On the opening night of the US tour in Hartford, Connecticut, Waters realised that whenever Clapton took a solo, the audience were on their feet, cheering and waving their cigarette lighters. 'And then, as soon as Eric finished, the lighters would go off and everyone would sit down,' says Renwick. 'And this very much annoyed Roger. He thought people were making too much noise and not paying enough attention to the lyrics. In Hartford, we came to the end of the first half, and Roger just threw down his bass on the floor of the stage – it was still plugged in so there was this dreadful cacophony – stuck his arm in the air, shouted, "The *great* Eric Clapton!" and stormed off.'

Backstage, an embarrassed Waters apologised to Clapton and the rest of the band. On stage for the second half of the show, he even apologised to the audience 'for being so unprofessional'.

'I know that, from that point on, Eric would have gone home if he could,' says Renwick. 'When they made the record, Roger had asked Eric if he'd do some stuff live, and he thought it would be a couple of shows, but it turned into several months. Being a man of his word, he couldn't go back on it . . .'

Following the last night of the tour in Quebec, Clapton bowed out amicably, taking keyboard player Chris Stainton and Tim Renwick with him for his own band. Waters was forced to address the issue that even with Eric in the band, many of the shows had been sparsely attended, while *The Pros and Cons* . . . album had stalled shy of the Billboard Top 30 in America. All of which made his decision to go back on the road in the US the following spring so confusing. The sixteen-date tour played in smaller venues than before and was bluntly titled 'Pros and Cons Plus Some Old Pink Floyd Stuff – North American Tour 1985'.

Guitarists Andy Fairweather-Low and Jay Stapley joined in place of Clapton and Renwick. Fairweather-Low had been a teen idol in the midsixties, as lead singer with Amen Corner, a band that had played alongside Pink Floyd on the 1967 Jimi Hendrix package tour. Stapley was a young session player, who had worked with the singer, jingle-writer and Carolyne Christie's cousin David Dundas.

'I was a kid at the time, so doing that tour was a real challenge,' says Stapley now. 'We all thought it was odd that Roger was touring again, but one story we heard was that he wanted to prove he could do it without having Eric in the band to help sell tickets. The trouble is I'd grown up listening to David Gilmour and Eric Clapton, but Roger took me aside and told me I shouldn't try and play like either. Unfortunately, for me, doing songs like "Money" felt a little bit like spitting in church.'

By Waters' own estimation, the Clapton-assisted tour had left him some £400,000 out of pocket. But as he proudly declared, 'It was something I *wanted* to do, not *needed* to do.'

A similar degree of financial security would allow Pink Floyd band members, both past and present, to take risks in their solo careers. By 1983, Waters' spurned bandmate Richard Wright had, he claimed, grown tired of sailing around the Greek Islands, and wanted to get back to making music.

Wright was far more daring in his choice of collaborator. Dave 'Dee' Harris was a singer and songwriter from the Midlands, and frontman with the group Fashion. A product of the 'New Romantic' scene, Fashion's David Bowie-inspired sounds and dandyish chic placed them alongside, if some way behind, the scene's standard-bearers – Duran Duran and Spandau Ballet. Harris had made two albums with Fashion, but was now growing restless. Attending a music business seminar in New York in 1982, he ran into *The Final Cut*'s saxophonist Raphael Ravenscroft, who told him that the Floyd's ex-keyboard player wanted to put a band together. A drummer and bassist were invited to attend a jamming session at Wright's house in Royston, but, ultimately, only Harris showed up.

'I said to Rick, "Why don't we just do this together?"' says Harris now. Wright's musical favourites at the time included Talking Heads and Brian Eno. 'He wanted a very electronic sound, which is why I think he wanted to work with me. He had a solo deal with Harvest and we agreed to split it.'

'It was a bit odd at first when Dave said he could remember going to see Floyd perform when he was fourteen,' said Wright, 'but, from the moment we actually started working together, we realised just how close we were.'

Quirky male duos were the rage in electronic pop, from Orchestral Manoeuvres in the Dark to Soft Cell. Wright and Harris would form a duo of their own called Zee. As they were recording at Wright's own studio, The Old Rectory, Harris and his wife Sue were invited to move into the keyboard player's rambling country pile ('Rick was tumbling around in this place') for eighteen months during the making of the album.

For Harris, who had only turned professional two years earlier, it would prove an eye-opening experience. As a Pink Floyd fan since his teens, he was hoping Wright could be persuaded into playing the Hammond, 'but getting him to do it was a nightmare'. Instead, the pair became completely preoccupied with the Fairlight digital sampling synthesiser. 'It was the toy of the moment and we got stuck on this thing, so everything we did ended up sounding like a fucking robot. Remember, this *was* the eighties.'

For much of the time, Harris was left to his own devices, while Wright coped with the fallout from his divorce and estrangement from Pink Floyd. 'Juliette, his ex-wife, was still around,' Harris recalls. 'She was fabulous, but there were lots of ups and downs. There was also a communication problem, because, understandably, Rick had other things going on. He'd be flying off to Greece one day, or having his boat built the next . . . I also realised I had no idea what he actually thought of what I was doing, as he never told me. A couple of times I said to Juliette, "I don't think Rick likes this", and she went and told him, and he was like, "No, no, I *love* it." What we really needed was an A&R man or a producer.'

A trip to Wright's house in Grasse in the south of France to write lyrics resulted in a fortnight of 'us just getting pissed the whole time'. Back in England, Harris worked all-nighters in the studio, under the watchful eye of the Wrights' housekeeper, Pink: 'He was this wonderful, flaming Canadian queen. A lovely guy, who was forever on the phone to the wives of the other guys in Pink Floyd. Every time you walked in, you'd hear him – "Oh . . . my . . . God" – as he discovered some fresh bit of gossip. I'd hear these stories and think: Christ, this is exactly like being in a semi-pro band, but with millionaires – the same bitching, the wives calling each other this and that . . .'

Zee's album, *Identity*, would be released in the UK and Europe only in March 1984. It met with resounding indifference. Harris plays a very Pink Floyd-sounding guitar on one track, 'Cuts Like a Diamond', but the over-use of the Fairlight has rendered the album very dated. Even then, when the duo's electro-pop sound chimed with the times, the combination of young blade Harris and the dashing, if forty-year-old Wright was perhaps unlikely to bump Duran Duran off the cover of *Smash Hits*. Meanwhile, Pink Floyd fans just wanted Wright to make music that sounded like Pink Floyd. Or, better still, rejoin Pink Floyd.

'Zee was a disaster,' said Wright later, 'an experimental mistake, but it was made at a time in my life when I was lost.'

'It always saddens me when Rick says it was a mistake,' protests Harris, 'because he never said that to me at the time.' However, when *Confusion* failed to sell, Harris jumped ship for a production job. 'I wasn't in the financial situation Rick was. My career was in a very different place. We fell out, and it's very sad, as I loved Rick dearly.'

Within months, Wright was dividing his time between houses in London, Rhodes and Athens, in the company of his new girlfriend, a fashion designer, former model and aspiring singer named Franka. Pink Floyd fans who were waiting for Wright to find himself and return to the fold would not have to wait much longer.

By the summer of 1985, with Waters and Gilmour back from their solo campaigns, the thorny issue of Pink Floyd's future became even more pressing. Strangely, the first collaboration between the band members since *The Final Cut* would take place on Nick Mason's next studio venture. In August 1985, Mason released his second album, *Profiles*, a collaboration with former 10cc guitarist Rick Fenn. Singer-songwriter Danny Peyronel, whose son attended the same school as Fenn's daughter in West London, was roped in to co-write some material and sing lead vocals on one track, 'Israel'. At Britannia Row, Peyronel told engineer Nick Griffiths that despite being an ardent Pink Floyd fan he sometimes had trouble telling David Gilmour and Roger Waters' voices apart. 'He told me it was easy to tell them apart,' says Peyronel. 'If it's in tune it's Gilmour . . .' Most of *Profiles* was a dummy run for the film and TV commercial music Mason and Fenn would dabble in, with the formation of their company Bamboo Music. A year on, the pair's music, alongside some vintage Pink Floyd, would be used in the short, autobiographical film, *Life Could Be a Dream*. The movie explored Mason's love of motor racing, culminating in footage of him competing in the 1984 Endurance race in Mospor, Canada.

However, one song on the album truly stood out. Entitled 'Lie for a Lie', it was a gentle, lilting pop song with last-minute lyrics from Danny Peyronel, which was released as a single. Featuring Mason on drums and Gilmour on lead vocals and guitar, it was the first recording of the partnership that now made up Pink Floyd Mark III.

After *About Face*, Gilmour had quickly realised that, at thirty-nine years old, he had no desire to start his career again as a solo artist. In the meantime, he threw himself into producing his new discovery, Dream Academy, a high-brow pop trio featuring Nick Laird-Clowes, a singer, songwriter and guitarist introduced to him some years earlier by Jeff Dexter. Dream Academy would enjoy a UK Top 10 hit that year with 'Life in a Northern Town'. Eager to keep his hand in, Gilmour played guitar for anyone that asked, including Pete Townshend, Paul McCartney and Grace Jones. Inevitably, Floyd were among the rock giants rumoured to be appearing at Live Aid. 'They asked me to put Pink Floyd back together and I said no, but I'd bring my new band to play,' said Waters. 'But they didn't want me.' Gilmour showed up at Wembley Stadium anyway, playing guitar for Bryan Ferry.

Waters, meanwhile, remained dogged in his belief that the band was now over, a spent force. He approached Steve O'Rourke to negotiate a new deal in which he would pay the manager a different percentage to the rest of the band. O'Rourke informed Gilmour and Mason of the approach, which angered Waters, who believed the negotiations should have been kept private.

O'Rourke and Waters' relationship had often been tense, with the manager's never-ending quest for a good deal jarring with the latter's so-called artistic integrity, not least over the issue of playing stadiums. 'Steve is an effective hustler, a man in a man's world,' allowed Waters in 1987. 'And, to give him his due, he never gave up his job of trying to get me to fill stadiums.'

As just one shareholder of the company Pink Floyd Music, Waters needed Gilmour and Mason's agreement to dismiss O'Rourke. They refused, as, in their eyes, Pink Floyd was still a going concern, and they wished to retain Steve as their manager. They also believed that dismissing him would strengthen Waters' position in dissolving the group (they later turned down Roger's proposal to fire O'Rourke in exchange for him allowing them to continue using the Pink Floyd name).

In October 1985, Waters fired the first shot. He took out a High Court application to prevent the Pink Floyd name ever being used again. Gilmour maintained that it was not Waters' place to decide whether Pink Floyd worked again, and insisted that he wished to continue the band. Waters didn't believe it was possible. 'Roger said, "You'll never fucking get it together to make a record,"' said Gilmour, 'and I said, "We will make a record." He said, "Well, I'm not leaving. I'll just sit at the back of the studio and criticise."'

Two months later, Waters sent a letter to EMI and Columbia informing them that he was leaving Pink Floyd, and asking them to release him from his contractual obligations as a member of the group. Gilmour thought that Waters had taken this decision believing it would expedite the demise of the Pink Floyd name, and also because he could then invoke the 'leaving member's clause' in his contract which allowed him to take up a solo career under a section of the same contract. 'Having done that, he declared Pink Floyd was over,' Gilmour told Karl Dallas. 'I declared that it wasn't.'

Interviewed in 2004, Waters claimed that he sent in his letter of resignation because of a clause in Pink Floyd's contract with Columbia relating to a 'product commitment'. This meant that if the band did not go on releasing albums under the terms of their contract, the record company could potentially sue them and also withhold royalties. While Waters described the clause as 'ambivalent', he claimed that the other band members threatened to sue him for potential loss of earnings and legal expenses, on the grounds that he was preventing Pink Floyd from making any more records. 'They forced me to resign from the band,' Waters told *Uncut* magazine, 'because if I hadn't, the financial repercussions would have wiped me out completely.'

The case to decide whether anyone could continue using the Pink Floyd name was not due to be heard for another twelve months. Gilmour and Mason deliberated on their next move. Waters terminated his contract with Steve O'Rourke, and appointed The Who's and The Rolling Stones' former tour manager Peter Rudge to handle his affairs. His first musical move was to launch himself into another solo project, a soundtrack to the upcoming movie, *When the Wind Blows*. An animated film based on the 1982 graphic novel by Raymond Briggs, it was a blackly humorous tale of an elderly couple (voiced by actors Dame Peggy Ashcroft and Sir John Mills) and their experiences in the aftermath of a Soviet nuclear strike. David Bowie had originally committed to produce the soundtrack, but when he pulled out, Waters stepped in, eventually sharing the album with contributions from Bowie, Genesis, Squeeze, Paul Hardcastle and The Stranglers' Hugh Cornwell.

Work commenced at Britannia Row and the Billiard Room, with members of Waters' backing group, now called The Bleeding Heart Band (after a lyric from *The Wall*). Guitarist Jay Stapley and saxophonist Mel Collins remained from the last US tour, joined by guest vocalists ex-Ace and Squeeze singer Paul Carrack and Clare Torry of 'Great Gig in the Sky' fame.

Clare, who had not worked with any of Pink Floyd since *Dark Side of the Moon*, was living near Waters in East Sheen. Both walked their dogs in the same park. Recording sessions, she remembers, took place in the Billiard Room 'after a sandwich and a pint of beer in our local pub, The Plough'.

Waters' lyrical contributions to the album are often more potent than the music itself, which, as part of a soundtrack, was sometimes lost beneath the snippets of dialogue, although 'Folded Flags' sounded like a cross between Floyd's 'Brain Damage' and 'Grantchester Meadows'. On 'Towers of Faith', Waters somehow managed to follow Woody Guthrie's famous quotation 'this land is our land' with 'this band is my band', a cheeky quip at his former bandmates, before returning to his indictment of US president Ronald Reagan's foreign policies and corporate greed among 'mohair-suited businessmen' in the World Trade Center.

'I always thought "Towers of Faith" was one of the best things Roger ever did,' ventures Clare Torry. 'I remembered the lyrics, and I telephoned him after 9/11, because I thought: My God, remember what you wrote in that song.'

Released in October 1986, the final album hardly troubled the charts, with the movie enjoying a limited run at the cinema. It was a less than auspicious start to Waters' solo career proper. Within days of the album's release he was back in the Billiard Room recording a follow-up. But by then, all hell had broken loose in his dispute with Pink Floyd.

In February that year, producer Bob Ezrin had received a surprise telephone call, while working in Los Angeles on a Rod Stewart album: 'It was Roger! I was stunned. We hadn't spoken since *The Wall*. He said, "I know I was awful to you, and I apologise, and I'm now a different guy from who I was back then . . . *and* I'd really like to talk to you about working together again."'

Ezrin was delighted and flattered. 'The truth is, I missed Roger Waters,' he admits. 'I *still* miss Roger Waters. He's a wonderful, challenging guy to work with.'

The challenging aspect of Waters' nature was apparent from the start of the conversation.

'Roger said, "Can you come here now, to England, to talk about this record?" I said, "No, I can't. Can you come here?" He was like, "I'm not bloody going *there*." So we agreed to meet halfway, in New York City.'

Waters and Ezrin met up in Waters' hotel suite. 'We had a good time, laughing and telling stories. He apologised for what had happened, saying he'd been going through a difficult time . . . he played me his new material and I knew exactly where I wanted to take it.

'So we started to work on a deal. He insisted we start work in England in the summer and we stay there working for three months until we were finished.' Ezrin pointed out that Waters had never done anything in just three months, and that it wasn't a realistic schedule. 'I said to him, "What am I going to do with my wife and kids?" I had four kids at home at the time [and had remarried]. He said he'd lend us one of his houses and arrange to get my children into the American school . . .'

Back in Los Angeles, Ezrin tried to persuade his family to agree to the move. 'I was so seduced by the notion of getting back with Roger Waters that I sold my wife hard on it. At first she absolutely refused. Then she slowly came round and said OK.' Ezrin told Waters the deal was on. 'And then, about ten days later, my wife just broke down in tears and said, "I'm sorry, but I just can't do it." So I called Roger's manager, Peter Rudge, and he said, "Don't do this to me!". . . He told Roger and he went nuclear, about me leading him on, wasting his time . . . And that was it. Roger was never going to talk to me again.'

Two weeks later, Ezrin took another surprise telephone call. This time, from David Gilmour. 'In my conversations with Roger, he'd told me Pink Floyd was no more, and that "the muffins", as he referred to them, would never dare carry on without him. Now here's Dave saying, "We are thinking of doing another Floyd album. I have some songs and I'd love to play them for you."'

The music in question had been coming together slowly over a period of a few months. Almost a year earlier at Live Aid, Gilmour had been introduced to Jon Carin, the keyboard player in Bryan Ferry's backing band. Carin was a twenty-one-year-old New Yorker, who'd begun his career with the electro-pop band Industry (one big hit: 1983's 'State of the Nation'). When Industry split, Carin went into playing sessions, crossing paths with Gilmour again on Bryan Ferry's *Boys and Girls* album.

Gilmour invited Carin to Hookend, where the two jammed in Gilmour's own studio. Carin worked up the beginnings of a piece that would later become the Floyd song, 'Learning to Fly'. He went back to America, aware that the piece was likely to be used by Gilmour for something, 'although there was no talk of Pink Floyd at this stage', as he told *Mojo* magazine in 2004.

In truth, Gilmour had been fired up by the dispute with Waters, and was determined to make another Pink Floyd album. 'Dave absolutely saw red, and finally got it together to go back to work,' said Nick Mason. 'One of the great spurs was the fact that Roger, hearing about the plans for a new album, had told him, "You'll never do it." '

In Waters' absence, Gilmour had also been casting around for new collaborators – something Waters would make much of in their subsequent war of words. Roxy Music guitarist Phil Manzanera (also managed by Steve O'Rourke) spent time with Gilmour co-writing what would become the song 'One Slip'. In the summer, ex-10cc guitarist Eric Stewart joined Gilmour at his request in Hookend, later informing a journalist he had been invited 'to work on a concept that was definitely intended for the next Pink Floyd album. We sat around writing for a period of time, but we couldn't get the different elements to gel. So the whole concept was scrapped. I don't want to divulge the concept because, especially knowing Dave, it may well be used in the future.'

'I don't think I ever got in Eric to write lyrics,' insisted Gilmour in 2006. 'He's a friend of mine, but in a way we're too similar; we're both from the sweeter end of things, we both like melody. We just had a day or two mucking about . . .'

That same summer, another would-be collaborator approached Gilmour. 'It was before we'd even started on the project,' recalled the guitarist, 'I was in Greece and I think I had a visit from Rick's then wife, Franka [whom he'd married in 1984], saying, "I hear you're starting a new album. Please, please, please can Rick be part of it?" I left it for a while because I wanted to be sure that I knew what I was doing before I got anyone's hopes too high.'

Aside from the problems the band had experienced with Wright during *The Wall* sessions, there were other issues to be considered. 'There were one or two legal reasons which made it a little trickier if Rick rejoined,' said Gilmour later. A clause in his leaving agreement disqualified him from rejoining the band as a full member. 'And, to be honest, Nick and I didn't particularly want to get in extra partners – we had put up all the money and taken the biggest risks, and so we wanted to take the largest cut.'

'I remember having a meeting with them and Steve [O'Rourke] in a restaurant in Hampstead,' said Wright. 'I think they wanted to see how I was. I passed the test.'

However, while Gilmour admitted that Richard Wright had been brought back in to make 'us stronger legally *and* musically' (with the legal aspect ahead of the musical), Wright's input on the album was minimal. He would not be invited to the sessions until February the following year, where he recorded some vocal harmonies, some Hammond organ and one solo, which was rejected from the final mix.

According to Waters in a 1988 *Penthouse* article, he, too, had a meeting with Gilmour in August that year, in a last-ditch attempt to resolve their differences. Waters informed the interviewer that Gilmour told him that Wright 'was useful to him', suggesting that his re-appointment to Pink Floyd was based on the fact that it would make the band look better in the eyes of the public to have three, rather than just two of the classic line-up.

Gilmour's call to Bob Ezrin came at the moment he decided he needed to consolidate what writing had been done.

'So Dave came over to see *me*,' laughs Ezrin. 'A totally different approach from Roger's. Dave came out with his young son, Matthew. We spent three days together and he said, "I'm a family man, you're a family man, we'll work it out."' A decision was made to record some of the album with Ezrin in England, before reconvening in Ezrin's hometown of Los Angeles, also allowing for holidays and days off. 'The total opposite from what Roger had proposed.'

Here on in, the precise circumstances surrounding the making of the album become blurred and contradictory, depending on who is telling the story and when they were spoken to. Interviewed specifically for this book in March 2007, Bob Ezrin insisted Gilmour approached him two weeks after he had turned down Waters. Interviewed for *Penthouse* magazine in 1988, he claimed he was approached a month later, while Waters insisted, in the same article, that he discovered Ezrin had been hired to work on a Pink Floyd album a *week* after being told he would not be available to work on Roger's new record. As Ezrin later admitted: 'It was a coincidence, but he thought it was a conspiracy.'

Nevertheless, when Ezrin arrived in England late that summer, he joined Gilmour for a month of what the guitarist described as 'mucking about with a lot of demos'. Ezrin was hired as co-producer alongside Gilmour, and, according to Waters, was now guaranteed a generous number of points from the gross sales of the next Pink Floyd album.

At least, the environment for making the record was more tranquil than the mood between Waters and his ex-bandmates. Recording sessions would take place on Gilmour's new houseboat studio, *Astoria*, a 90ft-long vessel moored on the River Thames near Hampton Court and once owned by music hall impresario and slapstick comedian Fred Karno. Gilmour had converted the boat's dining room into a studio, while turning the connecting living room into a control room.

'Working there was just magical, so inspirational; kids sculling down the river, geese flying by . . .' says Ezrin, who joined Gilmour, Mason and the newly enlisted Jon Carin. Despite being nearly twenty years Gilmour's junior, Carin was, Ezrin recalls, 'an old soul, who, in some ways, was closer to vintage Pink Floyd in his tastes than we were'. Working with the latest technology on the *Astoria*, the band began using samples, experimenting with a seemingly endless number of possibilities for each track. As well as 'Learning to Fly', Gilmour also had the bones of what would become 'The Dogs of War', 'Terminal Frost' and 'Signs of Life' (for which Ezrin would record the sound of Gilmour's boatman, Langley Iddens, rowing across the Thames). In the absence of Waters, Ezrin played bass, enjoying 'the endless laughter and the sense of adventure. Here we were on the river – like we were on a boys' camp.'

Yet the mood was still being interrupted by the ongoing legal dispute with Roger Waters. In June, Steve O'Rourke, believing his management contract with Waters had been terminated illegally, had filed a suit against Waters to the tune of £25,000 for retrospective commissions; a dispute made more complex by the fact that O'Rourke had only ever had a verbal contract with the band. In October, Waters began High Court proceedings to seek the dissolution of the Pink Floyd partnership; an action again made more complex by the verbal nature of the agreement. As Gilmour explained: 'The phone would be going every five minutes with this lawyer and that lawyer wanting to know this and that.'

There was also a problem with Nick Mason: his drumming.

'I hadn't played for four years and I didn't even like the sound or feel of my own playing,' wrote Mason later.

'Nick seemed to not really be able to play,' agreed Gilmour. 'His ability and confidence seemed to have disappeared.'

'Roger worked on everybody's confidence,' suggested Ezrin. 'In Rick's case it destroyed him. With Nick it had been a matter of him being marginalised on *The Final Cut*. He hadn't been practising, and he just wasn't sounding like himself.'

The use of sampled drums and computer technology removed the need for a human drummer, at least for the time being. The need for a lyricist posed more of an immediate problem. Gilmour's next approach was to Liverpudlian poet and songwriter Roger McGough, who'd enjoyed a brief taste of pop stardom in the mid-sixties band Scaffold. While Gilmour denied that he was 'looking for a concept' for the album, he admitted to meeting with McGough: 'I can't remember exactly what happened with him,' he later told writer Phil Sutcliffe, 'but he's the sort of person I wouldn't be averse to working with.'

According to Roger Waters, in November, Bob Ezrin and Columbia Records executive Stephen Ralbovsky expressed concerns about the Floyd's new music. Waters later told *Billboard*'s Timothy White that they suggested that Gilmour start again.

'A tissue of lies,' Gilmour told this writer in 2008. 'I never stopped and started again. We have had a long history of saying to record companies, "Fuck off! We will deliver our record when we are ready to, and you can sell it". Steve Ralbovsky did come down and wanted to hear a few things. He was a mate. It's entirely possible he wasn't impressed with it. We'd only been at it for three weeks, and there was a track I'd played him a year before that I'd done at home with [session drummer] Simon Phillips. It was a ripping track but it wasn't going to fit with anything. Steve said, "What happened to that one?" I said it wasn't going to make it. Whatever his thoughts were, he kept them to himself. We carried on, and by Christmas we had upped our gear and were on our way forward.'

Everybody, though, accepted that Waters' absence had created a hole in the project. 'There was never a question about the quality of the music or the vocals,' says Ezrin. 'But we acknowledged we'd lost our main lyricist.'

'It was tough not having Roger there to say, "Shall we do this or *this*," ' conceded Gilmour. 'It was a slow process until the stuff we'd got sounded like we were getting somewhere.'

In January 1987, Canadian songwriter Carole Pope flew to England at Ezrin's behest. Pope had previously been part of a folk-rock duo called Rough Trade. 'I had suggestions for concept albums in the Pink Floyd style,' Pope later explained. 'By the time I left England in February, they still couldn't decide what to do.' Pope also recalled one song, which never made it on to the finished album, entitled 'Peace Be With You', 'a nice, mid-tempo thing about Roger Waters'.

'Carole had a very different style, very poetic, and it didn't come to anything,' recalls Ezrin now. 'A lot of people went through my mind. And it's interesting, because, if you're Pink Floyd, you can go ask for anything. It was great to be able to stretch and say, "Boy, I'd really like to try that one and that one . . ." '

Finally, Gilmour struck lucky through his own connections. Anthony Moore was a singer-songwriter who'd previously played in the experimental rock bands Slapp Happy and Henry Cow. Roughly the same age as Gilmour and from a similar background, he had also been managed by Peter Jenner. By this time, Gilmour was, he said, happy for the album to 'be a bunch of songs, and if a mood or theme came along to tie it all together, so much the better'. Moore wrote the bulk of the lyrics for three songs: 'On the Turning Away', 'The Dogs of War', and 'Learning to Fly'.

Co-written with Ezrin and Jon Carin, 'Learning to Fly' was a quite literal song about Gilmour's latest hobby. Following Nick Mason's lead, the guitarist had been taking flying lessons (the two bandmates would later jointly buy a plane of their own), often providing an escape from the legal and musical turmoil in his life. Mason supplied the necessary sound effects, while, between them, the song acquired a familiar guitar and keyboard pattern that earmarked it as *very* Pink Floyd. Finally, some serious progress was being made. 'It was a turning point,' said Ezrin. 'It felt like a complete Floyd work, and that made everybody feel gratified, because that was what we'd been told by Roger we were incapable of doing.'

Aside from his visit to Gilmour in August, Waters also dropped by the *Astoria* a second time to see Bob Ezrin. Michael Kamen had tried to broker a truce between Waters and Ezrin. Gilmour wasn't present, but Ezrin confirms a visit from Waters and Carolyne Christie – then his new bride – and experiencing the feeling that 'we were being checked out'.

To complicate matters, Waters was still a shareholder and director of Pink Floyd Music. Gilmour and Mason were unable to form a new company with so many legal issues still unresolved. Waters, therefore, began exercising his right to block any decisions being made by his former bandmates. 'At the moment, we have to have a board meeting for every single decision we want to do as a group,' complained Gilmour at the time, 'and Roger comes and he votes against it.'

In February, following a stint at London's Mayfair and Audio International Studios, the sessions moved to Los Angeles, under the terms of Gilmour's deal with Ezrin. On one level, at least, it was a relief. 'It was fantastic because office hours are not in sync,' recalled Gilmour, 'so the lawyers couldn't call in the middle of recording unless they were calling in the middle of the night.'

In LA, Mason graciously handed over the reins to session drummers Carmine Appice and Jim Keltner, a decision he was to rue on the subsequent tour when he found himself having to learn the parts anyway. Appice and Keltner would be just two of the countless hired hands that would eventually leave their mark on the next Pink Floyd album. 'Musicians in Los Angeles are reliable,' Gilmour told *Q* magazine. 'They turn up, know exactly what you want and work quickly.'

The issue of just *how* quickly was of particular importance. With Waters in the process of finishing his next solo album and with legal battles already raging, Gilmour wanted to release another Pink Floyd record as soon as possible. Working with a drummer who was having trouble drumming, with a keyboard player who wasn't legally entitled to rejoin the band as a full member, and locked in a legal battle with the band's departed main lyricist, it's little wonder that the process of making the album was so laboured. In short, Gilmour needed all the help he could get.

'We were both rather nervous about how the album would be

received,' admits Mason. 'And I think that's why we spent so much time and worked with so many people to make sure we got the thing right.'

Stage two of the campaign now involved booking a tour. And quickly. Before the album had even been completed, the band approached promoters to book dates. At which point Waters sent out letters to every single promoter in North America saying he would sue them if they put Floyd tickets on sale.

While Gilmour and Mason were due an advance from the record company once they'd delivered the new album, that would only cover the cost of making the record. With Waters threatening to put an injunction on the band and, potentially, freezing their bank accounts, the tour could be jeopardised. To cover the cost of initial dates, Gilmour and Mason had to stump up the money themselves. Mason was now separated from his wife Lindy, and found himself a 'bit short of the ready cash' for the millions required. Instead he put his treasured 1962 GTO Ferrari down as collateral and cobbled together his half of the funds.

In Pink Floyd's favour, most promoters took umbrage at Waters' threat. Ezrin's friend, Canadian promoter Michael Cohl, was the first to step in, agreeing to put tickets on sale for a date at the Canadian National Exhibition Stadium in Toronto almost six months later in October. All 60,000 tickets sold out in a matter of hours, leading to two further shows being added, securing a figure in the region of $3 million gross income. Other promoters came on board. Confidence boosted, the band still had to ensure that they had a team of lawyers primed and ready to go to court should Waters manage to persuade a judge that it was illegal for this version of Pink Floyd to perform.

With the album completed, despite the best efforts of the respective legal teams ('the only *real* winners in all this', as Mason later remarked), the band now found themselves stumped for an album title. Acutely aware that any title could be misconstrued as relating to the band's situation or leave them open to mockery from Waters, they rejected three possibles – *Signs of Life*, *Of Promises Broken* and *Delusions of Maturity* – in favour of *A Momentary Lapse of Reason*, a phrase lifted from the lyrics to 'One Slip'. In the end, Waters would still make hay ('a lapse of reason, indeed' etc).

The last piece of the puzzle would be artist Storm Thorgerson, whose last proper Pink Floyd commission (excluding *A Collection of Great Dance Songs*) had been 1975's *Wish You Were Here.* 'I was brought back to help give *Momentary Lapse* . . . a Floyd look and a Floyd feeling,' said Thorgerson. Inspired by a lyric from the new album's 'Yet Another Movie' ('a vision of an empty bed'), Thorgerson suggested staging a scene of 700 empty beds arranged on a beach. 'David said, "Sure, just do it,"' recalls Thorgerson. They transported the props to their chosen location, Saunton Sands in North Devon, and laid out the beds one by one. Then rain stopped play. The photograph was finally taken a fortnight later. It was a suitably grand and expensive concept for what would be a grand and expensive album and tour.

In June, with Pink Floyd still applying the finishing touches to their record, Roger Waters unveiled his new album. The gloves were off again. *Radio K.A.O.S.* was another concept album. But what a concept. The story's central character was a disabled Welsh boy named Billy gifted with telepathic powers. Billy's carer is his twin brother, a coal miner, who is imprisoned during the miners' strike (an industrial dispute which then Prime Minister Thatcher attacked with much the same gusto as she did Argentina in the Falklands War). Billy is sent to stay with his uncle in Los Angeles, where he discovers that his telepathic gifts enable him to hack into computer systems. Billy befriends a local DJ (voiced by Jim Ladd, one of the original MCs on *The Wall* tour) on the fictitious Radio K.A.O.S. station, and tells him of his and his twin brother's plight. Billy hacks into a military satellite, and tricks the world into believing that ballistic missiles are about to be detonated in major cities throughout the globe. The closing track, 'The Tide is Turning (After Live Aid)', arrives at the conclusion that war is futile, and that the love of one's family and the world in general is more important than anything else. (Although it was later reported that Waters added this happy ending at the suggestion of EMI, who believed the album was too bleak without it.) For added complication, the album's sub-plot addressed the fictional Radio K.A.O.S. station's attempts to stand up against the rigid formatting of American radio at the time. The entire album was dedicated to 'All those who find themselves at the violent end of monetarism.' Even Waters wasn't convinced: 'I accepted halfway through the record that, as a narrative form, the album was doomed to failure.' He also admitted that 'the part where Billy pretends he's just started the Third World War I now find faintly embarrassing.'

For guitarist Jay Stapley, *Radio K.A.O.S.* saw Waters in his element. 'The studio was Roger's *métier*. I remember hearing an interview with Dave Gilmour in which he said that you'd sit there with Roger in the studio, and there'd be an introduction to a song playing and he would be able to say, "Right, something needs to happen *now*." He had this perfect sense of theatre applied to music. I think he was sometimes insecure about his own ability, as he's not a trained musician. But we all admired Roger's ability to do what we couldn't – write amazing lyrics and conceive amazing stage shows.'

But Waters had set himself a tough challenge. With its references to the British miners' strike, the US bombing of Tripoli, Ronald Reagan, ballistic missiles and even cordless telephones, *Radio K.A.O.S.* is undeniably a product of 1987. Unfortunately, the music was, too. Dominated by Fairlights, reverb-heavy drums and Billy's synthesised voice, *Radio K.A.O.S.* is an auditory struggle in the twenty-first century, even before you get to the convoluted narrative. In Bob Ezrin's absence, Waters had co-produced the record with Nick Griffiths and former Deaf School saxophonist Ian Ritchie.

'Between Ian Ritchie and myself we really fucked that record up,' admits Waters. 'We tried too hard to make it sound modern.' Most of the worthy lyrics and ideas are lost beneath its glossy production and vogueish drum sounds, though its closing ballad, 'The Tide is Turning (After Live Aid)', with the full-throated accompaniment of the Pontardulais Male Voice Choir, was a surprisingly tuneful single that found an unlikely fan. 'I heard "The Tide is Turning", which I really liked,' claimed David Gilmour. 'The rest of it's not really done to my tastes. But I'm obviously biased.'

The album was not to the record-buying public's tastes, either. *Radio K.A.O.S.* peaked at number 50 in the US and number 25 in the UK, some places lower than *The Pros and Cons of Hitch-hiking*. 'Waters raises a lot of knotty issues over communication but he never really wrestles them to the ground,' claimed *Rolling Stone*'s review, while also praising the album as 'his most listenable work since *The Wall*'. Waters would remain bullish in his defence of artistry over sales ('If you're going to use sales as a criterion, it makes *Grease* a better record than *Graceland*'), but he also realised that he was now a victim of his own carefully cultivated anonymity. 'It's frustrating to find out how many people don't know who I am or what I actually did in Pink Floyd,' he told writer David Fricke. 'I wanted anonymity. I treasure it. But now it's as if the past twenty years meant nothing.'

The presence of a new Pink Floyd hardly helped his position. Waters launched the *Radio K.A.O.S.* tour in New York in August, a month before the release of *A Momentary Lapse of Reason* and two months before the next Pink Floyd tour. A full bells-and-whistles production, Waters wheeled out some new props alongside the usual animations, back projections and quadraphonic sound. A telephone box was installed in the middle of the audience, for Waters to take questions from fans; an astonishing U-turn from a man who, ten years earlier, had spat on one fan. In another highly surprising move, Moosehead, the Canadian beer company, sponsored the North American leg of the tour.

On stage, Waters broke up selections from the *Radio K.A.O.S.* album with a medley of Pink Floyd songs, including 'Have a Cigar' and 'Mother', as well as screening the group's promo film for 'Arnold Layne'. Keyboard player and vocalist Paul Carrack was one of the newest recruits to The Bleeding Heart Band. Part of his duties included singing such Floyd songs as 'Money'. 'My version actually came out as a B-side, and I got death threats for it,' laughs Carrack. 'They said I should be shot. We saw rather a lot of madness on the *K.A.O.S.* tour. I can remember arriving at one gig and there was a guy outside who was convinced he was the character of Billy from the album, and that the whole thing had been written about him.'

As a bandleader, Roger Waters proved a saner presence. Just. 'I know he can be intimidating and demanding,' admits Carrack. 'But I wasn't having any of it, and I think he appreciated it. Roger's strength is the big concept. He really means it, and you can't fault his commitment, but he can make hard work of it. I think he sometimes finds it difficult to put over to the band what he wants, because basically his music is very simple and some of the musicians sometimes get a bit scared of what to play and how to play, because he doesn't always know how to put over what he's after.'

Camaraderie within The Bleeding Heart Band was good. When the Far East leg of the tour blew out due to poor ticket sales, Waters, undeterred, took the band to Nassau's Compass Point Studios to record songs for his next album. However, by the time they went back on the road in November, Pink Floyd were on the move.

Come the summer, even David Gilmour realised they could tinker no more. *A Momentary Lapse of Reason* finally arrived in the shops at the beginning of September 1987. Leaving their audience in no doubt about who was actually *in* Pink Floyd, the group broke with tradition and included a photograph on the inside sleeve, taken by David Bailey, of a suited and booted Gilmour and Mason smiling smugly into the lens. Richard Wright's name appeared only among the numerous other session musician credits.

However depleted the team may have been, record-buyers didn't care. *A Momentary Lapse* . . . went to number 3 on both sides of the Atlantic, held off the top in the UK by Michael Jackson's *Bad* and the Pet Shop Boys' *Actually*, and in the US by *Bad* and rejuvenated hard-rockers Whitesnake's *1987*. Mason would later admit that the timing of the album's release could have been better, rather than going up against such heavy competition. Back then, though, it seemed like an album built to take on such competition, with everything sounding bigger, louder and more expensive, as if every last dollar's worth was being eked from its numerous hired hands.

The opening track, 'Signs of Life', placed a funereal keyboard figure over the sound of Gilmour's boatman sculling up the River Thames. In grand Pink Floyd tradition it hung on for dramatic effect before allowing the guitarist to pick out his first notes, *à la* 'Shine On You Crazy Diamond'. The album's signature song, 'Learning to Fly', wove its strong melody around the sound of an airborne Nick Mason and lyrics about, in Bob Ezrin's words, 'leaving your earthbound tendencies behind and liberating your spirit'. The closing song, 'Sorrow', shared a similar sense of purpose and confidence. Written by Gilmour one weekend on the *Astoria*, it housed the album's best guitar solo, a real note-bending extravaganza, and a lyric some fans, rightly or wrongly, took to be about Roger Waters.

What the album did make clear was just who was now in the driving seat. The wordy politicising of *The Final Cut* and the persistent despair of *The Wall* were nowhere to be found.

Lyrically, nothing here was likely to give Waters sleepless nights, a fact in which he later took great pleasure. Instead, the melancholy mood of most of *A Momentary Lapse* . . . suggests a forty-year-old Gilmour, several glasses of red wine down, reflecting on his life; including his relationships with Waters and his wife Ginger, from whom he was also becoming increasingly estranged. The couple would separate within a year. In 'Yet Another Movie', the lyric referring to an empty bed had been inspired by a scene in the couple's house in Lindos. The guitarist was quick to tell critics that he viewed the album as a return to the glory days of *Dark Side of the Moon*, when, in his view, the music hadn't taken such a back seat to Waters' lyrics. 'That's what I'm trying to do,' he insisted. 'Focus more on the music, restore the balance.'

Not everyone in the band agreed that he had succeeded. Interviewed in 2000, the under-used Richard Wright admitted: 'Roger's criticisms are fair. It's not a band album at all.'

A Momentary Lapse of Reason was, however, the right Pink Floyd album for the times. Where it falls down is that, like *Radio K.A.O.S.*, it's stuck in that time. Like most forty-something rockers, one of Gilmour and Mason's greatest fears must have been that they would sound *passé*. To start, those booming, reverbed drums are the very essence of the mid-eighties, but a world away from the more appealing sound of a loose-limbed, flailing Nick Mason on *Live At Pompeii*. The same drums, burbling bass and synthesisers on 'One Slip' are interchangeable with those on Peter Gabriel's *So* album from a year before, but then session bassist extraordinaire Tony Levin played on both albums. Gilmour's song-writing partners were similarly rooted in the era. Pat Leonard, his collaborator on 'Yet Another Movie', had been the brains behind Madonna's hits, 'Like a Prayer' and 'Live to Tell'. In the album's defence, Gilmour plays his heart out, but many of the songs themselves have no such heart. 'I didn't think it was the best Pink Floyd album ever made,' he said later. 'But I gave it the best damn shot I could.'

Reviewers agreed. The newly launched *Q* magazine, which would draw its readers from a pool of music fans weaned on the likes of Pink Floyd, acknowledged that it was 'Gilmour's album, to much the same degree that the four before were Waters', regarding it as a release of the guitarist's 'repressed talent'. Even Waters' confidant Karl Dallas came down on the Floyd's side of the fence, despite his earlier promise that

Waters' second album would 'flip your wig'. 'The new Floyd album is a classic, and Roger's is . . . well . . . Roger's.'

Waters showed no reticence in offering his views on *A Momentary Lapse of Reason*. 'I think it's very facile, but a quite clever forgery,' he told writer David Fricke. 'The songs are poor in general; the lyrics I can't quite believe. Gilmour's lyrics are very third-rate.'

However, outstripping *Radio K.A.O.S.* in the record shops, and with the Floyd selling out arenas to Waters' theatres, there was already the smell of victory in the air. Then came the pressing matter of just *how* they were going to perform live.

Keyboard player Jon Carin had already been confirmed for the tour, performing alongside Richard Wright. The absence of Waters also left a noticeable gap on stage to Gilmour's left. The role of Pink Floyd bassist would be taken by Guy Pratt. A 25-year-old session man whose previous clients had included Robert Palmer, Bryan Ferry and The Smiths, his musical talents had been inherited from his father, actor and song-writer Mike Pratt, who had a title role in the sixties drama series *Randall and Hopkirk (Deceased)* and had co-written Tommy Steele's hit 'Little White Bull'.

Pratt's Pink Floyd initiation had come as a teenager when he attended one of *The Wall* shows at London's Earls Court, while tripping on LSD. 'The one thing I remember was Roger in his number 1 T-shirt, having this big tirade against Alan Jones from *Melody Maker*,' says Guy. 'I was like, "Wow, he's *really* playing this rock star character well." I didn't know he was being himself. I also managed to blag backstage the night they had their crew party. They had all these strippers and all these inflatables from the old tours. Unfortunately, I was on acid, and wandering around dressed like one of The Clash. In those days, I would never have imagined I could play with Pink Floyd. It was out of the question.' Guy had first come to Gilmour's attention when he played on Bryan Ferry's *Bête Noire* album and later when he performed with the guitarist's protégés Dream Academy.

Like Wright, Nick Mason would perform alongside another musician. In his case, twenty-three-year-old percussionist Gary Wallis, whose highly visual performing style – attacking an array of gongs, drums and cymbals mounted around him in a cage – was the perfect contrast to Mason's considerably more restrained approach.

Saxophonist Scott Page, who'd already played on *A Momentary Lapse of Reason*, was another addition to the team. By no means a Pink Floyd fan ('Honest to God, I must be the only person in the world who's never even heard *Dark Side of the Moon*'), he would be rendered instantly recognisable to fans in even the cheapest stadium seats by his lavish mullet hairstyle. Adding some much-needed glamour were backing singers Rachel Fury, Margaret Taylor and, later, Durga McBroom. Taylor was later replaced by Durga's sister Lorelei.

One familiar older face among the young pups was Gilmour's Cambridge friend, the guitarist Tim Renwick. A survivor from Waters' *Pros and Cons of Hitch-hiking* tour, Renwick had been playing in the house band for the Cliff Richard musical *Time*, at London's Dominion Theatre, when he gratefully took Gilmour's call.

However, arriving in Toronto for rehearsals, the band encountered some problems. Guy Pratt quickly discovered that he hadn't actually been Pink Floyd's first choice of bassist. 'When we turned up to rehearse there were a few newspapers running articles about how Pink Floyd were in town to start their new tour and a lot of them said, "featuring Tony Levin on bass". So I was there only because Tony hadn't been available at the last minute. I was like, "Oh, *great!*"'

The band had hired a hangar at Lester B. Pearson airport in which to rehearse, but there was a noticeable lack of discipline. 'The Pink Floyd bass gig is not the most difficult one in the world,' says Guy, 'but Nick hadn't played the drums for years, Rick hadn't done anything for years, and David didn't seem to really like being in charge that much.'

'It was a disaster,' admits Tim Renwick. 'Nobody could remember how to play anything. It was all so disparate.'

But Gilmour knew whom to call.

'David rang me in August, and they were due to open in October,' remembers Bob Ezrin. 'He said, "Bob, in my usual inimitable style, I never fail to try and do these things on my own and, as always, I realise I need help. Can you come and help me?"' he laughs. 'I found the show to be in some disarray. The problem was there was no producer or director on stage, and David was busy working out which guitar to play. He couldn't do all this other stuff. There was no sense of flow to the show, the setlist needed rearranging . . .'

Ezrin took charge, viewing proceedings from in front of the stage and communicating with the motley crew via a megaphone.

'Bob really started knocking us into shape,' says Renwick. 'Jack-booting around this aircraft hangar, shouting orders, being very loud and demonstrative. One of the first things he did was make sure that if you weren't playing, you couldn't be seen loitering on stage; you were blacked out, or offstage.' Ezrin would remain with the tour until 'the baby was walking and I could go back to making some money in my own career'.

Aside from the issue of co-ordinating eleven people on stage, there was also the stage set itself to be considered. Gilmour and Mason first approached *The Wall* tour's design team, Jonathan Park and Mark Fisher, but both had already allied themselves to the *Radio K.A.O.S.* tour. Instead, set designer Paul Staples was brought into the fold to work alongside Floyd mainstays, lighting designer Marc Brickman and pro-duction director Robbie Williams, veterans from, respectively, *The Wall* and *Dark Side of the Moon* campaigns. Their aim was simple. As Marc Brickman explained, 'The idea is always to pull the last kid in the last seat of the stadium into the show.'

The Floyd's stage set would be effectively housed inside a steel framework, around 80ft high and spanning the width of the stage, from which pods of light were then suspended. Additional lighting and dry ice machines also operated from tracks above the stage. Trapdoors in the stage itself also opened to reveal extra robotic-looking lighting pods (nicknamed 'Floyd Droids' and given individual names Manny, Moe, Jack and Cloyd) that elevated into view at key moments in the show. The back of the stage was filled, as usual, with the band's familiar circular screen onto which new and old images were projected, including Storm Thorgerson's specially commissioned films for 'Learning to Fly' and 'On the Run'. The flying pig, aeroplane and a giant mirror ball completed the visual extravaganza. It would take a supporting team of some 160 technicians, riggers, electricians and more to keep the show on the road.

The tour opened on 9 September in Ottawa's Lansdowne Park Stadium. The set's greatest surprise came with its choice of opening number, 'Echoes' from *Meddle*, which was given its first airing in over a decade. A challenge for all concerned, the piece would be dropped before the end of the month, with Nick Mason later claiming that the band's new young musicians were simply too good to replicate the shoddy, hippie-ish feel of the original recording.

'There's a bit in "Echoes" we call "the wind section" where it all falls apart, and then comes back in,' explains Guy Pratt. 'Some of the younger players, mentioning no names, couldn't get their heads around it not being a set number of bars. It was like, "You have to feel it and know instinctively when to come back in." David's great line about that was, "The trouble with modern musicians is that they don't know how to disintegrate." '

Including the whole of *A Momentary Lapse of Reason* made commercial sense, but meant that the first half of the show was unfamiliar to most, and overshadowed by the second half, which ran the gamut of 'One of These Days' to a final encore of 'Run Like Hell', stopping off at 'Wish You Were Here', 'Another Brick in the Wall Part 2' and 'Comfortably Numb' en route. 'One of These Days' would be the oldest song played (Mason later explaining that the sixties-era Floyd sounded 'too early'). *The Final Cut* and *Animals* were also overlooked, although 'Sheep' came close to being included, until Gilmour decided that vocally it was too much Roger Waters' song.

Aside from the dazzling special effects, the presence of younger and more flamboyant band members made a huge difference. The athletic leaps and bounds made by percussionist Gary Wallis to strike the highest cymbals in his drum cage diverted attention from the staid-looking, middle-aged gentleman playing the drum kit beside him. The elaborately coiffured saxophonist Scott Page was also given to strapping on a guitar and appearing on stage when he wasn't actually needed. 'Scott and Gary came with the territory,' says Bob Ezrin. 'This was meant to be a more visual show. There's a lot of "Ooh-aah factor" to a Pink Floyd concert. People want to say, "Wow, look at that!" So they gave it to them.'

The age difference between the original Floyd and some of the hired hands was, initially, not a problem. 'They treated us very well,' recalls Guy Pratt. 'Mind you, I was terrified of David. Nick was the easiest to get on with, as he was such a lovely, amusing man.'

By their own admission, Guy and Jon Carin were also committed Pink Floyd fans, eager to hear stories from past campaigns. 'I was always plugging David for stories,' admits Guy. 'The problem was, he'd start telling a story and, because I was such a Pink Floyd anorak, I'd start correcting him on it. Rick is actually fantastic for reminiscences, whereas David sometimes pretends to have forgotten.'

However, being fifteen years younger than his bosses presented Guy with one immediate problem, when Richard Wright's beautiful teenage daughter Gala turned up later during the Australian leg of the tour: 'There's a certain ethical code of the road. You don't get involved with anyone that's part of the management, you don't get involved with anyone in catering, unless it's an absolute last resort, and if you get involved with one of the backing singers it will always end in tears. *But* there's no ruling about daughters of the band – and that was when the age difference did become apparent.

'We weren't officially an item on that tour, but it was obvious there was something going on, and it certainly didn't make me popular, as *everyone* was in love with Gala.' However, her father didn't feel inclined to take Guy aside. 'I was more worried about David and Nick. No one actually cautioned me, but there was a bit of eyebrow-raising.'

As the Floyd moved through North America, the gap closed between their shows and the *Radio K.A.O.S.* tour. 'We were playing Toronto when Floyd were rehearsing just up the road,' remembers Paul Carrack. 'Having them nearby added a bit of spice. There *was* tension there, and we all knew Roger was under a lot of pressure, but I think he felt vindicated because he was doing something different. We did some Floyd tunes, but not many.'

Roger had expressly banned members of Pink Floyd from attending any of his gigs, so Floyd's monitor technician was despatched undercover to one to report on how much pyrotechnics and special effects Waters was using. While rehearsing in Toronto, Scott Page, Jon Carin and Waters' old solo bandmate Tim Renwick were among those who walked unrecognised into Waters' gig. 'We wanted to see the competition,' says Renwick. 'And, pardon the pun, but I thought it was a bit watery. It was more like a tribute band.' During one part of the show, a spotlight scanned the audience landing on random members of the crowd. 'And I remember praying,' laughs Guy Pratt, 'absolutely *praying* that it landed on Tim Renwick.'

Ticket sales for some of Waters' shows were not all they could have been. Playing to an audience of 3,000 people in a 6,000-seater hall in

Cincinnati was not good for his ego, but Waters remained upbeat, despite knowing that Pink Floyd were playing to 80,000 people the following night. 'I felt like Henry the Fifth,' he laughed. '"We happy few, we band of brothers . . ." I felt a huge kinship with [the audience], because there was only a few of them.'

Nevertheless, there would still be dissenting voices in the Pink Floyd audience. 'There would be people who would make their feelings known about Roger not being there, just by shouting very loudly during moments when the rest of the audience was being very quiet,' Gilmour told Q magazine, while also revealing that on one occasion, he spotted a whole row of fans wearing 'Fuck Roger' T-shirts.

Unable to stop any of the Floyd shows going ahead, Waters was still hurling legal missiles from the sidelines, including a writ for over $35,000 in copyright fees for the Floyd's use of his flying pig. Unknown to the band, Waters had also bought up the rights to animated films by Ian Eames and Gerald Scarfe, which he had then placed with a company he owned. However, as Gilmour pointed out, 'We never agreed that he owned the rights. Pink Floyd, all of us, had commissioned those pieces of work and paid for them.' To circumvent the problem with the pig, Floyd ensured that their new version included a pair of hefty testicles to distinguish it from Waters' original female version. As Gilmour glumly explained: 'A pig's a pig, for Christ's sake, but adding the testicles *was* amusing for us.'

However, as the year ground to an end, it seemed as if the legal battle between the two parties was finally coming to an end. Interviewed for *Rolling Stone* magazine in November, Waters was all but admitting defeat: 'I've finally understood that no court in the land is interested in this airy-fairy nonsense of what is or isn't Pink Floyd. All I could possibly get out of it is a slice.'

The size of the slice would be decided on 23 December 1987, when Gilmour, Waters and Gilmour's accountant convened on the *Astoria* houseboat to end the matter once and for all. 'We hammered it out over a few hours, printed it out, signed it and that's the legal document we are bound by today,' explained Gilmour. The terms of the agreement released Waters from any arrangements with Steve O'Rourke, and allowed Gilmour and Mason to use the Pink Floyd name in perpetuity.

Waters would get his slice, maintaining his control over, as Gilmour explained, 'various bits and pieces', most notably *The Wall*.

Waters would no longer attend board meetings or attempt to veto Gilmour's and Mason's plans. Instead he retreated to plan his next move, while sniping at his former bandmates in the press. Gilmour, for his part, invariably took the bait.

Both warring factions would grace the pages of the music press. Waters would usually appear looking stick-thin and imposing in the black sunglasses and black-suit-white-T-shirt uniform of the older rock star. 'With Carolyne, Roger got into a very American rock story,' reflected his ex-manager Peter Jenner. 'Helicopters, nannies and the south of France.'

'I was still essentially the tall guy in black, standing in the corner scowling at everyone, saying, "Leave me alone,"' admitted Waters years later.

Gilmour and Mason would appear less intimidating: all billowy white shirts and pleated trousers. The guitarist especially looked a good deal heavier than the last time Pink Floyd had toured; Mason offered the knowing smile of a kindly, hip uncle, or a man who perhaps couldn't quite believe his luck. As Waters would remark on the drummer's reason for staying in Pink Floyd: 'Nick likes the money and the attention.'

Veteran rock critic Timothy White's damning article in the September 1988 edition of *Penthouse* found Waters blowing the whistle on what he had called 'the fair forgery' of *A Momentary Lapse of Reason*: reeling off the names of songwriters approached by Gilmour to help make a Pink Floyd album; outlining the precise date and location of the guitarist's meeting with a concerned record company executive; and, best of all, revealing the juicy titbit that Richard Wright was being paid a weekly wage of $11,000. Fans, whose own weekly wages would have amounted to considerably less, wondered whether, in rock star terms, this was good, bad or just average.

Gilmour and Mason would gamely rise to the challenge. They would both make light of Waters' claims that they had struggled to make a Pink Floyd album without him, basking instead in their new album's impressive sales figures and the fact that the tour was still lapping the globe and selling out stadiums. As Mason explained, 'Roger could have finished Pink Floyd off by never leaving. But by leaving it, the ashes suddenly picked up.' Gilmour was harsher: 'If Roger put half as much energy into his career as he has into fighting us, he'd be doing a whole lot better than he is now. I can't understand how he can't see the stupidity of it all.'

In 1988 the tour moved through New Zealand and Australia and an eight-night stand in Japan, where they were forced to ditch 'On the Run' from the set, as it exceeded permissible levels of electricity use. In Melbourne, Gilmour joined Tim Renwick and the newer band members for an after-hours jam at their hotel, playing to around two hundred people under the nom-de-plume The Fishermen's ('based on an old Peter Cook joke,' explained bassist Guy Pratt, 'where he invented a rhyming slang language').

The Fishermen's would make other impromptu appearances around the world. In contrast to previous Pink Floyd tours, the musicians did not split into different cliques. The three original members happily rubbed shoulders offstage with the newer band members, of which Guy Pratt was, according to Mason, 'invariably the last one out of the bar at night – or first thing in the morning'.

'My attitude was horrific,' admits Pratt. 'I got it all wrong. As a musician you're hired as a professional to do your job to the best of your ability. I just thought I was one of the band and could go off and get twatted. I heard from someone five months in that David had really wanted to sack me, but he couldn't as I was the most consistent musician in the band, even after staying up for two or three days at a time. It got to the point where I'd get nervous playing without a hangover.'

Offstage, promoters would routinely supply a couple of limousines only to find Gilmour, Mason and Wright piling into one of the vans with the rest of the band. 'So you'd have this ridiculous situation where the promoter was in the first limo with a couple of birds he wanted to impress and flanked by a police outrider,' says Guy, 'an empty limo behind, and then behind *that*, the band in a van with all the booze for the dressing room.'

There was, as Tim Renwick explains, 'a tremendous spirit in the band, and a real sense of liberation'. For Gilmour, now shouldering the respon-sibility of running the show, this involved letting off plenty of steam and enjoying all the perks of the job: from flying planes and hang-gliding on his days off, to a suitable rock star-ish consumption of drugs and alcohol.

As Guy Pratt admitted, the touring party included a euphemistically titled 'ambience co-ordinator' whose tasks included taking care of any band members' visiting parents *and* procuring drugs. Interviewed in 2006 and asked what piece of advice he would have given to himself twenty years ago, Gilmour promptly answered: 'Stop taking cocaine.'

'It *was* party time,' confesses Tim Renwick. 'Dave had fairly recently split from Ginger. Steve O'Rourke was also on a long leash as well. So, if the powers that be were into whooping it up, then the rest of us joined in with great spirit and gusto. It was quite a wild time. Dave, in particular, was a full-on party animal.'

Gilmour had his reasons. 'I was in a marriage that seemed to be breaking up for rather a long time,' he later said. He and Ginger would eventually divorce in 1990. After selling Hookend Manor, the couple had moved to a six-bedroom Georgian house in Sunbury overlooking the River Thames. Ginger stayed on, while Gilmour moved into town, resuming a bachelor's lifestyle in a townhouse in London's 'Little Venice'. Ginger would later blame their conflicting lifestyles for the split: 'I was getting more alternative – starting to meditate – and he was doing more cocaine and hanging out with all kinds of people.'

Marital problems, the fallout from the Norton Warburg scandal and the legal battle with Roger Waters had all taken their toll. 'I got carried away with the cocaine lifestyle,' Gilmour later explained. 'I thought the coke made me more loquacious, but the reality was rather more awful.'

Pink Floyd's past drug problems would make the headlines again in 1988. In October, EMI issued *Opel*, a collection of Syd Barrett out-takes and rarities. Syd's brother-in-law, Paul Breen, was interviewed for a radio programme about Barrett. 'I think [Pink Floyd] is a part of his life which he prefers to forget now,' he explained. 'There is a level of contentment now which he probably hasn't felt since he got involved with music.' Syd had, he revealed, also started painting again.

In the same month, the *News of the World* trailed Barrett to Cambridge, and took a photograph of him outside his house. Neighbours supposedly told the reporter that Syd was 'a hopeless case . . .' and 'had been in and out of mental hospitals'. It was claimed that fans who turned up at the house found him daubed in a strange white powder and talking gibberish. Jonathan Meades repeated his claims that Syd's Egerton Court flatmates had locked him in the linen cupboard. As it was the height of the press's preoccupation with illegal rave parties and acid house music, the story featured that trademark smiley face, but with the mouth turned down, alongside the headline, ACID DROVE PINK FLOYD ROCK STAR UP THE WALL. No member of Pink Floyd, past or present, gave any comment.

In the same year, Barrett's and Gilmour's one-time close friend Ian 'Pip' Carter was killed during a fight outside a pub in Cambridge. Pip had been, along with Emo, one of Syd's most attentive courtiers. 'Pip was a bad boy,' recalls Libby Gausden. 'But Syd loved him.' David Gilmour was among those who attended Carter's funeral.

'We wanted to be world-conquering,' reflected David Gilmour on the *Momentary Lapse . . .* tour. 'We wanted to leave no one in any doubts that we meant business.' Back out on the road, the Pink Floyd machine rolled through Europe, the UK (including two shows at London's Wembley Stadium) and Scandinavia. Even the naturally reticent Richard Wright was now telling journalists that it was the happiest tour he'd ever been on. It was a contrast to the impression he gave some at the start of the jaunt. 'When I first saw Rick, we were in Toronto,' said Jon Carin. 'I came out of the hotel and saw him getting out of a limo and what I saw was a lot of pain. I don't know if he felt that way, but I really sympathised.'

'Jon Carin and Gary Wallis were fairly essential in keeping us going at the beginning of the tour,' admitted Gilmour in *Mojo* magazine. 'But within a month, those roles reverted back to Nick and Rick taking over their proper parts in what was going on.'

'What I never realised until I started playing with Pink Floyd was just how much of that sound is down to David and Rick,' says Guy Pratt. 'It's all about the musical relationship between those two, the sound of those two communicating with each other.'

In November, the band released *Delicate Sound of Thunder*, a live album recorded over the last five nights of the tour at New York's Nassau Veterans Memorial Coliseum. By the beginning of the New Year it had been certified platinum in the US and gold in the UK. Yet without the lasers, the pig and the 'Floyd Droids' to attract the attention, it seemed a strangely soulless affair.

As a suitably extravagant publicity stunt, Gilmour and Mason were invited to Moscow to attend the launch of the Soyuz TM-7 rocket. The astronauts took a cassette copy of *Delicate Sound of Thunder* with them on their flight to a Russian space station, making it the first rock album ever to have been played in space.

A final lap of honour, the 'Another Lapse' European tour, was underway by the spring of 1989. In May, the band flew to Moscow again, this time to play five nights in Lushniki. With a shortage of currency, Floyd were essentially playing for free, although basic costs were covered and the Russian government arranged their transport and hotel accommodation. Rumours circulated of payment in caviar and timber (Gilmour: 'not true'). In truth, the band had chosen to lose money if only for the experience of playing a full, no-holds-barred rock show in the Soviet Union.

Just weeks later, inspired by a scene in a Marx Brothers movie, Gilmour persuaded Steve O'Rourke that it would be a great idea for Pink Floyd to play a free concert on a floating barge moored off Piazza San Marco on Venice's Grand Canal. O'Rourke had been against the idea since it was mooted months earlier. The show was broadcast live via satellite around the world, but very nearly didn't happen at all. In a flashback to an early US tour, when the manager had paid the local police to get the band's stolen equipment back, the Floyd found themselves greasing the palms of local officials to make things happen. A gang of itinerant gondoliers showed up just before showtime and demanded $10,000 to stop them blowing their whistles throughout the gig. Unaware perhaps that any noise they made would be rendered inaudible by the Floyd's monstrous sound system, they were, in the words of David Gilmour, 'told to piss off'. Gilmour's sentiments would be similar when confronted with claims by the local council that the volume of the performance had somehow damaged ancient buildings in the vicinity.

The final show took place in Marseilles on 18 July 1989. It had now been almost eighteen months since the tour had begun. 'It was over-the-top large,' says Tim Renwick, 'and I had started to feel like a pretty small cog in it. On the last week you'd be introduced to people you'd already been around the world with. You lived in this bubble. Back home, taking out the trash was a chore. I came back to earth with a bump.'

Grossing $135 million and playing to a total of 5.5 million people, the sheer scale of the tour and the ambition of the production had set a new benchmark for live rock shows. *Forbes* magazine declared Pink Floyd the world's highest paid rock band. By now, *A Momentary Lapse of Reason* and *Delicate Sound of Thunder* had both been certified platinum several times over. Just as Pink Floyd's comeback album had been built to go head to head with the likes of Michael Jackson, Bruce Springsteen and Prince, so too did their live gigs send their would-be competitors back to the drawing board. As the 1980s wound to a close, Roger Waters was already plotting a concert that would raise that game even higher. The lawyers may have been called off, but the game of one-upmanship continued.

CHAPTER TEN THE GRASS WAS GREENER

'You can't give up. You have to keep bashing
away or else you're finished as a human being.'

Roger Waters

Today, Roger Waters is the perfect host. The man who routinely ate
music critics for breakfast, that's if he deigned to speak to them at
all, has mellowed. A bit, anyway. In the flesh, he still looks like Roger
Waters but taller, the hair now flecked with grey, the chipped-tooth
smile still a little unnerving. On spying my copy of a recently published
book about his former band, his face darkens, before offering a rather
disconcerting smile; the same grin afforded the upstart interviewer in
Live At Pompeii. 'Have you read this, Roger?' The interview ended a few
minutes ago, so if he walks out now, it won't harm the story.

There is a pause. Waters picks up the book carefully, as if handling an
unexploded bomb or, possibly, some faecal matter, before handing it
back. His driver-cum-bodyguard, a wiry, ex-military type, is waiting in

the doorway, staring disconsolately in my direction. 'Don't believe everything you read,' says Waters, smiles again, waves his hand and is off.

A few minutes later, I spot him in the back seat of a chauffeured car, grinning as he talks to his driver. The vehicle purrs past the flotilla of boats moored in Chelsea Harbour and out of the car park of London's Conrad Hotel. Waters once lived near here, briefly, in the den of iniquity that was 101 Cromwell Road before common sense and his first wife prevailed and he found himself the flat in Shepherds Bush. Waters has now split from his second wife, but is, as he mentioned earlier 'in love again'. It suits him. The taciturn, prickly orator, the reluctant interviewee, is having a good day. It is the summer of 1992 and Roger Waters is charm personified. But then, as he explained earlier, he's just made what he believes to be one of the best albums of his career.

Roger Waters attacked the 1990s with his customary gusto. For grand gestures, he would prove hard to beat. Pink Floyd saw in the new decade with a headline appearance at Knebworth Park; the open-air venue they'd last played just before releasing *Wish You Were Here*. A charity event to raise money for the Nordoff-Robbins Music Therapy Centre, Floyd headlined a resignedly old-fashioned bill of Cliff Richard, Phil Collins, Eric Clapton, Led Zeppelin's reunited partners Jimmy Page and Robert Plant, and a reluctant second on the bill, Paul McCartney. Torrential downpours dampened the mood out front and in the backstage enclosure, where middle-aged pop stars and record execs in baggy tailored suits and floppily expensive haircuts huddled in the drinks tent or beneath buckled umbrellas. Pink Floyd arrived in helicopters.

On stage, Floyd's circular screen filled up with so much rainwater it had to be abandoned. Paul McCartney, perhaps wondering why an ex-Beatle was playing below Pink Floyd, extended his set with encore after encore, delaying the headliners' arrival time.

When they did appear, Floyd's truncated set was delivered to sheets of rain and strong winds, carrying away the opening notes of 'Shine On You Crazy Diamond'. Emerging from billowing clouds of dry ice, Gilmour, in baggy tailored suit and expensively floppy hair cut, braved the elements at the front of the stage and did his best. They bowed out with 'Comfortably Numb' and 'Run Like Hell'; only one song, 'Sorrow', from *A Momentary Lapse of Reason*, broke up the run of standards. With helicopters primed backstage for a swift getaway, it would be Pink Floyd's last public appearance for three years.

In contrast to a charity show in front of a mere 125,000, Waters would time his next live performance with an event of global and historic importance. In November 1989, East Germany's Communist government began to relinquish control of the Berlin Wall, the 28-mile barrier constructed twenty-eight years earlier to divide the German city in two and keep workers in the East. The East German government's decision to let their residents cross the border was followed by the physical dismantling of the wall itself by jubilant East Germans and their Western counterparts. By June 1990, the East German military had begun the official destruction of the wall. It was an extraordinary moment in modern history.

A year earlier, composer Leonard Bernstein (who had once declared himself 'bored stiff' by a performance of Pink Floyd's *Atom Heart Mother* in New York) had conducted a celebratory concert on both sides of the Berlin Wall. In July 1990, Roger Waters decided to stage a follow-up celebration: a performance of *The Wall*, near the Brandenburg Gate at Berlin's Potsdamer Platz in the ruins of the real wall. 'It's *not* a "Top that!" to David Gilmour and Nick Mason,' insisted Waters at the time, 'but it will be gratifying that a few more people in the world will understand that *The Wall* is *my* work and always has been . . . Though after hearing them at Knebworth I don't think I should worry.'

Rock entrepreneur Mick Worwood, who'd previously helped stage Live Aid, had approached Waters. Worwood was acting in response to an approach from Leonard Cheshire of the Memorial Fund for Disaster Relief, a charity set up in the aftermath of the Armenian earthquake and other recent disasters. Their target was to raise £500 million, based on £5 for each person killed in any war during the twentieth century.

Waters was introduced to Leonard Cheshire. The seventy-two-year-old fundraiser was a highly decorated former group captain in the RAF, who had flown many bombing missions over Berlin during the Second World War, and had been the UK's official representative and observer at the bombing of Nagasaki. Appalled by what he had witnessed during the war, Cheshire returned to the UK, and devoted himself to establishing the Cheshire Foundation of Care Homes across the country. To Waters, still preoccupied by the death of his own father in the Second World War, Cheshire was an inspirational figure.

Two years before, when asked if he'd ever stage a production of *The Wall* again, Waters said no, but quipped that he 'might do it outdoors if they ever take the wall down in Berlin'. News of this comment found its way back to Worwood and Cheshire. 'I said I would do what I could, but I thought it was unlikely that it would come off,' said Waters. 'This was before Berlin opened up and so we were looking at other venues.' In the meantime, Waters had been in discussions with producer Tony Hollingsworth, who had recently helped oversee the Nelson Mandela seventieth birthday tribute concert, an event which had been broadcast in sixty-seven different countries. Hollingsworth was now heading up a conference entitled 'Looking East', which aimed to bring Western entertainers to Eastern Bloc countries. While Waters was pondering the logistics of staging *The Wall* on New York's Wall Street or in Arizona's Grand Canyon, they received the unexpected news in November that the wall was officially coming down.

Ticket prices alone wouldn't cover the estimated $8 million needed to stage the show, and Hollingsworth was called in to produce the event for a global TV audience. As well as a planned live album and video, the idea was also sold to TV, with the show eventually broadcast live by satellite to thirty-five countries. Waters also put up his own $500,000 publishing advance. He planned to perform *The Wall* with a supporting cast of special musical guests in place of Pink Floyd. It was also agreed that all participants would donate their royalties from the live album and video to the fund. Despite rumours beforehand, Pink Floyd were not invited, though, according to Nick Mason, Waters made a point of sending invites to all of their ex-wives.

The Floyd's former set designers, Jonathan Park and Mark Fisher, were brought back to help stage the show. The wall itself was now 82ft high, 591ft long and constructed out of 2,500 fire-retardant bricks. Three cranes were positioned behind it to help with the dismantling during the show. One of the cranes also supported a giant-sized version of Gerald Scarfe's schoolteacher puppet. Scarfe, meanwhile, pitched in with a new design: a giant inflatable pig's head with spotlights for eyes.

Even by Pink Floyd standards, this was a grandiose project. In addition, before work could begin on Potsdamer Platz, which was essentially 'no man's land' on the East Berlin side of the wall, the authorities had to scan the area for unexploded mines and bombs lying dormant since the Second World War. During their examination, they discovered a mound of earth that had once housed the main entrance to one of Hitler's bunkers. 'It's an extraordinary, historic piece of land,' raved Waters.

However, with just eight weeks to go and with countless TV deals in place, the only act definitely confirmed to appear were German heavy rock band the Scorpions. Waters called an emergency meeting and agreed to accompany Tony Hollingsworth on a talent-scouting trip to Los Angeles.

Ex-Bleeding Heart Band member Paul Carrack was now playing in Genesis' bass guitarist Mike Rutherford's side project, Mike and The Mechanics, when he took the call. 'Roger gave me this twenty-minute spiel about how it was going to be the biggest concert of all time, and so on,' recalls Carrack. 'Finally, he came to the point and asked me: did I have Huey Lewis's phone number. I did and I gave it to him, then asked, "What about me, Roger?" and he just said, "You're not famous enough!" There was no attempt to spare my feelings,' laughs Carrack. 'In fact, Roger probably took great delight in telling me that. I thought it was perfectly reasonable, though. Nobody did know who the bloody hell I was.'

Progress was slow, though, as various musicians, including Neil Young and Eric Clapton, were unable to commit, and others agreed in principle but failed to respond later. Nevertheless, with Hollingsworth's diligence, Waters' unswerving self-belief and Cheshire's saint-like reputation, they were able to commandeer the use of two US military helicopters to recreate the intro for 'Another Brick in the Wall Part 2', a hundred-strong Soviet Army marching band and the Rundfunk East Berlin Radio Orchestra and choir. Six weeks before the show, when builders working on the site threatened to down tools unless they were paid the $200,000 they were owed, in cash, within an hour, Cheshire was able to sweet-talk a London bank into helping them out.

However, the retired group captain felt compelled to intervene when Waters proposed 'buzzing' the audience with two Second World War bombers. 'He felt bad about it, knowing he'd once been up there, dropping bombs on the poor bastards,' Waters told *Q* magazine. 'He said, "You can't do that!" ' Waters reluctantly backed down.

On the night, the cast of supporting extras included, Levon Helm, Garth Hudson and Rick Danko from The Band, Van Morrison, Bryan Adams, Cyndi Lauper, Sinead O'Connor and Joni Mitchell. Actors Tim Curry and Albert Finney played the prosecuting lawyer and judge for 'The Trial' (though Sean Connery had been one of the first choices for the Finney role until Waters vetoed it), Marianne Faithfull (playing Pink's mother), Jerry Hall (as the groupie in 'One of My Turns'), German torch singer Ute Lemper (as Pink's wife) and Thomas Dolby, as the schoolteacher. And, lurking behind the wall, Paul Carrack.

'A week before the gig, Roger rang me up again,' says Paul. 'They were already over there rehearsing, and I think they were having one or two problems with the special guests. Roger said, "I want you to listen to these six songs and learn them, just in case." And then, two days before it all kicked off, I got the call to go over.'

Leonard Cheshire officially opened the 21 July show with the blowing of a First World War whistle. From here on, it was straight into 'In the Flesh', Waters' spoof heavy metal song performed by the Scorpions. Midway through 'The Thin Ice', disaster struck when the sound blew out, leaving Waters alone and unheard on stage. Showing a welcome and all-too-rare glimpse of humour, he broke into a tap dance before the sound resumed and they jumped straight to 'Another Brick in the Wall Part 2', with an irritating guest vocal from eighties pop star Cyndi Lauper, and some extended soloing from Bleeding Heart Band guitarists Andy Fairweather-Low, Snowy White and Rick di Fonzo. Sadly, the presence of so many satellite TV links to the site meant that sound problems and power failures persisted. Meanwhile, Sinead O'Connor emoted wildly on 'Mother', Joni Mitchell tried hard on 'Goodbye Blue Sky', Jerry Hall fouled up the 'Wow, what a fabulous room . . .' routine as the air-headed groupie on 'One of My Turns', and Van Morrison growled his way through an edgy version of 'Comfortably Numb', with support from various members of The Band; the Dylan-approved folk-country rockers that had wowed all of Pink Floyd back in the early seventies.

Huey Lewis was nowhere to be seen. Meanwhile, faithful understudy Paul Carrack sang 'Hey You' from behind the wall itself. 'Had I known I'd have offered to wear a paper bag over my head,' he jokes. 'It was very scary, it really *was* the biggest gig of all time. If the cameras could have seen me, they'd have caught my knees knocking.'

Staying faithful to the original stage show, much of the original drama was maintained, despite the ever-changing cast of special guests. Using the wall again as a giant screen on which to project images, Waters updated the original films. During 'Bring the Boys Back Home' the wall showed a roll call of all those soldiers that had died during the war. However, more than one eyewitness pointed out the uncomfortable parallels between the scenes later in the show, when rock star Pink imagines himself as a fascist dictator, and events in Germany's still recent past. Seeing Waters, in military uniform and black sunglasses, jackbooting and ranting through 'Waiting for the Worms' ('Would you like to see our coloured cousins home again?'), might have stirred some disturbing memories for those old enough to remember life in Berlin before the wall. 'Everybody understands that that's satire,' claimed Waters.

The audience were nevertheless united for 'The Trial' and the closing chant of 'tear down the wall', the Berliners imbuing the words with more personal sentiment than the standard Pink Floyd fan. In this context, the choice of the *Radio K.A.O.S.* ballad 'The Tide is Turning' – a song celebrating faith in the human race – as the show's finale made sense. The official attendance figure for the gig was given as 200,000, with others maintaining that there were twice that number on site, with an estimated billion more watching on TV around the world.

In the aftermath, one rumour began circulating that the whole show had to be re-staged due to those earlier power failures; something Paul Carrack staunchly denies. However some parts had to be repeated for the video cameras. While most of the guests obliged, Sinead O'Connor refused to re-sing her performance of 'Mother', resulting in her dress rehearsal performance being used in the final video.

'Everyone was fabulous to work with,' said Waters later. 'Bryan Adams, Van Morrison, Cyndi Lauper, all brilliant. All except Sinead O'Connor.'

The forthright Irish singer-songwriter had also, according to Waters, complained about the lack of 'young people on the show', and suggested that Waters should have hired 'Ice-T or one of those people to rework one of my songs as a rap number'.

Yet still the lack of the Pink Floyd brand proved a problem. Released in September, neither the commemorative live album nor video did the level of business Waters or Leonard Cheshire might have hoped for. The album scraped into the Top 30 in the UK, but remained outside the American Top 50, generating a fraction of the anticipated amount for the Memorial Fund for Disaster Relief. Asked for their opinions on the staging of *The Wall* in Berlin, Pink Floyd were guarded, if quietly critical: 'I was rather entertained by it,' insisted Nick Mason. 'If I had a criticism it would have been that I'd have liked a different guitarist.' Gilmour was sniffier: 'I suspect that the motivation for putting *The Wall* show on in Berlin was not charitable.'

In October 1987, Waters had taken The Bleeding Heart Band to Nassau to record songs for a follow-up to *Radio K.A.O.S.* His plan then had been to revive the character of Billy and to continue the narrative. The working title for this new album was *Amused to Death*, taken from a book titled *Amusing Ourselves to Death* by Neil Postman, a critique of television's hold over the Western world. Rumours circulated that Gerald Scarfe had designed an album sleeve, featuring three figures (the current members of Pink Floyd?) floating in a Martini glass. Although Scarfe denies this.

Work resumed on the album after the *Radio K.A.O.S.* tour, and in fits and starts throughout 1988 and the early part of 1989, until news filtered out that Waters had put the album on hold. Around the same time, rumours circulated that he was also working on an opera based on the history of the French Revolution. It would be a further fourteen years before that came to completion.

Mindful of *Radio K.A.O.S.*'s poor sales, EMI were, it transpired, in no mood for *Radio K.A.O.S. Part 2.* Waters' relationship with the label had also soured during the legal war with Pink Floyd, as he believed that the company would always be more supportive of Pink Floyd to the detriment of his solo career. Following the Berlin Wall show, Waters would withdraw from public view, while dealing with upheaval in his professional and personal life.

In 1990, he appointed a new manager, Mark Fenwick, part of the Fenwick's department store dynasty, who had previously co-run the EG Records label, home to Robert Fripp and Brian Eno. That same year, Waters left EMI and signed a new worldwide deal with his US label Columbia. A year later he turned up for his first live performance since

Berlin, playing 'Another Brick in the Wall Part 2' and other Floyd classics at the Guitar Legends concert in Seville. There was further turmoil in his private life. Waters left his second wife Carolyne Christie after sixteen years together. He had, he claimed, met someone else, American actress Pricilla Phillips. Waters would divorce Carolyne in 1992 and marry Pricilla a year later. The two also would go on to have a son, Jack Fletcher, together in 1997.

In August 1992, *Amused to Death*, the product of several years' work in ten different recording studios, was released. It arrived five years after *Radio K.A.O.S.*, the longest gap between albums in Waters' career. The Floyd-in-a-Martini-glass cover had been dumped for a picture of an ape staring at a single eye peering back at him through a TV set. The sleeve mirrored the theme of the album, and the thinking behind Neil Postman's book. While some of the remaining ideas dated back to 1987, Waters had revised many of the songs following specific world events. The most topical themes were the 1989 massacre in Tiananmen Square and the first Gulf War, both of which had been heavily televised. Waters was in his element.

'I've always been intrigued by this notion of war as an entertainment to mollify the folks back home, and the Gulf War fuelled that idea,' he explains. '*Amused to Death* deals with the idea of whether TV is good or bad.' As a positive, Waters recalled a TV documentary about the First World War ('an example of television taking its responsibilities seriously'), in which veterans from the conflict recounted their experiences. The album's first track, 'The Ballad of Bill Hubbard', featured dialogue from the programme, in which an old soldier, Alf Razzell of the Royal Fusiliers, can be heard detailing his failed attempts to save a comrade's life.

For much of the album, Waters focused on the negative effects of the medium. 'I had this rather depressing image of some alien creature seeing the death of this planet and coming down in their spaceships and finding all our skeletons sitting around our TV sets,' he announced. The televising of the Gulf War on CNN had demonstrated the power of the global communications network, and Waters was not impressed. Also in his sights was US President George Bush Snr ('I get gobsmacked when I hear him saying that God was on their side during the Gulf War'), whose predecessor Ronald Reagan had been given a thorough drubbing on *Radio K.A.O.S.*

Amused to Death was certainly a better album than its predecessor. While Waters had written it alone, he'd roped in a stellar cast of session men and special guests, alongside The Bleeding Heart Band. The hired hands included drummer Jeff Porcaro and arranger Michael Kamen (both of whom had featured on *The Wall*), while the guests included The Eagles' Don Henley, country singer Rita Coolidge and guitar hero Jeff Beck, the man once mooted for the Pink Floyd job before David Gilmour.

Beck's playing on the album's signature song 'What God Wants Part 1' was a singular highlight, and clearly another concerted effort by Waters to snag a guitarist with a reputation to rival David Gilmour's. Beck later explained that he and Waters had bonded after he'd been allowed to drive Waters' vintage Maserati through Richmond Park. Waters had also enlisted a co-producer, Pat Leonard, the songwriter who'd penned hits for Madonna and played keyboards on *A Momentary Lapse of Reason*. 'Whatever Pat had done before didn't interest me,' claims Waters. 'He had sat in a Chicago theatre, aged fourteen, watching Pink Floyd play *Dark Side of the Moon*. He knew all my work and I was impressed.'

One of Waters' old Bleeding Heart Band members once recalled a conversation in which Waters had declared, 'I'm just in the process of choosing someone to perform the menial task of producer on my next record.' Nevertheless, Leonard made his mark on *Amused to Death*, helping to give it the similarly widescreen sound Bob Ezrin had achieved on *A Momentary Lapse* . . . Not that Ezrin went unmentioned on *Amused to Death*. On one song, 'Too Much Rope', Waters crooned the line, 'Each man has his price, Bob, and yours was pretty low', which most took to refer to their falling-out over Ezrin's decision to produce Pink Floyd five years earlier. Waters explains that 'the original line was, "Each man has his price, my friends", so make of that what you will.' ('Isn't that childish? Isn't that just amazing?' commented Ezrin.)

Ezrin wasn't the only high-profile figure on Waters' hit list. While recording the album, he'd approached film-maker Stanley Kubrick for permission to use dialogue from Kubrick's *2001: A Space Odyssey* on the album. Kubrick refused, and found himself mentioned in a garbled message recorded backwards at the start of the song 'Perfect Sense Part 1'. Though perhaps Kubrick was paying back Waters for his refusal to allow him to use *Atom Heart Mother* for one of his films over twenty years previously.

On completing the album, Waters invited old friend Ron Geesin over to his Kimbridge manor house. 'I turned up at half-past twelve and by half-one he still wasn't there,' says Geesin now. 'Roger used to do this when I first knew him. You'd arrive at the time he'd suggested and he still wasn't back from playing squash. I used to call it the C.L.F. – Calculated Lateness Factor. It was his way of trying to keep you on your toes.'

When Waters finally arrived, he played Geesin some sketches from the opera he'd been working on. 'I made some vague suggestion, like, "Oh, maybe the brass section should do this or that . . ." and he turned round and said, "I didn't invite you here to find out what you think . . ."'

Before leaving, Waters handed Geesin a CD copy of *Amused to Death*. When he went to play it back at home, Ron discovered that the box was empty. 'So I made this little piece of art, shaped like a CD, on which I wrote a poem about the disc not being in there, and sent it back to him. After three days I phoned him up and he said to me, "What's this thing in here? I don't understand it." He knew perfectly well that it was just an affectionate gift and a joke about how the disc had been missing. We'd done things like this for years. He was just being difficult. Next thing, Roger said to me, "What's this I hear about you reviewing the album?" I told him that I was doing nothing of the sort, and nor would I have the outlet to do so. He said, "Well, that's what I've heard." So this went back and forth, and in the end I just said, "Roger, that'll be that then. Now fuck off."'

The two have not spoken since.

To help sell *Amused to Death*, Waters submitted to the sort of promotional campaign that would have met with his withering contempt back in the days of Pink Floyd. He made for a fantastic interviewee: passionately explaining his new album, while taking verbal pot shots at world leaders, TV stations, Pink Floyd, everyone . . . Waters blithely informed one interviewer the only music he was currently listening to was that of vintage soul singer Joe Tex. Elsewhere, he decried Madonna as 'an awful, ugly, dull person', and clearly felt no need to prove himself hip: 'I hope people get fed up with teenagers with baseball hats on back to front and rappers talking over other people's music.'

That said, he still bit the bullet and submitted a video clip to MTV. 'I see the irony,' he told *Details* magazine. 'But I had to decide whether to get hard-nosed and say, "I will not make a video", and substantially reduce the chances of people becoming aware of this record.' The music channel had been in its infancy when Waters began his solo career. Unfortunately, Roger had once clammed up during an MTV interview about *The Pros and Cons of Hitch-hiking* (when they asked for his comments about Pink Floyd), and had been sorely under-represented on the channel ever since. Two years later, the relaunched Pink Floyd would enjoy widespread coverage on MTV.

For a man perceived as so single-minded and unyielding, it was also gratifying to hear him admitting to feelings of insecurity about his work. 'I let people push me down roads I shouldn't have gone down really,' he told the *LA Times*. 'With *Radio K.A.O.S.* I got sidetracked by the technology and the notion that I ought to get a bit more with it. I was right in the middle of all the Pink Floyd litigation and I guess I got a bit insecure about what I was worth and who I was . . .'

Waters also revealed that he had been in therapy throughout most of the 1980s, to learn how to, in his words, 'free himself from the dictates of destructive sub-personalities'. This admission related to therapy inspired by the psychologist Carl Jung, in which the subject learns how to individuate. The parallels with Waters' ideas on *Dark Side of the Moon* were obvious. Jung believed that while society prepares most people for the first half of their life, it fails to do so for middle age and beyond. Individuation was therefore a way of preparing the psyche for the second half of life. 'You stand a better chance of walking your own path,' said Waters. 'We've all got crosses to bear. My biggest one was my father's death and having to grow up in a female-dominated society, and because of that, causing my subsequent relationship with women to become very difficult.' Most hacks, of course, just wanted to know if he was ever going to get back together with Pink Floyd.

Amused to Death garnered some of the better reviews of Waters' career. However, the *Daily Telegraph*'s was not one of them: 'Had he been blessed with even a rudimentary sense of humour and rather more verbal fluency . . . Roger Waters might well be pop's Martin Amis,' wrote Charles Shaar Murray. Waters spent one subsequent magazine interview lashing out at Murray and other music critics ('they can't fucking write'). *Billboard* magazine, however, decided that *Amused to Death* was 'one of the most provocative and musically dazzling records of the decade'.

The album certainly suggested that Waters had deeply held convictions about the world around him. This was not the work of a complacent millionaire rock star. In contrast, the last Pink Floyd album had stood for very little. Waters, as ever, had the ideas, the philosophies, the obsessions, but he couldn't match his bandmates for broader musical appeal. Roger's music still had to fight it out with the words and the special effects, of which there were many on *Amused to Death*. 'Perfect Sense Part 1' encapsulated the problem, with the esteemed soul singer P.P. Arnold wrestling with too many tongue-twisting lyrics, just to get the message across. Nevertheless, this was Roger Waters' style of making music, for which he felt no need to apologise. With three solo albums proper to his name, the record-buying public should have grown used to it by now. Except they hadn't. *A Momentary Lapse of Reason* may have been a triumph of style over very little substance, but for many, *Amused to Death* offered too much substance.

Asked in 1992 whether he would tour the album, Waters said he would 'if it sold between three to four million'. In the end, *Amused to Death* would end up selling nearer to a million copies. Peaking in the UK at number 8, it was his highest charting album to date. For its creator, as ever, sales and critics meant little. 'I think it's a stunning piece of work,' he reflected later, ranking it alongside *Dark Side of the Moon* and *The Wall* as one of the best albums of his career. In more verbose moments, Waters would claim, not unreasonably, that had *Amused to Death* been a Pink Floyd record, it would have sold 10 million copies. For all his defiance, the album's lack of success must have hurt. Waters would not play live for another seven years.

While not quite floating in the Martini glass of Roger Waters' imagination, Pink Floyd had lain dormant since playing Knebworth. They had lives to live. David Gilmour got divorced, while Nick Mason married TV actress and presenter Annette Lynton, with whom he would have two more children, sons Guy and Carey.

In 1990, the Floyd partners and Steve O'Rourke competed in the Carrera Pan America sports car race in Mexico. O'Rourke had pre-sold the rights to a film of their participation to cover the costs of competing. Three days in, disaster struck, when a Jaguar being driven by Gilmour, with O'Rourke in the passenger seat, sped over the edge of an embankment near the town of San Luis Potisi, leaving the guitarist battered and bruised and the manager with a compound fracture of the leg. Having escaped death, they returned to England, to record a soundtrack to the film.

Realising they needed some help, Gilmour, Mason and Wright rounded up young guns Gary Wallis, Jon Carin and Guy Pratt, and repaired to West London's Olympic Studios. The sessions offered a stark contrast to the agonisingly slow process of making *A Momentary Lapse of Reason*. Without the pressure of having to create a Pink Floyd album, the musicians simply jammed together, with guitarist Tim Renwick helping out between stints on Bryan Ferry's new album. They produced seven pieces of new music needed for the soundtrack. It was the quickest Pink Floyd had worked since making the soundtrack to *Obscured by Clouds*. Released in April 1992, neither the film nor the soundtrack would trouble anyone but the most ardent Pink Floyd watcher. Nevertheless, this new way of working would prove crucial to the next Floyd album. Not that David Gilmour was in any hurry to start making that album. Instead, he'd resumed his sideline as a trusty guitarist-for-hire (suggesting to all clients that they donate his fee to charity). Gilmour's guitar playing graced albums from, among others, Warren Zevon, Propaganda, Paul Young, All About Eve and old pal Roy Harper. He also composed one new song, 'Me and J.C.', for the film version of *The Cement Garden*, Ian McEwan's eerie tale of murder and incest.

In 1992, Gilmour and Mason would reunite only to play a couple of charity gigs in London, including the Chelsea Arts Ball at the Royal Albert Hall, where Richard Wright joined them on stage. In November, EMI issued 'Shine On', a boxed set of seven Floyd albums, from *A Saucerful of Secrets* to *A Momentary Lapse of Reason*, plus an extra disc containing their early singles. Critics quickly fanned the embers of the Waters versus Floyd dispute, with both parties taking the bait. Again.

Gilmour informed *Musician* magazine that he had played a lot of the bass guitar on Pink Floyd's albums and that Waters jokingly thanked him whenever he won a Best Bass Player poll. Waters, meanwhile, quashed the rumour that he had had 150 rolls of toilet paper produced with Gilmour's face on them, while conceding that he thought it a good idea. There was a pattern to the sniping: that Waters was a poor musician; and that Gilmour and Mason lacked creativity. As the drummer said some years later, 'If our children behaved this way, we would have been very cross.'

On a more upbeat note, Pink Floyd began 1993 by starting work again. Better still, they started playing together in the studio, without the threat of lawsuits or telephone calls from lawyers to break their concentration. The sessions began at Britannia Row, with just Gilmour, Mason and Wright jamming together, before bassist Guy Pratt was invited to join in.

'It was thrilling to know you were playing on a Pink Floyd record,' admits Guy. 'Sometimes David would come up with ideas and I'd come up with basslines, only to realise how out of step my playing was. David would always have a better alternative – "Yes, that's great . . . but lose ninety per cent of the notes in it."' These sessions produced random chord sequences, riffs, and ideas. While engineer Andy Jackson was also back in the fold, Gilmour would keep a tape machine near to where he was playing, and simply hit the 'record' button whenever he felt the band were getting somewhere. Before long, they decided to call in a co-producer.

'I sort of assumed we'd do it again,' said Bob Ezrin, 'as David and I had stayed in touch on a friendly basis. So Steve O'Rourke rang me and said would I do it, and then told me how much less he would pay me. He always tried that.'

The band eventually found themselves with around sixty-five individual pieces of music from the piles of tapes. They decided to take a novel approach to whittling down the material. 'We had what we called "the big listen",' explained Gilmour, 'where we listened to all of these pieces, and everyone voted on each piece of music to see how popular it was.'

According to Gilmour, the pieces were then whittled down to 'a top twenty-five, which in fact became the top twenty-seven, as a couple more got added in'. The process continued, with the individual pieces either scrapped altogether or merged with other ideas. The final selection ran to some fifteen ideas, of which a further four would be discarded before the final tracklisting of eleven songs was agreed.

This process had its drawbacks when, according to Nick Mason, Richard Wright accorded each of his ideas the maximum number of points, skewing the voting. Despite his involvement, Wright was still not contractually a full member of the band; something that clearly rankled. 'It came very close to a point where I wasn't going to do the album,' he said in 2000, 'because I didn't feel that what we'd agreed was fair.'

However aggrieved he may have felt, Wright chose to remain, and would be rewarded with five co-writes on the finished album; the first time he'd received a songwriting credit on any new Pink Floyd album since *Wish You Were Here*. However, like Gilmour, Wright did not consider himself a natural lyricist. Dream Academy's Nick Laird-Clowes and *Momentary Lapse* . . . lyricist Anthony Moore would end up contributing, but Gilmour also now had a full-time writing partner, his new girlfriend.

Polly Samson was a newspaper journalist who'd been introduced to Gilmour at a dinner party. The daughter of Communist parents — a Chinese mother and German father — she had enjoyed an unconventional upbringing. Samson had been expelled from school before drifting into a job in publishing, which led to a stint as a *Sunday Times* gossip columnist in the early nineties. In the meantime, she was bringing up her young son, Charlie, alone, after the departure of his father, playwright Heathcote Williams. Mutual friends had tried to pair her up with Gilmour for some time, before he finally telephoned and invited her to a U2 concert.

At first Samson's role on the new album was simply one of encouragement. 'She was trying to persuade me to get on and point me in the direction of where to put my energy,' recalled Gilmour. The album's turning point was a song that would eventually be titled 'High Hopes', in which Gilmour, with his girlfriend's encouragement, reflected on his childhood and early life in Cambridge. 'She helped me get started on "High Hopes", but it quickly became obvious that it was better if she took part. She tried *not* to take part at first, but I wanted her to and she did.'

Gilmour would work with the rest of the band in the studio, before going back home and spending the evening writing with Polly. 'There was a whole invisible side to the process,' he explained. 'Something that Nick, Rick and Bob weren't aware of.'

Polly's presence soon led to tension among some in the Gilmour circle. 'It wasn't easy at first,' admits Bob Ezrin. 'It put a strain on the boys' club, and it was almost clichéd to have the new woman coming in and then get involved in the career. But she inspired David and gave him a sense of confidence and challenged him. Whatever David was thinking at the time she helped him find a way of saying it.'

'Polly has a tendency to ruffle everyone's feathers,' Gilmour admitted in *Mojo* magazine. 'I'm not aware of her having ruffled Nick or Rick's feathers, but she certainly ruffled the management's.'

'High Hopes' would, nevertheless, give the album the push it needed. 'It pulled the whole album together,' said Bob Ezrin. 'It was the most emotionally complete and clear song we had. We were on the river, in the winter, in good grey England. There's a special mood about England at that time of year. It makes people go inside, it's so introspective, and that song captured it.'

Polly Samson's relationship with Gilmour wasn't the only one the band had to contend with. Since the end of the *Momentary Lapse . . .* tour, Guy Pratt and Gala Wright had officially become an item. 'It was an odd time for me,' says Guy, 'because Gala and I had just gone on holiday and I think there was a feeling in the camp that we'd get it out of our systems and then it would all go back to normal. Except that didn't happen. Maybe it was a bigger deal in my mind than it really was, but I felt like I was walking on eggshells all the time.'

To add to the tension, Pratt also lived very near to Richard Wright in Kensington. 'So, in the usual caring, sharing Pink Floyd style, I was designated Rick's driver. So I had an hour of silence every morning, with Rick sitting in this horrible tatty VW Golf I was driving at the time.'

Jon Carin and Gary Wallis were brought in to witness Guy's suffering and complete the band, before recording of the final selected tracks began. Additional support came from a team of five backing vocalists including Sam Brown and *Momentary Lapse . . .* tour singer Durga McBroom, and orchestral arranger Michael Kamen. Tim Renwick came back to play additional guitar, alongside another Floyd veteran, Dick Parry. The saxophonist's last Pink Floyd album had been *Wish You Were Here*. He had only just resumed playing the instrument again after working for several years as a farrier, when he sent Gilmour a Christmas card.

'I just rang him up and asked him if he felt like auditioning for the tour,' said Gilmour. Parry visited the *Astoria*, and, within seconds, it was apparent that he was still up to scratch. He ended up playing on one song, 'Wearing the Inside Out'.

Meanwhile, keyboard player Carin pestered Gilmour's guitar tech Phil Taylor into locating some of the band's old keyboards from the seventies, including a Farfisa organ. Taken out of the warehouse in which they'd been stored, he then sampled sounds, some of which ended up being used on the tracks 'Take it Back' and 'Marooned'. As Andy Jackson later explained, 'It felt like a proper Pink Floyd album again.'

While Gilmour pulled back from the idea of making a concept album, a theme of sorts began to emerge as the songs developed further. In the light of Pink Floyd's past troubles there was a certain irony in song titles such as 'Keep Talking' and 'Lost for Words'. But while reluctant to dissect the ideas behind the songs, Gilmour later conceded that much of the album dealt with the theme of communication; and the notion that people simply talking to each other could solve more of life's problems. 'Maybe I needed to unload my subconscious,' he admitted.

Surprisingly, the band broke cover for a rare live performance in September. Floyd played three songs – 'Run Like Hell', 'Wish You Were Here' and 'Comfortably Numb' – at Sussex's Cowdray Ruins Castle as a fundraiser for the local hospital. Those who'd stumped up the £140 ticket price also got to see star turns from Eric Clapton, Genesis and the surviving members of Queen.

By December, the album was near completion. However, despite Bob Ezrin's involvement, *Dark Side of the Moon*'s mixing supervisor Chris Thomas would undertake the final mix. 'That *was* disappointing,' admits Ezrin. 'But everybody feels they could do better.' Now all they had to do was choose an album title. While not feeling quite so concerned about the title as they had been for *A Momentary Lapse of Reason*, nobody could agree on a solution. Over dinner one night, the band's friend, Douglas Adams, author of *The Hitch-hiker's Guide to the Galaxy*, suggested *The Division Bell*, named after the bell used in the House of Commons to summon absent members of parliament to the chambers for voting (Gilmour: 'it divides the yeses from the nos'). Adams had simply looked over some of the album's lyrics and spotted the phrase in the words to 'High Hopes'. In exchange, the band gifted £5,000 to Polly Samson's favoured charity, the Environmental Investigation Agency.

The author's suggestion had come at just the right moment: the night before the deadline imposed by EMI. Storm Thorgerson would oversee another grandiose idea on the band's behalf. Inspired by the theme of communication, Storm had sketched out an image of 'two heads facing, or talking to each other, making up a third face'. The cryptic third face, which may or may not be seen by the viewer, depending on how they were looking, represented, in Storm's words, 'the absent face – the ghost of Pink Floyd's past, Syd and Roger'. Gilmour was unconvinced.

After being presented with another set of sketches, he finally warmed to the idea. Two 3m-high sets of sculptured heads, in the imposing style of the Aku-Aku statues on Easter Island, were then constructed. One set would be built out of stone, the other from metal. They were then transported to a field in Ely, near to where David Gilmour had grown up, where they remained under camouflage netting and twenty-four-hour security until the weather conditions and light were deemed suitable for photographing them. When Thorgerson decided that they needed a row of lights between the two 'mouths' to represent speech, they acquired four cheap spotlights and wired them up to the photographer's car battery. The stone effigies would be used on the cassette version of *The Division Bell*, the metal-plated versions on the CD cover. The metal heads would end up standing guard outside London's Earls Court when the group next played there.

The mid-eighties had found Gilmour and Mason, like Roger Waters, chasing their respective tails to make music that sounded of the moment. When that moment passed, though, both *A Momentary Lapse of Reason* and Waters' *Radio K.A.O.S.* would suffer as a consequence. *The Division Bell* tried less hard and made no obvious concessions to the modern age, even if some modern bands were keen to declare their love of Pink Floyd. Since the last time Floyd made a studio album, dance music and 'rave culture' had made their mark on the musical landscape. (Gilmour told *Q* magazine that he *had* been to an acid house party but 'not a really big one'.) In 1993, he agreed to be interviewed with Alex Paterson of techno dance duo The Orb for a *Melody Maker* cover story. Gilmour professed to having seen The Orb in concert and to owning a couple of their albums; Paterson raved about Pink Floyd's *Meddle*. It was no great meeting of like-minded souls, however, even if Nick Mason would later reveal that the early jamming sessions for *The Division Bell* had yielded a set of Orb-style meanderings, jokingly titled 'The Big Spliff'.

Elsewhere, young American rock band Nirvana's amalgam of punk and heavy rock, added to the scuzzy good looks of their singer Kurt Cobain, had helped them sell millions of records. A host of like-minded 'grunge' rock bands followed, with old-timer Neil Young even making an album with Nirvana's rivals Pearl Jam. *The Division Bell* was littered with guitar solos, but there was no 'grunge' to be found here, thank you. As Gilmour explained, 'The Floyd is a big old lumbering beast, but it's *my* big old lumbering beast, and I like it.'

Released in March 1994, the 'New Floyd' cruised to number 1 on both sides of the Atlantic. Nobody could have been surprised. Within months, Gilmour was telling the press that *The Division Bell* sounded more like a genuine Pink Floyd album than anything since *Wish You Were Here*. The opening instrumental, 'Cluster One', with its static crackles and extra-terrestrial twittering – like signals from another galaxy – was certainly familiar Pink Floyd territory. Anyone flipping through the track selector on their CD player might also notice that most of its eleven songs began with some abstract keyboard whirl or sonorous note of unidentifiable origin.

However fearful some may have been of Pink Floyd acquiring their own Yoko Ono, the lyrics on *The Division Bell* had greater clarity than most of those on *A Momentary Lapse of Reason*. Gilmour was unwilling to explain, but it seemed as if his new partner had coerced him into exploring his feelings in greater detail than usual. 'A Great Day for Freedom' seemed, at first, to address the demise of the Berlin Wall, but there was another message, of lost optimism and hopes dashed. Similar themes of new beginnings countered with mournful reflection seemed to inform the whole album. Gilmour was in love, perhaps, but still feeling guarded.

'High Hopes' was the album's runaway highlight. With its tolling church bells, keening vocals and remembrance of times past, it was as if the older, world-wearier voice of *Atom Heart Mother*'s 'Fat Old Sun' had come back twenty-five years later to update the story. 'What Do You Want From Me?' was more combative, musically and lyrically. A slow blues over which Gilmour fired off questions – 'Do you want my blood, do you want my tears?' – it had, he admitted, been inspired after a row with Polly Samson, over lack of communication. 'Marooned' combined whale song with the sound of an Ibizan beach bar at sunrise, and later landed the band a Grammy Award for Best Rock Instrumental Performance. *The Division Bell* was more interesting, though, when Gilmour was forced out of his guitar-hero bunker, and made to start singing again, about love and, possibly, sex on 'Coming Back to Life', and his own inarticulate nature on 'Keep Talking', supplemented by a sample of the computer-aided voice of Professor Stephen Hawking, author of *A Brief History of Time*.

The album floundered on 'Take it Back', a Simple Minds/U2-style arena anthem that would have fitted better on *A Momentary Lapse of Reason* or even Gilmour's solo album, *About Face*. Or neither. Yet for the hardcore fans, the most notable coup was Richard Wright taking his first lead vocal since *Dark Side of the Moon*. 'Wearing the Inside Out' had been co-written by Wright with Anthony Moore. It had, commented one Floyd insider, 'taken Moore to climb inside Rick's head and get the words out'. Anyone even fleetingly familiar with Wright's past experiences in Pink Floyd and, one suspects, life in general would have been drawn to the words. The quavering tone and painfully raw lyrics suggested a man finding his way back to civilisation for the first time in a long while. 'There's a lot of emotional honesty there,' offers Bob Ezrin. 'Fans pick up on the sad and vulnerable side to Rick.'

'Poles Apart' was the one song that connected most directly with the ghosts of Pink Floyd's past. Gilmour wouldn't be drawn on it, but Samson later confirmed that it was about Syd Barrett in the first verse and Roger Waters in the second. There was even a mêlée of Wurlitzer sounds, a psychedelic motif from the era of *The Piper at the Gates of Dawn*, to separate the two. Gilmour sounded genuinely reflective, about shared experiences, and friendships lost along the way.

While Pink Floyd had become a whipping boy for critics bemoaning the bloated self-satisfaction of ageing rock stars, their original singer had suffered no such disapproval. Disappearing when he was still young and pretty, Barrett had enchanted many punks in the late seventies and left-field rock bands in the eighties and nineties, on both sides of the pond. Michael Stipe, lead singer with R.E.M., was a staunch Syd devotee. Roger Waters met R.E.M. backstage after an early show in London, and found Stipe very unwelcoming. 'He sat in the corner with his back to me,' remembered Waters. 'Then he went back on stage and did an encore, an *a cappella* version of Syd's song "Dark Globe", which might have been his way of saying, "Syd was all right, but you're an arsehole." '

In England, another Cambridge band, The Soft Boys, had since 1980 been modelling their neo-psychedelic sound on classic Syd. By the time Pink Floyd released *The Division Bell*, a wave of newer young English groups, including Blur, had emerged, taking their cue from The Who, The Kinks, The Beatles and Syd-era Floyd. The Barrett myth remained undiminished.

In 1992, Atlantic Records had contacted Syd's family, offering them £75,000 for any new recordings they might be able to make of Barrett. The family turned them down. In spring 1993, EMI followed a twentieth anniversary reissue of *Dark Side of the Moon* with *Crazy Diamond*, a boxed set of all Syd's known recordings. A month later, *Syd's First Trip*, the film of Barrett supposedly tripping in Cambridge, was released on video. The original film was bolstered with extra footage of the band with Andrew King outside Abbey Road. Everyone seemed astonishingly fresh-faced and good-looking, dolled up in their best pop star finery. Some years later, Pink Floyd purchased the rights from film-maker Nigel Lesmoir-Gordon and had it withdrawn from circulation.

'I sold the film via Steve O'Rourke,' says Nigel. 'They wanted it because I wanted to sell it to them, as I needed the money. I never called the film *Syd's First Trip*, though. I don't think it was the first time Syd had taken acid. Syd was dead keen to take LSD and dead keen to be filmed.'

The Division Bell had helped finally realise Steve O'Rourke's wish to be featured on a Pink Floyd album. At the end of 'High Hopes', he could be heard talking on the phone to Polly's young son, Charlie, who suddenly hangs up on him. To date, O'Rourke's voice is the last one heard on what may well prove to be the last ever Pink Floyd album. Not that anyone, even David Gilmour, was announcing it as such at the time. Rumours began, again, of a reunion with Roger Waters. 'We haven't discussed it, and there's absolutely no likelihood of that happening at all,' warned Gilmour. With another world tour booked, the guitarist had no desire to share the stewardship of the 'big old lumbering beast' with anyone else.

The lumbering beast analogy would be reflected in some reviews of the new record. 'The album gives off the uncomfortable whiff of middle-age and graying sensibilities,' complained Tom Graves in *Rolling Stone*. David Bennun in *Melody Maker* likened it to 'chewing on a bucket of gravel'. Stuart Maconie in *Q* was more obliging: 'Musically, it's that immutable Floyd style, awash with reminders and back-references. They remain unique and uniquely enigmatic.' The fiercest critic of all would be Roger Waters. 'Lyrics written by the new wife?' he bellyached to writer John Harris. 'I mean, give me a fucking break! Come on. And what a nerve, to call that Pink Floyd. It was an *awful* record.'

The guitarist dismissed his estranged bandmate's griping as sour grapes. Perhaps he was too much of a gentleman to point out that Waters was the only member of the band ever to have included a photograph of his wife on a Pink Floyd album (*Ummagumma*). Or perhaps he'd just forgotten.

While not yet Gilmour's wife, Polly soon would be. He had already asked her to marry him, and, after deliberating, she agreed. 'David got me to write some songs for Pink Floyd, which was his very clever way of giving me my self-respect,' she told writer Suzi MacKenzie. Having been living 'on her wits for a couple of years' and bringing up her son alone, Samson had, she claimed, been wary of looking for a husband that would automatically remove her money worries. By writing on *The Division Bell*, she earned a lot of money, and was, she said, 'able to go into the marriage well-off'. The two would marry in July 1994 at Marylebone Register Office.

For all Waters' protestations to the contrary, *The Division Bell* was a better and more confident album than *A Momentary Lapse of Reason*. The band faced the same obstacle as any group from their generation: how to make new music that could compete in fans' affections with the music they had made in the past. They could never top *Wish You Were Here* or *Dark Side of the Moon*. Instead *The Division Bell* offered careful nods to those benchmark albums, while ensuring that at least some of its songs – 'High Hopes' and 'Poles Apart' – wouldn't immediately send audience members scurrying to the refreshment stands and bathrooms next time they hit the stadium trail.

'There is lots about *The Division Bell* that I still love,' offers Guy Pratt. 'It still suffers from some eighties production hangovers. "Keep Talking" I find unlistenable, it's a great mess, but a lot of it reminded me of the pre-*Wall* Pink Floyd. "High Hopes" is one of those songs I never get bored of.'

The scale and spectacle of the *Momentary Lapse* . . . tour presented an immediate challenge when faced with doing it all again. The band's first response was to commission the building of a Skyship 600 airship, complete with Pink Floyd insignia. The airship accompanied a press reception for the album and tour in the US. A similar A60 airship was then unveiled for the launch in England. In the meantime, the band submitted to three weeks of intense rehearsals at an airforce base in North Carolina.

'David, Nick and Rick have no limit on the budget for this tour,' claimed Steve O'Rourke. Just as well. *The Division Bell* tour would require a 200-strong crew, and the use of a Russian military freight plane and two Boeing 747 cargo planes just to transport the stage set, designed by Mark Fisher, from the USA to the UK.

The set revisited familiar Pink Floyd themes, but simply upgraded and updated everything. A 'Bigger, Better, More' policy was in full effect. There were new films for 'Money', 'Time' and 'Shine On You Crazy Diamond', courtesy of Storm Thorgerson. There were three stages, so that while one was being set up in one stadium, the other two could be set up in place for the next two shows. There were *two* giant pigs, 400 Varilights, 300 speakers, a 40ft circular projection screen, two pulse lasers . . . and, to help fund the extravaganza, a hefty sponsorship deal from Volkswagen.

Gilmour immediately rued the decision. 'I confess to not having entirely thought it through before we did it. Having our name allied to Volkswagen is something I have no taste for. Any money I made from it went to charity.'

The tour opened on 29 March at Miami's Joe Robbie Stadium. The extended band was the same as it had been for the *Momentary Lapse . . .* tour, but now included saxophonist Dick Parry in place of Scott Page, with backing singers Durga McBroom, Sam Brown and Claudia Fontaine. Another veteran of Pink Floyd gigs past was tour manager Tony Howard, once the band's booking agent back in the days when they were signed to the Morrison Agency.

Tony Howard's presence wasn't the only link to the past. The Floyd's show opened that night with 'Astronomy Domine', the first song from the first Pink Floyd album. Looking for a visual effect to accompany it, the band got in touch with the Floyd's original lighting designer, Peter Wynne-Willson. Since 1967, Wynne-Willson had been responsible for some groundbreaking lighting designs and inventions.

But *The Division Bell* tour would be his first encounter with Pink Floyd since 1968, when he ran into them unexpectedly in Amsterdam, where he was working with an impoverished theatre troupe: 'Dave Gilmour, very sweetly, told Floyd's management to get me a plane ticket back to the UK, as I was living a fairly meagre existence.' Twenty-seven years later, Wynne-Willson was called on to replicate the lighting and oil slide effects that had once dazzled the stoned faithful at the UFO club.

On the band's last tour, they'd played the whole of their new album. This time, excerpts from *The Division Bell* were spaced out between the likes of 'Another Brick in the Wall Part 2', 'One of These Days', 'Wish You Were Here' and 'Money'. Still dwarfed by the myriad special effects whizzing around them, the band had changed since *A Momentary Lapse* . . . Nick Mason was no longer quite so overshadowed by second drummer Gary Wallis. While the shimmying backing singers offered the only hint of glamour, a shorn, slimmed-down Gilmour, now on an exercise regime, looked healthier than he had done in years.

In Houston, Texas, the final encore of 'Run Like Hell' was abandoned when a thunderstorm left the stage drenched. As the tour progressed through Mexico, California and back to Texas, the most notable change was the audience. Pink Floyd were now selling tickets to entire families and to those too young to have seen them back in the seventies. The US industry trade mag *Billboard* believed that the recent re-release of *Dark Side of the Moon* and its reappearance in the charts had brought the band to a younger generation. Gilmour was delighted: 'There are people who say we should make room for younger bands. That's not the way it works. They can make their own room.'

But as guitarist Tim Renwick recalls, '*The Division Bell* tour was much more staid than the one before.' The presence of Polly Samson, Nick Mason's new wife 'Nettie', and Richard Wright's soon-to-be third wife Millie ensured that 'everyone now had to go to bed a lot earlier'.

'On the last tour, the whole attitude had been, "Right, what club are we hitting tonight?"' recalls Tim. 'The next tour was a complete contrast. Security was much tighter as well; as they didn't want too many party animals turning up from the last tour. It was still enjoyable, but I think there was some resentment from some of the younger members.' They also knew whom to blame.

'There was a certain amount of anti-Polly stuff going on,' admitted Gilmour. 'Whether it was anti-woman or anti-newcomer, but there was power-struggling going on. It was a boys' club before Polly. I think she was seen as the fun police, unfairly, but she got a lot of flak for that.'

When the two had first begun their relationship, Gilmour had agreed to stop taking cocaine. 'I became too fond of the coke,' he admits. 'I think it happened because I got divorced and decided to go on the razzle and it all coincided with the Floyd coming back. There were various reasons. Taking the decision to stop was the hard bit, but once I'd done that I found it easy. But lots of people were invested in the person I was, the person who had the coke, and had no interest in me becoming a different and better person.'

Polly's day job as a writer and journalist also gave her a different view of the show. 'I think she gave reviews of the show more credence than we did,' says Guy Pratt. 'But this meant that we ended up changing some things in the show because a reviewer didn't like it. That certainly annoyed me, and I did let my feelings be known on a couple of occasions. Although I managed to do it without losing a friendship.' He adds, 'That tour was riven with tension. But I think it was all the better for it. Pink Floyd was borne out of tension for so many years that I think it still functioned at its best when it wasn't just a band of happy misfits.'

There was another potentially divisive factor to be considered. Unlike on the last tour, at the end of the show now, the three originals stepped forward to take the first bow alone. Which, according to Nick Mason, left some of the supporting players feeling aggrieved.

In turn, the others and various crew members established their own little clique, a mocked-up club beneath the stage, where they played after the show or sometimes even during the interval. The club was nicknamed 'The Donkey's Knob'.

The presence of the band's children on some dates was another stark reminder of their lives away from Pink Floyd. Nick Mason's eldest daughter was now working for him on the tour; some of Gilmour's children would join him on the dates; while bassist Guy Pratt would cement intra-band relations further by later marrying Gala Wright. 'It was the most un-rock 'n' roll tour,' says one insider. 'They were all in new relationships and they were being family men again.'

There would be one significant throwback to the old days, though. On 15 July, at Detroit's Pontiac Silverdome, the band changed their setlist. The whole of the second half of the show was now given over to *Dark Side of the Moon* in its entirety. The band had been considering playing the whole album since 1987. Now, they'd finally committed themselves to do it. Nick Mason found it an emotional experience. 'It reminds me of our history, the way we were then,' he said. 'It made us a big *American* band. But we reached a new plateau and immediately suffered for it from not knowing what to do next. The band disagreements, which never existed before, started then.'

Dark Side . . . would be played again two nights later at the Giants Stadium in New Jersey, and at random throughout the rest of the tour. In the meantime, the advent of the Internet had given the more technically advanced Pink Floyd fans a new medium with which to communicate. A couple of months into *The Division Bell* tour, postings began to appear on a Pink Floyd Internet newsgroup by an unknown individual known only as Publius. He/she invited fans to scrutinise the artwork, lyrics and music on *The Division Bell* for clues to an enigma or puzzle hidden within the album, hinting at a prize to anyone that could solve the riddle. The initial postings were greeted with scepticism, until, as promised by Publius in a posting beforehand, the words 'Enigma Publius' were spelled out in lights at the base of the stage during the show at the Giants Stadium.

Later on in the tour, as predicted, a similar message flashed up on the stage at London's Earls Court. When interviewed, the band members denied all knowledge, as did Storm Thorgerson and Steve O'Rourke, who were considered the likeliest culprits. However, a set of Floyd reissues at the end of 1994 threw up more 'evidence'. One photograph included in new CD insert artwork for *A Momentary Lapse of Reason* included the word 'Enigma' in the bottom right-hand corner; another contained the word 'Publius'.

The mystery would remain unsolved, though lighting director Marc Brickman later claimed that he had been told by O'Rourke to arrange the stage signals at the shows in New Jersey and London. Nick Mason was the only band member ever to comment on the riddle. Questioned about it in 2005, he explained that it had, in fact, been the idea of a puzzle fanatic employed at EMI Records, but that no prize had ever been won. As a testament to the tenacity and obsessiveness of some fans, the Publius Enigma still commands its own dedicated website.

By the end of July, *The Division Bell* tour had reached Europe, and Polly Samson had become Mrs Gilmour. The Czech president, Vaclav Havel, attended the show at Prague's Starhov Stadium and invited the band to dinner. Yet one invitation issued by the band would not be accepted. With the tour due to end with a run of fourteen nights at London's Earls Court, the group invited Roger Waters to join them on stage for *Dark Side of the Moon*.

'I thought it would be a good thing for the fans,' explained Gilmour, 'but also with the safety cushion of knowing that he wouldn't do it. It was a genuine offer, though.'

Waters declined. He had maintained a dignified silence throughout *The Division Bell* tour, but would later denounce what he saw as 'the inherent betrayal' of Pink Floyd playing songs, especially those from *The Wall*, in football stadiums: 'There would have to be some other reason for me to stand on stage with Dave Gilmour and play *Dark Side of the Moon*. There's too much history.'

The first night at Earls Court proved a disaster. No sooner had Jon Carin struck up the opening notes to 'Shine On You Crazy Diamond', than he found himself pulled off stage again. A 1,200-capacity stand at the rear of the arena had collapsed just as the show began. No one was seriously injured, however, and the band rescheduled the gig for the following week. On another night at Earls Court, author Douglas Adams, who was celebrating his birthday, was invited to strap on an acoustic guitar and join the band on stage for 'Brain Damage'.

The last gig at Earls Court would be the last of the tour, and, as it transpired, the final night of any Pink Floyd tour. The complete opposite to the *Momentary Lapse* . . . eighteen-month marathon, this one had lasted less than twelve. 'Some people were pissed off that it hadn't been made the full year,' ventures Tim Renwick. 'I can't say what the full reasons were but I suspect it was partly because Polly was new to the whole thing and found it all quite difficult.'

In truth, perhaps Gilmour simply felt there was nothing more to prove. Having played to over 5 million people and grossed some £150 million, how much more did Pink Floyd need? 'Wasn't it one of the most successful rock tours in history?' ventures Bob Ezrin. 'In David's mind there must have been some feeling of wanting to prove that he could do it without Roger Waters. He wouldn't be human if he didn't have that sense of, "So *there*, Rog." '

'Pink Floyd is not only me,' offered Gilmour. 'I'm bound up by other people's desires and choices and politics, as well as my own. I have more say than anyone else, but I'm the one to whom that position has fallen. But not through choice.'

He was clearly in no hurry to do it all again.

Summer 1995 would see the death of another of the Cambridge contingent's old associates. In July, Gilmour attended the funeral of Julian Hough. A theatre and television actor during the 1970s and '80s, Hough had been another victim of what Anthony Stern describes as 'The Cambridge Syndrome'. The son of a brilliant academic, the literary historian Graham Hough, Julian had been stricken with depression and drifted into a life of homelessness. He had not been heard from in months when his body was finally found and identified.

In June 1995, less than a year after the final show on *The Division Bell* tour, Pink Floyd released *Pulse*, a double live album. A video of the show from Earls Court followed soon after. The first 2 million copies of the album were issued in a limited edition box with an LED flashing light on the spine, a novelty that soon riled anyone watching TV in their living room, constantly aware of a red light blinking away on the shelf. It topped the charts in both America and the UK.

Arriving so soon after 1988's *Delicate Sound of Thunder*, *Pulse* seemed superfluous. Its only real point of interest was a live version of *Dark Side of the Moon*. Nick Mason admitted that it was a crying shame they'd never thought to sanction an official live version of the piece in the seventies.

Listening at home, without Storm Thorgerson's mind-blowing movies and 400 Varilights to dazzle the senses, there were also plenty of moments when you noticed the Waters-shaped hole in the band. While Guy Pratt tried hard, nobody else could do that hectoring, maniacal vocal on 'Run Like Hell' with quite such gusto. 'Comfortably Numb' slowed to a torpid crawl, with Richard Wright bluffing away in place of an absent Waters. As compensation, the keyboard player positively excelled on 'Astronomy Domine', another nagging reminder of how integral he had been to Pink Floyd's sound in the early days.

At the end of the year, it was announced that Pink Floyd were to be inducted into the Rock and Roll Hall of Fame. In January 1996, all three attended the ceremony at New York's Waldorf-Astoria Hotel. The band were presented with their award by Billy Corgan, frontman with Smashing Pumpkins, an American hard rock band whose latest release had been a sprawling, conceptual affair partly inspired by *The Wall*. Corgan sat in with Wright and Gilmour for an acoustic version of 'Wish You Were Here', looking as if he couldn't quite believe his luck.

Unusually Richard Wright would become the most active member of Pink Floyd that year. While he had written and played on *The Division Bell*, he still had reservations about it: 'I liked the record, but it was also frustrating, because I felt that it wasn't going in the right direction all the time.' Wright had wanted to make 'A Floyd album, like we used to — more thematic, with all the music having a logical link.' It's not known whether he suggested any concepts of his own. Once again, without Waters, thematic ideas seemed a little thin on the ground.

Before *The Division Bell* tour had ended, though, Wright was telling interviewers of his immediate plans to make another solo album. That year, Wright licensed the music to 'The Great Gig in the Sky', enabling it to be re-recorded for use in a TV ad for a painkiller (Gilmour: 'That's Rick's business. I didn't approve of it but I had no control over it').

By spring 1995, Wright was in Studio Harmoine in Paris, working on a new album. He corralled some familiar names into helping out, including lyricist Anthony Moore and guitarist Tim Renwick, along with drummer Manu Katche, whom Wright had seen playing on Peter Gabriel's world tour, and guest vocalist, and occasional thorn in Roger Waters' side, Sinead O'Connor. The album, *Broken China*, would be released the following year.

The inspiration behind the record came from much closer to home. Following the break-up of his first marriage, Wright had moved to Greece to be nearer his girlfriend Franka. The two married, but the relationship didn't last. By 1989, Wright had become involved with a twenty-eight-year-old model named Mildred Hobbs, known to all as

Millie, who would go on to become his third wife. Millie had been hospitalised suffering from clinical depression during the making of *The Division Bell*. *Broken China* told her story, though at first Wright was reluctant to reveal her identity, only telling interviewers that it was about a 'close friend that suffered from depression'.

'It was a moral dilemma,' he explained later. 'I wasn't using Millie's name in the beginning because I didn't want it to be seen as me using her to promote the album.' Odder still, Wright would also reveal that his wife's former therapist, Gerry Gordon, had contributed lyrics to two of the songs on the album.

There was clearly something purgative about *Broken China*, as it charted his wife's experiences through the different stages of her illness. Musically, it explored the more ambient aspects of Pink Floyd's sound. The instrumentals, 'Sweet July' and 'Interlude', could have soundtracked a reflective spell in a flotation tank. 'Runaway' was more *outré*, with voguish percussion that wouldn't have sounded out of place on an album by the then ultra-hip Massive Attack. (The Orb would later remix the song.) David Gilmour played guitar on 'Breakthrough', but, according to Wright, didn't make the final mix (although Gilmour would later perform the song live himself). Sinead O'Connor proved a sympathetic collaborator, delivering a piteous vocal on both 'Breakthrough' and 'Reaching for the Rail'. Wright's lead vocal on *The Division Bell* had been a high point, but his voice was less enduring over the long run, even if, on 'Hidden Fear' there was almost something of Scott Walker in his haughty, sombre tone. As someone who would admit to his own periods of depression, Wright's empathy with the subject matter was obvious.

In its Storm Thorgerson-designed sleeve, *Broken China* looked very much like a Pink Floyd album. The trouble is, it wasn't.

Suffering a similar fate to most Floyd members' solo works, the album failed to sell beyond the staunchest Floyd supporters. By the end of the year, Wright had dropped back out of view, concentrating on being a father to his young son, Benjamin, and heading off to the Virgin Islands on his yacht. Asked about the current status of Pink Floyd, Wright's pithy reply seemed wholly accurate: 'Pink Floyd is like a marriage that's on permanent trial separation.'

Observers could catch only fleeting glimpses of Pink Floyd as the decade wound to an end. Gilmour became a father again. Having adopted Polly's son Charlie, the couple would go on to have three more children: Joe, Gabriel and Romany. Being a member of Pink Floyd in the seventies and eighties had helped destroy all of the band members' first marriages. As Gilmour later explained, 'Raising my children is my priority now, and not missing their youth. That happened with my first children.'

Gilmour would also trade in the classic cars and vintage aeroplanes he'd once owned, withdrawing from Intrepid Aviation, the company he'd started to help fund his flying hobby. What had begun as a pastime had quickly become too much of a business. 'You collect Ferraris and then you've got to collect people to look after your Ferraris,' he observed. 'Life gets very complicated.'

Gilmour turned fifty in 1996, and hired London's Fulham Town Hall for an exclusive performance by the Floyd tribute band, The Australian Pink Floyd, and their Fab Four counterparts, The Bootleg Beatles. The presence of George Harrison among Gilmour's guests added an extra frisson to the occasion. Guy Pratt and Richard Wright joined the fake Floyd on stage for a rousing encore of 'Comfortably Numb'. The subsequent changes in Gilmour's life and choice of friends were summed up by one of those that attended the party: 'There are some of us who were invited to Dave's fiftieth but didn't get invited to his sixtieth. I think the fiftieth was the cut-off point for some of the people in his life.'

In 1999 Polly Samson published her first collection of short stories, *Lying in Bed*. She and Gilmour were now more likely to appear in the pages of society magazines than music papers. When snapped at some exclusive event, Gilmour, however, would usually look ill at ease. Once asked how he dealt with being recognised in the street, he explained that his automatic response was to 'duck my head or look in a shop window'.

In the same year, Gilmour submitted to a rare interview with *Q* magazine, answering readers' questions. Asked what he did all day, he replied: 'Change a nappy, take a child to school, strum a guitar . . .' He didn't even know if he still had a solo record deal: 'I'll have to ask my lawyer.' Gilmour seemed in no hurry to return to the fray, preferring family life in his new West Sussex farmhouse. Several Floyd fans wrote to the magazine complaining about his disappointing attitude. But were they really surprised?

'Dave's problem is he worked damn hard on *A Momentary Lapse of*

Reason and he took the whole thing on his shoulders,' offered Richard Wright. 'When it came to *The Division Bell*, he felt he was taking the whole thing on his shoulders again, and I don't think he's in any hurry to do it again.'

'To be honest, I just don't know what I want to do,' said Gilmour. 'And I'm afraid the others will just have to wait for me. It's hard. Pink Floyd is a lumbering great behemoth to rouse out of its torpor.' Instead, it was easier for Gilmour to keep his hand in, playing on other people's records. In 1999, he guested on Paul McCartney's rock 'n' roll album *Run Devil Run*, showing up in his backing band for an appearance on the TV chat show *Parkinson*.

Nick Mason was now living with his new family in Camilla Parker-Bowles's old house in the Wiltshire village of Corsham ('She was very helpful and gave me many tips about gardening'). His enduring love of speed and cars found him becoming a regular competitor in the London to Brighton vintage car rally. In 2000, he clambered back behind the drum kit for a fund-raising party for the fiftieth anniversary of Formula 1. Having described himself at various times as the band's 'ship's cook' and 'sous chef', Mason's willingness to play down his role in Pink Floyd was rather disingenuous. He was the closest the band had to an archivist, having diligently kept scrapbooks during the group's earliest years.

Just after *The Division Bell* tour, Mason began writing his own book about the band. 'Then I ran up against a lot of disapproval from Dave,' he reveals, 'because at one point it was going to be the official history of Pink Floyd.' Gilmour's main objections were that he thought Mason would treat the subject with too much levity and that any official history of the band would have to involve input from all the members, past and present.

'There was a period of mild deception,' Gilmour complained later, 'as there was a chap taking pictures on *The Division Bell* tour without me knowing anything about it. I got rather grumpy about the book, because I didn't think that what I saw conveyed enough of the artistic process, and asked him to can it, which he did.' Some suggested that Mason not performing on stage with Gilmour and Wright at the Rock and Roll Hall of Fame ceremony was evidence of Gilmour's disapproval.

Although temporarily shelved, Mason's book, *Inside Out: A Personal History of Pink Floyd*, would surface in 2004, after each of the band members, including Roger Waters, had read the manuscript. Further amendments would be made between the book's hardback and paperback publications.

'Ten or fifteen years ago I was the tall guy in black, standing in the corner, scowling at everyone. And I don't feel like that now,' Roger Waters lectures Trent Reznor, rock music's latest version of the tall guy in black. In 1999 the two were put together for a shared interview in the American magazine, *Revolver*.

Waters had never heard Reznor's band, the angsty, agitated Nine Inch Nails. However, Reznor, twenty-three years Waters' junior, had spent his troubled childhood on a farm in the middle of Pennsylvania, where Pink Floyd's *The Wall* was something of a lifeline. Waters seemed genuinely touched on learning this.

On being told that Reznor's last album had sold poorly, he offered some more fatherly advice: 'Modigliani never sold any pictures; Van Gogh peddled his for a bowl of soup. I've been through some of the same things.'

It had been nine years since Waters performed *The Wall* in Berlin. Nine years in which Pink Floyd had made another album and promoted it with one of the highest grossing tours in history. In the meantime, Waters had returned to family life and tinkering, endlessly it seemed, with his planned opera about the history of the French Revolution.

'I think at some point we've all had the "opera conversation",' admits ex-Bleeding Heart Band guitarist Jay Stapley. Waters had first publicly discussed his plans in 1989. In September 1995, word spread that the work, entitled *Ça Ira*, and co-written with Waters' friends, the French librettist Étienne Roda-Gil and his wife Nadine Delahaye, would be released the following year. By the summer of 1997, it had still not materialised, although it was said that Waters was now in discussions about a stage play of *The Wall*, and also making another solo rock album.

Ça Ira had begun in 1988 when Roda-Gil presented Waters with a libretto, suggesting that he set it to music. Waters ended up demoing a two-and-a-half-hour piece at the Billiard Room in East Sheen. This had found its way to the then French president, François Mitterand, who suggested the Paris Opera record it as part of the upcoming bicentennial celebration of the French Revolution. And then, nothing. 'It sat on the shelf for six years,' explained Waters. This was partly due to the sudden death of Nadine, but also to some resistance elsewhere because, according to Waters, 'me being English stuck in the Gallic craw'.

Étienne Roda-Gil died in 2004, and a year later Waters recruited a co-producer, Rick Wentworth, and went into Abbey Road Studios with an orchestra to record several sections from the opera, as a taster for his new label, Columbia. The company offered him a deal for the album but suggested he write an English version. Waters went back to the score, adding in new scenes and later recording in both French and English.

Finally, in 1999, he broke his silence: not with *Ça Ira*, or a new solo album, but with a series of live dates. 'Roger Waters in the Flesh' opened in Wisconsin in July 1999 and continued for just over a month, before resuming the following summer. Promotional posters for the show trumpeted Waters as 'The Creative Genius of Pink Floyd', and the setlist was designed to drive this message home. Several chunks of *The Wall* vied for space with 'Shine On You Crazy Diamond', 'Brain Damage', 'Wish You Were Here' and the obligatory segments from *The Final Cut* and his solo records. Partway into the tour, Waters began playing a new song, 'Each Small Candle', as his final encore.

Eric Clapton's former guitarist Doyle Bramhall II now joined mainstays Andy Fairweather-Low and Snowy White, while keyboard player Andy Wallace was now sharing the stage with Pink Floyd's Jon Carin. Producer James Guthrie had worked with both Floyd and Waters, and had brokered the exchange between the two camps. Gilmour gave his blessing ('You must do it,' he told Carin. 'He's a brilliant man'). On stage Jon would also cover some of the vocal parts formerly sung by his old boss, most notably on a version of 'Dogs' from the *Animals* album.

Aside from 1991's Guitar Legends festival, Waters had played live only once since *The Wall* in Berlin: at a benefit show in aid of the preservation of Walden Woods, in Massachusetts in 1992. The Eagles' Don Henley, whose band backed Waters on a handful of Floyd songs, had arranged the charity concert. This gig had been the catalyst for the current tour.

'I really enjoyed the contact with the audience that night,' admitted Waters, 'and thought maybe I should have another go at it. After I toured *Radio K.A.O.S.*, I stopped in the face of a lack of demand. I felt like I was banging my head against a brick wall.'

In the event, some of Waters' gigs had to be moved to larger venues to accommodate the crowds, and also the size of the projection screen being used behind the stage. For some watchers, there was still the issue of rearranged Floyd songs to be overcome, especially a sprightly, funked-up version of 'Another Brick in the Wall Part 2', which concluded with a tag-team guitar solo by Snowy White and Doyle Bramhall II. Assuming his customary persona of the 'tall guy in black', Waters soon had a familiar routine: part circus ringmaster, part orchestral conductor, and part rock star. When Bramhall or Jon Carin were singing, he would mouth the words, smile dotingly from the sidelines, or loom over Andy Fairweather-Low, wringing the neck of his bass like a farmer seeing off a particularly plucky Christmas turkey. In a stark contrast to his onstage persona with Pink Floyd, Waters appeared to be having the time of his life.

'He has his eye and ear on everything,' said Fairweather-Low. 'At the end of the show, if a single lighting cue is wrong, Roger's aware of it. I have never worked with anyone like it.'

Jon Carin talked Richard Wright into attending one of the shows. 'I found it difficult listening to him performing Pink Floyd songs because I wanted to be up there,' Wright told writer Jerry Ewing. 'When they were playing "Comfortably Numb" and "Wish You Were Here" it just wasn't as good, but when it got to his solo work, I could relax.'

Carin and Wright's wife Millie persuaded him to go backstage after the show. 'I hadn't seen Roger in, what, eighteen or nineteen years,' said Wright. 'So I shook his hand, said, "How are you?" and we both felt awkward. And that was it. There was no great meaningful conversation. But I thought: We're grown men now; all this bullshit should stop.'

With the first leg of the tour over, Waters helped oversee a remastered version of *The Wall* movie, providing a running commentary with Gerald Scarfe. Director Alan Parker, the third 'megalomaniac' in the equation, also contributed. EMI and Pink Floyd had no intention of allowing the twentieth anniversary of *The Wall* album to pass unnoticed. March 2000 saw the release of *Is There Anybody Out There? The Wall Live: Pink Floyd 1980–81*, pieced together over seven nights at Earls Court.

In an unusual display of détente between the estranged parties, Waters and Pink Floyd were all interviewed about the album, though neither could resist the occasional snipe at each other. If the others weren't quite so taken with it, Waters' opinion of *The Wall* remained undiminished. He told everyone that, if pushed, he thought it was still his finest achievement to date. Back on tour throughout the US that summer, Waters would feature five songs from the album in his set, commemorated with a live album and video also entitled *In the Flesh*.

In 2001 there were some harsh reminders of everyone's mortality. The year would see the premature deaths of Roger's first wife, Judy Trim, Gilmour's friend the author Douglas Adams, and the band's former booking agent and tour manager Tony Howard. Gilmour would perform at a memorial service for Adams later that summer. Also that year, he would be invited by old friend Robert Wyatt to participate in the annual Meltdown Festival at London's Royal Festival Hall. Wyatt was the curator of the week-long event that also featured performances by Elvis Costello and Tricky. In his first solo show since 1984, Gilmour mixed old Floyd faithfuls, including 'Comfortably Numb' and 'Shine On You Crazy Diamond', with the Syd Barrett gem 'Terrapin' and such oddities as 'Hush-A-Bye Mountain' from the movie *Chitty Chitty Bang Bang*. Also included was a brand-new composition, 'Smile'.

Gilmour would return to the Royal Festival Hall for three nights, six months later. Playing the same eclectic set, he was joined by Richard Wright for one song. A week later he played two further nights in Paris. Asked if Pink Floyd had now split up, Gilmour's answer was the most decisive it had been: 'I can't see us doing anything in the near future. I have something else I'm doing, and that's what my mind is concentrating on.' He was now plotting another solo album.

The first hesitant steps towards reconciling the past and present members of the band would be taken in January 2002. At a beach party on the Caribbean holiday island of Mustique, Nick Mason had an unexpected encounter with Roger Waters. 'I suddenly felt a forceful pair of hands grasp my shoulders and then my neck,' Mason wrote later. The two old friends would spend the afternoon together, having their first proper conversation in years.

A month later, Waters was back out on tour, with two shows planned at London Wembley Arena in June. Mason was invited to play drums on 'Set the Controls for the Heart of the Sun' at both shows. He accepted the offer, pattering around the kit on the Floyd's vintage space odyssey. It was the first time the two former friends had played on stage since *The Wall* in 1981. Waters' son Harry, whose voice as a three-year-old could be heard on *The Wall*, was now playing keyboards in his father's band. Harry was Mason's godson.

Playing live again was an opportunity for Waters to take his mind off events elsewhere in his life. He was going through another period of profound change. His third marriage, to Pricilla, had now broken down and they would soon divorce, but he now had a new partner, the actress and film-maker Laurie Durning.

Waters addressed the upheaval in his life with unflinching honesty. 'Through twenty years of psychotherapy, I've finally managed to learn to live in the moment,' he told *The Times*. 'I had some very powerful feelings of abandonment when I was a child, which I'm only beginning to extricate myself from now. I'm nearly sixty and I'm just beginning to feel I can operate as an adult.'

Pink Floyd's legacy would be revisited again before the year was out. In November, EMI released *Echoes: The Best of Pink Floyd*. Choosing the twenty-six tracks proved something of a chore. Interviewed just before the album's release, Gilmour explained that Waters had all but given up on the song selection. 'He gets very grumpy because he thinks I tell Nick and Rick what they've got to do and outvote him,' said the guitarist. 'But I don't think six tracks from *The Final Cut* is what people want. I wanted "Fat Old Sun" on there but none of the others were having it . . .'

The final selection acknowledged all eras of the band's history. Syd Barrett received a royalties boost with the inclusion of five of his songs. Waters, meanwhile, smarted over the presence of tracks from *A Momentary Lapse of Reason* and *The Division Bell*. 'It pisses me off no end that tracks from those records get included. But there's nothing I can do about it.'

Waters, nevertheless, had the opportunity to indulge himself with his own compilation, *Flickering Flame: The Solo Years Part 1*. Splicing together the best songs from each of his albums, it was a more inviting listening experience than any of the original records. As Waters wearily told inter-viewers when discussing his challenging solo albums, 'I now realise that not everyone wants to go that deep.' The one new song, 'Flickering Flame', included a stream-of-consciousness lyric that was in parts incredibly bombastic, especially when Waters likened himself to legend-ary Native Americans such as Geronimo and Crazy Horse, insisting that, like them, he'll be 'the last one to lay down my gun'. Elsewhere in the song, though, he acknowledged his marital problems and the death of his friend Philippe Constantin (whose 1976 interview with Waters remains one of the most revealing ever). The final telling lines offered a plea to his own ego to 'let go of the bone', with the hope that he might then, finally, be free.

The thirtieth anniversary reissue of *Dark Side of the Moon*, now retitled *The Dark Side of the Moon*, was the only Pink Floyd activity in 2003. Instead of the album's original engineer Alan Parsons, long-time Floyd collaborator James Guthrie oversaw the 5.1 Surround Sound mix. Waters, Gilmour, Mason and Wright roused themselves to talk to the press. For once, the backbiting was kept to a minimum. Instead, the band sounded genuinely proud of their achievement, even if only Waters claimed to have known all along just how good it really was: 'One of the truly great moments in the history of rock 'n' roll.'

David Gilmour, however, found himself in the newspapers for his non-Floyd activities. The year before he had sold his Georgian house in London's Little Venice to Earl Spencer and publicly donated the money, £3.6 million, to the homeless charity Crisis. Just as surprising was his atypical willingness to talk publicly about the donation. 'Quite frankly, I don't need that money,' he said, 'I have more than enough.' At the end of the year, Gilmour was awarded a CBE medal for his philanthropy and services to music. Photographed outside Buckingham Palace, immaculately groomed and impeccably dressed in a morning suit, Gilmour looked less like a rock star and more like a retired captain of industry.

However, the year would be marred again by the death of two more of the Floyd's close confidants. In October, manager Steve O'Rourke had a stroke in Miami, Florida, and died soon after. O'Rourke had been the band's sole manager since 1968. When Bryan Morrison sold the management wing of his agency to Brian Epstein's company, NEMS Enterprises, O'Rourke went with Pink Floyd, later managing them through his own company, EMKA Productions. A fanatical motor racing enthusiast, O'Rourke had been competing until 2000 with his own EMKA racing team, when a heart problem forced him to stop driving. He was described by one former colleague as 'a larger than life character, who knew both his own strengths and weaknesses'. Gilmour, Mason and Wright would perform 'Fat Old Sun' and 'The Great Gig in the Sky' at his funeral service. Waters, who'd fallen out with O'Rourke in the early eighties, did not attend. Barely a month later, orchestral arranger, composer and regular Floyd collaborator Michael Kamen would suffer a fatal heart attack. The deaths of his close friends would inform many of the songs on Gilmour's next solo record.

Nick Mason's long-delayed book about Pink Floyd would be published in the summer of 2004. *Inside Out: A Personal History of Pink Floyd* was a fascinating account of life inside the band. Later, Roger Waters would complain of Mason's artistic licence in approaching the facts and a tendency to suggest that the band, rather than Waters alone, were responsible for many key decisions. In truth, there were enough points of trivia to appease the most committed fan, including numerous photographs from the drummer's own archives, and enough witty, knockabout anecdotes to keep the less earnest reader interested. Film director Alan Parker, who, it seems, never quite got over the experience of working with Roger Waters on *The Wall*, claimed that the book made him laugh so much his wife feared he had Tourette's Syndrome. There were plenty of places Mason's book chose not to go – sex and drugs being two of them – but how much was down to his own decision or those of his bandmates was never revealed. To support its publication, the drummer also embarked on a most un-Floydlike promotional campaign; book signings, readings, meet-and-greets and numerous interviews.

News that his book was coming out prompted the commissioning of a special issue of *Q* magazine dedicated to Pink Floyd. David Gilmour twice declined a request for an interview. Richard Wright's whereabouts seemed unknown ('We think he's sailing,' somebody at EMI explained). Roger Waters was no longer on tour, but in the news again after declaring his support for War On Want's campaign against the recently built Peace Wall, now dividing the Palestinian community in Israel. Waters had been pictured spray-painting the words 'No thought control' on the offending structure.

Waters agreed to talk, and his manager Mark Fenwick explained that he would call the magazine's writer at some point over a given weekend and that he should await the call (a sly variation, perhaps, on the 'Calculated Lateness Factor'). When it was pointed out that it might be a little harsh to expect someone to sit by the telephone for forty-eight hours, he relented and agreed to a specific time. Waters was as good as his word. At the end of the interview, when asked if he could anticipate any thaw in relations between himself and Gilmour, he replied, 'I can't think why. We're both quite truculent individuals.' Waters now had other matters to focus on. A month later, it was announced that he had sold the rights to develop and produce a Broadway musical of *The Wall* to the Miramax film company and music entrepreneur Tommy Mottola. 'Great,' Waters quipped. 'Now I can write in some laughs.'

Nick Mason was his usual effusive self. Calling in from home, dogs snuffling and barking in the background, Mason joshed his way through the band's history, carefully sidestepping questions about sex and drugs ('I think that territory has moved from rock 'n' roll to football now'), but confessing that, yes, he'd love it if Pink Floyd played live again: 'It would be fantastic if we could do it for something like another Live Aid; a significant event of that nature would justify it.' A year later, that remark would come back to haunt him.

In May 2005, Tim Renwick, David Gilmour's stunt double and Cambridge compadre, got married again. Gilmour was a guest at the wedding reception. 'Dave said, "Live 8's happening on 2 July, put it in your diary," ' recalls Tim now. 'I said, "Oh, are you doing it?" He said, "We are definitely not doing it, but just to let you know if you wanted to keep that date free." '

On 31 May, Live 8 organiser Bob Geldof made the official announcement that ten benefit concerts would be staged worldwide to raise money for the Make Poverty History campaign. Looking for some suitably legendary names to join the likes of Madonna, U2 and Sir Paul McCartney at the gig in London's Hyde Park, Geldof later recalled hearing about Mason's comment that Pink Floyd might consider reforming for 'another Live Aid'. In Geldof's mind, this meant re-forming with Roger Waters, which was just the sort of historic reunion the concert needed.

Guy and Gala Pratt were on holiday in Formentera with the Gilmours when Guy read in the *Daily Telegraph* that Floyd were reuniting for Live 8. He had just signed up to play bass on the next Roxy Music tour, and was immediately contacted by Roxy's tour manager. 'I was like, "It is not happening!" ' laughs Guy. ' "I'm with David now. It will take more than Bob Geldof's ego to get that lot back together." '

Geldof telephoned Mason, who told him he thought he was probably wasting his time. Geldof called Gilmour and made his request outright. The guitarist turned him down flat. 'I told him I was right in the middle of making my album,' said Gilmour. 'He said, "I'll come down and see you." So he jumped on the train . . .'

Gilmour phoned Geldof on his mobile phone and told him to turn back. Having now arrived at East Croydon station, in the heart of the Surrey commuter belt, Geldof was near enough for Gilmour to begrudgingly agree to drive from his Sussex farmhouse and pick him up.

'He was a bit grumpy but he turned up in this lovely old Merc, and we went back to his place,' Geldof told *The Word* magazine. Back at the farm, Geldof went into his pitch, while Gilmour listened attentively. Eventually, he asked for a few days to mull it over before making his final decision.

In the meantime, Nick Mason had e-mailed Roger Waters, cagily explaining that Geldof had approached them about re-forming Pink Floyd for Live 8. Waters took the bait and called Geldof directly. 'Bob was just about to take his better half out for a birthday dinner,' recalled Waters. 'So our conversation was a little disjointed. Lots of saving the world interspersed with, "That looks great, try it with the other shoes . . ."'

Waters heard nothing more from Geldof for over two weeks, during which time Geldof wrote an impassioned letter to Gilmour asking him to reconsider. Mason believed that the only thing that would make the guitarist change his mind would be a call from Waters. Roger agreed and picked up the phone.

The last time he and Gilmour had spoken since their final lawyers' meeting in 1987 had been a couple of years earlier. Back then, they'd had an argument about a TV programme on the making of *Dark Side of the Moon*. According to Gilmour, 'Roger's memory had failed him slightly on one minor point, and we had to try to sort it out.' The result had been a four-way conference call with the two shouting at each other. Since then, nothing.

'It was . . . surprising,' Gilmour admitted. 'We chatted quite pleasantly for a minute or two and I said I'd call him back the next day when I'd thought about it. I thought about it, and thought that I'd probably always regret it if I didn't do it.' Twenty-four hours later he telephoned Waters and said, 'OK, let's do it.'

Bob Geldof was stunned. 'I said to Gilmour, "You've made an old man very happy . . . Not that I can stand you cunts." Cos I never liked their music really.'

With the arch-rivals reunited, Richard Wright immediately agreed to take part.

Back in London, Guy Pratt answered his phone to find Gilmour at the other end: 'David said, "Are you sitting down?"' Waters had told Gilmour that ideally he wanted to play acoustic guitar on two songs, meaning they needed a bass player. However, Guy was committed to the Roxy Music tour and would be playing a gig with them at the German Live 8 concert. 'So I had two hours of pacing up and down thinking: What am I going to do?' says Guy. 'At one point, [Roxy's guitarist] Phil Manzanera phoned up to see how my pacing was going.' In the end, Guy decided to fulfil his commitment to Roxy Music.

David Gilmour, believing that the worthiness of the cause far outweighed a petty dispute between rock stars, issued a brief statement to the press: 'Any squabbles Roger and the band have had in the past are so petty in this context. If re-forming for this concert will help focus attention, then it's got to be worthwhile.' Waters was terser: 'The cynics will scoff. Screw 'em.'

A band meeting took place at London's Connaught Hotel to work out a setlist. Waters brought video recordings of his own band; Gilmour showed up with recordings from the Floyd's last two tours. There were, as Nick Mason later recalled, 'smiles and jokes all round', but also arguments over which songs to play.

'The first meeting was pretty stilted and cagey,' admitted Gilmour. 'It was weird going into that same room. The songs that Roger wanted to do were not the same ones that I thought we should do. Roger wanted to do "Another Brick in the Wall", but I didn't think it was appropriate. This was a thing for Africa and I didn't really think that little children in Africa should be singing, "We don't need no education." There was no argument about it. I was absolutely right.'

Gilmour said that Waters had also been keen to perform 'In the Flesh', while Nick Mason claimed Roger wanted to play 'Run Like Hell'. Both were songs from *The Wall*: angry, confrontational rock 'n' roll songs, appropriate in the context of the album's unstinting tale of music biz psychosis, but rejected, according to Mason, on the grounds that 'such fascist anthems might be bit brutal for the occasion'.

Waters relented and agreed to 'roll over for one night only'. He was also acutely aware of the irony of the Pink Floyd situation when compared to the Live 8 cause. 'It did seem that to be wandering around, espousing this idea of communicating and solving problems while not talking to Gilmour *was* hypocritical.'

Three days of rehearsals were booked at London's Black Island Studios. In the meantime, Gilmour put himself through his paces, rehearsing the set several times a day on his own at home. Extra assistance was also needed. Invited to join the four on stage were backing singer Carol Kenyon (who'd sung on *The Division Bell*), saxophonist Dick Parry, keyboard player Jon Carin and guitarist Tim Renwick. Waters would, however, play bass himself. For Carin and Renwick this was history repeating itself: Jon had played at Live Aid at Wembley with Bryan Ferry, while Tim had backed Eric Clapton at the show in Philadelphia.

'Two weeks before Live 8 I got this call,' says Renwick. 'And it was Dave, laughing. He said, "We're doing it now, and we're doing it with Roger." I was completely gobsmacked. I never imagined it. Dave said, "It'll be a real laugh" – except it wasn't a laugh at all.

'Roger was at least an hour late turning up each day. Then he'd turn up with this attitude of, "Right, I'm here now, we can begin" – which is what he used to do years ago. Then he'd be making wild suggestions about rearranging things because with his band he'd done things at different tempos. David, bless him, was very accommodating, but in the end he had to turn around and say, "Look, we're doing four numbers and at the end of the day, people are expecting to hear the hits *exactly* the way they sounded in the old days."'

The setlist squabbles only served to emphasise the polar opposites that Waters and Gilmour had become. For the bass-playing ideas man, it was all about the concept, the grand idea. For the guitarist, the music, and the audience, came first.

'It was awkward and uncomfortable,' admitted Gilmour later. 'My view was that I wanted it to be small, compact, the four of us with whatever help we needed, and Roger wanted to expand it a bit.'

'There wasn't a single person in that room that Roger hadn't upset at some point in his career,' laughs Renwick. 'So there was a lot of people standing around, looking very tight-lipped and being incredibly professional but keeping their heads down.'

The night before the show, Floyd convened for a final dress rehearsal at Hyde Park. In the event, the setlist was decided with 'Breathe', 'Breathe Reprise', 'Money' (partly at Bob Geldof's request), 'Wish You Were Here' and 'Comfortably Numb'. Pink Floyd were slated to appear as second on the bill, just below headliner Paul McCartney; a reversal of the roles at 1990's Knebworth. The Beatle would also open the show. Setting the tone for a day of one-off collaborations and fleeting reunions, McCartney struck up the opening fanfare of *Sgt Pepper's Lonely Hearts Club Band* backed by a rather rusty U2. 'Did that really happen?' asked Bono afterwards.

Backstage, only Nick Mason would allow himself to be buttonholed by roving BBC reporters. While refusing to succumb to any diva-ish tendencies, Floyd also discovered that, for some of the day at least, they would have to share their dressing room with, according to Gilmour, 'Snow Patrol or someone'. There was, as Tim Renwick recalls, 'an awful lot of hanging around'.

Out front, at 3 p.m., Elton John struggled manfully to perform a duet of T.Rex's 'Children of the Revolution' with disorientated rock casualty Pete Doherty. Four hours later, by the time Madonna dragged baffled Ethiopian famine survivor Birhan Woldo on stage for 'Like a Prayer', any timetable or sense of reason had long been abandoned. By 10.30 p.m., with the show almost an hour behind schedule, the bureaucratic forces of evil had threatened a curfew.

With a last-minute reprieve, the familiar sound of a human heartbeat could be heard booming across the darkened park: the beginning of *Dark Side of the Moon*. Pink Floyd could be glimpsed in the wings; a smattering of worn jeans, greying hair, nervous smiles – incongruous rock stars one and all. Behind the stage, a pig floated over Battersea Power Station. For the first time in almost twenty-five years, the four members of the classic Pink Floyd walked out on stage together. Hostilities suspended. For once, the lawsuits, recriminations, clashing egos and musical squabbles were forgotten. For the next few glorious minutes it was all about the music.

CHAPTER ELEVEN HEROES FOR GHOSTS

'You can't carry on World War Three for ever.'

Nick Mason

There was talk of tears backstage at Live 8. But only among some of the observers. Whether this was solely down to Pink Floyd or the slow erosion of inhibitions after a long day boozing in the Golden Circle, who knows? Anyone that anticipated David Gilmour and Roger Waters falling into a watery-eyed embrace would have had a long wait ahead of them. While some around the band later claimed to have been moved to tears by the band's performance, Pink Floyd retained the collective stiff upper lip that has been both their saving grace and greatest downfall. Yet, as they'd lined up for a final bow, they had all allowed themselves to look pleased, and, in Waters' case, rather triumphant.

Pink Floyd's eighteen minutes on stage eclipsed every performance before it that day, and the one after. By the following morning, a teeth-baring, madly grinning Roger Waters had become the most repeated photograph from Live 8 in all the Sunday newspapers.

Will they do it again? For the next few weeks, stories circulated of promoters promising ever more ridiculous sums of money, ranging from $150 to $250 million, depending on which newspaper or magazine you happened to be reading. Gilmour told anyone that asked that he turned them all down. He has, he insists, achieved closure. Though not without slipping in one last dig at his former nemesis: 'I've been offered the same amount of money to tour Pink Floyd with or without Roger.'

Waters couldn't resist responding: 'Maybe he doesn't quite get how important the symbiosis between the four of us was during the "golden years". We all made a contribution, but it was the combination of the four separate talents. It was a very, very, special thing.'

For the man who once denounced his bandmates as 'the muffins' and had, he claimed on occasion, been its sole driving force, this was a remarkable change of heart. In the months immediately following Live 8, Waters would seem to be the one extending the olive branch. 'I hope we can do it again,' he said. 'If there was another special occasion – something with a political or charitable connection. I could even imagine us doing *Dark Side of the Moon* again.'

Richard Wright remained silent, but Nick Mason couldn't quite help himself: 'My bag is packed and ready to go.' Ever the arbitrator, Mason was just as quick to explain why he didn't think Gilmour was in a hurry to do it all again. 'David had the most to lose by doing Live 8. He's been working on his solo album for some time now, and I think he felt, quite rightly, that doing Pink Floyd again would take all the attention away from that.'

In November, the Floyd drummer and guitarist appeared together in London for Pink Floyd's induction into the UK Music Hall of Fame. Floyd fan Pete Townshend delivered a glowing introductory speech. Wright was unable to attend as he was having an eye operation ('poor sausage,' explained Gilmour). Waters was in Rome for a performance of *Ça Ira*, but was visible above Mason and Gilmour as a looming Orwellian presence on the overhead video screen. It was a moment of dark comedy. Gilmour's off-the-cuff dedication to Roger, Syd and 'all the passengers on this fabulous ride we've been on' saw Waters' face darken briefly. 'I confess I never felt like a passenger,' he shot back. Mason ended the performance with a rather excruciating drummer joke. Gilmour looked, as ever, as if he couldn't wait to go home.

Almost a year after Live 8, though, the guitarist had something to smile about. His third solo album, *On an Island*, was a number 1 hit in the UK, breaking the traditional run of lacklustre sales for Floyd solo records. The inconvenience of playing Live 8 had clearly paid off. In the absence of Pink Floyd, people had gone out and bought the next best thing: a David Gilmour album.

On an Island was a marking post in the guitarist's life. Released on 6 March 2006, his sixtieth birthday, it seemed to revisit his past while suggesting a settled, happy present and future. Among the contributors were fellow Cantabrigians, ex-Jokers Wild and *The Wall* surrogate band drummer Willie Wilson and guitarist Rado Klose, once part of The Pink Floyd Sound. Now working as a photographer, Klose has remained Gilmour's friend since childhood. 'David phoned up and said, "Are you still playing?"' says Klose. 'We hadn't played together in forty years. It was an interesting experience.' Klose bailed out of Pink Floyd in 1965, 'but I watched, sometimes with open-mouthed amazement, at what happened afterwards. In Cambridge, Floyd are like this huge gravitational object, with a lot of different tribes orbiting around it. I preferred to watch them from a distance.'

Among the album's other guests were singers David Crosby and Graham Nash, Roxy Music guitarist Phil Manzanera, songwriter Robert Wyatt and Poland's leading film composer Zbigniew Preisner. Their presence never impinged on Gilmour's, though. *On an Island* was a vehicle for his voice and guitar playing. There was none of the flash of his last solo album, *About Face*, or the uncertainty of the first. Instead, it was a laid-back, elegiac and terribly English-sounding record. Once again, his co-writer Polly Samson has helped eke out Gilmour's innermost thoughts, or at least tried to. 'Polly thinks I'm a little autistic,' Gilmour told one interviewer.

'The album has a feeling of contentment to it,' he said. 'Tied with elements of melancholy, nostalgia and regret.' Dedicated to the memory of the late Michael Kamen and Tony Howard, songs such as 'The Blue' revisited a dust-to-dust, ashes-to-ashes theme of mortality that had often crept into Gilmour's work. 'I've always thought a lot about mortality and it used to scare me deeply.' Sadly, in the month of the album's release, yet another of Pink Floyd's foot-soldiers, engineer Nick Griffiths, died following a transplant operation.

As a contrast, on the song 'Smile' Gilmour sounded at the pinnacle of family-man contentment. On 'This Heaven' he explored his feelings about spirituality, albeit from an atheist's perspective: 'It's about heaven being here on earth. That thing of being in a church or a place of worship where you can feel the power in the building.' Only one song, 'Take a Breath', worked up a head of steam, though: the guitar clanging away in a manner oddly reminiscent of Syd Barrett's more electric moments on *The Piper at the Gates of Dawn*. *On an Island* was an album made to please one person: Gilmour himself. Anyone else was a bonus. 'We sometimes sit here, with a glass of wine of an evening and listen to the album from start to finish,' he revealed. 'And I still think it sounds fantastic.'

Gilmour launched the album with a BBC-recorded show at London's Mermaid Theatre, before embarking on a world tour. His choice of bandmates did little to quell the clamour for a Pink Floyd reunion. While drummer Steve DiStanislao and Phil Manzanera were relative new boys, Guy Pratt, Dick Parry, Jon Carin and Richard Wright were familiar names. Carin, Parry and Wright had all played on the album also. With Wright performing stage left to Gilmour, shadowed by Jon Carin, it was a familiar set-up to anyone that had seen a Pink Floyd show in the eighties or nineties.

'Rick plays beautifully, he has soul and I like having him around,' offers Gilmour. 'My difficulty with him on this record was persuading him to get off his arse and come down and do some work. He came down and played Hammond. But then I wanted him to sing on one of them, and that was like pulling teeth. It's not laziness, just lack of confidence.'

Nevertheless, the notoriously diffident keyboard player would excel during the tour. Gilmour played a set loaded with Pink Floyd songs, revisiting *Obscured By Clouds* for 'Wot's . . . Uh The Deal', and *Atom Heart Mother* for his beloved 'Fat Old Sun'. Wright took the lead on his own Floyd song, 'Wearing the Inside Out', traded vocals with Gilmour on 'Time', and received a spontaneous round of applause every time he struck the opening note of 'Echoes', the mind-bending, prog-rock extravaganza from 1971. 'There was a beautiful heckle one night,' recalls Guy Pratt. ' "Give us a ping, Rick!" ' On the Continent, the audience's enthusiasm for Wright ensured that, even offstage, the keyboardist was jokingly referred to as

'Reeechard' in honour of the frequently heard shouts from the crowd.

In May, Gilmour played three nights at London's Royal Albert Hall. On one, David Bowie stepped up for a nervy version of 'Arnold Layne' and 'Comfortably Numb'. On the final night, Nick Mason took over on the drums for 'Wish You Were Here' and 'Comfortably Numb', making it a brief reunion for Pink Floyd Mark III. Mason was, however, otherwise engaged as Roger Waters' very occasional drummer. Fired up by Live 8, Waters had wasted little time in reviving the 'In the Flesh' tour. Opening in Lisbon at the beginning of June, Waters marched his troops through Italy, Iceland, Greece and Scandinavia, and on to London's Hyde Park. His band still included Floyd faithful Jon Carin, just finished playing on the Gilmour tour, and trusty lieutenants Andy Fairweather-Low, Snowy White and drummer Graham Broad, plus a new would-be guitar hero, David Kilminster, whose CV included previous stints with the likes of Emerson Lake & Palmer's Keith Emerson. Kilminster's art-rock credentials seemed appropriate, as the second half of Waters' show was now given over to the whole of *Dark Side of the Moon*. When their respective schedules or the handy timing of a motor racing event permitted it, Mason would play drums for the full rendition of Pink Floyd's classic 1973 album. With members split between the two rival camps, fans could now get two surrogate Floyds for their money.

On an Island's preoccupation with mortality seemed even more apt in the summer of 2006. On Friday 7 July, Syd died quietly in Cambridge. His health had been deteriorating for some time, and he had gone voluntarily to the hospital in which his father had once worked.

Friends and former bandmates learned of the news at the beginning of the following week. 'David Gilmour phoned me,' recalls Aubrey 'Po' Powell. 'He was the one who'd stayed in touch with the family more than any of the others. David knew he'd been ill, so he wasn't surprised. But I was. I felt incredibly shocked, even though this was somebody I hadn't seen for thirty-five years. I started thinking about when we'd gone to the first Windsor Rhythm and Blues Festival together. We'd all jumped in Syd's mum's old Austin 10, and got lost on the way. It was the first time Cream ever played. Syd was completely starstruck and rooted to the spot during the whole gig. It all came flooding back.'

In Cambridge, Clive Welham, Syd's one-time drummer in The

Mottoes, heard the news on the television: 'And then before the story had finished, the phone started ringing.' Welham had seen Barrett in town not long before, standing just a few feet in front of him, queuing in a shop. 'I didn't say anything to him,' says Clive. 'I did think about it, but then I thought: Why? He doesn't want to be disturbed.'

One day in Cambridge, Libby Gausden had chosen to approach the man who had once been her first boyfriend. 'I said, "Do you know who I am, Syd?" And he replied, "Of course I know who you are, you're Libby". He understood, but he wasn't quite right. My father had suffered a stroke, and it had hit his brain, and Syd's behaviour reminded me of that.'

Years later, Libby's daughter Abigail, then studying at Cambridge University, saw a man pedalling past her on a bicycle. Abigail was wearing one of her mother's Biba dresses from the 1960s. 'Hello little Lib,' he called out. 'Hello,' she replied, unaware of who he was. A friend pointed out that it was Syd Barrett.

Barrett had, however, been a part of these people's lives a long time ago. To all but his closest family members, he had become a ghost long before he died.

Pink Floyd kept their distance but released a simple statement to the press: 'The band are naturally very upset and sad to learn of Syd Barrett's death. Syd was the guiding light of the early band line-up and leaves a legacy which continues to inspire.'

Coincidentally, writer Tom Stoppard's latest play, *Rock 'n' Roll*, which included references to Barrett and extracts of Pink Floyd's music, had opened in London just weeks before Syd's death. Initially set in Cambridge in the 1960s, the play tackled the impact of rock music in Czechoslovakia and a disillusioned university don's struggle to cope with the erosion of his Communist beliefs. The play's opening scene found the don's daughter, the embodiment of a sixties 'hippie chick', pondering a chance encounter with the elusive Barrett to the strains of Syd's solo song, 'Golden Hair'. Both Nick Mason and David Gilmour attended performances of the play.

A quiet family funeral for Barrett took place at Cambridge Crematorium on 18 July. None of the band attended. Tributes to Barrett filled the national press as well as the usual music magazines. Contemporaries ranging from Elton John and David Bowie offered their memories and reflections. From the next generation of musicians,

Paul Weller offered a wry observation in *Mojo* magazine: 'Syd shone so bright for such a short space of time, everyone's vision is still trapped in that time.'

Meanwhile, in his conscious desire to 'smear politics and philosophy over my music', Roger Waters was now upsetting Middle America and distancing himself from Middle England. He had taken to performing a new song in concert. 'Leaving Beirut' was a piece inspired by his travels in the Middle East as a teenager; a throwback to the time when he and a crew of would-be Cambridge beatniks had crossed Europe in search of adventure. The song's anti-war message would be misinterpreted in some parts of America, where sensitivity about the country's involvement in the Iraq War was paramount. Waters was unapologetic. 'I paint what I see,' he told writer Jon Shults. 'I'd like to be remembered as somebody who spoke his truth and stuck by it through thick and thin.'

Waters' principles put him back into the newspapers again before the end of the year. He was now permanently resident in The Hamptons in upstate New York, home of his new partner, Laurie Durning. England, it transpired, had lost its appeal. 'I've become disenchanted with the political and philosophical atmosphere,' he told a visiting journalist from *The Times*. The passing of the anti-hunting bill a year before had been a deciding factor. Despite previously voicing his support for animal rights, Waters refused to buy all his politics and philosophical beliefs off the liberal peg. He attended marches with the Countryside Alliance and denounced the bill as 'one of the most divisive pieces of legislation we've ever had in Great Britain. It's not a case of whether or not I agree with fox hunting, but I will defend to the hilt their right to take part in it.'

Ça Ira finally appeared in September 2006. Loosely translated from the French as 'there is hope', this was Waters' three-act opera re-telling the story of the French Revolution. Waters did not perform himself on the album. Instead, Welsh baritone Bryn Terfel and Chinese soprano Ying Huang were among the performers. Though, as one reviewer pointed out, 'the sound is more Puccini than Pink Floyd'.

As many fans were aware, the opera had been in development since the end of the 1980s. The piece was premiered in its entirety in Rome in November 2005. A complete operatic performance was then staged in Poznan, Poland in August 2006, a month before the album was released.

Waters appeared on stage in a non-speaking part, playing the Pope (a performance sadly not preserved on film for posterity).

Despite customary suspicion among critics at any collaboration between the rock and classical worlds, reviews of *Ça Ira* were complimentary. 'The grand romanticism might throw some Waters die-hards,' wrote *Rolling Stone*, 'but the opera does reflect some of the man's long-term obsessions with war and peace, love and loss.'

'I've always been a big fan of Beethoven's choral music, Berlioz and Borodin,' explained Waters. 'This is unashamedly romantic and resides in that early nineteenth-century tradition, because that's where my tastes lie in classical and choral music.' *Ça Ira* topped the classical music charts, even if most of his fanbase had wished for a more traditional rock album instead. For Waters, however, the album's historical theme didn't detract from its relevance to a modern audience: 'It's about freedom, learning, reason, egalitarianism. How to find our way through modern life and come out the other end with more people happier more of the time.' Whatever the medium, this was familiar Roger Waters territory. Also, as an in-joke to his more dedicated fans, one piece, 'The Letter', used a melody line borrowed from 'Every Stranger's Eyes', a ballad on *The Pros and Cons of Hitch-hiking* ('For those that want to look for it: happy hunting').

Waters busied himself with promoting the album, even appearing on daytime TV chat shows to discuss the work and, inevitably, his relationship with Pink Floyd. The discussions followed a pattern of tackling the opera for 10 per cent of the time and Pink Floyd for the remaining 90 per cent, but Waters took it in his stride; a testament to his mellower old age or twenty years of dedicated psychotherapy. What *Ça Ira* proved above all else was Waters' ease with the role of composer and conceptualist; creating a piece of art for others to perform. This seemed a fitting new approach for a reluctant rock star who had just turned sixty-three.

In November, Syd Barrett's family auctioned his possessions through Cheffins auction house in Cambridge. Number 6 St Margaret's Square was also put up for sale. Among the idiosyncratic home furnishings were strangely customised door handles, offbeat colour schemes and Syd's hand-painted bicycles. Paul Weller's observation of a man trapped in a short space of time seemed all the more poignant when you glimpsed the place. This was the home of Roger Barrett, not 'Syd'. This man had lived frugally and, as it later transpired, below his means, surrounded by books, his own writings, including an unfinished history of art, and a clutch of CDs. No rock music, just jazz such as Miles Davis and Charlie Parker. His scatterbrained approach to DIY – a coffee table with a homemade compartment nailed underneath – seemed proof of his jumbled frame of mind. There was another bleaker side to his life. Unable or unwilling to tackle his health problems, Barrett had often neglected to take his medication and had, his sister Rosemary revealed, lost several fingers due to complications arising from his diabetes.

In December, David Gilmour announced plans to release a tribute single to Barrett: a live performance of 'Arnold Layne'. Earlier that month, the *Mail on Sunday* ran a story, headlined 'THE GENIUS NEXT DOOR', from David Sore, formerly Syd's neighbour in St Margaret's Square. He spoke of how intimidating he had found Syd's behaviour as a child growing up in the 1980s, recalling Barrett's sometimes very public rages, and bonfires in the back garden in which he burned his paintings and other possessions. Pink Floyd fans were intrigued, if a little amused, by Sore's claim that he had once heard Barrett shouting, 'Fucking Roger Waters! I'm going to fucking kill him!'

While many devotees had romanticised about Syd the recluse, rarely venturing beyond the local shops, the reality was rather different. Barrett had been catching the train to London unaccompanied for years, visiting art galleries and the Royal Botanical Gardens at Kew, near to where he'd once lived in Richmond Hill. He had also, as old friend Anthony Stern points out, 'become another great Cambridge eccentric – bicycling around the town'.

'Syd turned into Arnold Layne in the end,' smiles Libby Gausden. 'Which seemed so ironic. When we were growing up, there was a Cambridge eccentric who used to walk around with a bucket on her head. And Syd used to laugh, but he also used to make us all wonder *why* she had a bucket on her head, what happened to her that made her that way. Now Syd had become another of those odd people in Cambridge.'

When the BBC screened a television documentary about Syd and the early Pink Floyd in 2001, Barrett watched it non-committally, only telling his sister that it had been good to see his old landlord Mike Leonard again.

In the same year, photographer Mick Rock had published a book of his

Barrett photographs entitled *Psychedelic Renegades*. A limited edition run of the title included a flyleaf signed by Syd himself. Rock had negotiated the deal with Barrett's family for an unspecified sum of money, and Syd had been willing to sign his name – R. Barrett – on 325 pieces of paper, which were then bound into each of the copies. This was not quite the hopeless lunatic of legend, then. As Rosemary told one journalist: 'He was very mad, but he was able to do anything and everything he wanted to do.'

He was, it also transpired, a very rich man. Barrett left over £1.25 million in his will to be divided between his brothers and sisters. The inclusion of his songs on the *Echoes* compilation, the reissue of his solo albums and the ongoing interest in his work had reaped its rewards. While never dealing directly with Syd, David Gilmour had taken a close interest in ensuring that Barrett received his royalties. The auction of his possessions raised more money for the family, with some fans paying over £10,000 for Barrett's two bicycles, and over £50,000 for his artworks. As one of his former business associates from the sixties had once grumblingly explained: 'Don't believe all that stuff about poor old Syd, there's nothing actually *poor* about him.'

In 2003, Roger Waters had talked of making another rock album. 'It's another loony concept thing,' he explained. 'It's about a conversation in a New York bar, and one of the characters is a taxi driver from the Balkans, and his marriage is falling apart . . .' By early 2007, it still hadn't appeared. In March, Waters released a new download-only single, 'Hello (I Love You)', taken from the soundtrack to the science fiction movie *The Last Mimzy*. A rather slight song, it punched a lot of familiar Pink Floyd buttons, twisting *The Wall*'s lyric 'Is there anybody out there?' into 'Is there anybody in there?' for the chorus. Waters went back on the road, trekking through Australia, New Zealand and South America, again performing *Dark Side of the Moon*, and telling interviewers that he was open to the idea of playing with Pink Floyd again.

In March, the *New York Daily News* claimed that Floyd would reunite to perform at one of the planned Live Earth charity concerts in June. The Live Earth shows were being staged in seven continents to help raise awareness of global warming. Gilmour quickly denied that Pink Floyd would be appearing, though Waters agreed to play at the US show in the Giants Stadium in New Jersey.

Once again, it seemed as though Waters was trying to broker another reunion, only to find Gilmour unwilling. As Waters admitted in one interview, Pink Floyd had been Gilmour's baby for the past twenty years, and the guitarist's legendary obstinacy would make him unlikely to relinquish his control. Old wounds had yet to heal, and Waters knew that better than anyone. 'I don't think any of us came out of the years from 1985 with any credit,' he commented. 'It was a bad, negative time. And I regret my part in that negativity.'

2007 also marked the fortieth anniversary of the so-called Summer of Love and the release of Pink Floyd's debut album, *The Piper at the Gates of Dawn*. If there was no new Pink Floyd album, the band's past achievements were deemed ripe for reassessment. In April, the Institute of Contemporary Arts staged a multi-media event to mark the anniversary of 'The 14-Hour Technicolor Dream'. Once described by Peter Jenner as 'the height of acid use in England', the event would be commemorated with the screening of film footage from the original show, DJ sets, a one-man play, *The Madcap*, and live performances, including an appearance by The Crazy World of Arthur Brown and The Pretty Things, two of the bands that had performed at the original event.

Details of two further concerts were also announced at the same time. On 26 May, Robyn Hitchcock, Cambridge singer-songwriter and one-time frontman of The Soft Boys, and former Blur guitarist Graham Coxon headlined a tribute to Pink Floyd's 'Games for May' concert at the Queen Elizabeth Hall. Forty years earlier the band had upset the classical music venue's management by switching on a bubble machine and showering the audience with flowers, smearing the hall's leather seats with burst bubbles and squashed flower stems. It had also been the night Floyd premiered their second single, 'See Emily Play'. Pink Floyd's 1967-era lighting designer Peter Wynne-Willson was on hand to provide an authentic psychedelic backdrop; a role he would also undertake two weeks earlier at a tribute night to Syd Barrett, held at London's Barbican Theatre on 10 May.

Billed as 'Madcap's Last Laugh', the idea had first been mooted by the Barbican's programmer Bryn Ormrod following Barrett's death the year before. Ormrod approached Pink Floyd's original producer and mentor Joe Boyd, who brought in musician and sometime Pink Floyd lyricist Nick Laird-Clowes, once of David Gilmour's eighties protégés The Dream Academy, and now working under the nom-de-plume, Trashmonk.

Floyd gave the planned gig their blessing and allowed Laird-Clowes access to their archives for securing old footage of the band and Syd. In the meantime, Boyd and Laird-Clowes set about booking acts to appear. Tickets went on sale and sold well, despite an unconfirmed bill. In the weeks running up to the event, the names were released of those slated to appear. These included the ubiquitous Robyn Hitchcock, Blur's Damon Albarn, Chrissie Hynde and the Soft Machine's original vocalist and Syd's old contemporary Kevin Ayers. Fans and critics speculated on whether any of Pink Floyd would perform; the more eagle-eyed noting that Waters' never-ending *In the Flesh* tour was due to resume, after a day off, at Earls Court the night after the show.

Six days before the event, artist and Floyd confidant Storm Thorgerson threw a launch party for his latest book, *Taken by Storm*, at Abbey Road Studios. David Gilmour, Nick Mason and Richard Wright all attended, snapped together by the paparazzi, which prompted further speculation over whether any of them would attend the Barrett tribute. Wright, it later transpired, was the first to sign up, asking to perform 'Arnold Layne', a song he'd sung on Gilmour's last solo tour. From here on, the usual whirl of 'Will they, won't they?' rumours continued over the next few days. Nothing was confirmed, nothing was denied. Joe Boyd later explained that he had met up with Waters in New York some weeks before. 'He was friendly and interested, but not certain of coming along,' he noted.

An hour before showtime the word had spread among the media that Roger Waters would now definitely be performing. Those dropping into the hall's backstage catering area were greeted by the sight of the Floyd and Waters' musical right-hand man Jon Carin eating a meal sandwiched between former Soft Boy and Barrett aficionado Robyn Hitchcock and Led Zeppelin's old bass player John Paul Jones. There was no sign of Gilmour, Wright, Mason or Waters.

Without fuss or fanfare, the show opened with the sound of North Carolina bluesman Blind Boy Fuller, and a backdrop of the sleevenotes to one of his albums, featuring the highlighted names of fellow bluesmen Pink Anderson and Floyd Council. When the lights came up, the Sense of Sound choir, an eighteen-voice ensemble from Liverpool, struck up an a cappella rendition of 'Bike', the nursery rhyme-like closing song on *The Piper at the Gates of Dawn*.

The Damned's Captain Sensible plugged in for a faithful version of 'Flaming' from the same album. Kevin Ayers responded with a ramshackle rendition of Syd's 'Here I Go' and his own ode to Barrett, 'Oh What a Dream'. Backing each of the individual musicians was a 'house band' comprising Oasis' bass guitarist, Andy Bell, keyboard player Adam Peters and drummer Simon Finley (both mainstays of Echo and The Bunnymen) alongside singer-songwriter Beth Orton's guitarist, Ted Barnes. The first half of the show progressed to a collage of dripping oil slides and retina-dazzling trickery from Peter Wynne-Willson beamed onto three huge screens behind the Barbican stage, a far larger canvas than anything he or Pink Floyd could have imagined in 1967. Wynne-Willson was also joined in his efforts by the Boyle Family, an artists' collective, whose late father, Mark, had produced some of the ground-breaking light shows at the UFO club.

The performers trooped on, with their names flashed up on the screen behind them, each one performing one or two songs at most. Folk singer Kate McGarrigle helped raise the first goosebumps of the night, with a charming 'See Emily Play', sharing the vocals with her daughter Martha Wainwright and niece Lily Lanken.

As the lights dimmed again for the last performance of the first half, a familiar, slightly stooped figure could be spotted in the wings, instantly recognisable before the stage lights had even come back on again. Roger Waters' arrival immediately prompted a standing ovation. Grinning nervously, he seated himself on a stool, acoustic guitar across his lap, and fussed with his microphone. To his left stood Jon Carin behind a keyboard.

'Of course, I'm terrified,' Waters quipped. 'These small occasions are much more frightening than the big ones where you can hide behind all the paraphernalia. But for those of us who suffer from a sense of shame, and doom, as I'm sure any of you who know my work will know I have all my life . . . this is all quite stressful.'

Waters continued his speech, throwing a little more light on his relationship with Syd Barrett. 'However, it would not have been stressful for Syd, because he did not suffer from those things in the same way that I do. Before the illness, he lived his life like he walked . . . he kind of . . . bounced, the whole time . . . and I think that his lack of a sense of shame enabled him to take all the risks that he did, musically, and that's why we owe him such an enormous debt. Certainly I do personally, because without Syd, I don't know what I'd be doing. Probably would have been a property developer or something.'

The candour was disarming, but in a frustratingly contrary move, Waters announced that he would not be playing one of Syd's songs, or even a Pink Floyd song, but one of his own. 'Typical Waters,' came one grumbled quip from somewhere in the stalls. The song 'Flickering Flame' had become a mainstay of Waters' recent solo performances, but to this partisan Barrett audience and in the context of the night its unfamiliarity made it a poor choice. The deeply personal lyrics were apt, but there was a palpable sense of disappointment as Waters bade his goodbyes and loped off stage at the end. Was that *it*?

'There are holes in our psychology,' he admitted months before. 'There is something that makes us still want to go out there and do it.' But for Waters, doing it now meant resurrecting *Dark Side of the Moon* at his own solo shows, with three guitarists standing where David Gilmour had once stood, attempting to do what Gilmour had once done so much better. For those that had seen the Floyd guitarist's own performances of 'Wish You Were Here', 'Breathe' and 'Comfortably Numb' during his solo shows there was still the niggling hangover of Live 8. It wasn't about who was playing the bass, it was about the fact that Roger Waters had been there that night; the man whose imagination and obsessive nature had so informed those songs. After Live 8, the alternatives were never going to be quite so exciting.

Backstage during the interval, the sight of David Gilmour's guitar tech Phil Taylor carrying his master's wares revealed that Waters would not be the only member of Pink Floyd, past or present, planning to make an appearance. In a closed-off dressing room, a little after 8.30 p.m., David Gilmour was photographed warming up with his guitar while Nick Mason kept time with a pair of drum sticks on a nearby armchair. The 'great behemoth', as the guitarist had once described Pink Floyd, was rousing itself from its torpor yet again, while having to make do with any available surface to practise on.

Out front, before an audience still playing guessing games, Roger Waters reappeared alongside Syd Barrett on the overhead screen. As mentioned earlier, the grainy, black and white footage showed the two being interviewed by Austrian musicologist Hans Keller ('Why does it all got to be so terribly loud?') for the BBC arts show, *Look of the Week*. Filmed in May 1967, Barrett and Waters spoke like the well-raised middle-class schoolboys they had been just a few years earlier. Barrett sounded erudite and appeared to be anything but stoned.

The music recommenced with Nick Laird-Clowes leading the Sense of Sound choir through an unearthly new arrangement of Pink Floyd's 'Chapter 24', a song originally inspired by those nocturnal sessions with the Chinese *I-Ching* at Barrett's Earlham Street flat, and revitalised by a choral accompaniment and haunting string arrangement. The Floyd's original promo video for 'Scarecrow' crackled into life on the screen above, in which an impossibly youthful-looking Pink Floyd frolicked in a field, before Laird-Clowes joined folk singer Vashti Bunyan for the song itself.

Damon Albarn's band Blur had dominated the UK charts in the 1990s with a strand of English pop partly derived from the Barrett-era Pink Floyd. Blur's 1994 album, *Parklife*, had even deposed Floyd's *The Division Bell* from the number 1 slot in the UK that year. Albarn wore his influences on his sleeve, dusting off 'Word Song' from Barrett's *Opel* album of offcuts and out-takes, and imbuing the track with a wit and sparkle sadly absent from the original, where Syd's freeform list of unrelated words sounded more like the verbal outpourings of a sick man than the 'early version of rap' Albarn claimed it to be.

Damon also coaxed Barrett's twenty-nine-year-old nephew, Ian, on to the stage to say a few words. Knowing that the entire audience was scrutinising him for a family resemblance hardly helped his nerves. Ian offered a few appreciative words before raising his glass of beer and scuttling gratefully back into the stalls.

Chrissie Hynde had been instrumental in helping pull the show together. Her roughshod takes of 'Dark Globe' and 'Late Night', with Pretenders guitarist Adam Seymour, stayed close to the dilapidated spirit of the originals. But after the resolutely English Damon Albarn, Kevin Ayers and Captain Sensible, it was strange to hear anybody singing in an American accent.

By the time producer Joe Boyd finally strode on to announce 'a suitable band to end the show', sharp-eyed Floyd fans knew what was coming. Now the names of David Gilmour, Nick Mason and Richard Wright flashed up on the screen above, as they trooped on stage, the same identity parade of tucked-in shirts and worn-in jeans last visible at Live 8. Mason wore a now familiar grin, Wright looked as jittery as ever, but clearly delighted by the crowd's standing ovation. Gilmour commandeered the centre stage, exuding a brisk, business-like air. Audience calls for Roger Waters were swiftly parried. 'He was here, too,' fired back the guitarist. 'Now the rest of us.'

Except why wasn't Waters here now? Whispers later circulated that Gilmour had invited him to join them on stage, only to be turned down. Later, Joe Boyd would claim that Waters had only confirmed that he would perform the night before the show, while explaining that he would have to leave the venue by 9 p.m. as he needed to meet his girlfriend, who was flying into London that evening. In the end, this reunion of sorts had come together after another flurry of last-minute calls. Wright had agreed first, Waters next, and Mason once Gilmour had announced his decision to play. However, the guitarist hadn't confirmed until 2 p.m. that day.

Just as at Live 8, bassist Guy Pratt would find himself otherwise booked, playing in Bryan Ferry's band at the Cambridge Corn Exchange that night; the venue in which Syd Barrett had made his last public performance thirty-five years earlier. Instead, Oasis' bass player, Andy Bell, found himself on stage with Pink Floyd, a career curveball he could never have anticipated.

'Arnold Layne' performed by the remaining Pink Floyd seemed the only logical ending to the show. The group's very first single, a creepy psychedelic ode to a Cambridge cross-dresser, it had been produced by Joe Boyd nearly forty years ago. The sound of Wright's Farfisa organ was lost in the mix, with his voice sometimes following suit. But they ploughed on regardless. Jon Carin was back on stage, playing keyboards and singing backing vocals, with Gilmour also stepping into the fray when Wright's voice faltered. At just three and a half minutes, the performance was gone in a flash. A simple pop song from a band who had made their mark and earned their millions trading on anything but simple pop.

And then the band were gone, too, back into the wings, as the lights dimmed and the stage was plunged into darkness. The audience, still on their feet, kept up their applause, a hundred barked conversations around the hall seeming to merge into one: 'Where's Waters?'

After several minutes, the stage lights came up, and the evening's performers paraded back on stage: Robyn Hitchcock, Martha Wainwright, Chrissie Hynde, Nick Laird-Clowes, Kevin Ayers . . . Eventually, Richard Wright appeared, resuming his place at the keyboard. David Gilmour came next, clutching his guitar like a trusty keepsake, followed by Nick Mason, still holding a pair of drumsticks. Realising that the house band's Simon Finley already occupied the drum kit, Nick took up his spot next to Wright's keyboards, much like a lounge-bar singer waiting for the pianist to strike up the next song. All that was missing was a martini glass.

Jostling for space on the now cramped stage, the ad-hoc ensemble lurched into 'Bike', the same song that had opened the show. Nick Laird-Clowes took the first verse, before flitting around Gilmour and nudging him to take over the vocals. 'Bike' had been one of the songs Gilmour recalled hearing when he briefly visited Pink Floyd during the making of *The Piper at the Gates of Dawn*. Still trying to eke out a living playing in a covers band in France, Gilmour could hardly have imagined that four decades later, he would be on stage singing the same song. Mason, tapping his drumsticks on the palm of his hands, was clearly unfamiliar with the words. Instead, the gamely smiling drummer looked not dissimilar to the Queen captured on TV at the Millennium Eve celebrations, unsure of the lyrics or handshaking ritual to 'Auld Lang Syne'.

Behind the three remaining members of Pink Floyd, the drums clattered, guitars were fitfully strummed, and a motley choir of acolytes, contemporaries and otherwise complete strangers bellowed the words to Syd Barrett's nonsense poem. It was a witty, heartfelt, messy performance, in keeping with the spirit of the occasion. You rather hoped that Pink Floyd's departed friend would have approved, had he still been around to witness it.

Yet one of Syd Barrett's oldest friends was still absent. As those in the audience kept wondering, where *was* Roger Waters, the only performer missing from the grand finale? Was he really on his way to the airport? Had he been invited to join his former bandmates, but chosen not to join in? As the final chord was struck, and the house lights came up, it seemed as if the moment had passed again. Was this really the last time Pink Floyd, or most of them, would be seen together on stage? Another reunion of sorts, then. But still, not quite. How *very* Pink Floyd.

CHAPTER TWELVE IF I HAD BEEN GOD

'Being in a rock 'n' roll band? It's the easiest job in the world.'

Roger Waters

Roger Waters is quite the thespian on this 12 May 2011 evening. Pink Floyd's former guitarist, songwriter and conceptualist has brought his production of *The Wall* to London's O₂ Arena for six nights. When Pink Floyd first staged *The Wall* thirty years ago, the band were shackled to their equipment. Tonight, though, Waters dispenses with his bass guitar for many songs, preferring to roam the stage, inhabiting the lead character of Pink, *The Wall*'s damaged rock star.

Waters arrived on stage earlier playing Pink at his delusional, egomaniacal worst. He delivered the hectoring lyrics to *The Wall*'s opening song, 'In the Flesh', while wearing black leather Gruppenführer-style greatcoat and a pair of jackboots. As the song staggered to a halt, a huge fibreglass Stuka bomber zoomed noisily over the audience before crashing into the wall, triggering plumes of smoke and fire. It was a spectacular entrance.

Now, though, he is alone on stage and performing 'Don't Leave Me Now', Pink's harrowing plea to his newly estranged wife. Waters is sixty-seven years old, still rail-thin, and dressed in a snug black T-shirt, snugger black jeans and a pair of box-fresh white trainers. There isn't a guitar to hide behind. Instead, he clutches a hand-held microphone and pours out Pink's tale of woe, as a single spotlight picks him out from the darkness. It's a performance at odds with Waters' stage persona during his time in Pink Floyd. Then, he was a most unwilling rock star. After all, the idea for *The Wall* originated from his dissatisfaction with stadium shows, and a desire to seal himself off from his audience. Tonight, though, Waters appears to relish the attention and his closeness to the crowd, all 20,000 of them.

However, as Waters delivers his soliloquy, not all of the audience sit in rapt silence. A lone voice can be heard from the stalls, twenty or so rows in front of the stage: 'Steve . . . Steve . . . Pass this drink to Natalie?' Heads turn to see one male fan gingerly clambering over the seats, bumping knees and feet with his neighbours while trying to ferry a tray of drinks in wobbly plastic glasses back to his friends.

Despite a chorus of disapproving sighs and tuts from those around him, the fan seems unaware of the disruption he is causing. As Waters pauses for breath, you half expect him to lean over and let fly with a volley of spittle, just as he did at one over-zealous devotee who tried to climb on stage at a Canadian Floyd show in 1977. But, no, times have changed. The fan sits down. The show goes on. In a strange way, it's rather disappointing.

'I used to get very snotty with audiences for getting drunk and shouting,' Waters told an interviewer a few weeks earlier. 'Now, I am way more relaxed and less critical than I was in those days.'

Waters' refusal to reprimand an inattentive fan isn't the only evidence of how much he has changed. In the audience at the O$_2$ this evening are *The Wall* album's sleeve designer Gerald Scarfe and his wife, the actor Jane Asher, Syd Barrett's former girlfriends Jenny Spires and Libby Gausden, and the Floyd's long-serving cover artist and confidant Storm Thorgerson. What they all know, but many of the audience don't, is that David Gilmour and Nick Mason will soon join Roger Waters on stage.

Sadly, though, there will be one other Pink Floyd member absent from tonight's reunion.

On 15 September 2008, Richard Wright died at his home in West London. He had been diagnosed with cancer nine months earlier. Wright was a notoriously private man, and his family and friends had not disclosed his condition to the public. As with Syd Barrett's death two years before, the media responded with numerous obituaries and hastily prepared articles examining the legacy of Pink Floyd's 'quiet man'. But the diffident keyboard player was a much harder sell than the reclusive, mysterious Barrett. As *The Times*' obituary bluntly explained: 'Had Rick Wright's profile been any lower, he would have been reported missing.'

'I like to use the George Harrison example,' Nick Mason told this writer, a week after Wright's death. 'Because, like George, Rick wrote, he sang, he did a lot of things, but he did become eclipsed by everyone else. Rick could be very droll and very funny, but he suffered from being quieter than the rest of us.'

When considering Wright's personality compared to those of his bandmates, it was hard not to recall an interview in the 1972 film, *Pink Floyd Live At Pompeii*. Here, the director Adrian Maben tried to quiz Pink Floyd about their working methods. Busy scoffing beer and oysters, they preferred to answer his questions with questions of their own, in between a barrage of in-jokes and schoolboy banter.

But when Maben asked if the band ever had any difficult moments, Wright immediately engaged. 'We have a great understanding and tolerance of each other,' he said, looking rather mournful, 'but there are a lot of things left unsaid . . . I feel . . . sometimes.'

Quite what those 'things left unsaid' were had intrigued Pink Floyd's audience ever since Wright made his exit from the band in 1981. In every interview he ever gave, Richard Wright blamed his inability to contribute to *The Wall* on 'personality issues' with Waters, and the emotional impact of his first marriage breaking up. The tension between Wright and Waters actually dated back to their time together as students sharing lodgings in Highgate. In recent years, Waters had jokily told interviewers about the time Wright had padlocked the kitchen cupboard containing his food, or refused to pay for his bandmates' extra order of prawns in a Tokyo restaurant.

The suggestion that Wright was frugal endured, however rich Pink Floyd became. 'We never grew up, we just grew older,' Mason admitted. 'Having given Rick this character we were quite happy to work on the same joke for forty-odd years. It never gets boring, especially when the person in question finds it irritating.'

By the mid-1970s, Wright, like Gilmour, had acquired a villa on Lindos, where he loved to spend time between recording and touring. The Floyd's friends, families and hangers-ons could wile away the summer months on a beautiful Greek island, enjoying all the perks of a rock star lifestyle. Days in Lindos would be spent racing catamarans around the bay, and the nights enjoying what one attendee remembers as 'full-moon parties'.

'There was an awful lot of cocaine around back then,' one associate admitted, 'and that didn't help. But Rick just stopped communicating. It was like he got gazumped by the others. At some point in the seventies he seemed to withdraw into himself.'

But Wright had returned to Pink Floyd in the mid-1980s and rediscovered his abilities as a musician and as a songwriter. When David Gilmour went on the road to promote his 2006 solo album *On an Island*, he brought Wright along to play keyboards.

Wright's passion was sailing, and he kept a 65-ft yacht called *Evrika* moored in the Virgin Islands. He seemed happier on the road than at home. In July 2007, writer Mark Paytress interviewed him for *Mojo* magazine. Wright had been living alone since the end of his third marriage. Paytress wrote of visiting his mews cottage in Kensington, and finding it to be 'a surprisingly bare residence – no coffee, half a handshake, two large white sofas . . .' and how 'the still handsome man who opened the door cut a lonely figure'.

It was perhaps better to remember Wright from his appearance in *Breaking Bread, Drinking Wine*, a charming documentary filmed on the *On an Island* tour. Wright featured prominently, and looked more at ease than ever. 'I think this is probably the most fun tour I've ever done in my life,' he said, on camera. A week after his death came Gilmour's *Live in Gdansk* album. It reiterated Wright's contribution to the tour, and featured a version of Floyd's 'Echoes', a song so closely identified with the keyboard player.

'In my view all the greatest Pink Floyd moments are the ones where

Rick is in full flow,' said Gilmour. 'Like Rick, I don't find it easy to express my feelings in words, but I loved him and will miss him enormously.'

Wright's old nemesis, Waters, released a statement of his own, praising 'Rick's ear for harmonic progression' before adding, 'I am very grateful for the opportunity that Live 8 afforded me to engage with him and David [Gilmour] and Nick [Mason] that one last time. I wish there had been more.' It confirmed the rumours that Waters had wanted to perform with Pink Floyd again.

There would be a further twist in the tale. In October 2008, David Gilmour attended the music magazine _Q_'s annual awards ceremony in London. In his acceptance speech for an Outstanding Contribution To Music award, the guitarist revealed that one of Wright's last wishes had been to play a big outdoor festival, such as Glastonbury. 'But we weren't able to do that due to all sorts of strange reasons,' he said.

The guitarist's comments referred to the Glastonbury Festival organiser Michael Eavis, who'd turned down Gilmour's request. Tickets for that year's festival had sold slowly compared to previous years, and there had been criticism of Eavis' decision to book the New York hip-hop artist Jay-Z, rather than a traditional, ie safer, rock act, as a headliner. The _Sun_ newspaper claimed that Eavis had turned Gilmour down because he 'wanted the event to appeal to a younger generation', but Eavis explained that there simply wasn't room on the bill.

Gilmour subsequently emphasised that he hadn't wanted to usurp any of the festival's headline acts, but had simply wanted to play anywhere on the bill, as it was likely to be Wright's last gig.

Mischievous tales of padlocked kitchen cupboards and disputed restaurant bills were soon overshadowed by the news that the musician had left £24 million to his family in his will. The money was distributed between his three children, with substantial amounts also going to his sisters and their offspring. Wright's daughter, Gala, inherited his Aston Martin DB5. Gala's husband, Pink Floyd's touring bassist Guy Pratt, was given his treasured Bösendorfer piano. Wright had also set aside £20,000 for what he called 'a really good party', which was later held in Westbourne Grove.

Guitarist Dominic Miller, who'd played on Wright's *Broken China* album, performed at the event, and recalled seeing 'everyone, roadies, managers, tour managers, designers, friends, girlfriends, wives, producers, retired drug dealers, even the guy who did the sax solo on *Dark Side* . . .' Gilmour, Mason and Jeff Beck (the guitarist Wright once claimed Pink Floyd had approached to replace Syd Barrett) all played.

Just weeks before Wright's death, David Gilmour had told this writer, 'At my age I am entirely selfish and want to please myself. I shan't tour with Pink Floyd again.' The subsequent loss of what Nick Mason called 'one of our dysfunctional family' made the possibility of Gilmour changing his mind seem even more unlikely.

Pink Floyd's brief re-formation at Live 8 was now being cited as an inspiration by other bands considering reunion tours. In December 2007, the three surviving members of Led Zeppelin had come back together to play a concert, with drummer Jason Bonham deputising for his late father, John. The media furore surrounding their charity show at London's O_2 Arena had been extraordinary, and it was said that some 20 million people had applied for tickets for the 20,000-capacity event.

The day after the gig, every national newspaper in the UK splashed photographs and reviews across its front pages. It was a reminder of how important the rock music of the 1970s still was to a current generation of media tastemakers, but also how Zeppelin, like Floyd, seemed to transcend age barriers and musical genres.

Despite big-money offers from promoters, Led Zeppelin's lead singer Robert Plant refused to commit to a Zeppelin reunion tour. Plant used Floyd's Live 8 reunion as an example of 'the way it should be done'. What Plant, like David Gilmour, understood was also the value of the old showbiz axiom: always leave them wanting more.

With Gilmour showing no desire to reactivate the Pink Floyd name, though, Roger Waters stepped forward to fill the void. It was a decision that galvanised his career more than anyone, including Waters himself, could possibly have anticipated. In December 2009, the thirtieth anniversary of Pink Floyd's *The Wall*, Waters announced his plans to tour his own production of the Floyd's elaborate and confrontational stage show.

'I started to get itchy feet,' Waters explained. 'My wife Laurie said, "You should go out on tour again, but if you do, there's only one thing you can do – *The Wall*."' At first, Waters was reluctant. 'I said, "Be quiet! You don't understand!" Then I started figuring out whether it was possible.'

For Waters, it was imperative that *The Wall* had something relevant to say to modern audiences. 'I started to think that maybe there is something in the story that could be seen as an allegory for the way nations behave towards one another, or religions behave towards one another. In other words, could the piece be developed to describe a broader, more universal condition than we did in 1980 and I did in 1990 in Berlin? So I started to think about it more and more, and I started jotting a few things down on paper, and eventually I said, "Y'know what? I'm gonna do this . . ."'

Mark Fisher, who'd designed the show in 1980, was brought in to oversee the new production. Fisher vividly recalled the mood thirty years earlier. '[Pink Floyd] were getting to the point where they couldn't stand the sight of each other,' he told *Rolling Stone*. 'It was all too convenient that they got to declare that the whole thing was a turkey and way too expensive and walk away from it on those grounds.'

But as Fisher also explained, 'The rock 'n' roll industry has been transformed since then. Back then, there were only individual promoters, not companies that arranged whole tours. Back then, being able to move something from town to town was way beyond us.' This industry sea change, together with huge technological advances, not to mention much higher ticket prices, now made it possible for the $60 million production to turn a substantial profit.

The Wall 2010 was an unbelievably ambitious enterprise. Showing his usual painstaking attention to detail, Waters pored over every aspect of the production, pushing Fisher and his team as well as himself to ensure that they delivered the best possible results. The tour's requirements read like the world's most expensive shopping list: 242 flat-pack cardboard bricks for a 24ft-high and 240ft-wide wall, 82 moveable lights, one 30ft-high helium-filled inflatable schoolmaster . . . The most immediate difference was visible in the wall itself. On the original tour, Pink Floyd had only 35mm cine-projectors with which to beam an image a maximum of 80ft wide in the middle of the wall. Waters now had twenty-three projectors beaming images across the full width of the

240ft wall, and on to a circular screen behind the stage. It was a visual feast, with Gerald Scarfe's ghoulish animations now brought to life in eye-watering high definition.

The only thing missing was Pink Floyd. 'I feel no compunction about doing *The Wall* with a band, only one member of which was in Pink Floyd,' Waters explained. 'The contributions the others made were fundamental. Nevertheless, it stands on its own as a piece.'

This time, Waters relied on a team of eleven musicians and backing vocalists. These included long-serving drummer Graham Broad, keyboard player Jon Carin and Snowy White, the guitarist who'd served time on several Waters tours since playing second guitar on Floyd's 1977 dates. Among the newer additions were Michigan-born session vocalist Robbie Wyckoff, who'd sung on albums by Barbra Streisand and Celine Dion. Described as 'a vocal chameleon', Wyckoff was brought in specifically to replicate the parts David Gilmour had sung on the original album.

With fifty-six shows already booked for the year ahead, Waters was leaving nothing to chance. Having committed to the tour, he hired a personal trainer, a vocal coach and a stylist, to, as one interviewer noted, 'help him select clothes in various shades of black'.

Although technology alone had helped make the tour physically and financially viable, Waters was soon more convinced than ever that *The Wall*'s message was pertinent in 2010. 'It has an attachment to anti-authoritarian, anti-totalitarian and anti-extreme ideology – whether political or religious,' he declared.

Events going on in the wider world backed up his claim. In July 2010, Waters broke off from rehearsals to add his support to The Hoping Foundation, a charity supporting Palestinian children affected by the conflict with Israel. Waters had been invited to perform at a fundraiser at Kiddington Hall in Oxfordshire by David Gilmour. Some negotiations took place beforehand, though. 'David said, and I quote, "If you do [The Teddy Bears' 1958 hit] 'To Know Him Is to Love Him' at The Hoping Foundation gig I'll come and do 'Comfortably Numb' on one of your Wall shows,"' revealed Waters.

On the night, the reunited couple performed a 28-minute set backed by a group that included Waters' son Harry playing keyboards. They rolled out 'Wish You Were Here' and 'Comfortably Numb'. But it was

'To Know Him Is to Love Him' that raised the biggest smile, 'what with us having famously been at each other's throats for years', as Waters explained. The song's high register was also much easier for Gilmour to reach than Waters. Internet footage of the performance rather suggested one man putting the other through his paces. The question now, was: at which of Waters' *Wall* shows would David Gilmour perform? Audiences would just have to wait.

The Wall tour opened with much fanfare in September 2010 with three sold-out dates at Toronto's 20,000-capacity Air Canada Centre. A children's choir from the city's Regent Park School of Music helped perform the hit single 'Another Brick in the Wall Part 2'. On 'Mother', Waters sang to grainy black-and-white footage of himself performing the same song with Pink Floyd at Earls Court in 1980, a time when, as he informed the audience, he was 'miserable and fucked up'.

These were moments of vulnerability and human interaction that set the production apart from the original *Wall* concerts. But the scale of the show and its visual impact alone was enough to gain column inches. The *Toronto Star* was quick to note some teething problems, but its reporter was still dazzled by the 'arresting digital animation and ceiling-high marionettes', and 'the requisite, giant, inflatable wild boar' that soared over the audience, emblazoned with the sarcastic slogan, 'Everything Will Be OK'. The first half of the show concluded with the plaintive 'Goodbye Cruel World', and the final brick placed in the wall, leaving the audience faced with a huge, imposing edifice.

The Wall was also loaded with moments of high personal drama that seemed even more poignant in the light of everything that had gone on since Waters had written the original story. His estrangement from Pink Floyd and his first wife, and the decline and death of Syd Barrett were all there. During the second act, the band performed the achingly lonely 'Hey You' while hidden behind the wall. For 'Nobody Home', Waters' tale of on-tour depression directly inspired by Barrett's behaviour on Pink Floyd's first American tour, he appeared, staring at a flickering TV screen in a makeshift motel room constructed in a gap in the wall. On the album's showstopper, 'Comfortably Numb', Waters paced the stage in front of the giant barrier before gesturing upwards to where Robbie Wyckoff and guitarist Dave Kilminster appeared overhead to sing and play what had once been Gilmour's parts.

From here on, the drama hardly diminished. Gerald Scarfe's original animated marching hammers had lost none of their grotesque power in the thirty-one years since they'd first been seen. But they were now joined by an image of Waters' father, Second Lieutenant Eric Waters, and the grim details of his death at Anzio during the Second World War. The tour programme also included a poem Waters had written about his father. Prior to the tour, Waters had requested that fans post him photos of their family members lost in any conflict. Known as 'Fallen Loved Ones', this scrapbook of personal images and stories made for poignant viewing when projected onto the wall. Among the many slogans and maxims that flashed up, former US president Dwight D. Eisenhower's words from his 1953 'Chance for Peace' speech seemed especially apt: 'Every gun that is made, every warship launched, every rocket fired, signifies in the final sense, a theft from those who hunger and are not fed, those who are cold and are not clothed.'

As the show progressed, Waters added pictures of world leaders, past and present, and, controversially, footage of the July 2007 Baghdad air strikes in which Iraqi civilians were killed and injured by the American military. The classified footage had been taken from the cockpit of one of the US army's helicopters and had been made public on the WikiLeaks website. Later on the tour, Waters would also include images of Jean Charles de Menezes, the Brazilian electrician shot dead by the police on a London tube train after being mistaken for a terrorist in 2005. Members of Menezes' family would later attend Waters' show in Porto Alegre, Brazil.

All 'the thunder and noise', as Waters described it, still couldn't drown out *The Wall*'s message or its relevance to the modern age. As the tour progressed, through Chicago and the American Midwest and on to a two-night stand at New York's Madison Square Garden, the political aspects of the show started to draw media attention as well as the crashing Stuka and the flying pig.

During 'Goodbye Blue Sky', images of fighter planes dropping bombs shaped like the former Soviet Union's hammer-and-sickle and corporate logos for Mercedes-Benz and Shell flashed up across the wall. A month into the tour, though, and Waters was under fire from the Anti-Defamation League, who believed that using images of bombs shaped like the Jewish Star of David next to bombs shaped like US-dollar signs was anti-Semitic.

Waters responded with an open letter in the *Independent* newspaper. 'There is no anti-Semitism in *The Wall* show,' he wrote. 'The point I am trying to make in the song is that the bombardment we are all subject to by conflicting religious, political, and economic ideologies only encourages us to turn against one another, and I mourn the concomitant loss of life.'

It was not the first time Waters had been criticised for his stance on Israel. In 2005, Pink Floyd's 'Another Brick in the Wall Part 2' had been turned into a protest anthem by Palestinian children protesting against the West Bank Barrier, the wall constructed by the Israelis to separate them from the Palestinian community.

A year later, Waters was booked to play a show in Tel Aviv, but had been contacted by Palestinians arranging a cultural boycott of Israel because of its construction of the wall. Waters accepted their invitation to visit and see first-hand what he later described as 'this appalling edifice'. As he told the *Guardian*, 'In solidarity, and somewhat impotently, I wrote on their wall that day, "We don't need no thought control".'

Waters cancelled the Tel Aviv gig and arranged instead to play Neve Shalom, a village jointly founded by Palestinian and Israeli peace supporters, where he played to some 60,000 people, making it the largest music event in Israeli history. The decision failed to quell the argument, and now led to criticism from the Palestinian Solidarity Campaign who criticised him for not boycotting Israel completely. Waters defended his decision: 'I would not rule out going to Israel because I disapprove of the foreign policy any more than I would refuse to play in the UK because I disapprove of Tony Blair's foreign policy.'

But in 2011, Waters announced his support for the international BDS (boycott, divestment and sanctions) campaign against Israel. 'My position is not anti-Semitic,' he wrote. 'This is not an attack on the people of Israel. My conviction is born in the idea that all people deserve basic human rights.'

Nevertheless, following the ADL's complaint, the juxtaposition of the Star of David and US-dollar-shaped 'bombs' was amended for the remaining shows. The first leg of *The Wall* tour finally came to a halt three days before Christmas at Mexico City's Palacio de los Deportes. Waters' deeply personal tale of psychological isolation had proved a money-spinner. The tour had grossed $89.5 million, putting it at

Number 2, behind stadium pop-rockers Bon Jovi, in the list of highest-grossing US tours of 2010. Next stop: Europe.

While Waters was busy building *The Wall* across North America, the UK electronic music duo The Orb released their new album, *Metallic Spheres*, featuring David Gilmour, in October. The two parties had first come together for a joint interview with *Melody Maker* in 1993. Back then, The Orb's Alex Paterson had drawn a line between *Meddle* and *The Dark Side of the Moon* and nineties ambient sounds. Gilmour, in turn, had cited The Orb's albums as his choice of 'late-night relaxing music'.

Gilmour recorded Metallic Spheres' tranquil-sounding guitar and lap steel at Youth's studio, The Dreaming Cave, a hideaway constructed at the end of the producer's garden in Wandsworth, South London. The album's bonus track, 'The Cult of Youth Ambient Mix', heightened the parallels between The Orb's signature sound and vintage Pink Floyd, with parts that even evoked the eerie middle section in 'Echoes'. An accompanying promo film showed Gilmour wandering around the garden, soaking up the sunshine and playing lap steel on the studio's porch. The mood of the session seemed as elegantly laid-back as the mood of *The Wall* was loud and declamatory.

Nevertheless, when Waters began the second run of *Wall* shows in Lisbon in March 2011, speculation increased about which of the forthcoming sixty-four European concerts David Gilmour would make his promised appearance at. 'I didn't say it would be in the UK,' teased Waters, when asked.

After Portugal, the tour wound through the rest of Europe and into Russia for shows in Moscow and St Petersburg. Playing in the former communist countries seemed to reinforce Waters' message that *The Wall* was 'anti-authoritarian, anti-totalitarian and anti-extreme ideology'. But he was now hinting in the press that the tour would be his last. 'I'm sixty-six, so I think there will come a point where I just don't want the physical demand,' he told *NME*. 'I can't imagine that aged eighty I'm gonna be one of those guys who does fifty-five-date tours.'

On stage, though, Waters showed little sign of physical decline. He basked in his role as the show's frontman, ringmaster and all-round MC. By the time *The Wall* reached Britain in May, Waters looked and sounded more confident than ever.

With six nights booked at London's O$_2$ Arena, the question was no longer where would David Gilmour appear, but, rather, on which night? The levels of expectation were such that on the first evening it was hard not to feel a twinge of sympathy for Wyckoff and Kilminster when they appeared on top of the wall during 'Comfortably Numb', and 20,000 people saw that they *weren't* David Gilmour.

After some deliberation, Gilmour agreed to play the second night at the O$_2$. Social media made it impossible for the news to stay secret for long. But then Waters himself had fully embraced the Internet and on the afternoon of the show revealed online that Gilmour was rehearsing at the venue.

The platform used to elevate the guitarist to the top of the wall was a more comfortable and hi-tech affair than the rather ramshackle hydraulic lift used in 1980. Back then, Gilmour's guitar tech Phil Taylor would place a flight case on casters, nicknamed 'Dave's Pulpit', on top of the platform to give Gilmour the extra inches to be seen over the wall. 'Try not to dive off, cos I'll be standing somewhere down there,' Waters quipped, as he watched Gilmour rehearse. 'I'll try,' the guitarist fired back.

That night, when Gilmour appeared during 'Comfortably Numb', there was a collective gasp from the audience followed by applause that almost threatened to drown out his vocals. Dressed in regulation black T-shirt, standing perfectly still and looking as unyielding as one of the giant heads on *The Division Bell* cover, Gilmour sang his lines and played the song's brief first solo before being plunged into darkness. Down below, Waters, arms outstretched, smiled wolfishly.

When Gilmour reappeared and launched into the song's second and final guitar solo, the anticipation in the arena was palpable. Meanwhile, a wonderfully unselfconscious Waters played air drums and froze in a mime-like pose. After a few seconds he started loping slowly across the stage before stopping and hammering at the wall with both fists, triggering an explosion of colours and images of flying bricks, just as Gilmour pitched into the final bars of the solo.

'It was OK,' Gilmour told this writer later. 'I was strangely more nervous than I thought I might be. I made a mistake with the lyrics, I don't think I've ever done that before. I sang a wrong second verse, my solo was not as good as it has been . . .'

With all the 'noise and thunder' of the show, few in the O_2 noticed the slip-ups. Fewer still cared. As such, it seemed to take a while for the mood to settle, as the regular band returned for the aptly named 'The Show Must Go On'. But Waters still had another surprise card to play.

The concert's spectacular finale came at the end of 'The Trial'. Waters, his band and the audience chanted the words, 'Tear down the wall', until, finally, the first bricks toppled forward and the whole structure collapsed as if struck by some huge invisible wrecking ball. On any other night, Waters would stroll out in front of the ruins before bringing on his backing group to perform the final song of the night, 'Outside the Wall'. This evening, though, he stopped and addressed the audience first. 'So, now we know, tonight was the night when David did me the enormous honour of coming to play "Comfortably Numb",' he said. On cue, the guitarist reappeared clutching a mandolin and smiling shyly during another round of tumultuous applause.

But Waters wasn't done yet. 'By another extraordinary and happy coincidence there is another remnant of our old band here tonight,' he declared. Enter: Nick Mason. The drummer, looking a little frazzled having only just flown back from America, sauntered on from the wings clutching a tambourine and grinning.

'I was going to go to the show anyway,' Mason told this writer. 'I came straight from the airport to the 02, and Dave said, "Why don't you come on at the end?" So I said, "Oh, OK then".' Flanked by the rest of Waters' band, the three old stagers performed 'Outside the Wall' while a joshing Waters stuck his microphone into Gilmour's face and urged him to sing, and grabbed hold of Mason and forced him to sway rather stiffly in time to the music.

It was hard to imagine anything like this happening in 1980; something Waters was swift to acknowledge. 'Thirty years ago when David and Nick and I first did this, with Rick, I was a rather grumpy person and disaffected with rock 'n' roll audiences . . . as young David will attest.' To his left, a smiling Gilmour nodded in agreement. Waters paused, with his hand on the guitarist's shoulder. 'But all that's changed!' he shouted. 'I could not be happier than to be here with these guys . . . and all of you here in this room tonight. Thank you very very much indeed!'

'It felt terrific on the night,' said Mason. 'And I now have a really nice photo of the three of us laughing.' Though he was unsure how genuine

Waters' statement about no longer feeling grumpy and disaffected had been. 'It was very odd. We can't decide whether he means it or whether he thinks that makes him sound like a nicer person.'

It was the end of another Pink Floyd reunion, but not *The Wall*. Waters went on to stage the show in Ireland and across Europe before finishing in Athens' Olympic Indoor Hall. Despite many of the nations visited being in the grip of a punishing economic recession, the box office data for the European dates showed that *The Wall* was financially bulletproof. The show's gross box office revenue was usually well in excess of $1.5 million a night, with profits from merchandising sales still to come. Unsurprisingly, then, Waters announced that he would be back with *The Wall* the following year.

While Roger Waters was on a financial winning streak, Pink Floyd's record company, EMI, was having a tougher time of it. In January 2010, the beleaguered label had reported pre-tax losses of £1.75 billion for the previous year. Two months later, it was reported that Pink Floyd were suing EMI for breaking the terms of an earlier contract by making individual Floyd songs available to purchase via the Internet.

As well as claiming that the band hadn't received all of the royalties due to them from online sales, the group's lawyers' main bone of contention was that, for artistic reasons alone, the songs should not be sold separately, and that Floyd albums should only be sold as a whole. EMI contested that this ruling only applied to physical product such as CDs and vinyl, but not to downloads.

The court heard in the band's favour. However, a year later, Floyd and EMI announced a new five-year partnership, which allowed the label to continue selling Floyd songs individually on iTunes. In spring 2011, the news that Pink Floyd had sanctioned reissues of *The Dark Side of the Moon*, *Wish You Were Here* and *The Wall* seemed like a well-timed move to help prop up the ailing label.

All three albums were re-released in their original format, plus a version with additional tracks and a sumptuous Immersion box-set edition, which retailed at an eye-popping £80. The box sets were packed with ephemera, including replica tickets, backstage passes and drinks coasters designed by Storm Thorgerson. But, more importantly, they contained a treasure-trove of bonus tracks, alternative mixes and live material. Some of the music had been circulating for years on bootlegs, but a lot had never been heard outside the Floyd camp, and much of it had been languishing in the EMI vaults for decades.

At last, Floyd completists could sample the fabled early mix of *Wish You Were Here*'s title track, featuring Stéphane Grappelli's rococo violin solo, and hear segments from the mysterious *Household Objects* project, where the band had twanged elastic bands to make a bass sound and created a melody with tuned wine glasses. Waters also bravely made available some of his earliest demos for *The Wall*. These demonstrated how much the rest of the band had improved his original ideas, but also how focused Waters' vision was even before he'd shared the material with co-producer Bob Ezrin.

Unfortunately, while the music press and Floyd obsessives anticipated the 5.1 surround-sound mix of 'Shine On You Crazy Diamond' and other gems, the rest of the media was preoccupied by events in David Gilmour's home life. Just as the press campaign for the reissues began, Gilmour's twenty-one-year-old stepson, Charlie, was sentenced to sixteen months in prison. He had been arrested seven months earlier, during protests in central London against proposed increases in student tuition fees. Charlie was photographed swinging on the union flag at the cenotaph, and was later caught on CCTV kicking a shop window in Oxford Street. The harshness of the sentence was widely criticised. He was later released on curfew after serving four months.

There was, inevitably, a sense of finality about the reissues, as if it was drawing a line under Pink Floyd's career. 'We thought, Fuck trying to hang on to anything anymore,' admitted Gilmour. 'The thinking was, If we don't do this now, we never will,' Mason told this writer, before joshing that sales of the costly box sets might help keep EMI in business 'for another fortnight'. In the end, even Pink Floyd couldn't save EMI. In September 2012, the label was swallowed up by the Universal Music Group in a £1.2 billion takeover deal.

With the traditional music industry in decline, the continuing success of Roger Waters' *Wall* tour seemed both heartening and extraordinary. At the beginning of 2012, he announced forthcoming dates in South America. But if there was ever a time to question how far Waters had strayed from *The Wall*'s original ethos and its criticism of the inhumane nature of stadium gigs, then it was now.

In 1980, Pink Floyd, at Waters' request, had turned down a $2 million guarantee from a US promoter to perform *The Wall* at Philadelphia's open-air JFK Stadium. 'It's three years since we did that last stadium,' Waters told the band, referring to the night in Montreal in 1977 when he'd spat at a fan. 'I said then that I would never do one again. *The Wall* was entirely sparked off by how awful it was . . . and that's why we've produced this show strictly for arenas.'

But that was then. As well as announcing outdoor stadium shows in Chile and Brazil, Waters declared a nine-night run at the open-air River Plate Stadium in Buenos Aires, Argentina. The combined fifteen South American dates in March would see Waters playing to a total of over 750,000 people and breaking box office attendance records previously set by The Rolling Stones in 1995. The gross revenue from the Buenos Aires run alone was later reported as $37,970,877.

Waters justified these 65,000-capacity stadium shows like so: 'My walls are coming down,' he said. 'There's something about connecting with that many people outdoors, which is actually extremely gratifying.'

'*The Wall* is not just about me,' he told *Mojo* magazine. 'It's not just about you, this is shared experience – our grief. It's now about social, economic and political issues.'

Waters brought *The Wall* back to North America for another run in summer 2012. The final performance was held at Quebec's Plains of Abraham on the site of a 1759 battle between British and French armed forces. Seventy thousand people watched the rise and fall of an 800-ft wall, in what was the second biggest production of *The Wall* yet, outdone only by Waters' 1990 performance in Berlin.

Back in Britain, the Olympics kept the nation enthralled for most of the summer, and fired up speculation that Pink Floyd, or at least David Gilmour, would appear at the closing ceremony. In the end, it was left to Nick Mason to fly the Floyd flag at a show that also featured The Who, Madness and what was left of Queen.

Mason bowled up to play drums on twenty-one-year-old folky-pop singer-songwriter Ed Sheeran's perfectly respectable rendition of 'Wish You Were Here'. Many of Sheeran's young audience took to Twitter to praise what they presumed was his new song. Some Floyd purists bristled, but as Mason rightly pointed out in an email to the singer: 'Sooner or later people will work out the origin of the song, and who knows, maybe check out our catalogue, just as hopefully our fans might check out yours.'

Mason and Waters' past lives came under the spotlight a month later, when the house they had lodged in as students was sold at auction for £1.2 million. In 1963, the Floyd's drummer and bassist moved into 33 Stanhope Gardens, Highgate, a house owned by art school lecturer and part-time musician Mike Leonard. When Mason moved out, Syd Barrett moved in. The early Floyd had rehearsed in Leonard's front room, and improvised music to accompany their landlord's light-show demonstrations at Hornsey Art School. Leonard's willingness to let the group rehearse at the house despite complaints from his neighbours was a godsend to Pink Floyd. Some of the band's old musical equipment was later discovered in the attic. 'Stanhope Gardens made a real difference to our musical activities,' explained Mason, who claimed to have buried the hood of one of his first cars, an Aston Martin International, in the garden of the house.

In December, Waters enjoyed his own Olympic-style victory. Year-end figures revealed that *The Wall* had been the third most profitable tour of 2012, just behind Bruce Springsteen and Madonna, but ahead of pop giants Coldplay and Lady Gaga. *The Wall*'s 192 shows had grossed a staggering $377 million. Images of Waters in his military-style leather greatcoat with its red and white 'marching hammers' armband now turned up in the business pages of newspapers as well as music magazines.

Waters may have performed a complete volte-face when it came to playing in stadiums, but there was so much to admire in the show's ambition and spectacle. He'd also achieved the rare feat of turning a production weighted with genuine social and political messages into a money-spinner. Many may have attended for the visual eye-candy alone, and there was certainly no other show on earth where one could experience a crashing plane, a rock star dressed like a military dictator and a massive wall tumbling down, but Waters had never once stinted on driving *The Wall*'s serious message home.

Predictably then, in November 2012, he revealed plans for further shows in Europe for the following summer. These would include a date at London's prestigious Wembley Stadium. Twenty-five years earlier, a newly solo Roger Waters could only watch as Pink Floyd filled the stadium twice over without him, after his own shows had recently struggled to fill the neighbouring arena. When asked whether any of his old bandmates, especially David Gilmour, might appear at the forthcoming hometown show, Waters replied, with a lovely hint of mischief, 'I think, by and large, David is retired.'

Gilmour may have been out of the spotlight but he was quietly working on new material. In his absence, though, Pink Floyd's more prolific and outspoken songwriter had reclaimed at least some of the group's legacy. Now thirty-four years old, Waters' favourite Floyd album *The Wall* had acquired a new lease of life, and so too had its now sixty-nine-year-old creator. Waters hadn't released a new album since 1992. But touring *The Wall* had spurred him into writing a brand-new song that, in turn, had convinced him that perhaps it wasn't time to stop just yet.

Pink Floyd were no more. EMI Records were no more. The music business as Pink Floyd knew it was no more. But Roger Waters was planning his studio comeback. The opening line to Waters' latest composition was, he revealed, 'If I had been God . . .'

'It may prove deeply unpopular in certain quarters,' he said, doubtless relishing any future objections. 'But, fuck it!' In an uncertain and changing world, it was reassuring to know that some things never change.

ACKNOWLEDGEMENTS

This book wouldn't have been possible without the help of friends and colleagues including Phil Alexander, Danny Eccleston, Gareth Grundy, Ted Kessler, Paul Rees and Stuart Williams. Further thanks to John Aizlewood, Johnny Black, Dave Brolan, Fred Dellar, Peter Doggett, Tom Doyle, Jerry Ewing, Sarah Ewing, Lora Findlay, Dawn Foley, Pat Gilbert, Ian Gittins, Ross Halfin, John Harris, Neil Jeffries, Philip Lloyd-Smee, Paul Loasby, Steve Malins, Toby Manning, Mark Paytress, Jenny Spires, Mark Sturdy, Phil Sutcliffe and Paul Trynka for phone numbers, information, interview transcripts, website expertise, encouragement and advice.

A warm handshake to Graham Coster at Aurum Press for effusive praise, tactful criticism and a nice E.M. Forster anecdote and to Rachel Leyshon for her sympathetic copy-editing. Thanks also to Matt Johns of the superlative Pink Floyd website brain-damage.co.uk and Warren Dosanjh of i-spysydincambridge.com for all their help and support.

Several people tolerated my frequent telephone calls and intrusions into their (past) lives. So a special thank you to Jeff Dexter, Iain 'Emo' Moore, Matthew Scurfield, Anthony Stern and John Watkins, who were especially gracious with their time and memories.

This book draws on my own interviews with David Gilmour, Nick Mason, Roger Waters and Richard Wright conducted between 1992 and 2011 for various magazines, including *Mojo* and *Q*. Thanks also to Nick Mason and David Gilmour for agreeing to be interviewed by me for further magazine articles since the book's original publication in 2007. Further thanks to David Gilmour for helping to fact-check this new edition.

Also my own interviews with and contributions from: Nick Barraclough, Andrew Bown, Joe Boyd, Mick Brockett, Peter Brown, Ivan Carling-Scanlon, Paul Carrack, Libby Chisman, Caroline Coon, Alice Cooper, David Crosby, Karl Dallas, John Davies, Chris Dennis, Jeff Dexter, Geoff Docherty, Harry Dodson, Warren Dosanjh, Bob Ezrin, Jenny Fabian, Mick Farren, Hugh Fielder, Duggie Fields, David Gale, Ron Geesin, John Gordon, Caroline Greeves, Jeff Griffin, Bob Harris, Dave 'De' Harris, Jeanette Holland, John 'Hoppy' Hopkins, Nicky Horne, Sam Hutt, Richard Jacobs, Jeff Jarratt, Nick Kent, Susan Kingsford, 'Bob' Rado Klose, John Leckie, Jenny Lesmoir-Gordon, Nigel Lesmoir-Gordon, Peter Jenner, Andrew King, Jonathan Meades, Tabitha Mellor, Bhaskar Menon, Clive Metcalfe, Peter Mew, Iain 'Emo' Moore, Seamus O'Connell, Davy O'List, Alan Parsons, Danny Peyronel, Aubrey 'Po' Powell, Guy Pratt, William Pryor, Stephen Pyle, Andrew Rawlinson, Alun Renshaw, Tim Renwick, Pete Revell, Mick Rock, Sheila Rock, Evelyn 'Iggy' Rose, Peter Rowan, Gerald Scarfe, Barbet Schroeder, Matthew Scurfield, Vic Singh, Christine Smith, Norman Smith (RIP), Jenny Spires, Jay Stapley, Anthony Stern, Steve Stollman, Storm Thorgerson, Clare Torry, Pete Townshend, John Watkins, Clive Welham (RIP), Peter Whitehead, John Whiteley, Andrew Whittuck, Rick Wills, Peter Wynne-Willson, John 'Willie' Wilson, Baron Wolman and Emily Young. Many thanks to everyone who spared the time to talk to me.

Countless magazine interviews and articles proved invaluable in writing this book, including many published in *Classic Rock*, *Melody Maker*, *Mojo*, *Musician*, *NME*, *Q*, *Record Collector*, *Rolling Stone*, *Sounds*, *Spin*, *Uncut*, *The Word* and more. Those deserving of a special mention are listed in the bibliography.

Finally, lots of love and gratitude to Claire and Matthew for infinite amounts of patience, particularly during the last big push.

SELECT BIBLIOGRAPHY

Pink Floyd and Syd Barrett Books

Cavanagh, John, *The Piper at the Gates of Dawn* (Continuum, 2003)

Dallas, Karl, *Pink Floyd: Bricks in the Wall* (Shapolsky Publishing, 1987)

Fitch, Vernon, *The Pink Floyd Encyclopedia* (Collector's Guide Publishing, 1998)

Fitch, Vernon, *Pink Floyd: The Press Reports 1966–1983* (Collector's Guide Publishing, 2001)

Fitch, Vernon and Richard Mahon, *Comfortably Numb, A History of The Wall, Pink Floyd 1978–1981* (PFA Publishing, 2006)

Harris, John, *The Dark Side of the Moon: The Making of the Pink Floyd Masterpiece* (Fourth Estate, 2005)

Hodges, Nick and Jan Priston, *Embryo: A Pink Floyd Chronology 1966–1971* (Cherry Red Books, 1999)

Mabbett, Andy, *The Complete Guide to the Music of Pink Floyd* (Omnibus, 1995)

Manning, Toby, *The Rough Guide to Pink Floyd* (Rough Guides, 2006)

Mason, Nick, *Inside Out: A Personal History of Pink Floyd* (Weidenfeld & Nicolson, 2004)

McDonald, Bruno (ed.), *Pink Floyd: Through the Eyes of ... The Band, Its Fans, Friends And Foes* (Sidgwick & Jackson, 1996)

Miles, Barry, *Pink Floyd, A Visual Documentary* (Omnibus Press, 1980)

Miles, Barry, *Pink Floyd, The Early Years* (Omnibus Press, 2006)

Palacios, Julian, *Lost in the Woods: Syd Barrett and the Pink Floyd* (Boxtree, 1998)

Parker, David, *Random Precision: Recording the Music of Syd Barrett 1965–1974* (Cherry Red Books, 2001)

Povey, Glenn and Ian Russell, *Pink Floyd: In the Flesh, The Complete Performance History* (Bloomsbury, 1997)

Povey, Glenn, *Echoes: The Complete History of Pink Floyd* (Mindhead Publishing, 2006)

Pratt, Guy, *My Bass and Other Animals* (Orion, 2007)

Rock, Mick, *Psychedelic Renegades* (Genesis Publications, 2002)

Sanders Rick, *The Pink Floyd* (Futura Publications, 1976)

Shaffner, Nicholas, *A Saucerful of Secrets: A Pink Floyd Odyssey* (Helter Skelter, 1992)

Thorgerson, Storm and Peter Curzon, *Mind Over Matter: The Images Of Pink Floyd* (Sanctuary, 1997)

Thorgerson, Storm and Peter Curzon, *Taken By Storm: The Album Art of Storm Thorgerson, A Retrospective* (Omnibus, 2007)

Watkinson, Mike and Pete Anderson, *Syd Barrett, Crazy Diamond* (Omnibus Press, 1991)

Willis, Tim, *Madcap: The Half-Life of Syd Barrett, Pink Floyd's Lost Genius* (Short Books, 2002)

Background

Ackroyd, Peter, *London: The Biography* (Chatto & Windus, 2000)

Bennett, Graham, *Soft Machine: Out-Bloody-Rageous* (SAF Publishing, 2005)

Bizot, Jean-François, *200 Trips from the Counterculture: Graphics and Stories from the Underground Press Syndicate* (Thames & Hudson, 2006)

Boyd, Joe, *White Bicycles: Making Music in the 1960s* (Serpent's Tail, 2005)

Donnelly, Mark, *Sixties Britain: Culture, Society and Politics* (Longman, 2005)

Farren, Mick, *Give the Anarchist a Cigarette* (Jonathan Cape, 2001)

Gorman, Paul, *The Look: Adventures in Pop and Rock Fashion* (Sanctuary, 2001)

Grahame, Kenneth, *The Wind in the Willows* (Methuen, originally published 1908)

Green, Jonathon, *Days in the Life: Voices from the English Underground 1961–1971* (William Heinemann, 1988)

Huxley, Aldous, *The Doors of Perception* (Vintage, originally published 1954)

Levy, Shaun, *Ready, Steady, Go!: Swinging London and the Invention of Cool* (Fourth Estate, 2003)

MacDonald, Ian, *Revolution in the Head: The Beatles Records in the Sixties* (Fourth Estate 1994)

Miles, Barry, *In the Sixties* (Jonathan Cape, 2002)

Miles, Barry, *Hippie* (Sterling, 2005)

Norman, Philip, *The Stones* (Elm Tree/Hamish Hamilton, 1984)

Nuttall, Jeff, *Bomb Culture* (MacGibbon & Kee, 1968)

Paytress, Mark, *Twentieth-Century Boy: The Marc Bolan Story* (Sidgwick & Jackson, 1992)

Phillips, Charlie & Mike, *Notting Hill in the Sixties* (Lawrence & Wishart, 1992)

Pryor, William, *The Survival of the Coolest: An Addiction Memoir* (Clear Books, 2003)

Rawlinson, Andrew, *The Book of Enlightened Masters: Western Teachers in Eastern Traditions* (Open Court Publishing, 1997)

Sandbrook, Christopher, *White Heat: A History of Britain in the Swinging Sixties* (Little, Brown, 2006)

Scurfield, Matthew, *I Could Be Anyone* (to be published in 2008)

Scully, Rock, with David Dalton, *Living with the Dead* (Little, Brown, 1996)

Sedgwick, Nick, *Light Blue with Bulges* (Fourth Estate, 1989)

Sounes, Howard, *The Sights, Sounds and Ideas of a Brilliant Decade* (Simon & Schuster, 2006)

Stevens, Jay, *Storming Heaven: LSD and the American Dream* (Paladin, 1989)

Street-Porter, Janet, *Fall Out: A Memoir of Friends Made and Friends Unmade* (Headline Review, 2007)

Vyner, Harriet, *Groovy Bob: The Life and Times of Robert Fraser* (Faber & Faber, 2001)

Magazine Articles

Black, Johnny, 'The Long March' (*Mojo,* November 2001)

Clerk, Carol, 'Lost in Space' (*Uncut*, June 2003)

Clerk, Carol, 'The Last Days of Pink Floyd' (*Uncut*, June 2004)

Constantin, Philippe, 'Really Wish You Were Here: The Politics of Absence' (*Street Life*, January 1976)

Ellen, Mark, 'The Deal Maker' (*The Word*, August 2005)

Ewing, Jerry, 'The Show Must Go On' (*Classic Rock*, January 2000)

Harris, John, 'In the Flesh' (*Q* & *Mojo* Pink Floyd Special Edition, August 2004)

Johns, Matt and Powell, Paul Jr, Adrian Maben interview (www.brain-damage.co.uk, 2003)

Kent, Nick, 'The Cracked Ballad of Syd Barrett' (*New Musical Express*, April 1974)

McKnight, Connor, 'Notes Towards the Illumination of the Floyd' (*Zigzag*, July 1973)

Salewicz, Chris, 'Over the Wall' (*Q*, August 1987)

Simmons, Sylvie, 'Danger! Demolition in Progress' (*Mojo*, December 1999)

Snow, Mat, 'The Rightful Heir' (*Q*, September 1990)

Sutcliffe, Phil, 'And This Is Me …' (*Mojo*, April 2006)

Sutcliffe, Phil, 'The First Men on the Moon' (*Mojo*, March 1998)

Sutcliffe, Phil, 'The Greatest Show on Earth' (*Mojo*, July 1995)

Recommended Websites

www.brain-damage.co.uk
www.pinkfloyd.com
www.neptunepinkfloyd.co.uk
www.pinkfloydz.com
www.pinkfloyd.net
www.davidgilmour.com
www.outsidethewall.net
www.pink-floyd.org
www.gilmourish.com
www.sydbarrett.org
www.floydianslip.com
www.roger-waters.com
www.rogerwaters.org
www.i-spysydincambridge.com

For more information about the author go to www.markrblake.com

INDEX